New Ways of Analyzing Variation in English

Charles-James N. Bailey
Roger W. Shuy

Editors

Georgetown University Press, Washington, D.C. 20007

Library of Congress Card Catalogue Number: 73-76753
ISBN 0-87840-01-28

TO

WILLIAM LABOV

who freed us from static analysis

CONTENTS

PROBLEMS IN VARIATION

OTHER STUDIES IN VARIATION

CREOLES

PREFACE

In October 1972, Georgetown University hosted the combined meetings of the Eighth Southeastern Conference on Linguistics (SECOL) and the first annual colloquium on New Ways of Analyzing Variation in English (NWAVE). A total of sixty-four papers was presented over a three-day period to an attendance of over 300 scholars. One of the guiding principles of the conference was to intermingle topics rather than to set them off in special sections such as phonology, creolization, or semantax. Consequently, many linguists who would not otherwise have attended a paper dealing with language variation were given easy access to such material. What worked well as a program format, however, seemed less desirable in the published version. For this reason, two separate volumes of selected papers from these meetings are being made available. In this volume, the papers relating to variation are collected. Although most of the papers are concerned with variation in English, we have added to those dealing with English creoles a few dealing with non-English creoles. The papers in the main body of the volume which deal with semantax, phonology, language contact, language acquisition, and historical concerns appear in Toward Tomorrow's Linguistics, edited by Roger W. Shuy and Charles-James N. Bailey. The editors regret that the conference papers presented by Jerry Morgan, William Stewart, J. L. Dillard, David Stampe, Beatrice and R. M. R. Hall, and Eric Hamp were not received in time for this publication.

Roger W. Shuy

INTRODUCTION

We owe an expression of thanks to Dean Robert Lado for his contributions to these meetings and to all the scholars whose avid participation has made them the success they have been. Not least do I owe my personal thanks to those friends all over the country who have responded so quickly and so favorably to my appeal for good papers from as many faculty and bright students helping in the development of the new framework as possible.

For our avowed purpose was to exhibit the solid existence of the new ways of doing linguistics. A few of us had been exchanging ideas among ourselves about the theoretical implications of the patterns of language variation which had been uncovered by William Labov and those following his lead, as well as by David DeCamp and other creolists. It was clear that 'gradience' (first brought to the attention of linguists by Dwight Bolinger years ago in connection with intonational analysis) had to be described and that models based on the omnipresence of discrete oppositions were inadequate for the job. And it was also clear that linguistic variation was closely associated with the social context and topic of conversation, as Dell Hymes and many other sociolinguists had long been contending. Variation had been examined by Labov, Roger Shuy, Walt Wolfram, Ralph Fasold, and others. We regarded Labov's variable rules as an epochal breakthrough for nonstatic models of linguistic description and are dedicating this volume to him because of the freedom which has accrued to linguistic analysis as a result of this development. Labov has also worked on discourse analysis and on what has come to be called semantic fuzziness. Creolists like John Reinecke, Robert LePage, Ian Hancock, Beryl Bailey, DeCamp, and Derek Bickerton have noted the existence of gradatums in linguistic data and the inadequacy of static models. Dale Elliott, Stanley Legum, and Sandra Annear Thompson found implications in variation some years ago, and Gary Parker, and I had been turning up similar

patterns in regional variation. Carol Odo and Richard Day were
finding implicational patterns in Hawaiian Creole. Brent Berlin and
Paul Kay's discovery of implications among the basic color terms
was becoming well known. Henry Hoenigswald, like Hymes and
McCawley, had found reasons for broadening the scope of linguistic
data, while Fred Householder and Wolfgang Dressler had begun to
follow the variationists in studying historical change in the sociolinguistic perspective. Charles Ferguson was contributing to many
aspects of the new outlook, and William Stewart and J. L. Dillard
had been unearthing new facts about the Creole origins of Black Vernacular English. Guy Carden had been systematizing isolectal variation in the ordering of rules, while Arnold Zwicky and Dressler
were avidly at work on low-level tempo and other variations in
phonology.

It was with surprise that variationists discovered that their conclusions about the effects of social context on variation and gradience
in linguistic description had also been arrived at by other linguists,
independently traveling quite different routes. And the surprise was
the greater when we saw that some of their models for dealing with
some of these matters were in advance of those put forward by
scholars who had been interested in the matter for a longer time.
Chomsky's sentence grammar had already been replaced by discourse analysis among generative semanticists as a result of their
interest in presupposition and illocutionary force. (The influence of
the philosophers J. L. Austin, P. T. Geach, P. F. Strawson, H. P.
Grice, and J. R. Searle had already had its effects.) And there were
now appearing studies by George and Robin Lakoff, James McCawley,
Bruce Fraser, Charles Fillmore, and others who had concluded that
the topic and the status of one's interlocutors in communicative situations influence formal grammars. The new interest of George
Lakoff in fuzzy logic and of John Ross in squishes complemented the
interest of variationists in gradience and of David Stampe, Matthew
Chen, H.-I. Hsieh, and other natural phonologists in implicational
patternings. Eric Hamp was finding squishes in Indo-European
etymology, and Edward Keenan's hierarchies of accessibility showed
similar implicational patterns in syntax. Gradience was also being
put forward by Lloyd Anderson, and Victor Yngve was becoming an
advocate of social or 'human' linguistics.

If the new outlook required viewing its human object as Aristotle's
'social critter', it also required a psychosomatic conception of man
in place of the recent view of man as mainly a mind endowed with
innate knowledge. Besides the natural phonologists just mentioned,
Gaberell Drachman, Chin-Wu Kim, John Ohala, and Victoria From-
kin were insisting that theoretical processes had to be grounded in
and explained in terms of man's neurological and anatomical makeup.

And Robert Krohn and Theo Vennemann were insisting on a more down-to-earth analysis of underlying phonological segments.

Finally, the role of time in linguistic description was becoming crucial for me, as well as for Labov, Stampe, William Wang, and Chen, who interested ourselves chiefly in explaining linguistic change. As early as 1967, Sven Öhman had demonstrated the utility of incorporating a time factor into phonetic rules. Early in 1969 at the UCLA Conference both Labov and I had discussed temporal models for linguistic description. The work of the creolists already mentioned came to influence both of us more and more. The effects of language mixture were also being investigated by Patricia Wolfe, Gillian Sankoff, Henrietta Cedergren, Eric Hamp, and Elizabeth Closs Traugott. Vennemann's observations on the restructuring effects of massive mixture in the form of borrowings from a past stage of the same language should also be mentioned here.

A time-based framework requires directionally oriented marking values in place of the plus and minus feature values of static grammars. Gary Parker, Matthew Chen, and I have studied markedness from this point of view, and our studies complement Stampe's theory of natural processes. For the rule-reorderings required in a dynamic grammar, there is some discussion of recent developments in the paper by Bailey at this meeting.

Uneasiness with strictly homogeneous monolectal grammars was being voiced also by Ronald Butters, Frank Anshen, Peter Trudgill, Bruce Fraser, Barbara Robson, and others whose work first became known to me at these meetings; and steps were being taken toward polylectal or polysystematic formulations by Bickerton and a few others. Wang was uncovering new facts about the way in which changes spread across the lexicon. There is also now to be reckoned with Jerry Morgan's proposal concerning random variation resulting from complex or conflicting situations in which the rules fail, being adequate only for the simpler, more usual cases.

This outline of recent developments has inevitably omitted other linguists worthy of notice, especially of the host of sociolinguists whose work has greatly contributed to the analysis of heterogeneous linguistic phenomena: J. L. Fischer, J. Gumperz, W. Bright, P. Friedrich, E. Goffman, and many others, including many who attended and participated in the Twenty-third Georgetown University Round Table on Languages and Linguistics. Hymes has suggested that the interest in the manner in which the least advantaged ranks of society speak--so vital to the development of the new framework-- is part and parcel of an enlarging interest in the way such people behave generally.

The net result of all this has been a convergence of our interests in time-based gradient variation and in what has variously been referred to as 'lectology' or as 'dynamic', 'secular', or 'non-discrete' linguistics. Different groups emphasize different aspects of the new framework, but it seems clear that the older atomistic dialectology has been replaced with unified grammars which systematically generate a variety of output patterns. As both Wallace Chafe and I had concluded, descriptive analysis had to employ diachronic models and concepts; and I had stressed that descriptive analysis did not differ from a broader view of what had been called dialectology previously. (I had proposed integrating all three disciplines.) Considering the diverse routes by which scholars have arrived at similar views of linguistic analysis, it seems that they cannot be far wrong. The fact that these different approaches have been espoused by leading linguists indicates that their time has come.

Several factors have made Washington a good location for this initial effort to give the new framework a visible existence. In addition to the location of our Sociolinguistics Program and other facilities here, there is our location on the East Coast at the meeting of North and South: for the South and East are where a great deal of the most interesting kinds of variation are 'at'.

After the general description of recent developments already given, permit me to turn to a more personal view of the new attitudes toward linguistic analysis. Tired of the extremes of empiricism and mentalism, which I feel have been given fair trials and found wanting, I welcome a classical balance of deduction and induction, universals and flux, intuitions and statistical evidence, mind and body, innate potentials and physical naturalness, substance and life, private intention and social meaning, essence and accidents, competence and performance, explanatory theory and methodology of description, abstract hypothesis and low-level analysis, and constancy and variation (as in the scholastic proportion: air : bird = water : fish).

So I am happy to be rid of static, homogeneous models and to be rid of the fudges represented by 'my dialect', 'performance component', 'optional', and the rest. There is a new experimental phonetics and a new phonology seeking to discover what is natural; there is a new transcriptional phonetics seeking to present a more realistic and helpful portrayal of many facets of the stream of speech than that of the past two decades; a new generative semantics; a new lectology; and a new historical analysis. From sources as varying as physiology, dialectology, creole studies, abstract syntax, and sociology: a kind of convergence. The greater the diversity and independence of these sources, the greater the likelihood of our being on the right track. The First Annual Colloquium on New Ways of Analyzing Variation in English has exhibited this convergence, and we are now documenting it.[1]

Charles-James N. Bailey

NOTE

[1]See also C.-J. N. Bailey, Contributions of the study of variation to the framework of the new linguistics. Read at a meeting of the International Linguistics Association, Arequipa, Peru, March 1973; to appear in a Spanish version.

ON WHAT BASIS VARIABLE RULES?

WALT WOLFRAM

Federal City College and Center for Applied Linguistics

Introduction. Since Labov's original formulation of variable rules as an integral part of a speaker's language competence (1969), the validity of this construct has been subjected to considerable debate. In some instances there has been ready adoption with or without minor changes in formulation, while in other cases there has been almost instant rejection. As is to be expected with any new proposal, the seriousness with which linguists have accepted or rejected the notion has run the gamut of critical assessment. There has been both uncritical acceptance and cavalier dismissal; but we have also seen critical assessments which come up on opposite sides of the argument.

This paper is not intended to make either a glorious defense or a damning rejection of the proposal. I shall leave that aspect to better polemicists. What I desire to do, however, is to set up some principles of LANGUAGE on which the theory must stand or fall. In a sense, then, I am regressing to the fundamental premises which must be accepted or rejected. Lest my role be construed as that of a neutral referee giving instructions for a fair fight, however, we should be reminded of the referees' decisions made at the recent Olympics. Unfortunately, bias is often detected only after the decision has been rendered.

In the following discussion, three premises crucial to the acceptance of variable rules are discussed, namely (1) inherent variability, (2) replicable regularity, and (3) language specificity. No doubt there are other premises or subcategories of those discussed here, but in this discussion, I shall limit myself to principles cited above.

1

1. Inherent variability. It seems appropriate that we start with the most fundamental issue of all, the acceptance of what Labov has termed 'inherent variability'. The establishment of variable rules must begin with the assertion that some fluctuation between variants is part of a unitary system. The alternative to this is the assertion that fluctuating variants are matters of code switching (including stylistic shifting) or borrowing of some type. Theoretically, one might dismiss the notion of variability by assuming that all instances of variation are simply matters of code-switching between co-existent systems (this, of course, is based on the further assumption of co-existent systems). From this perspective, the fluctuating variants are assigned to different systems or subsystems within a speaker's linguistic repertoire and he simply shifts from one to the other. We should mention here that switching is typically associated with a SET of features rather than isolated variants and that switching usually takes place in response to some stylistic, situational, interlocutor, topic, or other functional shift. On a linguistic level, we would expect some change in the linguistic environment to account for the distribution of variants. What we are faced with, however, is the observation that variation takes place while extralinguistic and linguistic context remain quite constant. Variation in a constant extralinguistic and linguistic context is difficult to dismiss. But even within the most constant of contexts it can still be claimed that our failure to uncover further conditioning detail to account for shift is only a function of our finite powers of observation. Hence, it may be claimed that the provision of more sociopsychological or linguistic detail would allow us to account for 'apparent' fluctuation in terms of a purely categorical framework. Although it may be a heuristically useful procedure to admit inherent variability only after an exhaustive attempt to account for fluctuating variants in categorical terms, we still are left with the fact that our best powers of observation leave us with inexplicable fluctuation. Ultimately, of course, it is impossible to prove that inherent variability does exist, since we are always subject to our finite observations. Unable to prove the claim logically, we must resort to the fact that the existing data on fluctuation do not support the categorical explanation. Hence, we assume inherent variability.

Given the assumption of inherent variability, some may still want to differentiate between what has been termed 'dialect mixture' and inherent variability. This distinction appears to be of considerable importance to students of languages in contact, whether it be on a inter- or intra-language level. Students of inter-language contact situations may maintain, for example, that it is possible for a speaker of L_1 to borrow a form from L_2 without integrating it completely into the system of L_2. Isn't it, for example, quite possible for a speaker of English to borrow a term from German following the morpheme structure sequence rules of German even if they 'violate' the English morpheme structure rules? By the same token, investigators of nonstandard language varieties have been confronted with this issue because of the affect that a superordinate variety may have on a subordinate one. Are not some of the fluctuating items used by speakers of the subordinate variety sometimes borrowed from the superordinate one? In some cases, heuristic procedures for differentiating dialect mixture from inherent variability have even been set up.[1] Thus, for example, some linguists (e.g. Labov et al. 1968: 164-67, Wolfram 1969:45-47, Fasold 1972), analyzing the sporadic use of -$\underline{Z}$ third-person, present tense forms, have cited the evidence of structural hypercorrection, frequency levels, and sociological context to show the difference between fluctuating forms which are 'borrowed' and 'inherent'. As attractive as these analyses may appear in terms of language contact situations, this distinction is dependent on the observation of both sociological and linguistic phenomena.[2] There appears to be no purely linguistic basis for such a differentiation, as unsatisfying as that may seem to students of language contact.

At this point, one may anticipate the discussion of linguistic constraints on variability and ask if sensitivity to linguistic environment may be used as a linguistic basis for distinguishing inherent variability and dialect mixture. That is, do fluctuating items which are inherently variable show a structured sensitivity to surrounding linguistic environment that is not matched for fluctuating items resulting from dialect mixture? Although it may be tempting to set up such a criterion, it should be cautioned that such a position may not be justified when looked at in closer detail. For example, suppose that L_1 does not have any word-final consonant cluster but L_2 does. A speaker of L_1 uses a word from L_2 which ends in a consonant cluster. In some instances, it is observed that the cluster is intact and in some instances it is reduced in order to conform to the morpheme structure rules of L_1; this is a very natural expectation in terms of linguistic change of any type. One may predict that the cluster would have a tendency to be reduced more frequently when followed by a vowel than when followed by a consonant for natural phonetic (i.e. universal) reasons. Similarly, we may expect the stress patterns to affect the incidence of the variants and be ordered hierarchically with the following vocalic/nonvocalic environment. On the basis of some exploratory evidence, this is what appears to happen with fluctuating items whether they are labeled 'inherently variable', 'borrowed', or 'interference'. Thus, our attempts to distinguish 'dialect mixture' and 'inherent variability' on a formal linguistic basis turn out somewhat futile. What we are left with is an assumption

concerning variability in which it does not appear linguistically
feasible to argue for the exclusion of 'dialect mixture'.[3]

2. Replicable regularity. Granted the assumption of inherent
variability, the step beyond traditional optional rules is premised
on the systematic patterning of variation. This regularity is demonstrated by the isolation of various linguistic and extralinguistic contexts which inhibit or favor the operation of a particular optional
rule. The constraints on variability are further shown to be ordered
with respect to each other so that a regular hierarchy of constraints
can be formalized for a given rule. Although frequency tabulations
serve as a basis for determining relationships, most proponents of
variable rules relegate the actual figures to the status of heuristics.
The significant relationships are matters of 'more' or 'less'.

Before going any further, we are confronted with the problem of
constraint isolation. Although it is apparently assumed that constraints will emerge fairly clearly from a close scrutiny of the data,
Bickerton (1971:486) asserts that we know far too little about co-
occurrence phenomena to insure the correct identification of constraints. What is more distressing, however, is Bickerton's selection of a most 'unlikely' constraint only to find that it can be fitted
into the geometrical hierarchy of constraints as neatly as some of
Labov's 'natural' constraints. And this was accomplished after
only the second attempt. This suggests that other equally irrelevant
constraints might have given equivalent results. How do we explain
such embarrassing data? One explanation is that contained somewhere in Bickerton's unlikely constraint, there actually is a valid
constraint. Certainly, some of the relevant constraints isolated
in variable studies are approximative in their observational accuracy.
For example, some of the isolated constraints on copula deletion in
terms of grammatical categories seem approximative of phonological
detail still to be specified. Personally, I do not find this explanation
very satisfying.

Another explanation is that the selection worked by chance. The
next twenty random choices would not work the same way if they
indeed were 'unlikely' constraints. But the fact that it was only the
second 'unlikely' candidate as a constraint is not very satisfying.
We would breathe a little easier if it had been the tenth choice instead of the second.

The third alternative is to claim that we know enough about
naturalness in language situations to avoid ever making such an
unlikely choice. By the same token that Bickerton made a decision
about unnaturalness in classifying his constraint as 'unlikely', it
may be maintained that we have the right to assume that our knowledge about naturalness in language will avoid such errors. But we

are still left with the fact that some of the constraints we consider likely may not be valid. The only counterevidence that I can offer to Bickerton's assertion is that I have gone through scores of likely constraints with respect to a given variable rule only to find that they did not show a consistent patterning. No doubt there are some constraints which may turn out to be invalid on the basis of further investigation, but this is not reflective of any inherent theoretical weakness.

Assuming, then, that it is possible to isolate valid constraints, we must demonstrate that the relationships between them are replicable if we are to maintain that they are systematic. On an individual level, this means that at a given point in time (since relationships, of course, change in time), we will get consistent distribution patterns in the constraints. For example, different speech samples from an individual will reveal the same patterning. On a group level, we may expect the constraint hierarchies to match within a homogeneous speech community. That is, if we take speaker A and B from language variety X, we will find that the effect of the constraints and the relative ordering of the constraints is quite regular. Compare, for example, the figures of constraints on consonant cluster reduction from my study of the black community in Detroit in Table 1. In this table, consonant cluster reduction in two main types of environments is given: (1) a following consonantal/non-consonantal environment, and (2) the cluster is bimorphemic or monomorphemic. The figures include one group, upper working-class informants. Both the individual and the group figures are included.

In Table 1 we see the same general pattern of ordering on an individual level that was observed when calculated for the group as a whole. In the light of data such as these, it is difficult to understand why some variationists have maintained that the speech of the social group is much more regular than the speech of an individual speaker. At least when we look at linguistic constraints we find that the regularity can be observed by looking at an individual speaker. For most speakers, we are impressed with how few examples are actually needed in order for the general pattern to emerge.

There are, however, two exceptions to this regularity which may make the characterization of the speech represented for the social group as a whole appear to be more systematic than the speech of the individual. In some cases, there are not sufficient examples in a given subcategory of constraints to reproduce the clear-cut effect of the constraint orders as it is represented for the group as a whole. This type of inconsistency arises simply from the limited number of examples available for a given informant and would be

TABLE 1. Frequency of simplified consonant cluster in the
speech of upper working-class blacks in Detroit,
by linguistic environments.

Informant	No Del/Tot C ##C	%	C## ##C	%	C ##(V)	%	C# ##(V)	%
1	6/8	.75	6/9	.67	7/12	.58	1/6	.17
2	7/7	1.00	5/7	.71	8/13	.62	1/3	.33
3	12/12	1.00	7/11	.64	5/8	.63	1/4	.25
4	9/9	1.00	2/4	.50	8/11	.73	1/1	(1.00)
5	8/8	1.00	9/9	1.00	10/12	.83	2/6	.33
6	6/6	1.00	6/9	.67	9/14	.64	1/6	.16
7	8/8	1.00	8/12	.75	8/12	.67	0/3	.00
8	8/8	1.00	6/11	.55	7/12	.58	2/4	.50
9	11/13	.85	4/5	.80	4/7	.57	1/3	.33
10	10/10	1.00	11/12	.92	8/10	.80	0/2	.00
11	6/8	.75	10/14	.71	6/12	.50	0/1	.00
12	9/10	.90	10/13	.77	7/10	.70	0/2	.00
Group Figure	100/107	.93	84/116	.72	87/113	.65	10/41	.24

remedied by a more adequate population of examples. In Table 1,
the individual deviations seem to be of this type.

To be honest, however, there are instances where there appear
to be sufficient examples for discovering the regularity, yet the
group figures come out more regular than the individual figures.
These cases seem somewhat more difficult to dismiss. It is important, however, to note that these instances of deviation are restricted to cases where the effect ratios of various constraints are
relatively close. For example, suppose that we have three hierarchically ordered constraints, one inhibiting a particular rule 75
per cent, another 25 per cent, and the third 15 per cent. Between
the first two constraints we would not expect any individual deviation
(given an adequate representation of examples) whereas, for the
second and third constraints we might expect some individual reordering of constraints even within a relatively homogeneous group
of speakers. The actual frequency levels which might make two
constraints susceptible to individual differences in ordering are, of
course, arbitrary at this point.

In a sense, the problem of determining when the isolation of constraint ordering is valid or not is a reflection of two more general
problems which apply to all linguistic organization. One is the fact
that there is not always a clear-cut motivation concerning the

relationships between rules. In the same sense that there is not always a clear-cut formal motivation for one rule sequence over another, we may expect that there will not always be a clear-cut indication of the ordering of constraints. And, when the effect ratios of two constraints are close, we may expect two different speakers even with a relatively homogeneous community to alter their ordering. The second problem is the difficulty in determining the cut-off point between those constraints to be included in the formalization of a speaker's language competence. How many constraints can be reliably isolated for a given speaker? In a sense, the difficulty in determining cut-off points for the constraint inclusion is a reflection of the hazy interface that sometimes exists between competence and performance.

From a purely practical standpoint, there are difficulties in dealing with a great number of constraints, since the number of subdivisions in geometric ordering is doubled every time another constraint is introduced. This means that if we isolate six constraints, it is possible to get 128 branchings in the hierarchy (i.e. 2, 2x2, 2x4, 2x16, 2x32, 2x64 = 128). The expectation of getting sufficient numbers of examples to adequately determine the ordering of constraints naturally diminishes as the number of branchings proliferates. In most cases, we find that the clear-cut affect on variability is quite high in the first several orders of constraints, but that it tends to diminish after that.

A problem of more theoretical consequence arises when all the branchings necessary to establish hierarchical orderings are not logically possible, either because of the features of a specific language variety or because of metatheoretical constraints on human language. The logical impossibility of some categories may disallow observing cross-products crucial for establishing the rank orders. This problem has arisen at various stages in my own studies and in the studies of Fasold (Fasold has one instance in which a crucial cross-product calls for the comparison of such categories as a voiced vocalic pause and a voiceless vocalic pause). Although we might calculate expected frequencies for hypothetical categories in order to force a decision with respect to geometric ordering, the theoretical implication of this observation is that the requirement of strict geometrical ordering may be too strong a requirement. [4]

In the above discussion, we have tried to account for certain apparent irregularities that may arise in comparing individuals within a relatively homogeneous group. It is, of course, necessary to recognize that structured reordering of constraints can take place in social or temporal space. It is quite possible for reordering to be a function of regular language change. In the case of regular

reordering, however, it seems quite possible to expect that suscepti-
bility to 'imminent change' may follow the same sort of distribution
we found in individual variation. For example, we would expect two
constraints with frequency levels of 60 and 70 per cent to be susceptible to imminent change while constraints of 25 and 75 per cent respectively would not be nearly as susceptible.

One must caution, at this point, that the mathematics of constraint
reordering must not be considered apart from (but it can be considered
complementary to) the notion of marking in constraint orders. If it is
true, as Bailey (1972) suggests, that constraints are typically reordered from marked to unmarked orders, then it is possible for constraint reordering to counteract reordering changes we might predict
from a purely mathematical base. Suppose, for example, we have
three environmental constraints in a given variable rule: $\underline{X}$ the first
order constraint effects a 50 per cent frequency level for the occurrence of a given form, $\underline{Y}$, the second order constraint, a 45 per cent
level, and $\underline{Z}$ the third order constraint, and 40 per cent frequency
level. If they are already in their unmarked order, the order would
not be expected to change, despite the closeness in the effect ratios.
(They may, of course, merge and reduce the number of constraint
orders). On the other hand, if $\underline{X}$ and $\underline{Y}$ are in an unmarked order
with reference to each other, both $\underline{X}$ and $\underline{Y}$ are in their marked order
with reference to $\underline{Z}$, then $\underline{Z}$ may be reordered before both of them
while the order of $\underline{X}$ and $\underline{Y}$ with respect to each other remains intact.
This phenomenon can be referred to as 'constraint hopping'.[5]

Finally, we may cite the evidence of independent studies on variability as evidence of regularity of constraints. Investigations of
variability in Black English by Labov et al. (1968), Wolfram (1969),
Kernan (1971), Legum et al. (1971), and Fasold (1972) all indicate
the replicable nature of the data. Particular analyses of copula
deletion and final consonant cluster reduction all indicate overwhelm-
ing convergence. It is indeed difficult to dismiss such converging
analyses as anything but confirmation for the highly systematic nature
of variable constraints.

3. Language specificity. By themselves, the premises discussed
above do not justify the incorporation of constraints on variability
into the grammar of a specific language. In order for us to justify
our formalization of variable rules in any given grammar, we need
to demonstrate that there are aspects of variable constraints which
are unique to a given language variety. If we found that constraints
could be predicted on the basis of a universal theory of optional rule
constraints, there would be no need to represent them in a specific
language. Instead, they could simply be postulated as part of a

general language metatheory. This is the view that Kiparsky is endorsing when he says:

> . . . if something is universally predictable, it is not learned and can be taken out of the grammar, i.e., it can be made to follow from some general principle about language with a capital L. What I am conjecturing is that Labov's data can be taken out of the grammar of English, the grammar of German, Spanish, etc., and derived from a theory about optional rules in general (1971:645).

This position maintains that although variable rules may have important insights for a theory of optional rules in general, it is unnecessarily redundant to include this sort of information for a specific language variety.

There are two aspects to the question of constraint universality. The first may be referred to as 'effect predictability' and the second 'order predictability'. When we use the term effect predictability, we are referring to the fact that a particular type of environment will always have a particular effect on variability. For example, we may predict that the effect of a following consonant on a consonant cluster will always effect reduction as opposed to a following vowel or pause. It appears quite plausible to suggest that some of these effects may be universally predictable. For example, syllable structure and distinctiveness of category which relate to a general theory of markedness in language may produce such predictability. (Such predictability is, of course, based on the assumption that it is possible to isolate those factors which do effect variability precisely and that these isolable factors conform to general principles of naturalness in language.) On the basis of the data that have been collected up to this point, it appears reasonable to suggest that effect predictability is universal. This does not mean that we have a complete inventory of constraint effects nor that the effects that have been studied are stated in sufficiently precise manner. Obviously, our inventory is illustrative rather than exhaustive at this stage, and we will have to redefine the effects we have isolated on the basis of more empirical data. For example, I have stated that we would typically expect the absence of grammatical marking to favor deletion on the basis of Labov's (1968) study of BE and my own study of PRE (Wolfram et al. 1971). But Cedergren (personal communication) suggests that this be qualified so that it only applied to grammatical marking which is not transformationally introduced. Such modifications appear to be matters of observational and descriptive adequacy which are not true counter evidence. Without clear counter evidence, it seems most reasonable to claim that effect predictability is part of the general metatheory of optional rules.

If constraining effects are universal, then it is unnecessary to indicate what the favoring effect is for a specific language. For example, it is unnecessary to indicate whether + or - values favor the operation of a rule since this is redundant information predicted on the basis of the metatheory. In this respect, some of the previous formulation of variable rules, including my own, appear to have included information which is unnecessary for a specific language description.

The second aspect of constraint universality, order predictability, refers to the specific hierarchical ordering of constraints. For such ordering to be part of a general theory of optional rules, we must be able to predict not only the effect of the constraint, but how it is ordered with respect to other constraints. For example, we would have to posit as universal a statement to the effect that a following consonant/nonconsonant will always be greater than stress/unstress in its effect on deletion of final consonants. If we cannot predict hierarchical orders on the basis of our general theory, then such information must be incorporated into our particular grammar of a language. · The empirical evidence that we have on constraint hierarchies indicates at least some of the hierarchical organization can be language-specific. Thus, for example, Labov indicates that at one age level consonant cluster reduction may indicate grammaticality as a first order constraint and following vocality the second order constraint whereas at another stage the order is reversed. Thus it is necessary to indicate such information in a specific grammar. An argument against this claim would either have to question the validity of the empirical data or demonstrate that the passage from one stage to another is inevitable within the life history of an individual so that it is completely predictable. Accepting the authenticity of the data, it appears that the ordering of constraints is language-specific information that must at least sometimes be formulated in a grammar.

It will be noted that I have qualified my assertion by saying 'sometimes'. It appears that there may be some conditions under which such information can be redundant. For example, if we maintain that there is a universal unmarked hierarchy, then it would only be necessary to specify those orders which are marked. A general theory of marking would account for the unspecified hierarchical marking. At this point, there are practical problems involved in formally following such a procedure, since we do not have a comprehensive catalog of unmarked hierarchical orders as part of our metatheory, but this is an empirical deficiency which does not affect the theoretical validity of this position.

NOTES

[1]In some instances (e.g. Loflin 1967, Fickett 1971) it appears that the operating principle for determining dialect mixture is that any obligatory rule in SE which would have to be considered as optional in Black English is dismissed as dialect mixture. Obviously, such a simplistic approach cannot help but come up with a very distorted picture of even the most ideal construct of BE.

[2]DeCamp (1972:77) correctly points out that hypercorrection is a concept which is dependent on both sociological and linguistic facts.

[3]This point becomes more clear when we look at the history of those things currently classified as inherently variable. If we follow the proposed distinction between dialect mixture and inherent variability, most inherently variable items were initiated as what would have been classified as dialect mixture.

[4]Geometrical ordering is based on the supposition that variable constraints operate independently. If we found that there were significant synergystic effects in the combination of constraints, a geometrically ordered hierarchy would have to be abandoned.

[5]Bailey (1972) cites Labov's data on æ-raising (1972) as an illustration of constraint hopping. Elsewhere this phenomenon has been referred to as 'acceleration'.

REFERENCES

Bailey, C.-J. N. Forthcoming. The patterning of language variation. In: Varieties of present-day American English. Ed. by R. W. Bailey and J. L. Robinson. New York, Macmillan.

Bickerton, Derek. 1971. Inherent variability and variable rules. Foundations of Language. 7.457-92.

DeCamp, David. 1972. Hypercorrection and rule generalization. Language in Society. 1.87-90.

Fickett, Joan G. 1970. Aspects of morphemics, syntax, and semology of an inner-city dialect: 'Merican'. New York, West Rush.

Fasold, Ralph W. 1972. Tense marking in Black English: A linguistic and social analysis. Washington, D.C., Center for Applied Linguistics.

Kernan, Claudia Mitchell. 1971. Language behavior in a Black urban community. Berkeley, Monographs of the Language-Behavior Research Laboratory, No. 2.

Kiparsky, Paul. 1971. Historical linguistics. In: A survey of linguistic science. Ed. by William Orr Dingwall. College Park, University of Maryland.

Labov, William. 1969. Contraction, deletion, and inherent variability of the English copula. Language. 45.715-62.

Labov, William. 1972. The internal evolution of linguistic rules. In: Linguistic change and generative theory: Essays from the UCLA Conference on Historical Linguistics in the Perspective of Transformational Theory, February 1969. Ed. by R. P. Stockwell and R. K. S. Macaulay. Bloomington, Indiana University Press. 101-71.

_____, Paul Cohen, Clarence Robins, and John Lewis. 1968. A study of nonstandard English used by Negro and Puerto Rican speakers in New York City. Final Report, Cooperative Research Project No. 2091. Office of Education.

Legum, Stanley W., Carol Pfaff, Gene Tinnie, and Michael Nicholas. 1971. The speech of young Black children in Los Angeles. Technical Report No. 33. Los Angeles, Southwest Regional Laboratory.

Wolfram, Walt. 1969. A sociolinguistic description of Detroit Negro speech. Washington, D.C., Center for Applied Linguistics.

_____, in collaboration with Marie Shiels Djouadi and Ralph W. Fasold. Overlapping influence in the English of second-generation Puerto Rican teenagers in East Harlem. Final Report, USOE Project No. 3-70-0033(508).

ON THE NATURE OF VARIABLE CONSTRAINTS

HENRIETTA J. CEDERGREN

Université du Québec à Montréal

Phonology has provided the first testing ground for theories of linguistic variability partly due to the possibility of constructing data sets large enough for simultaneous analysis along many dimensions of variation. With massive data, we are more likely to be bound to the patterning existing in the data, and less likely to resort to generating biased artificial data in order to fill vacant 'cells' in tables, to be tempted into lengthy 'a posteriori' speculations to explain away each piece of data which does not fit our models, or to dismiss systematically patterned exceptions as 'performance error'.

This paper reports some results of a sociolinguistic survey of the Spanish of Panama City involving a sample of seventy-nine speakers (Cedergren 1973). The particular variable described was measured some 22,000 times, a number sufficient for a consideration of all the relevant dimensions of variation.

The analytical framework. Quantitative studies of language use in the speech community have demonstrated regular cooccurrence patterns between language variables and features of both linguistic and extralinguistic dimensions such as style, status, age, and regional origin. To describe this phenomenon, Labov (1969) introduced variable rules, thus replacing optional rules, in order to account for the regular patterns of covariation between the frequency of rule execution and contextual elements. For each variable rule in every environment there exists a quantity p which represents the probability of rule execution.

As a working hypothesis, it has been proposed (Cedergren and D. Sankoff 1972) that it is a universal tendency for p to be in the form of:

$$p = 1 - (1 - p_0)(1 - \alpha)(1 - \beta) \ldots (1 - \omega)$$

where p_0 is an input probability independent of context and $\alpha, \beta \ldots \omega$ represent the contribution of each relevant feature in the environment. This formalization assumes that each of the environmental factors affects the probability of rule application in a consistent and independent manner, regardless of the presence or absence of other features relevant to the rule. Note, that we incorporate social and stylistic constraints into this hypothesis in the same way as linguistic factors, thereby permitting the comparison of linguistic and non-linguistic constraints and the investigation of language independence from the social system.

In empirical studies, the unmarked relation of variable constraints is indeed noninteraction or independence. This situation predominates among stable sociolinguistic variables in the speech community. Numerous examples are found in the literature. Here we will present a slightly more complicated case and discuss the methodological implication of non-negligible interaction.

Syllable final S. The variability of syllable final S is a well-known phenomenon in Spanish dialectology and has an extensive geographical distribution covering wide areas of American and European Spanish-speaking communities. Historically the alternation dates at least from the XVI century (Alonso 1962:47).

Quantitative studies of Puerto Rican Spanish by Ma and Herasimchuk (1971) and of Cuban Spanish by Vallejo-Claros (1970) indicate the different phonetic realizations of S are subject to variable linguistic and external stylistic and social constraints.

Three relevant variants of S, a strident, an aspirate, or null are considered in the analysis. The distribution of these variants in our corpus is displayed in Table 1.

TABLE 1. Distribution of variants.

Variants	%
s	11
h	41
∅	48
N	22, 167

We have postulated a variable rule of the form

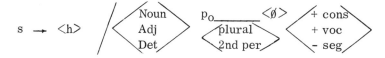

to account for the aspiration of S where the frequency of rule execution is shown to be the result of a combination of factors: the nature of the following segment, the existence of word boundary, the morphemic status of S, the type of S suffix, and the grammatical form co-occurring with the plural.

The raw data cross-classified according to all possible linguistic environment is presented in Table 2.

A maximum likelihood procedure for estimating the probabilistic contributions as in the formula for the variable rule, produces the values in Table 3. We can deduce from Table 3 that the single environmental factor most conducive to the application of the S-aspiration rule is a following consonant with a probability coefficient of 0.89. Another feature which encourages rule application is internal position in the word. Monomorphemes are quite susceptible to aspiration and among form classes in the noun phrase the plural forms of nouns favor rule execution. The degree of formality of the conversational topic is not as great as the linguistic conditioning but it is not negligible.

Table 2 also reveals the extent to which the model captures the systematicity observed in the data. Generally speaking the fit is quite reasonable for a situation where only nine parameters have been estimated to predict twenty-eight cells in a table; independence is thereby verified. However, it should be noted that determiners generally act in a nonindependent manner. Noticeable divergences appear between the distribution of determiners and the expected incidence in the model in either prevocalic or preconsonantal position.

Ma and Herasimchuk also found that the class of determiners exhibited an extraordinary proportion of standard forms in prevocalic position. In attempting to explain this phenomenon, they hypothesized that the S morpheme is retained more often because the initial position in the noun phrase would make the determiner the first element to transmit the information of plurality. Nouns need not preserve the redundant information of the plural morpheme. In an earlier partial study of the variable we obtained similar results. Both these studies, however, lacked the methodology for estimating the appropriate probabilistic parameters underlying the problem.

In terms of the formal characteristics of our model, the discrepancies that were found for determiners indicate the nonindependent

TABLE 2. Observed frequency of s̲ per total cases of S with predicted values in parenthesis.

Style A: Informal	Cons	Voc	Pause
Internal	$\frac{34}{1791}$ (30)		
Monomorphemic	$\frac{89}{1701}$ (67)	$\frac{157}{976}$ (174)	$\frac{153}{500}$ (174)
Verb	$\frac{3}{30}$ (2)	$\frac{5}{13}$ (5)	
Determiner	$\frac{22}{862}$ (61)	$\frac{89}{179}$ (57)	
Adjective	$\frac{3}{142}$ (5)	$\frac{13}{59}$ (8)	$\frac{13}{68}$ (19)
Noun	$\frac{36}{754}$ (22)	$\frac{69}{498}$ (67)	$\frac{146}{544}$ (142)
Style B: Formal			
Internal	$\frac{61}{3654}$ (65)		
Monomorphemic	$\frac{158}{2617}$ (122)	$\frac{219}{1346}$ (284)	$\frac{503}{1120}$ (459)
Verb	$\frac{21}{88}$ (8)	$\frac{21}{72}$ (30)	
Determiner	$\frac{51}{1238}$ (103)	$\frac{167}{359}$ (135)	
Adjective	$\frac{12}{466}$ (17)	$\frac{23}{96}$ (16)	$\frac{34}{101}$ (33)
Noun	$\frac{60}{1247}$ (44)	$\frac{98}{617}$ (97)	$\frac{233}{849}$ (261)

TABLE 3. Contribution of each factor influencing S aspiration.

$p_0 = 0.21$
[Det]   0   [Adj]   0.66   [Noun]   0.58
[monomorphemic]   0.49   [plural]   0.08   [verb]   0
[final]   0   [internal]   0.62
[cons]   0.89   [voc]   0.49   [pause]   0
[informal]   0.15   [formal]   0

interaction between the environmental factors of the rule. A closer look at the set of determiners in the corpus was warranted to explicate the type of interaction between the phonological constraints and the determiners. The hypothesis which emerged was that the distribution of variants is conditioned not by a single phonological factor, but by the conjoined presence of stress and a following vowel.

To verify this hypothesis, data from eleven informants was searched. Each occurrence of determiner was cross-classified for the nature of the phonological environment and the presence of stress in the following syllable. The results displayed in Table 4 unmistakeably show that stress is a variable constraint affecting the distribution of determiners. We therefore assume that this feature should be incorporated into the structural environment of our rule.

An exhaustive search of all S tokens, not just determiners was also effected to delimit the range of the stress effect. The result confirmed that the effect of stress was limited only to determiners and led us to conclude that the configuration of determiner-vowel-stress was governed by a separate rule in the grammar.

TABLE 4. Distribution of s for determiners by following segment and stress (N = 11).

Consonant		Vowel	
stressed	unstressed	stressed	unstressed
$\frac{3}{134}$ 2%	$\frac{3}{170}$ 2%	$\frac{28}{40}$ 70%	$\frac{7}{42}$ 17%

This illustration reveals the use of variable rules as an adjunct to discovery procedures for the detection of hidden linguistic constraints.

S is a well developed sociolinguistic variable in covariation with both stylistic and social features. The exact contribution of each nonlinguistic factor was also estimated following the established procedure. The effect of sex, age group, socioeconomic status, and local origin of speaker were separately correlated with the linguistic constraints. In each and every case, the analysis revealed that the linguistic constraints do not interact with the social constraints; for the probability coefficients assigned to the linguistic features do not noticeably change in the different analyses. This independence is an important characteristic of the relation between language structure and social structure. Also it serves as evidence against the hypothesis that linguistic variation along sociolinguistic dimensions always proceeds by successive reweighting of the features or constraints in rules. Here the configuration of constraints with respect to one another remains relatively fixed, while the input probability varies from one socioeconomic group to another or from one person to another.

CH lenition. The acceleration of rule application rates can occur in selected linguistic environments across certain social and age groups in the context of a rapid sound change. An example of an ongoing sound change in the history of the community is the lenition of CH. This variable presents three variants which are the standard form [č], reduced occlusion [š̑] and a sibilant [š]. We have postulated (Cedergren 1973) two rules to account for the distribution of the newer variants, which represent the step-wise phonetic implementation of the sound change.

Table 5 displays the distribution of the variants when aggregated by the relevant linguistic environments and age groups of the sample. The estimated coefficient values assigned to the social variable clearly indicate that the frequency of CH lenition is not evenly distributed among the speakers of the sample, as seen in Table 6.

The younger speakers under 35, groups I and II, favor the execution of both rules and are the vehicles of the change. The 20-35 age group reveals slightly atypical values for the variable constraints. This group, as seen in Table 5, is more sensitive to the effect of word boundary than the youngest group of speakers, indicating a reweighting of linguistic constraints as the rule is being generalized in the community.

In such cases of relatively rapid rule spread, the variable rule calculation enables us to estimate the rate of increase of rule application in different time periods. From Table 6 we can calculate that the first rule, reduced occlusion, applies, in least favorable environments, 13 per cent of the time for the oldest group, average age 60, 15 per cent for the group of average age 42, 51 per cent for the group of average age 28, and 56 per cent for the group of average age 18. Under the assumption that these represent variable constraints

TABLE 5. Distribution of CH variants by age groups and the preceding linguistic environment. I, age 14-20; II, age 21-35; III, age 36-50; IV, age 51+.

Age group	Variant	Initial CH			Internal CH	
		V	K	P	V	K
I	CH-1	40	40	17	36	76
	CH-2	7	10	14	3	0
	CH-3	53	50	69	60	23
	N	(30)	(29)	(10)	(339)	(13)
II	CH-1	65	52	58	29	50
	CH-2	8	17	12	6	13
	CH-3	27	31	30	63	35
	N	(62)	(29)	(43)	(357)	(30)
III	CH-1	65	75	63	66	90
	CH-2	17	13	26	7	6
	CH-3	28	12	11	25	3
	N	(46)	(16)	(43)	(322)	(33)
IV	CH-1	77	70	71	69	78
	CH-2	7	20	29	11	10
	CH-3	16	10	0	19	10
	N	(30)	(10)	(17)	(198)	(19)

acquired during childhood, we estimate that from about 1938 to 1952, this rule probability increased at an average rate of .025 or 2 1/2 per cent per year, and has more or less ceased to increase since then. The second rule on the other hand increased even more, 3 per cent per year during the 1940s and has continued to increase at half that rate since then until it now applies to about every eligible input string.

We would contend that insofar as rule diffusion rates can be estimated from synchronic data, this is the methodology of choice. Methods not based on age-related variability, on the other hand, run the risk of imputing or exaggerating dynamic qualities in situations

TABLE 6. Linguistic and age factors influencing CH lenition.

Rule 1: Reduced occlusion							
$p_0 = 0.13$							
[k-]	0	[v]	0.18	[p-]	0.21		
[internal]	0.06	[initial]	0				
[I]	0.47	[II]	0.44	[III]	0.02	[IV]	0

Rule 2: Lenition							
$p_0 = 0$							
[k-]	0.16	[v-]	0.49	[p-]	0		
[internal]	0.35	[initial]	0				
[I]	0.84	[II]	0.69	[III]	0.27	[IV]	0

which may well have exhibited stable variability over many centuries, e.g. S variation in Spanish.

Recurrent linguistic patterns. Our work on variability in Panamanian Spanish and Montreal French provides an opportunity to independently corroborate or refine certain sociolinguistic principles which have been proposed by Labov (1971) and Wolfram (1971). The factors contributing to the deletion of L in Montreal French (Sankoff and Cedergren 1971), word final D and N deletion, and S aspiration in Spanish (Cedergren 1973) all indicate that the following phonological environment of consonant reduction or deletion rules does not affect rule executability idiosyncratically. If the following segment is not a vowel, the probability of rule application increases.

The presence of a grammatical feature is another condition which receives cross-linguistic validation of interaction patterns. The S suffixes in Spanish tend to constrain the aspiration and deletion of the variable. This conservative effect on rule application converges with the results of the study of consonant cluster deletion in Black English (Labov et al. 1968, Wolfram 1969). However, the deletion of intervocalic D and final R in Spanish appears to provide counter examples to this principle. In both instances, the presence of a grammatical form favors rule execution rather than constraining it. Intervocalic D of the past participle formative as in pasado and cantado, and the formative R, as in the infinitive cantar and chupar tend to delete more than monomorphemic forms. These grammatical forms, however, are both introduced by obligatory transformational rules, and thus it is likely that predictable grammatical surface markers should be susceptible to variability. As a result, statements about the typical behavior of grammatical forms should be refined in terms of the surface predictability of the form.

Conclusions. We have provided empirical evidence about certain characteristics of variable constraints. These constraints tend not to interact. Cases of non-negligible interaction indicate the possible presence of hidden constraints or discontinuity in the grammar of the speech community due to rapid on-going sound changes. The variable rule calculation permits us to estimate the rate of increase of rule application across time. The probability coefficients contributed by factors influencing certain types of variable rules in Spanish and French confirm sociolinguistic principles that have been proposed from the study of English.

ACKNOWLEDGMENTS

I would like to particularly thank David Sankoff who developed the procedure for estimating rule probabilities. I am also grateful to Gillian and David Sankoff for their helpful suggestions and comments on work which led to this paper.

REFERENCES

Alonso, Dámaso. 1962. Sobre la -s final de sílaba en el mundo hispánico. In: Enciclopedia de Lingüística Hispánica. Suplemento.
Cedergren, Henrietta J. 1971. Una descripción sociolingüística del español de Panamá. Manuscript.
_____. 1973. The interplay of social and linguistic factors in Panama. Unpublished Ph.D. dissertation, Cornell University.
_____ and David Sankoff. 1972. Variable rules: Performance as a statistical reflection of competence. Manuscript.
Labov, William. 1969. Contraction, deletion and inherent variability of the English copula. Language. 45.715-62.
_____. 1971. Methodology. In: A survey of linguistic science. Ed. by W. O. Dingwall.
_____, Paul Cohen, Clarence Robins, and John Lewis. 1968. A study of the non-standard English of Negro and Puerto Rican speakers in New York City. Cooperative Research Report 3288.
Ma, Roxana and Eleanor Herasimchuk. 1971. The linguistic dimensions of a bilingual neighborhood. In: Bilingualism in the barrio. Ed. by Fishman, Cooper, and Ma. The Hague, Mouton.
Sankoff, Gillian and Henrietta J. Cedergren. 1971. Some results of a sociolinguistic study of Montreal French. In: Linguistic diversity in Canada. Ed. by R. Darnell.

Vallejo-Claros, Bernardo. 1970. La distribución y estratificación de /r/ /r̄/ y /s/ en el Español Cubano. Unpublished Ph. D. dissertation, University of Texas at Austin.

Wolfram, Walter. 1969. A sociolinguistic description of Detroit Negro Speech. Urban Language Series 5. Washington, D. C., Center for Applied Linguistics.

_____. 1971. Overlapping influence in the English of second generation Puerto Rican teenagers in East Harlem. Final Report, U. S. Office of Education Grant No. 3-70-0033(508). Washington, D. C., Center for Applied Linguistics.

QUANTITATIVE VERSUS DYNAMIC PARADIGMS: THE CASE OF MONTREAL QUE

DEREK BICKERTON

University of Hawaii

Cynics have long divided our profession into two mutually exclusive classes--'God's truth' linguists and 'hocus-pocus' linguists. Like all dichotomies, this is overly simplistic, and yet it does capture a deep truth about the field. For the root of the paradox lies within language itself, where extremes of orderliness and variability are somehow reconciled; the dichotomy arises simply because each of the two classes tends to concentrate on one of these to the exclusion of the other. Thus the 'God's truth' linguist seizes the extant patterns, extends and enlarges on them, and rationalizes away any stubborn facts that do not fit them, while the 'hocus-pocus' linguist gathers the facts, all the facts, and regards as artefacts of analysis any patterns that do not emerge ready-made from their scrutiny. Note that, relative to this fundamental dichotomy, the wars of the schools are superficial and fleeting: neogrammarian 'God's truth' yields to structuralist 'hocus-pocus', which in turn is vanquished by transformational 'God's truth' again. Common sense alone should tell us, at this juncture, to beware a further swing of the pendulum disguised as the ultimate revelation.

Fortunately there has been, during the past five years, a growing realization among linguists that if the discipline is ever to fulfill its perhaps premature and exaggerated claims to being a science, [1] it must somehow escape from this double bind, cease to oscillate between metaphysics and botanising, and proceed somehow to reconcile order with variability, just as its subject-matter contrives to do. But to do this satisfactorily is far from being an easy task, and I shall later reluctantly suggest that one of the two apparently most

promising approaches to date runs the risk of following through the
pendulum-swing and losing sight of the principle of order in a welter
of empirical fact.

Whether or not this is the case, the two approaches--which have
been referred to by their partisans as the 'dynamic paradigm' and the
'quantitative paradigm' respectively[2]--differ so much in both pre-
suppositions and techniques that it becomes rather important to
adjudicate between them. For this reason, the present paper chooses
to concentrate on a single, but critical, case, in order to determine
which of the two paradigms handles it the most successfully. The
case at issue is the deletion of the complementizer que by speakers
of Montreal French, discussed in G. Sankoff (MS) and Cedergren and
D. Sankoff (MS).

It may be as well to begin with a brief resume of the two approaches.
Both stem from the belief that variability in primary speech data cannot be dismissed as entirely a feature of performance but must to a
considerable extent reflect the competence of its producers. In consequence, it becomes necessary to introduce into grammars rules that
will generate at least part of the variable output observed. These
points have been abundantly discussed in the literature, [3] and no attempt will be made to argue them here.

The difference between the approaches becomes apparent when the
stage of rule-writing is reached. It is well at this point to anticipate the objection that only notational differences are involved. In
fact, differences in rule-schema reflect profound differences in the
nature of our assumptions about how the human mind works. For
those who believe, as the present writer does, that the major task
at present before linguistics is the empirical exploration of human
mental capacities, such differences must therefore be of considerable interest.

The dynamic paradigm requires the least radical alteration in our
present views of mental capacity. It proposes that variability, insofar as this stems from competence, simply results from the spread
of language changes through time and space (social as well as geographic). Thus, at any given point in time, the output of a speaker A
(whom a given rule had not yet 'reached') would differ from that of a
speaker B (whom the same rule had 'passed') with respect at least
to the operation of that rule, and would leave open the possibility of
a third speaker, C, whom the rule was just 'reaching', and who in
consequence would sometimes produce A's output, sometimes B's.
Such a model would account both for interpersonal variation (that between A's and B's outputs) and also for intrapersonal or inherent
variation (that in which C's output differs from itself). Moreover,
it could do so on the basis of a grammar that contained only categorical rules, with two provisos: first, that not every member of

a speech community would be assumed to share the same set of rules, and second, that there be accepted a convention by which two quasi-equivalent rules (i. e. an 'old' rule and its replacement) would apply alternately for those persons in the process of losing the former and acquiring the latter. The cost of this modification, in terms of grammars as we hitherto know them, would simply be the necessity of writing 'polylectal grammars' for the community as a whole (cf. Bailey 1968, Bickerton 1972). It has been argued that such grammars would not be psychologically real, but then psychological reality has never been claimed for them. What is psychologically real is the subset of the set of rules constituting such a grammar which is held by each individual--such subsets differing slightly from one another perhaps (though not necessarily) for every member of a given community. In other words, the dynamic paradigm retains the concept of the autonomous grammar-forming individual at the cost of rejecting the principle (held tacitly or explicitly by virtually all other persuasions) that individual and community grammars are isomorphic.

The quantitative paradigm, however, takes a more radical approach to mental capacity, and a less radical one to the relationship between communal and individual grammars. With regard to the first, it assumes that the human mind has the power to handle variability on a very large scale, and in particular is able to maintain proportional relationships between competing phenomena over long periods of time. As I discussed this question at length in Bickerton (1971) I shall not return to it here; moreover, the second point is more relevant to our immediate argument. Cedergren and D. Sankoff (MS:39) state

> We have written our rules in terms of individual speakers'
> grammars, and not in terms of group or social grammars;
> but these constructs can be attained if desired by appropriate
> adjustments of input probabilities [emphasis added].

At first sight, this might seem to deny the isomorphism of communal and individual grammars; but in fact the basic principle is preserved. As between the two, only relative PROBABILITIES of rule-application are seen as varying; the actual rules that are applied are shared by both.

In fact, isomorphism is preserved at the cost of introducing the 'variable rule' concept. Variable rules (first proposed in Labov et al. 1968, Labov 1969, and now presented in a mathematically more sophisticated version in Cedergren and D. Sankoff MS) attempt to deal with variation directly: that is to say, when confronted with a situation in which for many if not all speakers two features equivalent in meaning and function are seen to alternate, they specify as precisely as possible the environments within which alternation occurs and, then, for each environment, estimate relative probabilities of occurrence for either feature. Such rules, for all their novelty, are cast in the traditional generative format; I shall, however, argue here that they are merely structuralist wolves in generative clothing--simple data-displaying devices which mask rather than reveal the real rules involved in the generation of variable data. I shall, moreover, do this on the basis of what has been presented as one of the quantitative paradigm's strongest cases.

The variable deletion by speakers of Montreal French of the complementizer que is dealt with in considerable detail by both G. Sankoff (MS) and Cedergren and D. Sankoff (MS). Data consist of the speech output, during the first half-hour of interview, of sixteen Montreal speakers, evenly divided into four subgroups by sex and class (working or professional). Details of group production are given in Cedergren and Sankoff's Table 6 (reprinted here as Table 1). Data for individuals are given in Sankoff's Figure 2 (reprinted here as Figure 1). In analyzing this data, G. Sankoff finds grammatical environments of no analytic relevance, and claims that constraining factors are purely phonological: the nature of the segments immediately preceding and following the complementizer. This part of the analysis is almost certainly correct. However, Sankoff then proceeds to conflate the nine environments of her Figure 2 (Figure 1, here) into three, to yield the arrangement shown in her Table 8 (reprinted here as Table 2).

TABLE 1. (Table 6, Cedergren and Sankoff MS) Presence of que in complement over total number of complements in nine phonological environments (S = sibilant, C = other consonant, V = vowel).

| | Working class | | | | | | Professional | | | | | |
| | men | | | women | | | men | | | women | | |
	S	C	V	S	C	V	S	C	V	S	C	V
S_	$\frac{0}{11}$	--	$\frac{4}{7}$	$\frac{0}{7}$	$\frac{1}{2}$	$\frac{6}{6}$	$\frac{3}{4}$	$\frac{7}{7}$	$\frac{9}{10}$	$\frac{11}{24}$	$\frac{4}{4}$	$\frac{14}{15}$
C_	$\frac{1}{12}$	$\frac{2}{2}$	$\frac{8}{8}$	$\frac{3}{15}$	$\frac{0}{2}$	$\frac{11}{11}$	$\frac{5}{7}$	$\frac{5}{6}$	$\frac{9}{9}$	$\frac{5}{9}$	$\frac{5}{6}$	$\frac{9}{9}$
V_	$\frac{6}{15}$	$\frac{4}{7}$	$\frac{6}{8}$	$\frac{20}{31}$	$\frac{17}{20}$	$\frac{37}{37}$	$\frac{26}{26}$	$\frac{11}{12}$	$\frac{16}{16}$	$\frac{20}{21}$	$\frac{15}{16}$	$\frac{42}{42}$

FIGURE 1. Deletion of que for sixteen subjects in nine phonological environments. Scale: one case = 1/16 inch. Black bars on left indicate que absent; white bars on right indicate que present.

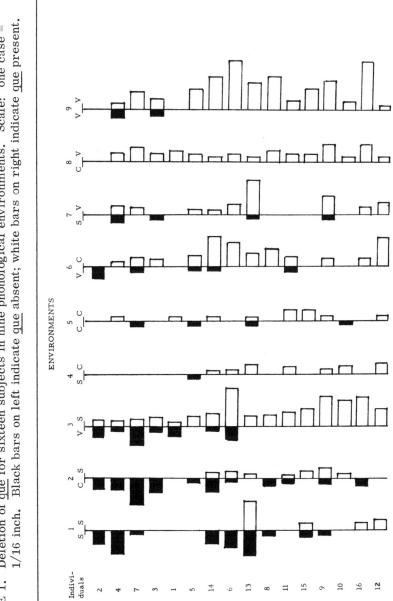

ENVIRONMENTS

TABLE 2. Percentage of deleted que for sixteen individuals in three environments.

Individuals	Environments			Overall deletion	N
	I	II	III		
	%	%	%	%	
2	100.0	87.5	0	82.4	17
4	91.7	25.0	37.5	55.5	27
7	100.0	66.7	0	53.1	32
3	100.0	16.7	28.5	41.2	17
1	. .	50.0	0	33.3	9
5	50.0	40.0	0	23.3	21
14	75.0	12.5	0	21.6	37
6	75.0	25.0	0	21.0	53
13	44.4	8.3	4.4	18.9	53
8	100.0	0.0	0	12.0	25
11	50.0	9.1	0	11.1	18
15	40.0	0	0	9.5	21
9	40.0	0	4.6	7.7	39
10	0	9.1	0	6.7	15
16	50.0	0	0	2.9	35
12	0	0	0	0	25
Overall deletion:	68.5%	19.2%	4.0%	23.0%	
N	89	177	178		444

The motivation for this is far from clear. In part it seems to stem from a desire to prove the consistency of the relationship I > II > III (i.e. that que in the group of environments labelled I will be deleted oftener than in the group labelled II, and oftener in the group labelled II than in that labelled III); in part from polemical reasons (the desire to show that quantitative methods can, in addition to much else, also replicate certain patterns of data shown in Bickerton 1971). Whatever the reason, there are two curious results. First, we note that the conflation of environments does not produce natural phonological sets. Such sets would have resulted from a three-by-three grouping of environments into the following:

(i)   S___S: C___S: V___S.
(ii) S___C: C___C: V___C.
(iii) S___V: C___V: V___V.

Instead, the last member of the first set is thrown into the second set to give the three unnatural and unequal sets:

(i)   S___S: C___S.
(ii) V___S: S___C: C___C: V___C.
(iii) S___V: C___V: V___V.

The only reason I can find for this curious maneuver is that, if natural sets had been used, the two 'errors in scale types' in San-koff's Table 8, i.e. instances where cells containing deletions occur to the right of cells without deletions, as with speakers 9 and 10, would have been increased to four (with the addition of speakers 3 and 4), so that the table would have been rather less credible as a demonstration of the claim that deletion in any category implies deletion in all leftward categories, while absence of deletion implies absence in all rightward ones.

The second result affects the quantity of variation shown. In G. Sankoff's Figure 2 (Figure 1 here), there are 113 filled cells, of which 89 contain only deletions or insertions, and therefore represent invariance in one environment for one speaker. In other words, when data for each individual in each environment are presented separately, the amount of variation present is 22 per cent. But if we now look at Sankoff's Table 8 (Table 2, here), we see that here there are 47 filled cells of which only 24 are invariant. This means that when we keep speakers as individuals and conflate environments, the apparent amount of variation increases to 49 per cent, i.e. more than doubles! But this is not all. If we next look at Cedergren and Sankoff's Table 6 (Table 1, here), we find 35 filled cells of which only 15 are invariant. This means that when we reverse the previous process--i.e. keep environments separate but conflate the output of individuals--the apparent amount of variation rises yet further, this time to a massive 57 per cent! In other words (as already suggested in Bickerton 1973), the very high amounts of variation found in quantitative-paradigm studies are largely artefacts of the mode of analysis.

Once the quantitativist has isolated the relevant environments and constraining factors, all that remains for him is to rank the latter in their order of force--a simple arithmetical calculation, given the numerical frequencies of occurrence for each variable in each environment--and state the result in terms of a variable rule, as Cedergren and Sankoff do for the variable constraints on deletion of que:

(1) [Cedergren and Sankoff (15)]

$$\text{que} \rightarrow \emptyset \ / \ \delta \left\{ \begin{array}{c} \left[\begin{array}{c} + \text{cor} \\ + \text{strd} \end{array} \right] \\ \left[\begin{array}{c} \alpha \ \text{cor} \\ -\alpha \ \text{strd} \end{array} \right] \\ \left[+ \text{syll} \right] \end{array} \right\} \ \#\# \ \emptyset \ O \ \underset{[+ \text{compl}]}{\underline{\hspace{2cm}}} \ \#\# \ \varepsilon \left\{ \begin{array}{c} \left[\begin{array}{c} + \text{cor} \\ + \text{strd} \end{array} \right] \\ \left[\begin{array}{c} \beta \ \text{cor} \\ -\beta \ \text{strd} \end{array} \right] \\ \left[+ \text{syll} \right] \end{array} \right\}^{4}$$

What we have here is, in fact, no more than a data-displaying
device--a sophisticated-looking but merely tabular statement of
the statistical values found in a particular set of data. As such,
its appearance of dynamism is illusory. It can represent change
by varying the order of constraints, but it cannot explain change, it
cannot show us why one thing happened rather than another, or predict the course that a given change will follow. In fact, as I shall
show, very precise and specific mechanisms of linguistic change
are at work here; but the quantitative paradigm loses these in its
anxiety to produce a single homogeneous statement that will be valid
for all speakers at once. This anxiety, though long endorsed by
tradition, lies, I believe, at the core of our inability to produce even
leakproof synchronic grammars, let alone dynamic grammars that
will show us how languages actually change.

I shall now reanalyze the data along dynamic-paradigm lines.
The first stage in such analysis is the construction of an implicational scale (cf. Elliott et al. 1969, DeCamp 1971, etc.). The
phrase 'first stage' is used advisedly. It is assumed by G. Sankoff
(MS:49-50) that an implicational scale is either deviance-free or use-
less as an analytic device, and indeed there is little in the literature
to suggest the contrary. There has, indeed, been an apparent failure to realize than an idealized implicational scale and the type of
scale that is formed by arranging raw data in a scale pattern are two
very different things. The first (which is by definition uniform and
deviance-free) is in fact an abstract unit of measurement, with which
the deviations of raw data from the ideal can be precisely determined.
It is perfectly true, as Sankoff states, that the two will only fit when
data is drawn from river valleys, creole continuums and other situations where change is unifocal and unidirectional. What she fails to
see is that this does not matter. It is precisely by interpreting the
differences between an ideal scale and the scaled data that we arrive
at an accurate understanding of the grammatical rules involved.

Table 3 shows both an ideal scale (set forth in the lects numbered
(a)) and the actual data for que (set forth in lects numbered (b)). We
will note that already the data look far less variable than they did. The

TABLE 3. Implicational scaling of que data. (1 = que insertion; 2 = que deletion; 12 = variable insertion/deletion; deviations ringed.)

Lect	Speaker	1 C-V	2 V-V	3 S-V	4 V-S	5 V-C	6 C-C	7 S-C	8 C-S	9 S-S
I(a)		1	1	1	1	1	1	1	1	1
I(b)	12	1	1	1	1	1	1	1	-	1
	16	1	1	1	1	1	-	-	②	1
II(a)		1	1	1	1	1	1	1	1	12
II(b)	13	1	1	⑫	1	1	⑫	1	1	12
	15	1	1	-	1	-	1	-	1	12
	10	1	1	-	1	-	②	1	1	-
	1	1	1	-	-	⑫	-	1	-	-
III(a)		1	1	1	1	1	1	1	1	2
IV(a)		1	1	1	1	1	1	1	12	2
IV(b)	11	1	1	-	1	⑫	1	1	12	-
	9	1	1	⑫	1	1	1	1	12	2
	6	1	1	1	⑫	1	-	1	12	2
	14	1	1	1	⑫	⑫	1	1	12	2
	4	1	⑫	⑫	⑫	1	1	-	12	2
V(a)		1	1	1	1	1	1	1	2	2
V(b)	8	1	1	-	1	1	-	-	2	2
	3	1	⑫	②	⑫	1	-	-	2	2
VI(a)		1	1	1	1	1	1	12	2	2
VII(a)		1	1	1	1	1	1	2	2	2
VIII(a)		1	1	1	1	1	12	2	2	2
IX(a)		1	1	1	1	1	2	2	2	2
X(a)		1	1	1	1	12	2	2	2	2
X(b)	5	1	1	1	1	12	2	2	2	2
XI(a)		1	1	1	1	2	2	2	2	2
XII(a)		1	1	1	12	2	2	2	2	2
XII(b)	7	1	1	1	12	⑫	2	-	2	2
	2	1	-	1	12	2	-	-	2	2

table is 85.2 per cent scalable, i.e. the amount of apparent variation
has now shrunk to 14.8 per cent. It is true that, hitherto, any figure
below 90 per cent scalability has been regarded as unsatisfactory--
but that, of course, was when a match between real and ideal was regarded as the whole aim of scaling. Once scaling is accepted as an
analytic tool rather than a final summation of analysis, achievement
of this or any other preset level becomes irrelevant.

In subsequent analysis of a constructed scale, one must first observe the distribution of deviations. There are fourteen deviations
in columns 2-5, as against only three in columns 6-9. Let us concentrate first on the less deviant sector. Column 9, entirely without
deviations, marks (for all speakers except possibly 16) the earliest
environment for the onset of change. It is also (as Baileyan wave
theory would lead us to expect) the most narrowly defined environment, i.e. that marked by the largest number of constraining features. The first stage in the deletion of que, then, is a rule which
has been acquired, or is in process of being acquired, by all but two
speakers in the sample, and it may be stated as:

$$(2) \quad \text{que} \rightarrow \emptyset \: / \: \begin{pmatrix} + \text{ cor} \\ + \text{ strd} \\ - \text{ syll} \end{pmatrix} \underline{\hspace{2cm}} \begin{pmatrix} + \text{ cor} \\ + \text{ strd} \\ - \text{ syll} \end{pmatrix}$$

The theory would then lead us to expect that the most heavily marked
feature (+ strd) would be dropped from either the preceding or the
following environment. It is impossible to tell from the data as given
whether or not this is the case; it is quite possible that the variability
of speakers 4, 6, 9, 11, 14 in the environment 'C-S' arises merely
because the Sankoff analysis has not taken (+ cor), (- strd) environments into account. Thus, while we may hypothesize that the next
step after (2) is really rule (3):

$$(3) \quad \text{que} \rightarrow \emptyset \: / \: \begin{pmatrix} + \text{ cor} \\ - \text{ syll} \end{pmatrix} \underline{\hspace{2cm}} \begin{pmatrix} + \text{ cor} \\ + \text{ strd} \\ + \text{ syll} \end{pmatrix}$$

in fact the first step as shown in available data is

$$(4) \quad \text{que} \rightarrow \emptyset \: / \: (- \text{ syll}) \underline{\hspace{2cm}} \begin{pmatrix} + \text{ cor} \\ + \text{ strd} \\ - \text{ syll} \end{pmatrix}$$

Table 3 now shows a curious feature. After rule (4) has become categorical for speakers 3 and 8 (in Lect 5) we find the four empty lects
VI-IX. Hitherto it has been hypothesized (in Bickerton 1973, for

example) that such empty lects might indicate some kind of boundary between systems. This may indeed be true in some cases; in others, however (as here), the empty lects stem inevitably from the choice of environments, which is mechanical and conflicts with the 'natural' environments as selected by the rule-change process itself.

We may best understand this point if we suppose what the scale by itself would lead us to expect, i. e. that change would spread to the environment of column 7 before reaching that of column 6. There is, we will appreciate, no way in which rule (4) could be simplified so as to spread change to the environment S-C without at the same time spreading it to C-C as well; to spread it to the former environment only, one would have to retain rule (4) unchanged and add rule (5):

(5) que → ∅ / (+ cor) _____ (- syll)
                (+ strd)
                (- syll)

But this would be, in terms of Baileyan theory, a counter-natural proceeding. Change normally proceeds from more-marked to less-marked; rule (5) would reverse this process, complicating the grammar rather than simplifying it. The fact that Lects VI-XI are empty is thus an important validation of the theory, indicating that such complications cannot take place, and that change MUST spread simultaneously to environments S-C and C-C, by the dropping of (+ cor), (+ strd) from rule (4) to give rule (6):

(6) que → ∅ / (- syll) _____ (- syll)

We may therefore summarize the evidence of columns 6-9 by stating that they show (with negligible deviation) the spread of a uniform syntactic change through the progressive generalization of the phonological environments in which it can occur, precisely as would be predicted by Baileyan theory.

However, the evidence of columns 2-5 is far less clear, and in order to interpret it correctly we must now make a further examination of the data, which may now be most conveniently arranged as in Figure 2. These data are, as we shall see, incomplete at one or two critical points, but as this is a defect of the original sample, there is nothing further we can do about it here. I am going to assume that, where data are missing, speaker output would have followed the rules suggested by the Baileyan model.

This may seem at first sight an extremely arbitrary procedure, but in reality it is far from being so. The study of language variation has so far suffered from a general ignorance as to what was, or what was not, adequate data to establish a given point beyond

FIGURE 2. Individual deletion patterns for sixteen speakers (1 = invariant insertion; 2 = invariant deletion; X = variability).

12

	S	C	V
S_	1	1	1
C_	-	1	1
V_	1	1	1

16

	S	C	V
S_	1	-	1
C_	2	-	1
V_	1	1	1

15

	S	C	V
S_	X	-	-
C_	1	1	1
V_	1	-	1

10

	S	C	V
S_	-	1	-
C_	1	2	1
V_	1	-	1

9

	S	C	V
S_	2	1	X
C_	X	1	1
V_	1	1	1

11

	S	C	V
S_	-	1	-
C_	X	1	1
V_	1	X	1

8

	S	C	V
S_	2	-	-
C_	2	-	1
V_	1	1	1

13

	S	C	V
S_	X	1	X
C_	1	X	1
V_	1	1	1

6

	S	C	V
S_	2	1	1
C_	X	-	1
V_	X	1	1

14

	S	C	V
S_	2	1	1
C_	X	1	1
V_	X	X	1

5

	S	C	V
S_	-	2	1
C_	2	2	1
V_	1	X	1

1

	S	C	V
S_	-	-	-
C_	-	1	1
V_	X	-	-

3

	S	C	V
S_	-	-	2
C_	2	-	1
V_	X	1	X

7

	S	C	V
S_	2	-	1
C_	2	2	1
V_	X	X	1

4

	S	C	V
S_	2	-	X
C_	X	1	1
V_	X	1	X

2

	S	C	V
S_	2	-	1
C_	2	-	-
V_	X	2	1

reasonable doubt. One could complain in general terms about other people's data or suggest (as G. Sankoff, MS:33 does with some of my data) on rather general grounds that it might be somehow inadequate. But an adequate model of language change enables one to specify exactly the information that data should yield, and where the original data are insufficient to give indications one way or the other, then the investigator can return to the speakers involved and reinterview or otherwise obtain sufficient data to resolve the points. Such a procedure has, in fact, far stronger safeguards than any hitherto adopted.

Examining Figure 2, we find that there are five speakers (2, 4, 6, 7, 14) who have deletion, optional or obligatory, in all three -S environments, while two more (1, 3) with vacant -S cells may be assumed also to have it. If we now turn back to the implicational scale of Table 3, and look at the column which contains most deviations (column 4, V-S environments) we note that its six deviations are all accounted for by speakers on the above list, i.e. 1, 3, 4, 6, 7, 14. This is far from being a coincidence, and in the light of the wave model it has a very clear and natural explanation.

We will recall that, for some speakers, rule (4) was simplified by loss of (+ cor), (+ strd) from following environments to yield rule (6). But this is not the only possible simplification of rule (4). It is equally possible to simplify it by dropping the feature (- syll) from the preceding environment, to give rule (7):

(7) que → ∅ / _____ (+ cor)
                            (+ strd)
                            (+ syll)

Both simplifications are natural, and, on the basis of present knowledge, there seems no reason why either should take precedence over the other.

However, since those speakers who have rule (6)--i.e. 2, 5, 7-- also have at least some deletion in V- environments, it could be argued that there is only a single line of development: that all speakers who progress past rule (4) in fact simplify it to (7) and then further simplify (7) to (8) by then dropping (+ cor), (+ strd) from preceding environments to give:

(8) que → ∅ / _____ (- syll)

so that rule (6) is in fact not required at all. While this is not impossible, there seem to be good reasons for supposing two distinct simplification paths. For example, speakers 2, 5, and 7 all have (if we ignore unfilled cells) obligatory deletion in S-S, C-S, and C-C environments, which is what we would expect if they shared rule (6), and only optional or null deletion in V-S environments. Now if we assume that, instead of acquiring (6) and then (8), they acquired (7) and then (8), this would mean that a later rule, (8), would be categorical (for speaker 2) or almost so (for 5 and 7) while an earlier rule, (7), remained variable. So far I am not aware of any cases in which an earlier rule remains variable while a later one becomes categorical, and, unless such cases are found, we must assume that speakers 2, 5, 7 first acquired categorical (6) and subsequently variable (8) (it will be obvious that the effects of (8) will vary depending on whether it is a simplification of (6) or of (7)).

If indeed two paths are followed to simplify (4), then we have a simple explanation of how 'dialect-splitting' can arise, not through some vague 'social' agency, but by purely internal mechanisms of linguistic change. Naturally, the speaker's choice of path will be influenced by the company he keeps, but there can be no 'social motivation' as such for dropping (+ cor), (+ strd) constraints from following environments rather than (- syll) from preceding ones, or vice versa. Yet an accumulation of such forked paths could very rapidly cause perceptible differences between the 'dialects' of two groups.

However, if we assume (8) follows (6) for the three speakers in question, some facts still require explanation. Acquisition of (8) should spread deletion simultaneously to the environments V-S, V-C; in fact, while 7 has variable deletion in both environments (indicating that (8) is in process of acquisition) 5 has variable deletion in V-C but null deletion in V-S, while 2 has categorical deletion in V-C but only variable deletion in V-S. However, if we look at Table 1, we find that in 5's two cells there is a low proportion of deletions (2/6) and in 2's, a high one (7/1). We must recall also that, as shown in the discussion of rules (5) and (6), some of the environments distinguished by Sankoff are 'unnatural' ones; here, for instance, no real purpose is served by distinguishing between V-S and V-C, since acquisition of rule (8) must spread deletion to both without distinction. The output of 2 and 5 merely indicates that, for the latter, the spread has only just begun, and, for the former, that it is almost complete, but that, for both, it is still in a variable stage. The fact that 2's single insertion fell in V-S rather than V-C, or that 5's two deletions fell in V-C rather than V-S may be assumed (pending evidence to the contrary) to be simply an accident of the sample, made all the likelier by the low count in the affected cells.

We are now left with only eleven deviant cells unaccounted for: the S-V, V-V cells of 3 and 4, the S-V cells of 9 and 13, the C-C cells of 10 and 13, the V-C cells of 11 and 14, and the C-S cell of 16. Note that these deviances now affect only half the sample, i. e. the other half follows without exception the rules so far given. For

the remainder, there are two possibilities. Either we can treat all
deviations as performance errors, in which case no further explanation is necessary, or we can attempt to account for them in terms
of the creation of new rules not connected with the major rule-change
so far discussed. The question is one which only more extensive
data on the speakers concerned can resolve adequately, but there is
in fact reason to believe that the second of the two possibilities may
be the right one.

The fact that four of the eleven deviances occur in the same cell--
S-V--immediately suggests the possibility that we have here a rule
quite unconnected with (2), i. e. :

(9) que → ø / (+ cor) _____ (+ syll)
                 (+ strd)
                 (- syll)

This possibility is reinforced by the fact that, of the four speakers
involved, one seems to have categorical deletion in this environment
(although this may be due to small sample size). Further, it is note-
worthy that, with the exception of 13, no speakers who have deletion
in -V environments have it in -C environments, while equally, those
speakers who have deletion in both -S and -C environments do not
have it in -V environments. This suggests the following: if only
four speakers have (9), and if no speaker has yet extended it, then
(9) must have been very recently acquired--certainly not earlier
than the acquisition of (6) by those who have acquired it. Now, while
(6) seems to simplify to (8), there would be, in theory, nothing to
prevent an alternative simplification to (10):

(10) que → ø / (- syll) _____

The result of this would be to spread deletion to S-V and C-V environments simultaneously. But no speaker in fact does this; and if, instead, a speaker were to add (9) to (6), the result would be as counter-
natural a grammar as would result from the addition of (5) to (4). In
other words, a rule would have been spread, not by simplification of
the original formula, but by addition of an 'extra' rule. However,
for the speaker who has not acquired (6)--who has only (2) or (4) as
his latest acquisition--(9) would present itself, not as an extension
of any already-acquired rule, but rather as a totally separate rule,
which could therefore be added to the grammar as freely as any
other. There is nothing strange in this; evidence has already been
given (Bickerton 1972) that rules can block other rules, and one
would here hypothesize that acquisition of (6) blocks (9), and vice

versa. The possibility is an interesting one, and deserves empirical
investigation.

With regard to the remaining seven apparent deviations, there
exists the further possibility that two of them--the V-V deletions of
speakers 3 and 4--derive from yet a third rule-change process,
which would consist of the addition of rule (11):

(11) que → ∅ / (+ syll) _____ (+ syll)

The possibility, one must admit, seems rather remote, and is really
only worth entertaining because, in this case, social circumstances
may give support to it. For, while the four speakers possibly acquiring rule (9) were widely distributed by class and sex, 3 and 4 are
both working-class males, therefore likelier to share rule-systems
than speakers of more disparate backgrounds. As with the putative
rule (9), only further empirical investigation of the outputs of the
speakers concerned can settle the issue one way or the other. It is
worth noting, though, that neither of the two possible outcomes can
adversely reflect on the dynamic paradigm itself: if deletions continue to appear in the relevant environments, then the rules exist as
given, and if not, the original deletions must simply be treated as
performance errors along with the five deviations still unaccounted
for.

For, even if we accept, as we may well do, that 'performance
consists essentially of samples of competence' (G. Sankoff, MS:4),
we are not thereby obliged to deny the existence of performance
error, and indeed we would be very unwise to do so. Unfortunately,
for all the discussion of the competence-performance distinction
that has taken place in the last decade and a half, no one has as yet
even hypothesized how much of a given speaker's output is likely to
constitute performance error (though Labov 1970 claims that only
about 2 per cent of colloquial speech is 'ungrammatical'). If in fact
we are left with only five deviations--those of speakers 10, 11, 13,
14 and 16--and if, as seems to be the case, these five deviations
arise simply through the occurrence of five individual deletions out
of a total of 444 insertion/deletions--just over 1 per cent of the
total--then this result should surely fall within the expected limits
of performance error: it would certainly be much odder if no such
'errors' were to be found in our data!

To sum up, the dynamic paradigm gives us a much more reasoned,
detailed, and informative account of the Montreal que-deletion data
than the quantitative paradigm can; an account, moreover, which is
in accordance with the theoretical predictions of the dynamic wave
model. Where quantitative analysis found no more than general
statistical trends, dynamic analysis has been able to show the

complete operation of a major rule change, spreading through the
community via regular and predictable stages; further, it has been
able to specify the conditions under which one could determine
whether the residue of unexplained variability derives solely from
performance error or partly from the inception of further rule
changes. The description it yields may be summarized as follows:

Overall rule system (9 and 11 conjectural)

(2) que → ∅ / (+ cor) _____ (+ cor)
           (+ strd)   (+ strd)
           (+ syll)   (- syll)

(4) que → ∅ / (- syll) _____ (+ cor)
                             (+ strd)
                             (- syll)

(7) que → ∅ / _____ (+ cor)
                             (+ strd)
                             (- syll)

(6) que → ∅ / (-syll) _____ (- syll)

(8) que → ∅ / _____ (- syll)

(9) que → ∅ / (+ cor) _____ (+ syll)
           (+ strd)
           (- syll)

(11) que → ∅ / (+ syll) _____ (+ syll)

Individual rule systems

Speakers	Rules
10, 12, 16:	No deletion rules
15	2 variable
13:	2 variable (9 variable)
11:	2 categorical, 4 variable
9:	2 categorical, 4 variable (9 variable)
6, 14:	2 categorical, 4 and 7 variable
4:	2 categorical, 4 and 7 variable (9 and 11 variable)
8:	4 categorical
1:	4 categorical, 7 variable
3:	4 categorical, 7 variable (9 categorical, 11 variable)
2, 5, 7:	6 categorical, 8 variable

If we present this information graphically, as in Figure 3, we are able to refute yet a further argument in favor of the quantitative paradigm. Arguing against DeCamp's insistence (1971:355) that the sociolinguist should correlate nonlinguistic variables to linguistic data, rather than vice versa, Sankoff (MS:55) claims her reason for not doing so is due to

> the desire of sociolinguists for their results to have some sociocultural validity, and to attempt to define categories which are socially meaningful for the people whose linguistic behavior is being investigated . . . In other words, sociolinguists who start by defining categories based on social or cultural criteria are not doing so to be arbitrary, but so that their results will correspond to socially or culturally meaningful categories.

I find this a strange argument. Either the relevant social and linguistic categories will exactly coincide (a happy, if unlikely event, which would render Sankoff's statement tautological) or they will not. If they do not, Sankoff's argument suggests, we should cleave to the 'culturally meaningful', a course which would, inter alia, eventually lead to the replacement of etymology by folk-etymology. But even for those sociolinguists who are ready to junk the second half of their hyphenation, the Sankoff argument does not apply in the case of que. For the dynamic paradigm, in addition to the advantages already detailed, also gives at least as accurate a social picture as the quantitative one. The latter merely shows deletion to be more frequent among working-class speakers; Figure 3, on the other hand, shows that it is also farther advanced, in terms of rule-changes, among that class. According to Baileyan wave theory, rules are farthest advanced at their point of origin, therefore, the figure not only indicates that the changes concerned originated in the working class, but also points to the subgroup within that class (2, 5, and 7) which was presumably the first to undergo change. Moreover, it does so without losing the ability to distinguish those individuals (8 in the working class, 14 in the professional class) who, as every honest sociolinguistic study since Labov (1966) has shown, deviate to a greater or lesser extent from their class norms. Thus the quantitative paradigm cannot even claim superiority on grounds of its greater fidelity to social truth. In contrast, the dynamic paradigm shows us the ongoing change processes which cause the surface facts of variation, provides a reasoned internal explanation for such changes in terms of wave theory and rule-simplification, and is able--in contrast with any other extant theory--to determine rules by means of precise and specific predictions which can then be

FIGURE 3. Wave-spread of rules. (o = male informant; Δ =
female informant; dotted line encircles members
of working class; unringed numbers indicate speakers;
ringed numbers, rules as given).

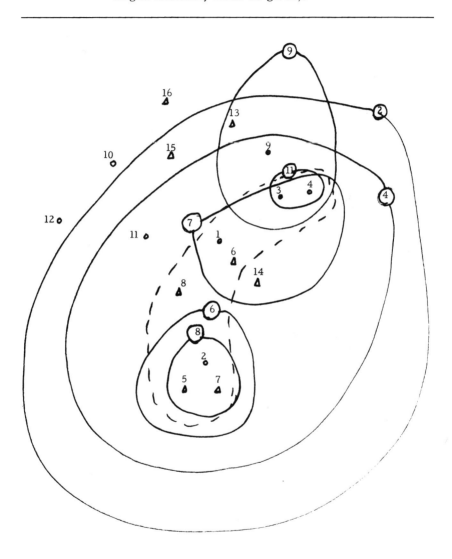

confirmed or disconfirmed by further examination of primary data. The latter factor represents the least we can mean, if we mean anything at all, when we speak of a 'scientific theory of language'.

NOTES

[1]See, for example, some extraordinary claims in Whorf's paper on 'Linguistics as a natural science' (Whorf 1956:220-32). Whorf's argument is based mainly on the power of linguistics to state facts about language structure that happen to be rather regular in themselves (e.g. English syllable structure). A parallel would be to claim geology as an exact science on the grounds that rocks are usually arranged neatly in strata instead of being all jumbled together!

[2]Named, respectively, in Bailey (1971) and G. Sankoff (MS). A more comprehensive survey of the former is contained in Bailey (1972).

[3]Elliott, Legum, and Thompson (1969), Labov (1969), Fasold (1970), Bailey (1971, 1972), DeCamp (1971), Bickerton (1971, 1972), to name but a few.

[4]The set of distinctive features used here is not necessarily that most appropriate; but as it is that used by both Sankoff and Cedergren and Sankoff, it seemed best to adhere to it throughout, as has been done here.

REFERENCES

Bailey, Charles-James N. 1971. Trying to talk in the new paradigm. Papers in Linguistics. 4(2).312-38.

_____. 1972. The patterning of language variation. To appear in: Varieties of present-day American English. Ed. by R. W. Bailey and J. L. Robinson.

Bickerton, Derek. 1971. Inherent variability and variable rules. Foundations of Language. 7(4).457-92.

_____. 1972. The structure of polylectal grammars. In: Georgetown University Monograph Series on Languages and Linguistics, Monograph 25. Edited by Roger W. Shuy. Washington, D.C., Georgetown University Press.

_____. 1973. On the nature of a creole continuum. To appear in: Language.

Cedergren, Henrietta and David Sankoff. Variable rules: Performance as a statistical reflection of competence. Mimeographed manuscript.

DeCamp, David. 1971. Toward a generative analysis of a post-creole speech continuum. In: Pidginization and creolization of languages. Ed. by Dell Hymes. Cambridge, Cambridge University Press. 349-70.

Elliott, Dale, Stanley Legum, and Sandra A. Thompson. 1969. Syntactic variation as linguistic data. Papers from the Fifth Regional Meeting of the Chicago Linguistic Society. Ed. by R. Binnick et al. Chicago, University of Chicago.

Fasold, Ralph W. 1970. Two models of socially significant language variation. Language. 46(3).531-63.

Labov, William. 1966. The social stratification of English in New York City. Washington, D.C., Center for Applied Linguistics.

_____. 1969. Contraction, deletion, and inherent variability of the English copula. Language. 45(4).715-62.

_____. 1970. The study of language in its social context. Studium Generale. 23.30-87.

_____, Paul Cohen, Clarence Robins, and John Lewis. 1968. A study of the non-standard English of Negro and Puerto Rican speakers in New York City. Cooperative Research Report No. 3288.

Sankoff, Gillian. A quantitative paradigm for the study of communicative competence. Mimeographed manuscript.

Whorf, Benjamin L. 1956. Language, thought, and reality. Cambridge, MIT Press.

ABOVE AND BEYOND PHONOLOGY IN VARIABLE RULES

GILLIAN SANKOFF

Université de Montréal

The principal goal of this paper is to extend the scope of an analytical framework which treats variation in linguistic behavior as being entirely natural, rather than anomalous, error-laden, or otherwise unmanageably messy. Perhaps the very success of such a framework in dealing with phonological data and with morphophonemic reduction rules has led many to believe that concepts of variation are applicable only in these domains, and that strict application of all-or-nothing principles are still defensible at other levels of grammar. I will argue that this is a misconception based in large part on an overly mechanistic view of language, which in turn stems from the traditional deterministic postulates underlying most of modern linguistics, including both structuralist and generative schools of various persuasions. Thus I think that work on systematic variability has often been misperceived by those who react to numbers and tables as being boring, trivial, or alarming, as being simply a detailed 'description' of 'performance'. My view is quite the opposite: I think from the beginning, and I refer principally to the continuing ground-breaking research of Labov and associates, the attempt has been to find more adequate ways of dealing with the great subtleties of competence in some of its most complex and interesting, i.e. noncategorical, aspects.

This is not to argue for chaos; quite the reverse. Perception of a set of observations as chaotic or otherwise disorderly may well stem from the inadequacy of the analyst's model to account for the kinds of diversity represented in the observations. It is to be hoped that the reason for a renewed interest of linguists in the study of language in context is not only to widen the field in which it is permissible to search for categorical constraints on linguistic behavior, e.g. to disambiguate referentially synonymous expressions 'categorically' by reference to social context. There is, in my view, mounting evidence that such semantic, discourse, or cultural constraints will be no more (or less) categorical than the type of linguistic constraints now agreed to be allowable. Both Hymes (1964, 1972) and Labov (1966, 1969, 1972a), from somewhat different traditions of enquiry, have for some years supported this point of view. Sherzer (n.d.) has recently provided some very cogent arguments as to why it is inadequate to deal with cultural and interactional context only in an ad hoc way and only when strictly 'necessary' (i.e. when all else appears to fail), why a systematic study of the latter is indicated, and careful work by Gumperz (c.g. Gumperz and Wilson 1971, Blom and Gumperz 1972) and others has shown the complexity of the two-way interactions between language behavior and its context. In brief, the study of the context of language use as an integral part of linguistic description is necessary on a number of grounds, but there is no reason to suppose that it will in any way simplify the linguist's task or provide easy, categorical solutions to current linguistic problems. The futility of the search for complete determinacy in language was not found at the level of the so-called idiolect, and it is difficult to imagine why it might be found to any greater degree at the level of speech act context.

Briefly, I posit that linguistic behavior, like other behavior, is subject to statistical variation which can best be accounted for by an underlying model which is probabilistic rather than deterministic in nature. This position has been argued recently by a number of researchers, and I will not go into any details here except to state one salient point: such a model contains no implication that any or all rules will be variable, i.e. it can deal with the kinds of structures involved in both variable and categorical rules.

In order to demonstrate that variability occurs and can be dealt with at levels of grammar above (or beyond) the phonological, I have chosen some examples from syntax and semantics, drawn from the current work of myself and coworkers on two linguistic communities: native, French-speaking Montrealers, and urban New Guineans who speak Tok Pisin, formerly a pidgin language with about 70 per cent English-derived vocabulary and which now boasts a first generation of native speakers.

1. The first example has to do with the placement of the future marker in New Guinea Tok Pisin (cf. Sankoff and Laberge 1972). This was a study in which we did an extensive series of recordings of members of about a dozen families in the town of Lae, as well as

a considerable number of other recordings of individuals, groups, public gatherings, and the like. There was no formal sample: families were chosen for intensive study on the basis of their having children of at least seven or eight years old who spoke Tok Pisin as a first language. The families were members of a close-knit multi-linguistic neighborhood. Few of the adults had a native language in common, and this included most spouses: all were fluent second-language speakers of Tok Pisin.

One of the results of an investigation of the syntactic marking of futures in the speech of eight adults and eight children in seven of the families was that bai, the marker, is variably placed before or after the subject NP. This has historical implications, as it seems that 50 or 60 years ago the standard order was to place baimbai or bai (now reduced to [ba] or [bə] by fluent speakers in informal conversation) before the subject NP. Though generational differences between our speakers appear in reduction of stress on bai, there appears to be no generational difference, nor a difference between individual speakers, with respect to order. Rather, there are a series of syntactic constraints, some of them categorical and others variable. Table 1 indicates the influence of the various pronominal subjects as well as nonpronominal noun phrases.

TABLE 1. Bai placement in terms of subject NP.

Subject NP Definition	Form	Position of bai __NP	__VP
1st sing.	mi	78	7
2nd sing.	yu	52	1
3rd pl.	ol	31	1
1st pl. incl.; {1st pl. excl. / 2nd pl.}	yumi; {mi / yu} pela	22	6
3rd sing.	em	11	47
other NP		22	36
Ø subject			53

We see that all pronouns except the 3rd person singular characteristically follow bai, whereas em and nonpronominal NP's generally precede, though with considerable variation. Further examination of the structure of nonpronominal subject NP's shows (Table 2) that there is a categorical rule which inserts bai after the NP when the latter contains an embedding whether the embedding contains a surface verb or not. The transformation for bai-movement is given as Rule 1.

Rule 1. bai + $\left\langle \begin{array}{c} NP \\ N\text{-}S \end{array} \right\rangle$ + VP

2:	NP	N-S
p	0.5	1.0

$$1 \qquad 2 \qquad\qquad 3 \;\Rightarrow\; <2+1+3>$$

TABLE 2. Bai placement in terms of structure of nonpronominal subject NP.

Structure of NP	Position of bai		
	_NP	NP_ _	_NP_
NP containing bilong (possessive)	--	8	2
NP containing embedding (with surface verb)	--	6	1
Other NP	17	17	2
Total	17	31	5

Thus a sentence like (1) applies the same bai-movement rule as a sentence like (2).

(1) Na meri bilong en bai igo bek.
    And his wife will go back. (Speaker #7)

(2) Igat planti man bai igo.
    There are lots of people who'll go. (Speaker #7)

In the case where the subject NP is nonpronominal and contains no embedding, the bai-movement rule operates with a probability of approximately .5, no further grammatical, social, or contextual constraints being evident. Thus the same speaker will use sentences like (3) and (4).

(3) Dispela kot ating bai i pinis nau.
    That court case will probably soon be finished. (Speaker #8)

(4) Bai wara igo insait.
    The water will get into it. (Speaker #8)

There is one further point of interest, and that is the existence of sentences containing a _bai_ both preceding and following the subject NP. Thus there seems to be a 'copying' alternative to the _bai_-movement rule based on the length of the subject NP, as this pattern seldom appears with NP's of less than three phonological words.
A rather long example is the following:

(5) _Bai_ man i wok gaden o mikim wonem istap long bus, _bai_ tingting.
   The people working in the fields or whatever they may be doing in the forest, will be thinking. (Speaker #14)

In summary, we can say that though we have not completed our investigation of the _bai_-movement rule, it is found to be quite stable in some syntactic environments, operating always (in the case of subject NP's containing embeddings) or almost never (in the case of most NP's consisting of a single pronoun other than _em_). Interestingly, most of the exceptions to the latter applied the _bai_-movement rule to indicate particular emphasis on the pronoun subject to the exclusion of other people, as in (6):

(6) _Mi_ bai kisim!
   _I_ [not you guys] will get it. (Speaker #3)

In the case of the pronoun _em_, however, _bai_-movement applies with a probability of approximately .85, and in the case of an NP consisting of more than a single pronoun, it applies with a probability of .5.

2. More on Montréal _que_. A preliminary analysis of the deletion of complementizer _que_ in the speech of sixteen Montrealers (Sankoff, Sarrasin, and Cedergren 1971) indicated a structure of variable phonological deletion constraints. Further work on other constructions containing _que_ has shown that not only is _que_ absent in a great many places where there is every indication that it is present earlier in the derivation, but also that it is present on the surface at places where one would not postulate its introduction by standard French transformations (Cedergren and Laberge 1972). Examples (7) and (8) show the alternation of _que_ after _quand_ for speaker #109; and examples (9) and (10) show the same kind of alternation with _comment_.

(7) _Quand_ qu'on sort, bien on va pas loin.
   When you leave, you don't go far. (Speaker #109)

(8) <u>Quand</u> tu as tout en main puis ça va bien, bien là tu te décourages moins.
When you have everything in hand and things are going well, you don't get so discouraged. (Speaker #109)

(9) Tu sais <u>comment</u> <u>qu'ça</u> se passe.
You know how it happens. (Speaker #6)

(10) Je sais pas <u>comment</u> ça se fait.
I don't know how it works. (Speaker #6)

Insertion of <u>que</u> results in a grammatically different structure, as the subordinator <u>quand</u> or <u>comment</u> appears to lose its subordinating function and act like an adverb, the subordinating function being taken over by an attached <u>que</u>. Examples (11) through (13) indicate, moreover, that more complexity is possible, with various representations of <u>est-ce</u> appearing between the WH-form and <u>que</u>.

(11) Je trouvais ça formidable <u>comment c'que c'est.</u>
I thought it was great, how it is. (Speaker #89)

(12) Je sais pas <u>comment c'est</u> qu'ils la faisaient dans ce temps-là.
I don't know how they did it in those days. (Speaker #24)

(13) Ils ont déterminé au juste <u>qu'est-c'est que c'est</u> j'avais.
They found out just what it was . . . that I had. (Speaker #52)

Sentence (13) contains the maximum number of <u>que</u>-attachments we have found, and Table 3 gives an idea of the complexity of the data.

We see that for some forms, most speakers categorically produce a <u>que</u>-less or a <u>que</u>-containing pattern, but that for most, the majority of speakers exhibit variation. We also see that there is the now familiar 'scaly' look to the pattern, and a reasonably good implicational relationship such that having <u>comme que</u> implies having <u>quand que</u>, and so on. Table 4 adds further information, showing that speakers tend to incorporate some sort of <u>que</u>-attachment consistently in the various possible environments. I have sketched a variable rule (Rule 2) involving <u>que</u>-attachment which takes into account only the syntactic constraints, and shows that <u>parce</u> is a very favorable (i. e. categorical) environment for <u>que</u>, whereas <u>comme</u> is a distinctly unfavorable environment.

TABLE 3. Ordering of speakers according to presence or absence of forms in their speech. [ETC¹ = other est-ce embeddings beginning with ce; ETC² = other embeddings beginning with que; que³ = qu'est-ce que]

Speakers	comme que	quand que	où	comment combien pourquoi ETC¹ que	ce	ETC¹	ETC²	que³
30	+	+	+		+			
25	+	+	+		+			
20	+	+	+		+		+	
68	+	+	+		+	+		+
87	+	+	+		+	+		+
75	+	+	+	+	+	+		
89	+	+	+	+	+	+		+
98	+	+	+	+	+			+
13	+	+	+	+	+	+	+	+
97	+	+	+	+	+	+	+	+
83	+	+	+	+	+	+	+	+
24	+	+	+	+	+	+	+	+
2	+	+	+	+	+	+	+	+
36	+	+	+	+	+	+	+	+
14	+	+	+	+	+	+	+	+
6	+	+	+	+	+		+	+
40	+	+	+	+	+	+	+	+
52	+	+	+	+	+	+	+	+
23	+	+	+	+	+	+	+	+
105	+	+	+	+			+	+
94	+	+	+	+		+		+
17	nil	+	+	nil	+			+
22	+	+	+	nil				+

TABLE 4. Ordering of speakers according to percentage of subordinators without que or other est-ce embeddings.

Speakers	comme	quand	comment combien pourquoi où	ce
30	1.00	1.00	1.00	1.00
25	1.00	1.00	1.00	1.00
20	1.00	1.00	1.00	.91
68	1.00	1.00	1.00	.96
87	1.00	1.00	1.00	.78
75	1.00	1.00	.71	1.00
89	1.00	1.00	.71	.79
98	1.00	1.00	.50	0
13	1.00	1.00	.57	.55
97	1.00	.89	.56	.43
83	1.00	.83	.50	.61
24	1.00	.98	.12	.64
2	1.00	1.00	.33	.12
36	1.00	.89	.33	.77
14	1.00	.75	.33	.66
6	.57	.57	.14	.56
40	.33	.33	.66	.40
52	.25	.68	.36	.15
23	.50	.50	.08	.13
105	.50	.36	.70	0
94	0	.23	0	0
17	–	.38	0	0
22	0	0	0	0

Rule 2: WH - raising rule

$$VP + [NP + V + Adv. \ Pron.]_S$$
$$\quad\quad 1 \quad\ 2 \quad\ 3 \quad\quad\ 4 \quad\quad\quad \Rightarrow 1 + 4 + <que> + 2 + 3$$

Approximate probability values for variable que:

term 4	comme	quand	où comment combien pourquoi	__ ce	parce
p	.1	.3	.4	.4	1.0

At this point, however, we encounter a major problem. Presence of que added as an adjunct with WH-raising appears in Table 5 to be highly unlikely in anything but a succeeding vocalic environment, in which its surface representation is generally the consonant [k]. The thought that this [k] may simply be a liaison-like phenomenon can rapidly be dismissed on the grounds of numerous full-form que's before consonants and pauses, as well as on the grounds that est-ce embeddings also occur almost entirely before vowels. How can we explain this? As a result, I think, of the same low level phonological rule that deletes que in constructions such as complements

TABLE 5.   [k] (= que) and [sk] (= est-ce-que) deletion according to succeeding phonological environments for speakers who use que and ETC (= other est-ce embeddings).

Forms	Succeeding phonological environments								
	[+sib]			$\begin{bmatrix} +cons \\ -sib \end{bmatrix}$			[-cons]		
	que	ETC-que	∅	que	ETC-que	∅	que	ETC-que	∅
comme; quand	2	--	113	1	--	56	96	--	50
où; pourquoi; combien; comment	2	1	41	3	--	16	26	53	54
Total	4	1	154	4	--	72	122	53	54

where it appears earlier in the derivation (Cedergren and Laberge 1972). This rule appears as Rule 3. Est-ce would be added as an optional complication of Rule 2, but would then be virtually always removed as a further consequence of Rule 3 in the favored environments. But if, as we have shown, presence of que is a result of both an optional attachment rule followed by an optional deletion rule, it becomes difficult to state the conditions under which attachment applies, since absence of que may result from it never having been attached in the first place, or from it having been attached and later deleted. It would seem at best inappropriate to postulate both attachment and deletion for those individuals and those forms where que never appears on the surface.

Rule 3: que-deletion rule

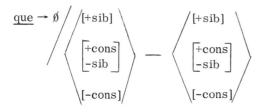

Effects:	[+sib]	$\begin{bmatrix} +\text{cons} \\ -\text{sib} \end{bmatrix}$	[-cons]
pre. seg.	.13	.02	0
fol. seg.	.36	.09	0

(1 - deletion prob.) = [1 - effect (pre. seg)] x [1 - effect (fol. seg.)]

Perhaps here we can look at some of the probabilities attached to various constraints in clear deletion cases (e.g. parce que, complements, relatives) and, comparing them to the observed data on possible attached, then deleted cases, infer what such frequencies might represent in terms of cases originally attached. For even if, turning back to the figures in Table 4, the phonological rule sweeps across surface que's of every grammatical stripe, it is clear that some of the forms are simply less amenable to que attachment. It seems, for example, that que is what some might call 'less good' with comme 'like' than it is with quand 'when'. Again, compare quand, which we see only occurring by itself and with que, but not taking any <u>est-ce</u> in between. Informants questioned about the acceptability of a construction like <u>quand</u> <u>est-ce</u> <u>que</u>, or <u>quand</u> <u>c'est</u> <u>que</u> all said this would be fine, but not with <u>comme</u>, thus *<u>comme ce</u> <u>que</u>, *<u>comme est-ce que</u>, etc. In fact the student who tabulated the forms in Tables 3 and 4 left columns for <u>est-ce</u> insertion for the <u>quand</u> form, but not for <u>comme</u>. Referring back to the table under Rule 2, which shows very approximate probabilities of <u>que</u> attachment for the various forms in the tables as well as for <u>parce</u>, we might also note that in comparing <u>que</u> deletion in complements versus relatives, we have found the latter to be a much more conservative environment--though the phonological constraints pattern in the same way. All speakers would be less likely to say a sentence like (14) than a sentence like (15).

(14) C'est la fille ∅ j'ai vue.
'That's the girl I saw' instead of 'That's the girl that I saw'

(15) Je pense ∅ ça a été plutôt un snobisme.
'I think it was more a kind of snobbery' instead of 'I think that it was more a kind of snobbery'

We have not yet investigated distinctions in the way a grammatical difference like restrictive versus nonrestrictive relatives would affect presence or absence of <u>que</u>, or, to turn the thing on its head, what <u>que</u> attachment can tell us about the nature of the NP which follows it, in terms of being more or less like other NP's. But we can already see that presence or absence of <u>que</u> is differentially allowable for different grammatical constructions in a way that is clearly important to an understanding of the grammar of French. This would seem to be the kind of area one might also investigate from the perspective of universals proposed by Wolfram at this conference. I might add that the difference between <u>est-ce</u> allowability with <u>quand</u> and <u>comme</u> might stem partially from the fact that <u>comme</u> can never be used in a surface direct question, whereas <u>quand</u> can.

Before passing to the last example, which is taken from the area of semantics, I would like to say a little more about the relationship between variability studies and the work of linguists who do not explicitly base their formulations on systematic studies of speech production. It is clear that Chomsky was correct in pointing out that there is no necessary connection between frequency of occurrence and grammaticality. Yet it is also clear that the questions of degrees of grammaticality or acceptability discussed so elegantly at this conference by Ross and by Sag fit very naturally into the overall framework of variability that we base our work on. The

problem comes back to a question of the interpretation one would be
able to give to a table like Table 4. What does it mean to note that
speaker 97, say, was never observed to use <u>comme que</u>, though he
did use <u>quand que</u> a little, and made considerable use of constructions like <u>comment que</u>? Is <u>comme que</u> disallowed by his grammar?
Would he react to its use by others as being 'funny'? Could we say
that <u>comme que</u> would be more likely to be grammatical for him in
some sense, even though he does not use it, than it would be for
speaker 20, who also does not use it, but does not use any of the
others either? Here we get into the problems of production versus
reception, the fact that we can receive correctly and without thought
that they are 'peculiar', messages in forms that we would never ourselves use, and so on, as Peter Trudgill pointed out during this conference. Further, questioning people about whether they find such
forms 'grammatical' runs into a great deal of interference due to
their recognition as nonstandard both by those who use them and
those who do not (cf. Labov 1970 on this general point).

3. My last example deals with pronoun semantics in Montreal
French, and is drawn from Laberge (1972). I am presenting only
one small part of the system: the variation Laberge found in the
surface representation of the pronoun she defined as 'indefinite
marked'. This is the indefinite par excellence, traditionally represented as <u>on</u> on the surface in French grammar, and which contains
no features indicating inclusion or exclusion of the speaker (ego) or
hearer, nor the singular/plural distinction. Some examples taken
from our recordings are listed here:

(16) <u>Tu</u> as beau parler de l'éléphant, du serpent, mais si <u>on</u>
      peut pas le décrire, hein?
    It's all very well to talk about elephants, about snakes,
    but if you can't describe them, eh? (Speaker #99)

(17) Quand <u>une personne</u> élevait une famille à ce temps-là,
      <u>vous</u> étiez pas capable d'avoir de luxe.
    When a person was bringing up a family at that time,
    you couldn't afford luxuries. (Speaker #37)

(18) <u>J</u>'aime mieux boire une bonne brosse, c'est mieux que
      fumer de la drogue, <u>je</u> trouve. Le lendemain matin
      <u>tu</u> as un gros mal de tête mais ça fait rien, <u>tu</u> es
      tout là. Tandis qu'avec la drogue, <u>tu</u> sais pas si <u>tu</u>
      vas être là le lendemain. <u>Tu</u> peux <u>te</u> prendre pour
      Batman ou Superman puis <u>tu te</u> pitch dans les
      poubelles.

> I'd rather have a good drink, it's better than smoking
> drugs, I find. The next morning you have a terrible
> headache but it doesn't matter, you're all there. But
> with drugs, you don't know if you're going to be there
> the next day. You might think you were Batman or
> Superman and throw yourself into the garbage pail.
> (Speaker #62)

Often what the speaker appears to be doing is talking about an experience of his own, but which he is generalizing to apply as a general rule. In sentence (17) the speaker does not imply that the 22-year-old addressee has herself raised a family during the depression; this is the indefinite vous which is distinguished clearly from personal vous in its underlying representation. Further evidence for this distinction (tu and vous personal versus tu and vous indefinite) comes from a comparison of speakers' address terms with their indefinite usage. Several older speakers consistently used the vous politeness form in addressing young interviewers, yet used tu (alternating with on) as an indefinite. This was the case for speakers 82 and 109 in the bar graph of Figure 1, and an example is given as sentence (19).

(19) Aussi, vous savez, quand tu as tout à la main puis ça va
      bien, bien là le courage vient.
    So, you know, when you have everything and things are
    going well, it's then that you get courage. (Speaker
    #109)

The graph shows that speaker 37 uses tu very occasionally to express the marked indefinite, that he uses vous for the marked indefinite about 60 per cent of the time, and on for the rest. Thus speakers over fifty are shown to use on frequently, alternating on with either tu (in the case of three speakers), or vous in the case of the other eleven. Speakers under twenty-five, however, use on very seldom indeed in the indefinite sense. More than half of them use over 80 per cent tu. For most younger speakers, as Laberge shows in a chapter not reported on here, on is used almost categorically to represent nous or 'we' as a verb subject. A typical example would be a sentence like (20).

(20) Dans notre famille, on a toujours fait ça.
    In our family, we always did that.

In over a thousand examples of underlying nous, Laberge found only one case of surface nous for one speaker under twenty-five.

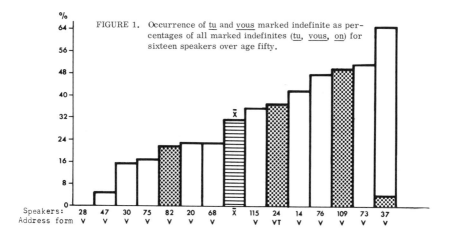

FIGURE 1. Occurrence of tu and vous marked indefinite as percentages of all marked indefinites (tu, vous, on) for
sixteen speakers over age fifty.

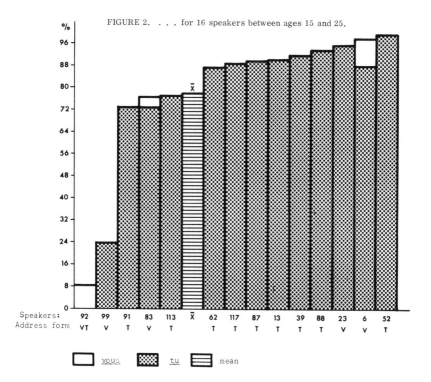

FIGURE 2. . . . for 16 speakers between ages 15 and 25.

Contrary to the que example, this example shows a dramatic and rapid usage change, which Laberge has described in terms of the articulation of the pronoun system as a whole. She has analyzed the alternation between on and either tu or vous as a variable rule with increasing input probabilities for younger speakers. This is not to suggest that younger speakers do not understand older speakers when they use on as in (16); and this again fits into some notion of passive competence. It is simply that such usage has become archaic, and gives every sign of disappearing. I might add that Laberge used only male speakers for the present analysis, as she felt the change tendencies would be clearer in the speech of men, given the greater conservative hypercorrection of women speakers in North American society, noted in our own previous work on Montreal French (Sankoff and Cedergren 1971) as well as in American English by Labov (1966), Shuy (1969), and Lakoff (n. d.).

4. The extension of probabilistic considerations from phonology to syntax is not a conceptually difficult jump. Whenever there are options open to a speaker, we can infer from his or her behavior an underlying set of probabilities. It seems clear to us that in the increasing number of situations which have been studied in depth, this inference is more than an exercise in data organization, since the underlying probabilities are consistently and systematically patterned according to internal (linguistic) and external (social and stylistic) constraints. There is no reason not to expect similar patterning elsewhere in grammar, aside from the phonological rules and syntactic transformations we have been discussing. Indeed, though there has been relatively little of the type of systematic data collection associated with variable rule studies, a certain amount of linguistic and probabilistic theorizing has been taking place à propos of other components of grammar.

On the level of phrase structure grammar, for example, considerable work has been done. The choice of one of a number of possible rules to rewrite a nonterminal node in a phrase marker is not strictly comparable to the application or nonapplication choice of a meaning-preserving transformation; nonetheless it frequently involves a certain freedom in the way a speaker organizes what he is saying. Furthermore, in the base component of many grammars, rewrite choices in phrase structure rules involve a strong stylistic component. The extension of phrase structure grammar to include probabilistic considerations has been suggested, largely independently and in ways which are mathematically almost identical, by Klein (1965), and by the mathematicians Grenander (1967), Horning (1970), Suppes (1970) working with Roger Brown's acquisition data, and D. Sankoff (1971, 1972). See also Peizer and Olmsted (1969).

Without going too far into problems of lexical choice and lexical insertion, it is not difficult to see how phenomena such as synonymy, overlapping meanings, specificity versus generality, and referents which are marginal or on the border between two semantic domains could all lead to probabilistic considerations of the lexicon. In this connection we can point particularly to the work of Lehrer (1970) on probabilistic weights of features in the semantic domain of 'containers'. The mathematical and probabilistic implications of this approach were investigated by D. Sankoff (1971b). Finally we may cite Labov's paper at this conference (1972b) as showing the role of probabilistic choice near the boundaries between semantic domains.

Much of the work done thus far, including our own, is fragmentary. Nevertheless, it seems readily discernible that there is a natural and behaviorally motivated trend to extend grammatical theory, which is primarily discrete and algebraic in character, by the introduction of well-defined probabilistic notions.

REFERENCES

Blom, J.-P. and J. J. Gumperz. 1972. Social meaning in linguistic structures: Code-switching in Norway. In: Directions in sociolinguistics. Ed. by J. J. Gumperz and D. Hymes. New York, Holt, Rinehart and Winston. 407-34.
Cedergren, H. J. and S. Laberge. 1972. Les règles variables du que explétif dans le français parlé à Montréal. Paper read at the Annual Meeting of the Canadian Linguistic Association.
Grenander, U. 1967. Syntax-controlled probabilities. Technical report, Brown University, Division of Applied Mathematics.
Gumperz, J. J. and R. Wilson. 1971. Convergence and creolization: A case from the Indo-Aryan/Dravidian border. In: Pidginization and creolization of languages. Ed. by D. Hymes. Cambridge, Cambridge University Press. 151-67.
Horning, J. J. 1969. A study of grammatical inference. Technical report No. CS-139, Stanford Artificial Intelligence Project, Memo A1-98. Stanford University, Computer Science Department.
Hymes, D. 1962. The ethnography of speaking. In: Anthropology and human behavior. Ed. by T. Gladwin and W. C. Sturtevant. Anthropological Society of Washington. 13-53.
_____. 1972. Models of the interaction of language and social life. In: Directions in sociolinguistics. Ed. by J. J. Gumperz and D. Hymes. New York, Holt, Rinehart and Winston. 35-71.
Klein, S. 1965. Control of style with a generative grammar. Language. 41.619-31.

Laberge, S. 1972. Observation d'un changement linguistique: Les pronoms indéfinis dans le français Montréalais. Unpublished M.A. Thesis, Département d'Anthropologie, Université de Montréal.

Labov, W. 1966. The social stratification of English in New York City. Washington, D.C., Center for Applied Linguistics.

_____. 1969. Contraction, deletion, and inherent variability of the English copula. Language. 45.715-62.

_____. 1972a. Where do grammars stop? In: Georgetown University Monograph Series on Languages and Linguistics, Monograph 25. Washington, D.C., Georgetown University Press.

_____. 1972b. The measurement of vagueness in semantic structures. Paper read at NWAVE Colloquium, Georgetown University.

Lakoff, R. n.d. Language and woman's place. Unpublished manuscript.

Lehrer, A. 1970. Indeterminacy in semantic description. Glossa. 4.87-110.

Peizer, D. B. and D. L. Olmsted. 1969. Modules of grammar acquisition. Language. 45.60-96.

Ross, J. R. 1972. The fake NP squish. Paper read at NWAVE Colloquium, Georgetown University.

Sag, I. 1972. On the state of progress on progressives and statives. Paper read at NWAVE Colloquium, Georgetown University.

Sankoff, D. 1971a. Branching processes with terminal types: Application to context-free grammars. Journal of Applied Probability. 8.233-40.

_____. 1971b. Dictionary structure and probability measures. Information and Control. 19.104-13.

_____. 1972. Context-free grammars and nonnegative matrices. Linear Algebra and its Applications. 5.277-81.

Sankoff, G. and H. J. Cedergren. 1971. Some results of a sociolinguistic study of Montreal French. In: Linguistic diversity in Canadian society. Ed. by R. Darnell. Linguistic Research, Inc. 61-87.

Sankoff, G. and S. Laberge. 1972. On the acquisition of native speakers by a language. To appear in: Kivung (Journal of the Linguistic Society of Papua New Guinea), vol. 5.

Sankoff, G., R. Sarrasin, and H. J. Cedergren. 1971. Quelques considérations sur la distribution de la variable que dans le français de Montréal. Paper read at the Congrès de l'Association Canadienne-française pour l'Avancement des Sciences.

Sherzer, J. n.d. Some current issues in linguistic theory: A sociolinguistic perspective. Unpublished manuscript.

Shuy, R. 1969. Sociolinguistic research at the Center for Applied Linguistics: The correlation of language and sex. International Days of Sociolinguistics. Rome, Istituto Luigi Sturzo. 849-58.

Trudgill, P. 1972. Diasystemic rules and variation in Norwich English. Paper read at NWAVE Colloquium, Georgetown University.

Wolfram, W. 1972. On what basis variable rules? Paper read at NWAVE Colloquium, Georgetown University.

SOME DATA WHICH
DO NOT FIT SOME MODELS

FRANK ANSHEN

State University of New York at Stony Brook

The purpose of this paper is to test some proposals for characterizing linguistic variation. I have identified three such proposals, that of David DeCamp, [1] that of Charles-James Bailey, developed by Derek Bickerton (1971), and that of William Labov (1969), extended by Sankoff (1972) and Cedergren and Sankoff (1972).

In considering these proposals I will first outline the claims they make about the ways in which variation may occur, and then consider the extent to which my data conform to these claims. In the case of Bailey's model it will be necessary to go further and consider the hypothesis which underlies his predictions

DeCamp's claim is the strongest of the three. He denies the importance of variation as a linguistic fact. Variation in groups is seen as an artifact of grouping individuals who themselves consistently use a given variant in a given environment. In general DeCamp feels that linguistic environments can be ordered $A_1, A_2 \ldots A_n$ so that the use of a given variant of a linguistic variable in any instance of A_k for an individual implies its use in every instance of A_k and A_k+1. Bailey admits the possibility of an individual showing variation in a given environment. He feels that environments of a linguistic variable $A_1 \ldots A_n$ may be ordered so that the appearance of a given linguistic variant in any instance of A_k for an individual implies that she will have some occurrence of that variant in A_k+1. Labov (for instance, 1968) offers a descriptive device which allows the incorporation of the facts of variation into linguistic rules. As it is a descriptive device which will fit any conceivable set of facts, it makes no predictions about the pattern of linguistic variation and

62

it is therefore untestable. It is reasonable to prefer a predictive
model such as DeCamp's or Bailey's if and only if the predictions
are accurate.

I will now consider some data which do not seem to fit the models
presented by DeCamp or Bailey. The data were gathered in interviews with black residents of Hillsborough, North Carolina in 1967.
The variable considered will be that old favorite postvocalic [r],
etymological r when followed by a consonant or word boundary.
Stressed instances of /ər/ were not considered as they exhibited
almost no variation. The data were elicited by having the informants
read a list of sentences, though this has the disadvantage of producing
a relatively formal speaking style, it has the advantage of producing
a large amount of directly comparable data. In all I have data from
67 speakers for 127 words. Percentage of use of [r] for the group
ranges from a high 54.2 for the word clearly to 0.0 for fifteen words.
A complete listing of words and the percent of [r] usage is presented
in Table 1. Averages for vowel type and following sound are shown
in Table 2. Table 3 shows that the following sound has at best a
minor influence on the occurrence of [r] while Table 4 indicates that
there is a strong influence exerted by the preceding vowel.

In order to test DeCamp's claims, each individual was scored
with respect to each preceding vowel whether he always used [r],
sometimes did, or never did. The results showed 160 instances of
individuals who used no [r] in a given environment, 238 instances of
some [r], and 4 instances of exclusive use at [r] by an individual in
a given environment. Clearly these data do not fit DeCamp's model.
Most people in most environments still exhibit variation. While
there are a substantial number of instances of no [r] usage there are
virtually no instances of categorical [r] usage by an individual in a
given environment. It is of course possible that I have not been able
to determine the correct environments. However, to take the extreme
case, there is no single word in which [r] was pronounced by everybody who used [r] in any word. It is therefore impossible for these
data to fit DeCamp's model.

Bailey's model makes a weaker claim. It does not require that
each person be categorical in each environment, only that the environments be ordered so that some use of [r] in an environment
implies its use in certain other environments. To test this model I
ordered the environments by preceding (1) front vowels; [i] and [e],
(2) central vowels; [a] and [ay], (3) back vowel [ɔ], and (4) unstressed
vowels, i.e. [ə]. This grouping of vowels was used as they seemed
to form natural groups not only articulatorily but also from the
figures in Table 4. This grouping makes it harder to falsify Bailey's
model than would considering each vowel separately. As might be
expected from Table 4, the best results come about when we postulate

TABLE 1. Words by per cent of [r] use.

#	Word	Sentence number	%	#	Word	Sentence number	%
1	clearly	51	54.2	41	hard	110	13.3
2	scared	26	48.2	42	yesterday	79	13.1
3	wear	90	47.6	43	car	83	13.1
4	here	93	47.1	44	Easter	52	12.5
5	care	40	46.2	45	wire	30	12.3
6	here	18	43.7	46	overhead	97	11.9
7	care	82	36.6	47	water	17	11.9
8	garden	9	30.8	48	worn	99	11.9
9	carefully	68	30.6	49	car	6	11.2
10	fired	97	26.3	50	sharp shooters	53	10.9
11	their	5	26.2	51	years	40	10.8
12	tires	91	26.2	52	corn	57	10.8
13	worn	91	22.4	53	ever	73	10.3
14	yesterday	76	21.3	54	tractor	40	10.0
15	worn	40	21.0	55	master	103	10.0
16	sisters	65	21.0	56	posture	108	10.0
17	hoarse	38	20.6	57	fire	75	9.8
18	there	8	20.0	58	horse's	42	9.5
19	market	106	20.0	59	dinner	48	9.5
20	care	21	19.7	60	for	18	9.5
21	stairs	29	19.4	61	supper	31	9.4
22	worn-out	96	19.3	62	car	39	9.4
23	queer	99	19.0	63	flowers	9	9.2
24	toward	71	18.3	64	restored	59	8.6
25	mourning	103	18.3	65	morning	69	8.3
26	ordered	59	17.0	66	horse	103	8.3
27	morning	19	16.9	67	airport	61	8.2
28	sister	52	16.9	68	mother	79	8.2
29	hoarse	19	16.7	69	whether	21	8.1
30	airport	61	16.4	70	forty	35	8.1
31	barn	32	15.6	71	Easter	38	7.6
32	minister	38	15.4	72	sharpshooter	53	7.6
33	there	84	15.0	73	yesterday	28	7.5
34	water	8	14.9	74	wharf	101	7.4
35	order	59	14.8	75	wore	99	6.9
36	yesterdays	89	14.8	76	hunter	97	6.8
37	air	46	14.0	77	after	69	6.6
38	are	25	13.8	78	further	41	6.5
39	tires	39	13.6	79	Rogers	63	6.5
40	toward	93	13.5	80	recorded	102	6.4

TABLE 1. Continued

#	Word	Sentence number	%	#	Word	Sentence number	%
81	over	6	6.3	105	after	17	3.0
82	tiger	20	6.3	106	after	32	3.0
83	mirror	5	6.2	107	either	51	3.0
84	are	25	6.2	108	floor	104	1.7
85	never	99	5.0	109	never	99	1.7
86	over	107	5.0	110	car	96	1.7
87	Cooper	30	4.9	111	war	107	1.6
88	order	59	4.9	112	brother	19	1.5
89	poor	96	4.9	113	another	17	0.0
90	sore	31	4.8	114	over	36	0.0
91	tire	6	4.6	115	floor	34	0.0
92	summer	30	4.6	116	underbrush	37	0.0
93	over	110	3.5	117	tower	41	0.0
94	Siler	93	3.4	118	sooner	48	0.0
95	sore	42	3.3	119	sooner	48	0.0
96	water	64	3.3	120	color	54	0.0
97	players	74	3.3	121	ordered	59	0.0
98	water	75	3.3	122	doctor	85	0.0
99	over	75	3.3	123	father	86	0.0
100	ever	77	3.3	124	after	98	0.0
101	super	106	3.3	125	after	102	0.0
102	daughters	5	3.1	126	humor	104	0.0
103	twenty-four	27	3.1	127	water	109	0.0
104	letters	14	3.0				

TABLE 2. Per cent of [r] use by preceding vowel and following sound.

	-K	-##K	-##V	Sentence final
i	32.5 (2)	31.4 (2)	--	47.1 (1)
e	28.7 (4)	28.4 (2)	41.4 (2)	14.5 (2)
ay	22.0 (3)	12.3 (1)	--	7.2 (2)
a	17.5 (5)	10.7 (5)	--	1.6 (1)
ɔ	12.6 (20)	3.3 (3)	2.4 (2)	5.3 (4)
ə	10.2 (14)	3.6 (31)	8.4 (7)	8.1 (9)

TABLE 3. Per cent of [r] use by following sound.

-K	-##K	-##V	Sentence final
20.6	15.0	17.4	14.0

TABLE 4. Per cent of [r] use by preceding vowel.

i	e	ay	a	ɔ	ə̆
35.0	28.3	15.5	13.0	9.9	6.4

that an occurrence of [r] after [ə] implies one after a back vowel; implies one after a central vowel; implies one after a front vowel. There are sixteen possible patterns of presence and absence of [r] in these four environments, of these five are predicted by Bailey's model. All patterns and the number of people in each are shown in Table 5. In the sample 46 of the 67 people fall into one of these five patterns. Note, however, that only two of the sixteen patterns are empty. Further, one of the patterns, representing five people, is the one in which no [r] is pronounced in any environment. It is reasonable to omit these people from a study of variation. This leaves 41 of 62 people who fall into patterns predicted by Bailey. The patterns in Table 5 are not equally likely and it is possible to calculate the expected percentage of the population for each pattern in the absence of any constraints such as those proposed by Bailey.[2] These expected values are given in the last column of Table 5 while

TABLE 5. Patterns of [r] presence.

Front vowel	Central vowel	Back vowel	ə	# of people	% of total	Expected %
*-	-	-	-	5	--	--
-	-	-	+	3	4.8	0.8
-	-	+	-	1	1.6	0.9
-	-	+	+	0	0.0	1.8
-	+	-	-	1	1.6	0.7
-	+	-	+	0	0.0	1.4
-	+	+	-	1	1.6	1.7
-	+	+	+	1	1.6	3.3
*+	-	-	-	7	11.3	3.3
+	-	-	+	1	1.6	6.4
+	-	+	-	2	3.2	5.3
+	-	+	+	8	12.9	14.5
*+	+	-	-	4	6.5	6.0
+	+	-	+	3	4.8	11.6
*+	+	+	-	5	8.1	13.5
*+	+	+	+	25	40.3	26.4
					100.5	99.7

* = predicted by Bailey's model; + = some [r] present; - = [r] absent

the actual values appear in the next to the last column. The expected
percentage of the population exhibiting the four predicted patterns is
49.2 while the observed percentage is 66.2. Put another way, about
one-third more people fit into Bailey's patterns than we would expect by chance. While I have not calculated the probability of this
occurring by chance, it seems that there is a clear tendency toward
conforming with Bailey's. More puzzling is the fact that the better
than expected fit does not come about by a generally equal increase
in all four of the predicted patterns but that all but 1.1 per cent of
the 17 per cent net increase is found in one pattern, that in which
an individual uses [r] in all four environments. Bailey's model gives
no hint why this should be true.

Even with all the caveats noted above Bailey does supply a better
prediction than any of the other models discussed in this paper and
it is thus worthwhile to consider his model in more depth. His prediction of the expected patterns stems from his concept of how a new
form enters the language. Starting with a restricted set of environments and a restricted set of people, the form adds, in time a new
set of people with the old environments, and a new set of environments

for the old people. In Anshen (1970) I examine the way in the pronunciation [r] entered the community. I show that a previously [r]-
less community adopted the idea that [r] pronunciation is correct
and that as a result people with more education use more [r]. The
crucial fact about this change though is that it apparently happened
very rapidly. The group over 55 years old showed no signs of it and
it is apparently complete for the next youngest group, with no evidence of transition. If my analysis is correct, then there was no
time for the type of expansion through people and time which Bailey
postulates. This leaves us with the peculiar conclusion that Bailey's
to an extent, makes predictions about these data which are more useful than either Labov's or DeCamp's but not to the extent which would
substantiate his model and these predictions do not seem to be true
for the reasons Bailey offers.

NOTES

[1]This view is severely modified by DeCamp in his article in this
volume.

[2]Eighty-nine per cent of the people had at least one instance of
[r] after a front vowel, 64.5 per cent after a central vowel, 69.4 per
cent after a back vowel, and 66.1 per cent after unstressed schwa.
The expected percentage of people with, for instance, [r] in the first
three environments but not the fourth would be 89 per cent x 64.5
per cent x 69.4 per cent x 33.9 (= 100 per cent - 66.1 per cent) =
13.5 per cent.

REFERENCES

Anshen, Frank. 1970. A sociolinguistic analysis of a sound change.
    Language Sciences. February. 20-21.
Bickerton, Derek. 1971. Inherent variability and variable rules.
    Foundations of Language. 7.457-92.
Cedergren, Henrietta and David Sankoff. 1972. Variable rules:
    Performance as a statistical reflection of competence. Unpub-
    lished manuscript.
Labov, William. 1969. Contraction, deletion, and inherent varia-
    bility of the English copula. Language. 45.715-62.
Sankoff, Gillian. 1972. A quantitative paradigm for the study of
    communicative competence. Paper delivered to the Texas Con-
    ference on the Enthnography of Speaking.

THE CLAUSE-INTERNAL SENTENCE SQUISH

DONALD H. ALBURY

University of Florida

In a series of recent papers, John Robert Ross has argued that grammar is essentially nondiscrete in nature. [1] As part of that argument, he has presented evidence that complements exhibit various degrees of nouniness in terms of the acceptability of certain syntactic phenomena associated with structures with embedded complements (Ross 1972a). On the basis of such evidence, Ross has claimed that complements fall into a linear sequence progressing from least nouny to most nouny, and has named this progression the sentence 'squish'. Further, Ross holds that the squishiness of complements is inherent, and present at all levels of grammar. The order of the complements in Ross' sentence squish is shown in Table 1, starting with the least nouny (and hence, the most sentence-like) at the top, and progressing through greater degrees of nouniness to the most nouny at the bottom.

TABLE 1. Ross' sentence squish.

Sentences
non-factive that complements
factive that complements
for-to complements
question word complements
accusative-ing complements
possessive-ing complements
action nominals
derived nominals
(noun phrases)

Most of the evidence cited by Ross in support of the sentence squish involves syntactic phenomena which encompass structures with embedded complements. In general, these phenomena show great regularity in structures with embedded complements from one end of the squish, less regularity in structures with embedded complements from the middle of the squish, and little or no regularity in structures with embedded complements from the other end of the squish. One such phenomenum is the rule of PREPOSITION DE-LETION. This rule applies obligatorily to structures in which the sentence-like _that_ and _for-to_ complements are embedded. Thus, the (a) sentences in (1) and (2) are not acceptable while the (b) sentences are. The rule applies optionally to sentences with an embedded question word complement, which is in the middle of the sentence squish, and so both the (a) and (b) sentences in (3) are acceptable. Finally, PREPOSITION DELETION does not apply at all to structures with the embedded noun phrase-like accusative-_ing_ and possessive-_ing_ complements. Thus, the (a) sentences in (4) and (5) are acceptable, while the (b) sentences are not.

(1a) *I was surprised at that you had hives.
(1b) I was surprised that you had hives.

(2a) *I was surprised at to find myself underwater.
(2b) I was surprised to find myself underwater.

(3a) I was surprised at how far I could throw the ball.
(3b) I was surprised how far I could throw the ball.

(4a) I was surprised at Jim retching.
(4b) *I was surprised Jim retching.

(5a) I was surprised at Jim's retching.
(5b) *I was surprised Jim's retching.

In this paper I will be concerned with what I believe to be a squish which is quite different from the one described by Ross. I will call Ross' squish the clause-external sentence squish, while I will be concerned here with the clause-internal sentence squish.[2] I will attempt to show that this squish results from the successive application of discrete rules to underlying forms in the derivation of the various types of complements. My squish is somewhat shorter than Ross', however. I will not make any distinction between factive and non-factive _that_ complements, or between action nominals and derived nominals, and I will arbitrarily exclude question word complements.[3]

Let us first consider how a that complement differs from a sentence. Most obvious, of course, is the presence of the complementizer that preceding the embedded sentence, which is optionally deleted in some environments. Somewhat less obvious is the rule of ADVERB PREPOSING. This is the rule which relates sentences (6a) to sentences (6b) and (6c).

Sentence (6a) has no acceptable corresponding that complement, the string in (7a) being unacceptable, but (6b) and (6c) both have acceptable corresponding that complements in (7b) and (7c). Indeed, the application of ADVERB PREPOSING to any complement yields unacceptable strings, as is illustrated by the (a) strings in (8), (9), (10), and (11). Thus, that complements, along with all other types of complements, are distinguished from sentences by the restriction of ADVERB PREPOSING to sentences. [4]

(6a)   Carefully, John aimed the rifle.
(6b)   John carefully aimed the rifle.
(6c)   John aimed the rifle carefully.

(7a)   *I saw that, carefully, John aimed the rifle.
             carefully, that

(7b)   I saw that John carefully aimed the rifle.
(7c)   I saw that John aimed the rifle carefully.

(8a)   *I want for, carefully, John to aim the rifle.
              carefully, for

(8b)   I want for John to carefully aim the rifle.
(8c)   I want for John to aim the rifle carefully.

(9a)   *I saw, carefully, John aiming the rifle.
(9b)   I saw John carefully aiming the rifle.
(9c)   I saw John aiming the rifle carefully.

(10a) *Carefully, John's aiming the rifle brought results.
(10b) John's carefully aiming the rifle brought results.
(10c) John's aiming the rifle carefully brought results.

(11a) *I liked careful(ly), John's aiming of the rifle.
(11b) I liked John's careful aiming of the rifle.
(11c) *I liked John's aiming of the rifle careful(ly).

Turning next to the relation of <u>for-to</u> complements to <u>that</u> complements and sentences, the most obvious characteristic after the complementizer is the absence of a tense marker in the complement.
Also, there are never any modals in <u>for-to</u> complements. As may
be seen by referring to examples (12) through (23), the absence of
tense markers and modals is characteristic of all complements other
than <u>that</u> complements. Finally, pronouns in subject position in
<u>for-to</u> complements occur in the accusative form, as is shown in
(20).

(12)   John closed the door a few minutes ago.

(13)   It is not true that John closed the door a few minutes ago.

(14a)   It was necessary for John to close the door a few
minutes ago.
(14b)   *It was necessary for John to closed the door a few
minutes ago.

(15a)   We are mad about John closing the door a few
minutes ago.
(15b)   *We are mad about John closed the door a few
minutes ago.

(16a)   John's closing the door a few minutes ago surprised me.
(16b)   *John's closed the door a few minutes ago surprised me.

(17a)   John's closing the door a few minutes ago startled me.
(17b)   *John's closed of the door a few minutes ago startled me.

(18)   They must have finished early.

(19)   It seems that they must have finished early.

(20a)   It is important for them to have finished early.
(20b)   *It is important for them to must have finished early.

(21a)   I am anticipating them having finished early.
(21b)   *I am anticipating them must(ing) have(ing) finished early.

(22a)   Their having finished early is unlikely.
(22b)   *Their must(ing) have(ing) finished early is unlikely.

(23a)   Their early finish surprises me.
(23b)   *Their (must) have early finish surprises me.

If we next consider the characteristics which set accusative-ing complements apart from other complements and from sentences, we see that accusative-ing complements do not have any complementizer like that or for-to, but that the suffix -ing appears wherever the tense marker would appear in a corresponding sentence, as may be seen in examples (15) and (21). Also, as in for-to complements, pronouns in subject position in the complements occur in the accusative form, as can be seen in (21a).

Possessive-ing complements are virtually identical to accusative-ing complements, with the exception that the subject noun in possessive-ing complements is always in the possessive form, as in (16) and (22). This last characteristic is shared by derived nominals.

The last type of complement which I will consider here is the derived nominal. Derived nominals have a number of characteristics which are not shared by other complements or by sentences. There is never any form of be or have in derived nominals. Object NP's in derived nominals are always preceded by a preposition, usually of, as in (17a). Derived nominals never have adverbs which are morphologically derived from verbs or adjectives, but instead have prenominal adjectives corresponding to such adverbs in other complements and in sentences, as is illustrated by comparing (23a) to the forms in (18) through (22). Derived nominals have a derivational suffix on the main verb of the clause, such as -ment, -al, -ness, or -th, but which may also be -ing, or nothing at all.

There are other ways in which derived nominals differ from other complements and from sentences. As has been pointed out by Chomsky (1970), there are many sentences which have corresponding possessive-ing complements, but which do not have corresponding derived nominals. This point is illustrated by the examples in (24) through (32), which are taken from Chomsky. The sentences in (24) have the corresponding possessive-ing complements in (25), and the corresponding derived nominals in (26), while the sentences in (27) have the corresponding possessive-ing complements in (28), but the expected corresponding derived nominals in (29) are not acceptable. Chomsky points out that the unacceptability of the derived nominals in (29) is not a property of the verbs involved, as is shown by the cases of the sentences in (30), which have the corresponding possessive-ing complements in (31), and the corresponding derived nominals in (32), all of which are acceptable.

(24a) John is eager to please.
(24b) John refused the offer.
(24c) John criticized the book.

(25a)   John's being eager to please.
(25b)   John's refusing the offer.
(25c)   John's criticizing the book.

(26a)   John's eagerness to please.
(26b)   John's refusal of the offer.
(26c)   John's criticism of the book.

(27a)   John is easy to please.
(27b)   John is certain to win the prize.
(27c)   John amused the children with his stories.

(28a)   John's being easy to please.
(28b)   John's being certain to win the prize.
(28c)   John's amusing the children with his stories.

(29a)   *John's easiness to please.
(29b)   *John's certainty to win the prize.
(29c)   *John's amusement of the children with his stories.

(30a)   John is certain that Bill will win the prize.
(30b)   John is amused at the children's antics.

(31a)   John's being certain that Bill will win the prize.
(31b)   John's being amused at the children's antics.

(32a)   John's certainty that Bill will win the prize.
(32b)   John's amusement at the children's antics.

However, a consideration of the sentences in (27) shows that they
have transformationally related paraphrases which do have acceptable corresponding derived nominals. Thus, related to (27a) and
(27b) are the sentences in (33) and (34), and the sentences in (33)
have the corresponding acceptable derived nominals in (35).

(33a)   It is easy to please John.
(33b)   It is certain that John will win the prize.

(34a)   To please John is easy.
(34b)   That John will win the prize is certain.

(35a)   the easiness of pleasing John
(35b)   the certainty that John will win the prize

The sentences in (27) are derived from the strings underlying the sentences in (33) by tough-MOVEMENT, and those underlying strings are in turn derived from the strings underlying the sentences in (34) by EXTRAPOSITION (at least, by the accepted formulation). An obvious generalization is that sentences which have undergone tough-MOVEMENT in their derivation cannot have corresponding derived nominals. The second generalization which apparently can be made here presents something of a paradox. Sentences which have undergone EXTRAPOSITION in their derivation, as in (33), have corresponding derived nominals, while sentences which met the structural description of EXTRAPOSITION at some point in their derivation, but did not undergo it, as in (34), do not have acceptable corresponding derived nominals. The paradox lies in the fact that other sentences which did not undergo EXTRAPOSITION in their derivations because their underlying forms never met the structural description for EXTRAPOSITION, as in (24), do have acceptable corresponding derived nominals. To state these facts in a rule of derived nominal formation would greatly complicate such a rule in a way which seems otherwise completely unmotivated.

There is a way around this paradox, but it involves the rejection of Rosenbaum's (1967) formulation of EXTRAPOSITION. Specifically, it requires that the sentences in (33) be regarded as representing the underlying order of the constituents, with the sentences in (34) being derived by a rule which I will temporarily call REVERSE-EXTRAPOSITION. Doing this permits the earlier generalization to be turned around to state that sentences which have undergone REVERSE-EXTRAPOSITION in their derivation do not have acceptable corresponding derived nominals. Note that, by this formulation, tough-MOVEMENT and REVERSE-EXTRAPOSITION are not ordered relative to each other, with each rule applying to the strings underlying the sentences in (33).

While the above proposal seems to contradict a well-motivated analysis, it becomes more acceptable if we consider it in the light of McCawley's (1970) proposal that English has underlying verb-initial order. The derived nominals in (35) show a verb-initial order. If we accept the hypothesis that these do represent the underlying order, rather than an order derived by two rules which first prepose the complements, and then return them to post-verbal position, we can explain the distribution of acceptable strings out of all the possible strings listed in (27a) and (27b), (29a) and (29b), (33), (34), and (35) by assuming that derived nominal formation is ordered before REVERSE-EXTRAPOSITION, and that REVERSE-EXTRAPOSITION is optional unless derived nominal formation has applied, in which case it cannot apply. To complete this analysis,

we need to account for the presence of it, which, however, is a
problem in other environments as well.

I implied above that REVERSE-EXTRAPOSITION would not be
retained as such. I will now turn to a related problem in order to
throw more light on the rule which derives the sentences in (34) from
the strings underlying the sentences in (33). Consider the passive
sentences in (36). They have the corresponding possessive-ing complements in (37), but the expected corresponding derived nominals
in (38) are not acceptable (at least, in my dialect).

(36a)   The offer was refused by John.
(36b)   The book was criticized by John.

(37a)   the offer's being refused by John
(37b)   the book's being criticized by John

(38a)   *the offer's refusal by John
(38b)   *the book's criticism by John

Not all passives lack acceptable corresponding derived nominals,
and the sentences in (39) have the corresponding derived nominals
in (40). The possibility of acceptable corresponding derived nominals seems to be an idiosyncratic feature of the verbs in the nominals, and to vary among speakers.

(39a)   The city was destroyed by the enemy.
(39b)   John was acquitted by the jury.

(40a)   the city's destruction by the enemy
(40b)   John's acquittal by the jury

There are derived nominals, however, which seem to have no
corresponding sentences, but which are related to derived nominals
corresponding to sentences, such as the derived nominals in (41),
which are related to the derived nominals in (26), and the derived
nominals in (42), which are related to the derived nominals in (40).
The derived nominals in (41) and (42) show verb-initial order, as do
those in (35). These derived nominals can show either a VOS order
or a VSO order, as in (43).

(41a)   the refusal of the offer by John
(41b)   the criticism of the book by John

(42a)   the destruction of the city by the enemy
(42b)   the acquittal of John by the jury

(43a)   the destruction by the enemy of the city
(43b)   the acquittal by the jury of John

The details of the rules which order the post-verbal noun phrases, and which prepose noun phrases to form active and passive sentences, are not clear. What is critical here, however, is that if the rule which moves the underlying subject into pre-verb position, which I will call AGENT PREPOSING, fails to apply, then the rule which moves the underlying object to pre-verb position to form a passive, which I will call OBJECT PREPOSING, applies optionally to derived nominals, and is even blocked from applying by some verbs in derived nominals.

Now observe that OBJECT PREPOSING does exactly the same thing as REVERSE-EXTRAPOSITION. We do not need a rule of REVERSE-EXTRAPOSITION if we regard all complements as being a string immediately dominated by an S node which is in turn immediately dominated by an NP node in underlying structure, and have OBJECT PREPOSING apply to object noun phrases without regard to whether the NP node dominates an embedded S node. [5]

The last case of a distinction between derived nominals and other complements which I will discuss here involves the sentences in (44) (repeated from (27c) and (30b) above). Sentence (44b) has the corresponding acceptable derived nominal in (45b), but the expected derived nominal in (45a), which corresponds to sentence (44a), is not acceptable. However, sentence (44a) has certain paraphrases in (46), and sentence (44b) has certain paraphrases in (47), which can be transformationally related by the rules of PSYCH MOVEMENT and FACTORING. [6] In essence, FACTORING moves a noun phrase out of another noun phrase. I will not try to motivate FACTORING here, but will simply point out that adopting FACTORING permits a simple principled explanation for some of the restrictions on the occurrence of derived nominals. The sentences in (46) have the expected corresponding derived nominals in (48), but only (48b) is acceptable, and the sentences in (47) have the expected corresponding derived nominals in (49), none of which is acceptable. The only acceptable derived nominals in (45), (48), and (49) are those corresponding to sentences which have not undergone PSYCH MOVEMENT, which are (45b), corresponding to (44b), and (48b), corresponding to (46b). All of the sentences which have undergone FACTORING have also undergone PSYCH MOVEMENT, and hence, do not have corresponding acceptable derived nominals.

(44a)   John amused the children with his stories.
(44b)   John is amused at the children's antics.

(45a) *John's amusement of the children with his stories
(45b) John's amusement at the children's antics

(46a) John's stories amused the children.
(46b) The children were amused at John's stories.
(46c) The children were amused by John's stories.

(47a) John is amused by the children's antics.
(47b) The children's antics amuse John.
(47c) The children amuse John with their antics.

(48a) *John's stories' amusement of the children
(48b) the children's amusement at John's stories
(48c) *the children's amusement by John's stories

(49a) *John's amusement by the children's antics
(49b) *the children's antics' amusement of John
(49c) *the children's amusement of John with their stories

If we chart the various types of complements against the rules discussed above, as in Table 2, we see that there are two quite different types of rules involved. One type of rule applies to sentences, and if such a rule applies to a particular complement, then it applies to all other complements ranked between that complement and the sentence. The other type of rule, which applies only to certain complements, is restricted in scope. Two of these rules change the case form of the subject noun or pronoun of certain complements, and two other rules add a suffix to the verb of the complement in certain complements. Moreover, in each case, one rule follows the other, and the second cannot apply if the first has applied.

I would like to propose a simple explanation for the data I have presented. My proposal is that the cycle consists of some rules which apply to strings immediately dominated by an S node, some rules which apply to strings immediately dominated by an NP node, and some rules which apply to any string, although conditions on the rule might vary depending on whether the string was immediately dominated by an S node or an NP node. The rule of OBJECT PREPOSING, for instance, would apply obligatorily to strings immediately dominated by an S node (unless the object noun phrase of the verb in the string was derived from an embedded sentence), and optionally to strings immediately dominated by an NP node (with the rule being blocked by the presence of certain verbs in those strings). Part of the process of forming each type of complement would be a rule which would delete an S node immediately dominating the string which would become the complement, so that a structure like that

TABLE 2. Types of complements versus rules.

Der Nom	Poss -ing	Acc -ing	for- to	that	Sen- tence	Rules
0	0	0	0	0	X	ADVERB PREPOSING
0	0	0	0	X	X	TENSE/MODAL PLACEMENT
0	X	X	X	X	X	be/have PLACEMENT
0	X	X	X	X	X	tough-MOVEMENT
0	X	X	X	X	X	PSYCH MOVEMENT
Opt	Obl	Obl	Obl	Obl	Obl	OBJECT PREPOSING
0	0	X	X	0	0	ACCUSATIVE CASE
X	X	0	0	0	0	POSSESSIVE CASE
0	X	X	0	0	0	-ing SUFFIXATION
X	0	0	0	0	0	DERIVED SUFFIXATION

The clause-internal sentence squish: 0 = does not apply; X = applies; Opt = optional; Obl = obligatory

in (50a) would be transformed into a structure like that in (50b). The different types of complements would be formed at different points in the cycle, so that there would be several occurrences in the cycle of the S node deletion rule. The rules in Table 2 which apply to sentences would then be rules which apply only to strings immediately dominated by an S node, while the rules which apply only to certain types of complements would be rules which apply only to strings immediately dominated by an NP node. [7] If the rules are then ordered as in Table 3, the data discussed above is neatly accounted for. For instance, the fact that no acceptable derived nominals correspond to sentences which have undergone tough-MOVEMENT is explained by the restriction of tough-MOVEMENT to strings immediately dominated by an S node, the deletion of the S node in DERIVED NOMINALIZATION, and the ordering of DERIVED NOMINALIZATION before tough-MOVEMENT. [8] In addition, the relative proportion of the cycle during which a string is immediately dominated by an NP node correlates with the relative degree of nouniness in Ross' sentence squish. Thus, Ross' sentence squish can be attributed to a combination of rule ordering and the discrete change of an embedded clause from a sentence to a noun phrase, and grammar therefore is not necessarily squishy all the way down.

(50a)   NP

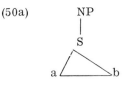

(50b)   NP

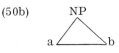

TABLE 3.

DERIVED NOMINALIZATION
DERIVED SUFFIXATION (NP)
OBJECT PREPOSING (S-Obl; NP-Opt)
PSYCH MOVEMENT (S)
tough-MOVEMENT (S)
be/have PLACEMENT (S)
POSSESSIVE-ing COMPLEMENTATION
POSSESSIVE CASE (NP)
ACCUSATIVE-ing COMPLEMENTATION
-ing SUFFIXATION (NP)
for-to COMPLEMENTATION
ACCUSATIVE CASE (NP)
TENSE/MODAL PLACEMENT (S)
that COMPLEMENTATION
ADVERB PREPOSING (S)

The proposed rule ordering: S = applies to strings dominated by an S; NP = applies to strings dominated by an NP

NOTES

[1]This paper is based in part on a paper written for Ross' course at the 1972 Linguistic Institute. It has been influenced by his comments on that paper, but I have not accepted all of his suggestions, and I retain full responsibility for the contents of this paper.

[2]Ross also lists some phenomena which do not extend beyond the complements they occur in, in other words, which are clause-internal, but these phenomena seem to be different from the rules I discuss here, and I have not included them. All but two of the phenomena are idioms, or involve it or there, and have also been discussed by Ross (1972b) as part of the fake NP squish. The other two phenomena, EXTRAPOSITION FROM NP and QUANTIFIER POSTPOSING, are rules which Ross indicates do not apply in certain complements, but it seems rather that the structures these

rules apply to do not occur in those complements, which is a somewhat different matter.

[3]I am not aware of any clause-internal syntactic evidence which
distinguishes between factive and nonfactive that complements. One
piece of evidence that what are called action nominals are actually
derived nominals is Albury (1972a).

[4]Ross (private communication) states that ADVERB PREPOSING
in that complements works for him after verbs like say and think.
My judgment differs here, and I will rely on my own dialect.

[5]A more detailed argument for this analysis of EXTRAPOSITION
is given in Albury (1972b).

[6]I am assuming here the form of PSYCH MOVEMENT as discussed
in Postal (1971). I have been told that Gregory Lee has given arguments for FACTORING, but I have not seen his work, and do not
have full references to it.

[7]It is possible that the distinction of rules which apply to sentences and to noun phrases also is a squish, but I do not have
sufficient evidence to make any kind of judgment on that point.

[8]The argument that rule ordering can account for the differences
between possessive-ing complements and derived nominals has been
made in Newmeyer (1971) and Albury (1971).

REFERENCES

Albury, Donald H. 1971. In defense of the transformational origin
of derived nominals. Paper presented to the Sixth Meeting of the
Southeastern Conference on Linguistics, Atlanta, Georgia.
_____. 1972a. On deriving nominals from causatives in English.
Paper presented to the Summer Meeting of the LSA, Chapel Hill,
North Carolina.
_____. 1972b. It-extraposition and the verb-initial hypothesis.
Paper to be presented to the Annual Meeting of the LSA, Atlanta,
Georgia.
Chomsky, Noam. 1970. Remarks on nominalization. In: Readings
in English transformational grammar. Ed. by R. A. Jacobs and
P. S. Rosenbaum. Waltham, Mass., Ginn.
McCawley, James D. 1970. English as a VSO language. Language.
46.286-99.
Newmeyer, Frederick J. 1971. The source of derived nominals in
English. Language. 47.786-96.
Postal, Paul. 1971. Cross-over phenomena. New York, Holt,
Rinehart and Winston.
Rosenbaum, Peter S. 1967. The grammar of English predicate
complement constructions. Cambridge, Mass., MIT Press.

Ross, John Robert. 1972a. Nouniness. Forum lecture, Linguistic Institute, Chapel Hill, North Carolina.

_____. 1972b. The fake NP squish. Paper presented to the Eighth Meeting of the Southeastern Conference on Linguistics/Colloquium on New Ways of Analyzing Variation in English, Washington, D. C.

ON THE STATE OF PROGRESS
ON PROGRESSIVES AND STATIVES[1]

IVAN A. SAG

University of Pennsylvania

1. Ever since the study of English grammar became a serious
academic pursuit, English grammarians have adopted the procedure
of taxonomic classification to explain the somewhat troublesome behavior of English verbs. This is apparent in the writings of Poutsma,
Jesperson, Bloch, Joos, Vendler, etc. One such classification per-
sisting throughout the works of almost all of these scholars has been
given various names: the state, statal, or stative verbs. Attempts
have been made, with varying degrees of success, to relate seemingly
unrelated syntactic phenomena by means of this classification.

The most recent treatment of the topic is by G. Lakoff (1966),
whose classificational criteria far exceed those of any of his prede-
cessors. His claims may be summarized as follows:

(1) Stative (S) verbs (and adjectives) do not take any of the
    following grammatical constructions, while nonstatives
    (NS) do:

    A. COMMAND IMPERATIVES:

        S: *Know that I am here!
        NS: Slice the salami!

    B. PROGRESSIVES:

        S: *John is knowing that.
        NS: John is slicing the salami.

83

C. DO-SOMETHING:

> S: *What I did was <u>hear</u> the concert.
> NS: What I did was <u>slice</u> the salami.
> S: *I <u>knew</u> the answer, though Bill told me not to
>   do so.
> NS: I <u>learned</u> the answer, though Bill told me not to
>   do so.

D. OCCURRENCE IN THE COMPLEMENTS OF
    <u>PERSUADE</u> AND <u>REMIND</u>:

> S: *I persuaded John to <u>hear</u> the music.
> NS: I persuaded John to <u>listen</u> to the music.

E. OCCURRENCE WITH MANNER ADVERBS THAT ARE
    SUBCATEGORIZED FOR ANIMATE SENTENCE
    SUBJECTS (<u>DELIBERATELY</u>, <u>RELUCTANTLY</u>,
    <u>MASTERFULLY</u>, <u>CAREFULLY</u>, <u>ENTHUSIASTICALLY</u>,
    <u>WELL</u>):

> S: *John <u>knew</u> the answer reluctantly.
> NS: John <u>sliced</u> the salami reluctantly.

F. <u>FOR</u> PHRASES:

> S: *John <u>knew</u> that fact for his teacher's sake.
> NS: John <u>sliced</u> the salami for his teacher's sake.

G. OCCURRENCE ON EITHER SIDE OF <u>INSTEAD OF</u>:

> S: *I <u>heard</u> the music instead of looking at the painting.
> NS: I <u>listened</u> to the music instead of <u>looking</u> at the
>   painting.
> S: *I looked at the painting instead of <u>hearing</u> the music.

Included in Lakoff's nonexhaustive list of stative verbs are the
following:

(2) believe, comprehend, consider (NP NP), desire, expect,
     guess (that), hate, have, hear, hope, know, love, owe,
     perceive, resemble, see, sound, want.

This stativity hypothesis is, of course, an insightful first attempt
at accounting for many seemingly disparate grammatical facts.

Therefore, in the absence of more detailed subsequent work on the topic, it is not surprising that it has been more or less generally accepted. I would like to provide evidence, however, that more than mere binary classification is required to explain the actual behavior of many of the verbs in question. So many factors are involved, in fact, that an accurate account of the facts is beyond the scope of the Aspects model, Generative Semantics, or any other theory hampered by its reliance on discrete categorization. As an illustration of the nondiscrete nature of these factors, consider first the case of progressives.

2. The progressive squish.[2] The fact that the progressive is somehow semantically different from the other stative tests has been correctly observed by P. G. Lee, who consequently draws a distinction between what he calls 'A-tests' (activity) and 'P-tests' (process). He remarks that 'know, for example, . . . fails the P-test [= progressive] because knowing is not a process' (Lee 1969:43).

The simple correlation of progressive with 'process', a common misconception, passes over several distinctions which, we shall see, are crucial to the analysis at hand. There are, of course, progressives that denote process, but other progressives express futurity, and still others, habituality. It will be convenient for us to distinguish these by means of the temporal adverbials at the moment, tomorrow, and nowadays, respectively. This is illustrated in sentences (3)-(5).

(3) At the moment, we're bombing a French mission. (PROCESS)
(4) We're bombing a French mission tomorrow. (FUTURATE)
(5) Nowadays we're bombing French missions. (HABITUAL)

Most verbs occur freely in all three basic types, but some of the proposed stative verbs may take certain progressives and not others. For example, expect occurs in all but the FUTURATE, as is shown in (6) to (8).

(6) *Tomorrow Stan's expecting McGovern to win in November.
(7) At the moment, Stan's expecting McGovern to win in November.
(8) Nowadays Stan's expecting McGovern to win in November.

The perception verbs see and hear are usually fine in all three. For example,

(9) Tomorrow I'm hearing what our opponents have to say.

(10) At the moment I'm hearing what our opponents have
      to say.

(11) Nowadays I'm hearing what our opponents have to say.

Notice, however, that with a Verb-_ing_ complement, the perception verbs cannot tolerate the FUTURATE progressive. Compare (12) and (13).

(12) *Tomorrow we're hearing Spiro misquoting George.

(13) Tomorrow we're hearing Spiro misquote George.

The moral here is that one must consider more than just some innate property of the verb in question. The overt syntactic structure may affect progressivizability.

There are certain other statives, like _owe_ and _want,_ which are bad in the FUTURATE, marginal in the PROCESS, and fine in the HABITUAL, as is indicated in (14) to (16).

(14) *Tomorrow the kids are wanting us to bring them toys.[3]

(15) ?At the moment the kids are wanting us to bring them toys.

(16) Nowadays the kids are wanting us to bring them toys.

There are, of course, a few statives which can take none of these progressives in simple sentences like the above. As might be expected, these are the ones most often cited, e. g. _know_, _resemble_, and _have_:

(17) *Tomorrow Judy's knowing the right answer.

(18) *At the moment, Judy's knowing the right answer.

(19) *Nowadays Judy's knowing the right answers.

I know of no verbs, however, which occur only in the FUTURATE, only in the PROCESS, only in the FUTURATE and the HABITUAL, or only in the FUTURATE and the PROCESS. Consequently, if we represent graphically the observations of (3) to (19) above, as is shown in (20), we see that it is possible to formulate the implicational hierarchy given in (21).

(20)

	FUTURATE	PROCESS	HABITUAL
hear, see	✓	✓	✓
hear, see (+ Verb-ing complement) expect	X	✓	✓
owe, want	X	?	✓
resemble, know, have	X	X	X

(21) FUTURATE   ⊃ PROCESS   ⊃ HABITUAL
      PROGRESSIVE   PROGRESSIVE   PROGRESSIVE

In other words, if a verb occurs in a certain progressive, then it will necessarily be the case that it also occurs in all progressives to the right of it in (21).

Thus far, we have been dealing with what has traditionally been called the 'present' progressive. It has been pointed out to me by Ellen Prince (personal communication) that similar variation can be observed in the case of the 'present-perfect' progressive, as is shown by (22) to (27).

(22) *The baby's resembling his father at the moment.
(23) ?The baby's been resembling his father for a month now.
(24) *Myra's loving her baby at the moment.
(25) ?Myra's been loving her baby for a month now.
(26) *At the moment I'm wanting an Edsel.
(27) I've been wanting an Edsel for years.

For some strange reason SUBJECT RAISING seems to improve the grammaticality of the progressivized forms of certain verbs. For instance, in (28) and (29) the (b) sentences are better than the (a) sentences.

(28a) *Little Linda is wanting something.
(28b) Little Linda seems to be wanting something.

(29a) ?Marvin's hating English class.
(29b) Marvin seems to be hating English class.

Additionally, some verbs which resist any progressive, even with SUBJECT RAISING, suddenly produce grammatical progressives

with certain adverbial constructions like more and more, rather
less now, and finally, as (30) to (35) show.

(30) *Irma's knowing a lot about contraception.
(31) ?Irma seems to be knowing a lot about contraception.
(32)   Irma's knowing more and more about contraception
          every day.
(33) *At the moment the baby's resembling his father.
(34) ?The baby seems to be resembling his father.
(35)   The baby's resembling his father more and more
          every day.

There are, it should be noted, at least two proposed stative verbs
which have obstinately failed every test discussed so far. These are
have and guess (that). Here we must be careful to distinguish stative
have and guess from their homophonous highly nonstative counterparts. That is, the have in expressions like have a party or have an
abortion passes all of the tests Lakoff proposed, and has never, I
hope, ever seriously been called a stative verb. The have in question indicates simple possession, as in sentences like (36).

(36)   Spiro has an 'I like Ike' button.

Similarly, we must distinguish the 'make a conjecture' sense of
guess from the 'be of the opinion' sense. It is only the latter of
these that concerns us here.
     Now consider the case of reduced relative clauses. Even stative
have and guess take progressives freely in sentences like (37) and
(38), where RELATIVE CLAUSE REDUCTION has applied.

(37)   Anyone having an 'I like Ike' button please keep it hidden.
(38)   Anyone guessing they won't succeed won't succeed.

In fact, the only verb I can find that won't take a progressive in this
construction is be, when followed by NP or certain adjectives, as is
illustrated in (39) to (41).

(39)   *Anyone being a communist will be shot.
(40)   *Anyone being unaware of the facts will vote for Nixon.
(41)   Anyone being stubborn will have his teddy bear taken away.

There is a great deal of regularity to be observed in the facts of
(6) to (41) above. The three basic types of progressives, taken together with the various other conditioning factors, constitute an
implicational hierarchy as shown in (42).

(42) $\begin{array}{c}\text{FUTURATE}\\\text{PROG}\end{array} \supset \begin{array}{c}\text{PROCESS}\\\text{PROG}\end{array} \supset \begin{array}{c}\text{HABITUAL}\\\text{PROG}\end{array} \supset \begin{array}{c}\text{PERFECT}\\\text{PROG}\end{array} \supset$

$\begin{array}{c}\text{RAISED SUBJ}\\\text{(+ PROG)}\end{array} \supset \begin{array}{c}\text{(PROG +)}\\\text{MORE \& MORE}\end{array} \supset \begin{array}{c}\text{REDUCED REL}\\\text{(+ PROG)}\end{array}$

If we plot these against various proposed stative verbs, we find the grammaticality variation to be as indicated in (43).

(43) THE PROGRESSIVE SQUISH

	FUT PROG	PROCESS PROG	HAB PROG	PERF PROG	RSD SUBJ	MORE & MORE	RED REL
be (+NP)	X	X	X	X	X	X	X
have, guess	X	X	X	X	X	X	✓
know	X	X	X	X	?X	✓	✓
resemble	X	X	X	?X	?	✓	✓
love	X	?X	?	?	✓	✓	✓
want, owe	X	?	✓	✓	✓	✓	✓
expect, sound, look, hear, see (+ V-ing complement)	X	✓	✓	✓	✓	✓	✓
hear, see	✓	✓	✓	✓	✓	✓	✓

↑ more stative   less   more
| less stative   receptive ⟶ receptive
environments   environments

It is important to note that the acceptability judgments indicated in (43) are relative rather than absolute. It is entirely possible that the reader's judgments will vary somewhat from those indicated. This, in and of itself, is not necessarily inconsistent with the above proposal, for it is quite possible that the strength of a given verb will vary from speaker to speaker. What this proposal predicts is that there will be variability, and that it will never be the case that a given speaker will find the same verb occurring more grammatically in a less receptive environment than in a more receptive one. To the extent to which this succeeds, the proposal is substantiated; to the extent to which this fails this is refuted. More specifically, if some speaker were to find (14) to (16) above all grammatical, this would not be counterevidence to my claim. If, however, he or she were to find (14) better than (15) or (16), then this would have to be considered as counterevidence.

In (43) I have indicated the top to bottom ranking of verbs as a progression from more stative to less stative. This, in a sense, is putting the cart before the horse. In order to show that there is any such class of verbs determined by the criteria that have been proposed, some kind of a correlation must be shown between the ranking of verbs in (43) and a ranking of the same verbs a propos of the other tests. With this in mind, let us turn to the do-something test ((1C) above).

3. Do-something. The most recent treatment of do is by Ross (1972). Speaking for himself and Lakoff, Ross posits a do in the underlying structure of all sentences containing nonstative verbs. By this proposal, underlying (44) would be a structure like (45).

(44)   We bomb dikes.

(45)

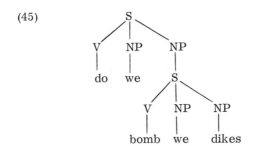

Sentences like (44) are produced by a rule of DO-GOBBLING. Before DO-GOBBLING applies, however, certain other transformations may intervene. The result is that only nonstative verbs can end up in sentences where the do never gets GOBBLED. Let us examine more closely some of the evidence cited for the DO-GOBBLING analysis to see if the scale of doability corresponds to the scale of progressivizability.

A. SWOOPING is cited as one piece of evidence for the correctness of the DO-GOBBLING analysis. When SWOOPING has applied, a do may be left unGOBBLED, as in (46).

(46)   That Bob resigned, which I think I should do, was a
         good idea.

But in (47) to (50) we see that the statives love, consider, expect, and perceive may also leave a do behind when SWOOPED.

(47) Marvin loves his ugly wife dearly, which I could never do.
(48) Larry considers Nixon his friend, which I could never do.
(49) Harry expects his children to wait on him hand and foot, which I could never bring myself to do.
(50) Our new accountant perceives problems with our tax returns, which our old one never used to do.

Other statives, like be, have, and want will not leave a do behind here. On this point compare the above with (51) to (53).

(51) *Shiela is a friend of Tom's, which I think I should do.
(52) *Nancy has an 'I like Ike' button, which none of my friends would ever do.
(53) *Veronica wants an Edsel, which Ignacz shouldn't do.

Notice that there are certain modifications which can be performed on this type of sentence so as to allow more statives to occur with a do. Know, for example, improves with the addition of always, as (54) and (55) illustrate.

(54) ?Mary knew the right answer, which I couldn't ever do.
(55) Mary always knew the right answer, which I could never do.

Similarly, the proform something may improve such sentences with know:

(56) Edwin knew the right answer, which was something I didn't ever do.

Notice, however, that neither of these modifications will improve this type of sentence with want, as (57) and (58) show.

(57) *Veronica always wanted an Edsel, which I would never do.
(58) *Veronica wanted an Edsel, which is something I would never do.

One other way to improve the SWOOPED do sentences with knów and resemble, and perhaps even with want, is to add temporal clauses. (59) to (62) illustrate this point.

(59) *My brother resembled Daddy, which I didn't do.
(60) My brother resembled Daddy by the time he was ten, which I didn't do until I was almost twenty.
(61) Margo knew all about the facts of life by the time she was ten, which I didn't do until I was twelve or thirteen.
(62) ?Henrietta wanted people to pay attention to her by the time she was five, which Sally didn't do until her early adolescence.

We therefore conclude that <u>want</u> is more resistant to <u>do</u> in this environment than <u>know</u> is. Recall, however, that in (43) above it was shown that <u>want</u> occurs in the progressive considerably more freely than <u>know</u>. Discrepancies such as this suggest that there may be no correlation between the notion of 'progressivizable' and the notion of 'doable'.

B. TOUGH-movement is cited as further evidence for DO-GOBBLING. However, alongside Ross' examples like (63), we find equally acceptable TOUGH-moved sentences with statives, like (64) to (66).

(63) Curling, which is tough to do, is also boring.
(64) Hating someone who's been your friend for years is sure tough to do.
(65) Perceiving problems with G. M.'s tax returns is a hard thing for a rookie accountant to do.
(66) Knowing what your teacher wants is hard to do sometimes.

For <u>see</u> and <u>hear</u>, just as in the case of the FUTURATE progressive, complement structure makes a difference. With a Verb-<u>ing</u> complement, the <u>do</u> is more difficult when TOUGH-movement takes place, as (67) and (68) show.

(67) *Seeing Margo sunbathing is fun to do.
(68) Seeing Margo sunbathe is fun to do. [4]

Notice, in addition, that <u>want</u> cannot occur in sentences of this type under any circumstances (that I know of):

(69) *Wanting a toy gun is hard to do.
(70) *Wanting someone to like you is easy to do sometimes.
(71) *Wanting the teacher to end school early is easy for a fourth-grader to do.

C. Just isn't done constructions are another case in point. Ross'
example (72) is fine, of course, but so are (73) and (74), which contain the statives owe and know respectively.

(72)   Kissing gorrillas just isn't done by today's debutantes.
(73)   Owing your close friends money just isn't done around
         here.
(74)   Knowing poems by heart just isn't done by today's
         college student.

Here again, the dubious grammaticality of (75) shows that want is
much more restricted than know vis-à-vis its occurrence with do.

(75)   ??Wanting his teachers to help him just isn't done by
         today's elementary school student.

D. The case of what NP did constructions is no different. Some
statives, like consider, see, and hear, occur freely in this context,
as is shown in (76) to (78).

(76)   What I did last night was see a good play.
(77)   What we did last night was hear Harry's rock band.
(78)   What McGovern shouldn't have done was consider
         Eagleton (as) his running mate.

If we add a clause indicating result after the did, however, the
grammaticality of many statives improves here, for (80) is better
than (79), and (82) is better than (81).

(79)   *What Harry did was resemble a Nazi.
(80)   ?What Harry did to get himself shot was resemble a Nazi.
(81)   *What Lucy did was know who fought the battle of
         Fallen Timbers.
(82)   ?What Lucy did to win the trip to Miami was know who
         fought the battle of Fallen Timbers.

But even with such result clauses, want is not 'doable':

(83)   *What Harry did to get himself elected was want the
         Senate to ratify the treaty.

All statives are 'doable', it is interesting to note, if the quantifier
all is added in addition to the result clause. This is illustrated in
(84) to (87).

(84)   All Harry did to get himself shot was resemble a Nazi.

(85)   All Margo did to win the trip to Miami was know who
       fought the battle of Fallen Timbers.

(86)   All Mary did to get herself arrested was owe the cop
       some money.

(87)   All you have to do to get busted is have a lid in your
       glove compartment.

E. As a final example, consider the case of <u>do so</u> constructions.
In relatively simple sentences of the form: S_1 and NP does so too,
only a couple of statives, like <u>consider</u> and <u>desire,</u> are acceptable,
as (88) and (89) show.

(88)   I consider Harvey a close friend, and Murray does so too.

(89)   Irma constantly desires sex, and Veronica does so too.

But if we play around with <u>do so</u> a little bit, we find sentence types
wherein only a few statives are excluded, as can be seen from (90)
to (94).

(90)   It's a shame that Peggy resembles her father, because
       for her to do so means her mother might kill her.

(91)   It's a good thing Hilda knows how much money is in the
       jackpot, because for her not to do so means she
       won't win the '73' El Dorado.

(92)   It's a good thing Marvin wants Nixon to win, because
       for him not to do so means he will be brutalized in
       the next FBI raid.

(93)   People who resemble their mothers, do so because of
       certain biogenetic laws.

(94)   Someone who knows all the answers does so because
       she's worked hard at it.

4. This is indeed a progress report. Little attempt has been
made to ascertain a hierarchy of <u>do</u> environments, because the
determining factors are not yet clear to me. Factors such as tense,
modality, and quantification seem to be playing more than a trivial
role in the above variation. Semantic properties like (self-) con-
trollability, which I have not touched upon here, appear to be relevant as well. My intention here, more than anything else, has been
simply to point out specific problems which any treatment of progressives or <u>do</u> must account for.
   Notice, however, that the proposals made by Lakoff and Ross
concerning stativity and <u>DO-GOBBLING</u> are quite general; they are
in fact equivalent to the claims that statives never take the present

progressive, and that statives never occur in the do constructions discussed in section 3 above. Therefore, the observations presented in this paper seem to indicate that neither stativity nor DO-GOBBLING is tenable in its present form.

Furthermore, we saw that know occurs in the do constructions of section 3 consistently more freely than want does, whereas the converse is true in the case of the progressive. It therefore seems unlikely that any hierarchical ranking of the verbs in question can be established which would be consistent with these two classificational criteria, let alone with the other five (or more) that have been proposed. In conclusion, it would not be at all surprising if the criteria proposed for ascertaining stativity turned out to be 'each a squish unto itself'.

NOTES

[1]This paper is part of a more comprehensive work on stativity now in preparation. I am greatly indebted to Arnold Zwicky and John Ross for stimulating discussion and insightful suggestions. An even greater gratitude is due my housemates: Sara Simons, Linda Sherman, Richard Cohen, and Dean Gibson, whose intuitions on stative verbs have by now been all but completely obliterated.

[2]For more on squishes, see Ross (1972).

[3](14) may be acceptable as the ADVERB PREPOSED transform of: The kids are wanting us to bring them toys tomorrow, where the progressive is PROCESS, not FUTURATE.

[4]In unearthing this ungodly pair, I was ably assisted by Peg Griffin and Patricia Sullivan.

REFERENCES

Lakoff, George. 1966. Stative verbs and adjectives in English. In: Harvard Computational Laboratory Report NSF-17.

Lee, P. Gregory. 1969. Subjects and Agents I. Ohio State Working Papers in Linguistics, Number 3. Ohio State University.

Ross, J. R. 1971. Act. In: Semantics of natural languages. Ed. by Davidson and Harman. Reidel.

_____. 1972. The category squish: Endstation hauptwart. CLS. VIII.

A FAKE NP SQUISH

JOHN ROBERT ROSS

Massachusetts Institute of Technology

1. Introduction

A popular exam question in Syntax One, these days, is: what part of speech is the expletive _there_? The answer is, 'Why it's an NP, of course! Just look at how, in (1), it has undergone RAISING, PASSIVE, NUMBER AGREEMENT, and TAG FORMATION, and at how the tensed auxiliary precedes it!

(1) At no time were there believed to have been files in this cake, were there?

And since copperclad, brass-bottomed NP's like _Harpo_ do exactly the same things (cf. (2), which exactly parallels (1)),

(2) At no time was Harpo believed to have been a drill sergeant, was he?

there must be a constituent of the same type as _Harpo_, i.e. an NP. Q.E.D.'

In the past, I have asked such questions not only about _there_, but also about 'weather _it_' and such idiom chunks as we find in the derived subject positions of the sentences in (3),

(3a) It is smoggy.
(3b) Careful tabs were kept on all 24 variables.
(3c) Headway was made on the Ellatization Project.
(3d) The cat's got your tongue.

and I have always marked such answers as the one given above as
correct.

And indeed, they are correct, in some sense, and provide a good
example of an important kind of syntactic argument.

However, in recent years, I have come across a larger body of
evidence which leads to the opposite conclusion: that in many respects, there, it, tabs, etc. do not behave like such indisputable
NP's as Harpo. This evidence will be presented in section 2.

So we find ourselves in a bind. There are good arguments that
there and its cronies are NP's; but there are others of the same
sort, which seem equally compelling, to the effect that they are
not NP's. What to do?

The data to be given in section 2 suggest a possible avenue of
escape. Roughly speaking, some of the problematic constituents
seem to be more like Harpo than others: they 'pass' more of the
NP tests than these others do. We can rank them on their 'noun-
phrasiness', as is done for some of them in (4).

(4)   More noun-phrasy
       Harpo > headway > there > tabs

The inequality sign in (4) is to be interpreted as an implication.
For any two items, A and B, if A > B, and if B 'passes' some test,
then A will also pass it. In other words, I am asserting that the
mystery items under discussion are 'fake' NP's: they only do a
subset of what NP's like Harpo do. I know of no syntactic processes
which are applicable to fake NP's, but not to standard-brand NP's
like Harpo.

What is even more interesting is the fact that the tests for noun-
phrasiness which will be the subject of section 2 can also be hierarchically ranked. An example of such a ranking is given in (5).[1, 2]

(5)   Choosier
       TAG FORMATION > TOUGH MOVEMENT > LEFT DISLOCATION

Again, the inequality sign has an implication interpretation. For any
two syntactic processes A and B, if A > B [read: 'B is choosier than
A' or 'A is stronger than B'], then whenever B can apply to a given
item, A will also be able to. The direction of the inequality sign is
purposely chosen to be the same in (4) and (5): just as NP's like
Harpo are found in a wider range of syntactic contexts than NP's
like tabs, so TAG FORMATION is applicable to a wider class of
structures than is LEFT DISLOCATION.

The two hierarchies above interact to mutually define each other. They form the type of matrix shown schematically in (6), which I will refer to as a 'squish'.

(6)

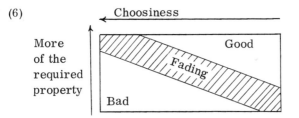

To give a concrete example, the hierarchies in (4) and (5) form the squish shown in (7).

(7)

	LEFT DISLOCATION	TOUGH MOVEMENT	TAG FORMATION
Harpo	OK	OK	OK
Headway	*	?	OK
There	*	*	OK
Tabs	*	*	?

To claim that fake NP's form a squish is to make a quite precise empirical claim. It is to claim that when all other fake NP's, such as those in (3), are 'blended into' (7), with as many rows being added as the facts necessitate, and when all other 'NP tests', i.e. syntactic processes involving NP's, are 'blended into' (7), with as many extra columns being added as there are processes that distinguish themselves, the resulting supermatrix will be 'well-behaved', as defined in (8).

(8) A matrix whose cells contain indications of degree of grammaticality is horizontally well-behaved if the degrees of grammaticality indicated in the cells of a row increase monotonically (i.e. without changes in direction of increment) or decrease monotonically. If one row has decreasing values, all must; if one row has increasing values, all must.

A matrix is vertically well-behaved if the degrees of grammaticality indicated in the cells of its columns increase or decrease monotonically in the manner specified above.

A matrix that is both horizontally and vertically
well-behaved is <u>well-behaved</u> .

   To claim that a body of data forms a squish is to claim that two
varying parameters can be found whose pattern of interaction is
given by a well-behaved matrix. We shall see in section 2 that while
the data on fake NP's suggest that a squish may at sometime be
demonstrable, at present, the associated matrix is not totally well-
behaved.

2. The evidence

   The data on which I base the claim that fake NP's form a squish
for me are shown in (9).
   Almost certainly, these judgments are true in their entirety for
no other speaker than me. Even making them relative, rather than
absolute, will attract few converts. <u>I suspect</u> that 'most' people's
idiolects will support the claim that <u>tack</u> is generally more noun-
phrasy than <u>tabs</u> is, and that the processes that form dislocated
S's are more choosy than those which form tagged S's; but I would
not flinch from data from speakers whose preferences were opposite
to mine even at the extremes of the matrix in (9). Having heard the
incredible variation among the reactions to matrices like (9) which I
have presented in classes and other lectures convinces me that there
is probably no significantly large submatrix of (9) which could be
said to represent 'the standard dialect'. Essentially, what we are
dealing with here is the degree to which the lexical idioms and
idiomatic constructions under scrutiny are syntactically frozen;
and it is to be expected, I fear, that no consensus will emerge in
such shadowlands. In such a situation, a definite article in the title
of this paper would be on the hybris side of chutzpah, I should think.
   What I would hope is that every idiolect's matrix will be well-
behaved. If so, we will have some basis for proceeding on the hope
that other areas of language will in general turn out to be provably
squishy, and some encouragement for an attempt to develop a quantitative theory of grammar which would be adequate to the task of explaining such relatively well-behaved matrices as (9).
   If not--that is, if fake NP's should turn out to be squishy for some
but not for others--then I would be completely baffled. The leap
from the present discrete view implicit in generative grammar to
a nondiscrete, squishy, theory of grammar is radical, but not be-
wildering. But a leap to something more radical than a theory of
squishes is something which at present outstrips my conceptual
apparatus.

	Animates	Forces of nature concretes	Events	Abstracts	TACK	HEADWAY	IT (BE MUGGY)	IT (S)	IT (rain)	THERE	TABS	HEED
TAG FORMATION	OK	OK	OK	OK	OK	OK	OK	OK	OK	OK	?·	?*
Head of relative clauses	OK	OK	OK	OK	OK	OK	DNA	DNA	DNA	DNA	?*	?·
Inside derived nominals	OK	OK	OK	OK	?·	?·	?·	?·	??	?·	??	?*
Get passives	OK	OK	OK	OK	OK	?·	*·	?·	*·	?*	??	??
TO BE DELETION	OK	OK	OK	OK	?·	??	?·	OK	??	??	?*	*·
CONJUNCTION REDUCTION	OK	OK	OK	OK	OK	OK	?·	*·	??	*	*	?*
Acc-Ing	OK	OK	OK	OK	OK	?·	??	??	?*	OK	?*	?*
. . . 's	OK	OK	OK	OK	?·	?·	??	??	?*	*	?*	*
PRONOMINALIZATION	OK	OK	OK	OK	?·	?*	DNA	DNA	DNA	DNA	*	*
EQUI	OK	OK	?·	OK	?·	?*	?·	*	??	*	*	*
TOUGH MOVEMENT TOPICALIZATION AND SWOOPING	OK	OK	OK	OK	OK	?·	*	*	*	*	*	*
NP SHIFT	OK	OK	OK	OK	??	?*	DNA	DNA	DNA	DNA	?*	*
RIGHT NODE RAISING	OK	OK	OK	OK	??	?*	DNA	DNA	DNA	DNA	*	*
LEFT and RIGHT DISLOCATION	OK	OK	OK	OK	??	*	*	*	*	*	*	*
BEING DELETION	OK	OK	OK	?·	??	*	*	*	*	*	*	*
What's . . . doing X	OK	?·	??	??	??	?*	*	*	?·	*	*	*
Think of . . . as X	OK	?·	??	??	?*	*·	?*	??	*	*	*	*
Double RAISING	OK	?·	??	??	?*	*	*	??	*	?*	*	*
PROMOTION and subject of be prevented	OK	?·	?*	*	*	*	*	*	*	*	*	*

NOTE: DNA = does not apply. Cells that interfere with horizontal good behavior contain parallel lines. Cells that interfere with vertical good behavior contain parallel lines.

(9)

2.1. PROMOTION and passivization of <u>prevent</u> and <u>allow</u>

The processes which form the basis of the judgments in the first
column of (9) are PROMOTION, a rule which I will assume converts
(10a) into (10b) and (10c) to (10d) [note that the argument at issue
here is not affected if I have chosen the wrong remote structure for
(10b)] and the rule of PASSIVE.

(10a) Harpo's being willing to retune surprised me.

       ↓PROMOTION

(10b) Harpo surprised me by being willing to retune.

(10c) Harpo's willingness to retune surprised me.

       ↓PROMOTION

(10d) Harpo surprised me with his willingness to retune.

When PROMOTION applies to postpose complements whose subjects
are fake NP's, we very soon find hash emerging. Cf. (11).

(11a)   My cat surprised me by knowing how to yodel.
(11b)   ?The heat surprised me by making the tar soft.
(11c)   ?*The concert surprised me by lasting two weeks.
(11d)   *This tack surprised me by being taken infrequently.
         etc.

Similarly, though PASSIVE is not normally subject to such restrictions, with the verbs <u>prevent</u> and <u>allow</u>, and possibly others, only
items toward the top of the noun-phrasiness edge of (9) can become
derived subjects. Thus the sentences in (12) are increasingly rotten,
though their active sources are fine.

(12a)   McX was prevented from thinning out the chipmunks.

(12b)   ?The gale was prevented from causing any damage.

(12c)   ?*Your induction will be prevented from taking more
         than 2 minutes.

(12d)   *This tack will not be allowed to be taken on any
         subsequent problems.

2.2. Double RAISING

RAISING is the rule which converts the subject of a complement clause into a constituent of the matrix clause. Thus (13a) can become (13b).

(13a)   It will be shown that John has cheated.

|
↓ RAISING

(13b)   John will be shown to have cheated.

If (13b) is the complement of a predicate which allows RAISING, as in (14a), then RAISING can apply again, producing (14b).

(14a)   It is likely that John will be shown to have cheated.

(14b)   John is likely to be shown to have cheated.

However, while all NP's can undergo RAISING once (as in (13)), none but the finest NP's can be raised twice.[3] Cf. (15).

(15a)   John is likely to be shown to have cheated.

(15b)   ?The wind is likely to be shown to have cracked the glass.

(15c)   ??The performance is likely to be shown to have begun late.

(15d)   ??The superset is likely to be shown to be recursive.

(15e)   ?*This tack is likely to be shown to have been taken on that.

(15f)   *No headway is likely to be shown to have been made.

(15g)   *It is likely to be shown to have been muggy.

(15h)   ??It is likely be shown to be possible to be in 6 1/2 places at once.

(15i)   *It is likely to be shown to have rained cats, dogs, and pigs.

(15j) ?*There is likely to be shown to be no way out of
       this shoe.

(15k) *Close tabs are likely to be shown to have been
       kept on Muskie.

(15l) *No heed is likely to be shown to have been paid
       to Cassandra.

The partial grammaticalities of (15h) and of (15j) are two places
where (9) is not vertically well-behaved. I have no explanation for
them.

2.3. Think of . . . as X

To the best of my knowledge, no one has argued for any particular
source for the type of complement that is found after <u>think</u> in such
sentences as (16).

(16) I thought of

a.   Freud as being wiggy
b.   ?the rock as being too heavy
c.   ??the show as being over-long
d.   ??generalizations as being wily and hard
          to capture
e.   ?*this tack as having been taken too often
f.   *significant headway as having already
          been made
g.   ?*it as being muggy
h.   ?? it as being likely that you would
          accept
i.   *it as {raining / having rained / etc.} .

The bad behavior of (16f) is probably to be attributed to the fact
that <u>headway</u> must be existentially quantified (cf. (17)), while the
post- <u>of</u> NP in sentences like (16) seems to exclude quantitication
with the nonspecific <u>some</u> [sm] (cf. (18)).

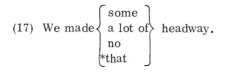

(17) We made {some / a lot of / no / *that} headway.

(18) I thought of $\left\{ \begin{array}{l} \text{*somebody} \\ \text{*sm people} \\ \underline{\text{some}}\text{ people} \\ \text{several people} \\ \text{??nobody} \\ \text{everybody} \end{array} \right\}$ as interesting.

(16h) is better than I would predict. I have no idea why.

2.4. What's . . . doing X?

This curious construction, unstudied in the literature I am familiar with, is synonymous with <u>why</u>-questions. Examples appear in (19).

(19) a. What's $\left\{ \begin{array}{l} \text{he} \\ \text{*someone} \end{array} \right\}$ doing (??not) $\left\{ \begin{array}{l} \text{in jail} \\ \text{?charged with} \\ \quad \text{decency} \\ \text{drunk/absent/} \\ \quad \text{high/drunker} \\ \quad \text{than Tom} \\ \text{?*the drunkest} \\ \quad \text{of all} \\ \text{?*a law student} \\ \quad \text{resembling a} \\ \quad \text{donut} \end{array} \right\}$

b. *What's this proof doing $\left\{ \begin{array}{l} \text{long} \\ \text{valid} \end{array} \right\}$?

c. ??What's he seem to be doing in Boston?[4]

Mysteries abound. Why can't negatives appear in this construction, while they can in <u>why</u>-questions like this one? What class of adjectives is possible in this construction? Is this construction somehow related to <u>there-</u> sentences? Cf. (20).

(20a) Several students were $\left\{ \begin{array}{l} \text{absent} \\ \text{tall} \\ \text{members.} \end{array} \right\}$.

(20b) There were several students $\left\{ \begin{array}{l} \text{absent} \\ \text{*tall} \\ \text{*members} \end{array} \right\}$.

At any rate, wherever these S's come from, and by whatever processes, their subjects can't be too fake. Cf. (21).

(21a)   What's the heat wave doing warping the love seat?

(21b)   ?What's the wind doing tipping over the canoe?

(21c)   ??What's the first set doing lasting two hours?

(21d)   ??What's his evasiveness doing becoming a campaign issue?

(21e)   ??What's this outmoded tack doing being taken on a complex social issue like ureic deriboflavinization?

(21f)   ?*What's satisfactory headway doing being made only on rearmament?[5]

(21g)   *What's it doing being muggy on Tuesday?

(21h)   *What's it doing being probable that the Pats will only drop 9.

(21i)   ?What's it doing sleeting?

(21j)   *What's there doing being no mistrial?

(21k)   *What are these exasperatingly close tabs doing being kept on people even after November 7?

(21l)   *What's close heed doing being paid to last year's returns?

What's (21i) doing being vertically ill-behaved?

2.5. Being DELETION

I will assume the existence of a rule, which I will refer to as Being DELETION, which converts (obligatorily?) such S's as (22a) into (22b).

(22a) ?? $\left\{ \begin{array}{c} \text{Me} \\ \text{You} \end{array} \right\}$ being in the tub is a funny sight.

(22b) $\left\{ \begin{array}{c} \text{Me} \\ \text{You} \end{array} \right\}$ in the tub is a funny sight.

This is argued for by the fact that the first-person pronoun never occurs with a following restrictive modifier, the only other conceivable source for such postnominal phrases as those in (22b). Such phrases cannot be derived from appositives, either, for these exclude any.

(23a)   You with any jewels on is a rare sight.

(23b)   *You, who have any jewels on, is a rare sight.

Finally, this type of NP only shows up in a subset of cases where obvious complements can appear. Cf. (24).

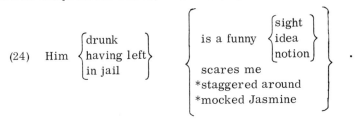

All in all, then, it seems highly probable that some such rule as Being DELETION produces the subject of (22b) from some full complement like the subject of (22a). But this rule must be prevented from applying after subjects that are not sufficiently noun-phrasy. Cf. (25).

$$
(25) \left\{
\begin{array}{l}
\text{Hinswood in the tub} \\
\text{The salt flowing} \\
\text{Explosions happening before} \\
\quad \text{breakfast} \\
?\text{The existence of Las Vegas} \\
\quad \text{provable} \\
??\text{This tack taken on filibustering} \\
*\text{Sufficient headway made} \\
\quad \text{on halitosis} \\
*\text{It muggy} \\
*\text{It likely that this line} \\
\quad \text{is bugged} \\
*\text{It snowing tomorrow} \\
*\text{There no more Schlitz}[6] \\
*\text{Close tabs kept on} \\
\quad \text{Kissinger} \\
*\text{Little heed paid to public} \\
\quad \text{apathy}
\end{array}
\right\} \text{is a funny thought.}
$$

Whether or not such absolute constructions as those that appear in (26) are produced by the same or by a different rule of Being DELETION, it is evident that this construction too dances to the drum of noun-phrasiness.

$$(26) \begin{cases} \text{Jack in bed} \\ \text{The significance of your} \\ \quad \text{refusal clear} \\ \text{*This tack taken} \\ \text{*Significant headway made} \\ \text{*It muggy} \\ \text{*It possible that it would} \\ \quad \text{rain} \\ \text{*Close tabs kept on the} \\ \quad \text{barometer} \end{cases} \text{, we settled back to wait for rain.}$$

2.6. LEFT DISLOCATION and RIGHT DISLOCATION

In colloquial speech, such S's as (27) can be converted by rules that I will refer to as LEFT DISLOCATION and RIGHT DISLOCATION to the sentences in (28) and (29), respectively. [7]

(27)   Those guys are smuggling my armadillo to Helen.

(28a)   Those guys, they're smuggling my armadillo to Helen.

(28b)   My armadillo, those guys are smuggling him to Helen.

(28c)   Helen, those guys are smuggling my armadillo to her.

(29a)   They're smuggling my armadillo to Helen, those guys.

(29b)   Those guys are smuggling him to Helen, my armadillo.

(29c)   ?Those guys are smuggling my armadillo to her, Helen.

That these rules are only viable with pretty genuine NP's is suggested by the sentences in (30).

(30a)   Max, he's sharp.

(30b)   It's strong here, the wind.

(30c)   The openness you're looking for--it's unattainable.

$$(30d) \quad \text{That tack,} \begin{cases} \text{??you shouldn't take it on} \\ \quad \text{this problem.} \\ \text{?it shouldn't be taken on} \\ \quad \text{easy problems.} \end{cases} . \text{[8]}$$

(30e)   Appreciable headway, I doubt that you'll make *it/?any. [9]

(30f)   *It, I don't think it ever rains. [10]

(30g)   *Such annoyingly close tabs, I don't think you should
         keep them even on presidential candidates, Sir.

2.7. RIGHT NODE RAISING

This rule, in conjoined structures, each of whose conjuncts has
an identical right extremity, deletes all of these identical right ex-
tremities, Chomsky-adjoining one copy to the conjoined node. Thus
(31a) becomes (31b), with a copy of NP_a being Chomsky-adjoined to
S_0.

(31a)

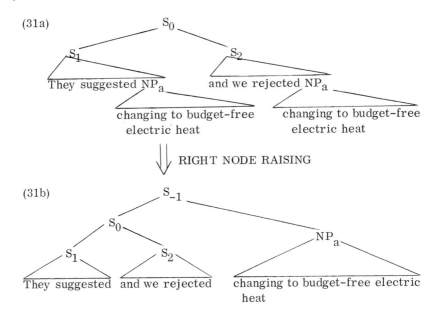

RIGHT NODE RAISING

(31b)

Of relevance for the present concern is the fact that this process
applies only to pretty bona-fide NP's. While prepositional phrases
can undergo this rule [cf. (32a)], [11] the precipitous but varying
putrescence of the remaining examples in (32) shows the influence
of fakeness on this rule.

(32a)   We talk to the students, and they talk to their pets,
          about ice.

(32b)   ? ?We have taken on this problem, and they will take on
        that one, a tack so kooky as to defy belief.

(32c)   ?*We made on the first problem, and you will probably
        make on the second, considerable headway.

(32d)   *They kept on George, and we kept on Dick, such close
        tabs that now each of them knows the other's catsup
        brand.

(32e)   *She paid to Fotheringay, and he to her, so little heed
        that I thought they were zombies.

2.8.   NP SHIFT

This rule moves to the right end of a sentence post-verbal NP's
that are complex and heavy enough that leaving them in their original position would have made difficult to process the sentence in
question. Thus (33a) becomes (33b).

(33a)   ??I explained [that I was Irish]   to the guards.
                                       NP
                  NP SHIFT

(33b)   I explained to the guards [that I was Irish]
                                                    NP

That fake NP's are poor candidates for this rule can be seen from
the sentences in (34).

(34a)   We elected to the presidency a man of great moral
          fiber (Acrilan).

(34b)   ??We have taken, on this problem, a tack so risky that
          I am sick.

(34c)   ?*We have made, on this problem, headway so funda-
          mental that a collapse of our theory is imminent.

(34d)   ?*Dick kept on Hubert close enough tabs to be able to
          know how often he had seen Patton.

(34e)   *I paid to Jane absolutely no heed whatever.

My reason for not narrowing the matrix in (9) by putting NP
SHIFT into the same column as RIGHT NODE RAISING is my per-
sistent, and unfortunate, (it makes the cell corresponding to (34d)
in (9) horizontally ill-behaved) intuition that (34d) is a tad better
than (32d). The two processes are also similar in refusing to apply
to any expletive pronoun, like it and there, but unless this other
difference can somehow be explained, they must be assigned different positions in the squish.

2.9. TOUGH MOVEMENT, TOPICALIZATION, AND SWOOPING

The effects of TOUGH MOVEMENT I have illustrated in footnote 1.
TOPICALIZATION we can find used in the first two sentences of this
paragraph. And (35) contains an example of SWOOPING, the rule
which forms nonrestrictive relative clauses from conjoined sentences
by adjoining the second of two adjacent clauses which both contain
occurrences of the same NP to the occurrence of this NP in the first
S.

(35a)　　I gave [Sandra]　my zwieback, and [she]　didn't want
　　　　　　　　　　　NP　　　　　　　　　　　NP
　　　　　any.

　　　　　　　⇓ SWOOPING

(35b)　　I gave　[Sandra],　and she didn't want any ,
　　　　　　　　　　NP　　　　　　　　　　　　　　NP
　　　　　my zwieback.

Later rules convert (35b) to (36).

(36)　　I gave Sandra, who didn't want any, my zwieback.

For me, these three processes seem equally loth to apply to
fake NP's. Cf. (37)-(44).

(37a)　　This tack on racism is tough to take.

(37b)　　This tack on racism I don't want to take.

(37c)　　He suggested taking this tack, which has never been
　　　　　taken before.

(38a)   ?Noticeable headway is tough to make on problems of
        this complexity.

(38b)   ?Significant headway I don't think we'll be able to make.

(38c)   ?We made dramatic headway, which we had been trying
        to make, on the problem of how many (n-5)-dimensional
        angels can dance on the head of an (2n-1)-dimensional
        pin.

(39a)   *It is very difficult to consider smoggy.

(39b)   *It I have never found too smoggy in LA. [12]

(39c)   *It, which is now smoggy in Denver, didn't use to be.

(40a)   *It is difficult to consider fair that they absconded. [13]

(40b)   *It I have never considered fair that they absconded.

(40c)   *It, which the police cannot prove, is obvious that
        they absconded.

(41a)   *It will be very difficult to prove likely to rain.

(41b)   *It I didn't think would rain.

(41c)   *It, which was raining, is now snowing.

(42a)   *There will be difficult to prove likely to be enough
        to eat.

(42b)   *There I don't consider to be enough booze in the
        eggnog.

(42c)   *I find there, which may have been previously, to be
        no grounds for contempt proceedings.

(43a)   *Close tabs are really impossible to keep on Kissinger.

(43b)   *Really close tabs we couldn't keep on any of them.

(43c)   *Close tabs, which we had previously tried to keep on
         Kissinger, were only intended to be kept on him while
         he was not actually on the Presidential Escalator.

(44a)   *Sufficient heed is not easy to pay to a real kvetsch.

(44b)   *Sufficient heed I think you have already paid to this
         kvetsch. [14]

(44c)   *We finally did pay heed, which you always said that
         someday we would have to pay, to the mice and
         lice in the rice.

As noted in (9), the relative well-formedness of (37) and (38)
produces two horizontally ill-behaved cells. I have no idea why.

2.10. EQUI

For the purposes of this paper, I will simply assume that the
optional process (es?) which may apply to the sentences in (45) to
convert them to those in (46) may be identified with the process
Postal refers to as EQUI (cf. Postal 1970). Whether or not this
identification will stand up under more detailed scrutiny is irrelevant to the point at hand, which is that EQUI is pretty choosy, pre-
ferring to delete only true-blue NP's. Cf. (47).

(45a) $\begin{Bmatrix} \text{Before} \\ \text{After} \end{Bmatrix}$ he laughed politely, Oliver wiped his moustache.

(45b)   Since I know what you're up to, I will sit this one out.

(45c)   Despite the fact that he had no open sores, Fred was
         insanely popular.

(46a) $\begin{Bmatrix} \text{Before} \\ \text{After} \end{Bmatrix}$ laughing politely, Oliver wiped his mustache.

(46b)   Knowing what you're up to, I will sit this one out.

(46c) Despite (*the fact[15]) having no open sores, Fred was insanely popular.

(47a) Knowing the answer, Max piped up.

(47b) Having totaled our farm, the hurricane moved off.

(47c) ?Before starting, the concert seemed likely to last two days.

(47d) Having no basis in fact, these generalizations should immediately be codified into a new linguistic theory.

(47e) ?Never having been taken previously, this tack will be taken for the first time on pollution.

(47f) ?*Before being made on the corollaries, significant headway will have to be made on the main theorem.

(47g) ?Being muggy, it isn't very chilly.

(47h) *Seeming that you will be invited, it will be necessary for you to knit yourself a tux.

(47i) ??Having snowed two feet, it began to hail.

(47j) *After being a confrontation, there's always some good old-time head-busting.

(47k) *Having been kept on Teddy, close tabs probably won't have to be kept on those other fascist peace-niks.

(47l) *Having been paid to the king, little heed was also paid to my Weimaraner.

As indicated in (9), the cells of the matrix corresponding to (47c), (47g), and (47i), are, for reasons unknown, both horizontally and vertically ill-behaved.

2.10. PRONOMINALIZATION

To say that whatever process(es) is/are used to ensure the generation of only well-formed anaphoric linkages in English is/are merely poorly understood would be to wildly understate the problem.

Whatever process(es) is/are involved, however, fake NP's do not all participate equally well in such linkages, as (48) shows.[16]

(48a)　?If George takes some tack on unemployment, inevitably Dick will take it soon thereafter.

(48b)　If you want to make headway on this, you'd better make $\left\{ \begin{array}{l} \text{?*it} \\ \text{some} \end{array} \right\}$ on that too.

(48c)　*Close tabs are always kept on left-wingers, but they never are on moderates like H. L. Hunt.

(48d)　We paid heed to his pleas, but we didn't pay $\left\{ \begin{array}{l} \text{*it} \\ \text{??any} \end{array} \right\}$ to his knees.

2.12 Prepossessing

The possessive morpheme, 's, does not attach itself with equal alacrity to all fake NP's. For me, the facts are as shown in (49).

(49a)　?That tack's having been taken again is incredible.

(49b)　?Significant headway's being made on others is wonderful news.

(49c)　??Its being so hot was a real shame.

(49d)　??Its being possible that murther will out is causing unrest in high places.

(49e)　?*Its having rained is tragic.

(49f)　*There's being no more rotten fruit surprised me.

(49g)　**Tabs's even being kept on Dick Gregory indicates that they are worried.[17]

(49h)　*No heed's being paid to her miffed Alice.

2.12 Acc-Ing

By this term, I refer to the accusative-gerund complement structures which are possible for me in the subjects of such sentences as (50).

(50a)   John being arrested incited a riot.

(50b)   The riot being televised caused a scandal.

(50c)   His aggression running wild plunged the nation into a
          moral Dark Ages.

Such complements are somewhat choosy, though not so much as
the Poss-Ing examples in (49), cf. (51).

(51a) $\left\{\begin{array}{l} \text{This tack being taken on devaluation.} \\ \text{?No headway being made for ten years.} \\ \text{??It being humid} \\ \text{??It being likely that you'll be evicted} \end{array}\right\}$ is scandalous.

(51b)   ?*It raining was a catastrophe.

(51c)   There being no more stagnant water must break your
        heart.

(51d)   ?*Accurate tabs being kept on state candidates too would
        deplete our secret slush fund too much, or we'd do it
        like a shot.

(51e)   ?*Little heed being paid to Jane riled her up good.

There are many people who totally reject all such Acc-Ing complements when in subject position (except (51c), which seems to be
generally well thought of), but who will accept them in object
position. This is possibly due to the fact that Acc-Ing subjects
are not popular among prescriptive grammarians, though I do not
think that all the heart-felt boggling that these sentences arouse can
be attributed to normative stigma. At any rate, it is clear that
there is a huge improvement when Acc-Ing complements are in
object position. All are totally well-formed, with the possible exception of the fakest NP. Cf. (52).

(52)   ?I can't imagine little heed being paid to Jane.

The widely accepted (51c) is a very clear case of a totally ill-
behaved cell. It is so universally beloved that one is forced to
postulate a special rule obligatorily deleting 's just after there.
Presumably, though here I have not checked to find what kind of
intermediate dialects exist, this is the core of a rule of POSSESSIVE
DELETION which spreads through Poss-Ing complements, producing

such arrays of data as that which obtain in my speech, the facts of
(51). But why should such a rule exist? And why should it start at
there ?

If the sequence of events just suggested above is in fact what
happened, it is counterevidence of the most serious sort against the
theory I am advocating here, which holds that all such rule-spread-
ing must start with animate NP's and spread down (9) row by row.
Probably such a theory is wrong, but I do not know what to suggest
as a replacement.

2.13 CONJUNCTION REDUCTION

This is the rule or rules which converts sentences containing conjoined clauses to sentences in which the coordinating conjunction is
attached to nonclausal elements. In its simplest form, it effects
such changes as those from (53) to (54).

(53a)   Manny wept and Sheila wept.

(53b)   We sighed and we cried.

(53c)   They ran into the houses and they ran out of the houses.

(54a)   Manny and Sheila wept.

(54b)   We sighed and cried.

(54c)   They ran into the houses and out of the houses.

Of relevance here is the fact that conversions that result in conjoined 'verb phrases', [18] such as the change from (53b) to (54b), are,
in my speech, constrained in such a way as to be progressively less
grammatical as the subject NP's become less and less genuine. Cf.
(55).

(55a)   This tack has been taken in the past, and may be taken
        again.

(55b)   Such significant headway has been made in the past,
        and will be made again before long.

(55c)   ?It is smoggy and may get muggy.

(55d)   *It is likely that he'll enter, and must therefore be possible that he'll win.

(55e)   ??It has rained and may snow.

(55f)   *There were diplodocuses, are platypuses, and may well also be diplatocodypuses.

(55g)   *Close tabs were kept on me, and may later be kept on you.

(55h)   ?*No heed was paid to Giovanni, (n)or will be to Erdmute.

(55i)   ?*Heed was paid to the Chairman's fears, and will be paid to yours.

The horizontal ill-behavior of (55b) and (55d), and the vertical ill-behavior of (55h, i) I cannot explain. Nor can I explain why it is that I, who have an idiolect which in most respects properly includes the idiolects of other speakers I have checked, should have such a choosy rule of CONJUNCTION REDUCTION, for there are many speakers who report that all sentences in (55) are perfect for them. [19]

2.14 To Be DELETION

It is clear that there exists a rule which, in the complements of certain verbs, deletes to be. This is indicated by the fact that (56) cannot be an underlying structure. (57) seems to be the most probable immediate source for it.

(56a)   I want significant headway made on this by the time I return.

(56b)   I want close tabs kept on him.

(57a)   I want significant headway to be made on this by the time I return.

(57b)   I want close tabs to be kept on him.

The argument is of a familiar kind, since headway and tabs occur in remote structures only as the objects of make and keep, respectively, and since PASSIVE would normally apply to such structures to produce the sentences in (57), the fact that we appear to find these fake NP's in unusual environments in (56) is simply explained by postulating the existence of a rule which obliterates the infinitivized form of the passive auxiliary.

With <u>want</u> and <u>would like</u>, the rule is relatively unrestricted, cf. (58).

(58a) I want the boys hungry.

(58b) I want the anchors heavy enough to break the crust.

(58c) I want the retreat delayed.

(58d) I want the facts accurate.

(58e) I want this tack taken on the question of furze.

(58f) I want significant headway made by sundown.

(58g) ?I want it believed to be muggy in Death Valley.

(58h) ?I want it believed to be easy to get along with Spiro.

(58i) ?I want it believed to be raining very lightly.

(58j) ?*I want there believed to be no radishes.

(58k) I want close tabs kept on everybody, including you!

(58l) I want no heed paid to her denials.

It is likely that the varying unacceptabilities of (58g)-(58j) are due to the fact that all the derived objects of <u>want</u> have undergone RAISING. Unless this rule has been applied, these NP's fail to meet the structural description of <u>To Be</u> DELETION, as the following sentences show.[20]

(59a) I want you *(to be) certain to bathe often.

(59b) I want it *(to be) certain to rain while the senator is visiting.

(59c) I want there *(to be) certain to be a dogfight during this movie.

Now contrast (59a) with (60), which derives from roughly the same source, and which differs from the former sentence only in not having undergone RAISING on the certain-cycle.

(60)   I want it (to be) certain that you will bathe often.

The restriction which seems to be operative here is this: to be cannot be deleted if its subject has been produced by a prior application of RAISING. This is, of course, a global rule.[21] I have not been able to devise any nonglobal formulation.

At any rate, the parallelism among the sentences in (59) indicates strongly that it is not the fakeness of the derived objects of want in the starred versions of (59b) and (59c) that renders them ungrammatical, but rather the effect of the above-mentioned global rule.

This means that the only way to check whether the expletives it and there block the application of To Be DELETION is with such dubious sentences as (58g)-(58j). And that their dubiousness is not unambiguously attributable to the fakeness of the derived objects of want can be seen from the awkwardness of the to be-less versions of (61).

(61a)   I want Dick ?(to be) believed to be honest.

(61b)   I want this donut ?(to be) believed to be magnetic.

Summing up the discussion so far, it appears clear that there exists a rule of To Be DELETION (this is obvious from (56)-(58)), that this rule is globally constrained, but that it is not constrained, except for (58j), by the fakeness of the NP after which to be is deleted. In short, the rule seems to be relatively insensitive to fakeness when operating after want (or would like).

However, the facts are not the same when this rule is applied after such verbs as consider, think, find, seem, etc. Applying to the complements of such verbs, To Be DELETION can be seen to be conditioned by the degree of phoniness of the subject NP of the to be that is being deleted, cf. (62).

(62a)   I considered Herman unthinkable.

(62b)   We found the soup delicious.

(62c)   They found the retreat dangerous.

(62d)   This proof seemed valid.

(62e)   ?We considered this tack unlikely to be taken.[22]

(62f)   ??We considered significant headway unlikely to be
         made.

(62g)   ?We considered it too muggy.

(62h)   We considered it possible that we would win.

(62i)   ??We considered it likely to rain enough to fill the
         tank.

(62j)   ??We considered there likely to be a riot.

(62k)   ?*We considered satisfactorily close tabs unlikely to
         be kept on him.

(62l)   *We considered heed unlikely to be paid to him.

It is the facts of (62) that I have entered in (9) and they are
roughly in accord with what one would be led to predict from the
hypothesis that (9) is a well-behaved matrix. However, as indicated
in (9), (62e), (62f), and (62h), and (62l) are horizontally ill-behaved,
with (62f) and (62h) being vertically ill-behaved. Needless to say, I
have no explanation for this ill-behavior.

2.15 Get PASSIVE

Many types of passive sentences whose main verb is be can also
occur with the main verb get. When get is not possible, the reason
seems to depend in part on the fakeness of the NP which becomes the
derived subject of get, cf. (63).

(63a)   Jane got busted.

(63b)   My watch got stolen again.

(63c)   His promotion got televised.

(63d)   His industriousness got commented on within weeks.

(63e)   This tack gets taken too much these days.

(63f)   ?Usually, significant headway doesn't get made on
         arranging ceasefires until just before an election.

(63g) *It got generally believed to be so humid in Moose Jaw
       that the Bear Relief Squad was put on stand-by alert.

(63h) ?It got pointed out that outside agitators have rights too.

(63i) *It got said to have rained torrentially.

(63j) ?*There got rumored to be some jobs available in
       Hyannis.

(63k) ??Really close tabs usually get kept only on candidates
       opposing an unresponsive and deceitful incumbent.

(63l) ??Unfortunately, far too little heed got paid to Eisenhower's
       prophetic warning.

The vertical ill-behavior of (63g), (63i), (which is also horizontally ill-behaved), and (63j), all expletive pronouns, is especially
puzzling in view of the fact that (63h), whose subject is also an
expletive, is only mildly objectionable.

2.16 Inside Derived Nominals.

I am sorry to report that Acc-Ing complements following such
nouns as likelihood, possibility, probability, chance, idea, etc., do
not behave either like those in subject position, nor like those in the
object of such verbs as imagine. Thus compare (51) and (52) with (64).

(64) The likelihood
      of
      {
        Dick Gregory winning
        the table cracking
        the meeting being long
        grammaticality being
          preserved
        ?this tack being taken
        ?significant headway
          being made on this
        ?it being cloudy
        ?it being true that
          Kissinger is only
          on a vacation trip
        ??it raining
        ?there being enough water
        ??close tabs being kept
          on you
        ?*no heed being taken
      }
      is too small to
      register on this
      portable Prob-
      ablometer--
      we'll have to go
      back to the
      Giant Likelo-
      tron 360.

While sentences like (64) are clearly worse across the board than sentences like (52), and generally better than sentences like (51), there is one case, that of there, where this pattern is inexplicably reversed, and two cases, headway and heed, where I cannot hear the difference I would expect.

This state of affairs is frustrating, because it indicates that whatever mechanism will eventually be devised to grind out the acceptability judgments in such cases must have more parameters than merely those cited in (65).

(65a)   Animates > Concretes > . . . > heed.

(65b)   Objects > . . . > insided derived nominals > . . . > subjects.

(65c)   Acc-Ing requires subjects of degree of noun-phrasiness X, where X ranges over some at present unspecificable domain.

What the additional parameters might be is, not surprisingly, a mystery, as are the reasons for the horizontal ill-behavior of tack and the vertical ill-behavior of there in (64).

2.17 Heads of Relative Clauses

Most nonpronominal NP's can be followed by a relative clause, even idiom chunks, as (66) indicates.

(66a)   The tack that you're taking is futile.

(66b)   The headway that you have made on Chapter 57 of your term paper is promising.

(66c)   ?*The tabs that we kept on the Shadow were not of any help to the NRLB.

(66d)   ?The little heed that I paid to the Medusa angered her.

The cell corresponding to (66c) is unexpectedly weak: it is both horizontally and vertically ill-behaved, while (66d)'s cell is horizontally ill-behaved.

2.18 Tag Questions

Even whatever non-choosy process(es) is/are used to form tag sentences will balk at constructing tags whose NP is excessively fake. Cf. (67).

(67a)   This tack has been taken before, hasn't it?

(67b)   Some headway has been made, hasn't it?

(67c)   It's rotten out, ain't it?

(67d)   It isn't likely that you'll show, is it?

(67e)   It really poured, didn't it?

(67f)   There sure are a lot of mothballs in this soup, aren't there?

(67g)   ? Pretty close tabs are being kept on Willy, aren't they?

(67h)   ?*Little heed was paid to her, was it?

2.19 Modifiability and Inside vs. Outside Passives

There are two other processes which interact with the squishoid in (9), but not in a way that can be diagrammed easily in its cells. Let us refer, for expository purposes, to the three nonverbal elements in (68) as NP_1, NP_2, and NP_3, as indicated.

(68)   The bosses took advantage of the wage freeze.
         NP_1 NP_2 NP_3

The 'inside passive' of (68) is (69a); the 'outside passive' is (69b).

(69a)   Advantage was taken of the wage freeze by the bosses.

(69b)   The wage freeze was taken advantage of by the bosses.

The first fact to be noted about NP_2 is that when it is modified, outside passives become more awkward. Compare (69) and (70).

(70a)   Ruthless advantage was taken of the wage freeze by the bosses.

(70b) ??The wage freeze was taken ruthless advantage of by the bosses.

It appears to be the case that the noun-phrasier the NP_2 of a given idiom is--that is, the higher up NP_2 appears in (9)--the more easily it can be modified. This can be seen from the sentences in (71).[23]

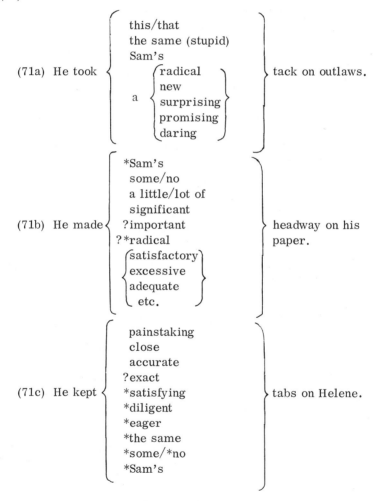

(71a) He took { this/that; the same (stupid); Sam's; a { radical, new, surprising, promising, daring } } tack on outlaws.

(71b) He made { *Sam's; some/no; a little/lot of; significant; ?important; ?*radical; { satisfactory, excessive, adequate, etc. } } headway on his paper.

(71c) He kept { painstaking; close; accurate; ?exact; *satisfying; *diligent; *eager; *the same; *some/*no; *Sam's } tabs on Helene.

(71d) He paid $\left\{\begin{array}{l} \text{no/\,?\,*some} \\ \text{little} \\ \text{?(in)sufficient} \\ \text{*inadequate} \\ \text{*unsatisfactory} \\ \text{*Sam's} \end{array}\right\}$ heed to the dangers.

The second fact to note is that the less fake NP_2 is, the worse outside passives are, cf. (72).

(72a) *Desegregation was taken this tack on.

(72b) ?*This area has been made headway on.

(73c) ?*He's been kept tabs on ever since he left South Dakota.

(73d) ?Your warning wasn't paid heed to.

The other side of this coin is the fact that while with very nounphrasy NP_2's, inside passives are possible with or without modification, with fake NP_2's, inside passives are weak unless NP_2 is modified. Cf. (73).

(73a) This (innovative) tack was taken on individuals.

(73b) (Significant) headway was made in the 479th talk.

(73c) $\left\{\begin{array}{l} \text{Close tabs} \\ \text{?\,?Tabs} \end{array}\right\}$ are being kept on Maximilian.

(73d) $\left\{\begin{array}{l} \left\{\begin{array}{l}\text{Little}\\ \text{No}\end{array}\right\}\ \text{heed} \\ \text{?*Heed} \end{array}\right\}$ was paid to the Chief's lamentations.

Thus it appears that what is going on here is the following: idioms of the form of (68) must be entered in the lexicon with some indication of the degree of noun-phrasiness possessed by NP_2. NP_2's headed by nouns like <u>tack</u> and <u>headway</u> will have high nounphrasiness scores, with NP_2's like <u>tabs</u> and <u>heed</u> having lower ones. The rule of PASSIVE, as can be seen from (74)-(77), must be formulated in such a way as to convert into a derived subject the first NP to the right of the verb.

(74a)   We talked to Ron about Henry's plans.

⇓ PASSIVE

(74b)   Ron was talked to by us about Henry's plans.

(74c)   *Henry's plans were talked to Ron about.

(75a)   We talked about Henry's plans to Ron.

⇓ PASSIVE

(75b)   ?Henry's plans were talked about to Ron by us.

(75c)   *Ron was talked about Henry's plans to.

(76a)   Many contributed large sums to the Hopscotch Marathon.

⇓ PASSIVE

(76b)   Large sums were contributed by many to the
         Hopscotch Marathon.

(76c)   *The Hopscotch Marathon was contributed large
         sums to by many.

(77a)   Many contributed to the Hopscotch Marathon.

⇓ PASSIVE

(77b)   The Hopscotch Marathon was contributed to by many.

Thus when (74a) is converted to (75a) by the cyclic rule of PP
SHIFT, the NP which PASSIVE converts into a derived subject changed
from the object of to, as in (74b), to the object of about, in (75b).
The generalization remains: the closest NP becomes the subject.

And in (76), though the object of to cannot be fronted, because the
NP large sums intervenes, in (77a), where the cyclic rule of UN-
SPECIFIED NP DELETION has applied to delete some underlying
object like something, we find that it is possible to front the object
of to.

Given this general approach to PASSIVE, it remains to account for contrasts like those in (70), and those in (73c) and (73d). The explanation I would propose is the following: though advantage is clearly noun-phrasy enough in its own right to be passivized, as (69a) shows, it is also fake enough so that 'Passive' can 'overlook' it when looking for the first NP to the right of the verb. However, when the optional rule of ADVERB TO ADJECTIVE (AA), which converts (78a) to (78b), has applied, [24]

(78a)   The bosses took advantage of the wage freeze ruthlessly.

⇓ AA

(78b)   The bosses took ruthless advantage of the wage freeze.

the prenominal modifier increases the noun-phrasiness of NP_2, making it less possible for PASSIVE to overlook it to produce an outside passive [cf. ? ?(70b)]. This same process of noun-phrasiness increasing through an application of AA is what I would use to explain the contrasts in (73c) and (73d): tabs and heed are lexically so fake--that is, they have such a low degree of noun-phrasiness-- that PASSIVE prefers to overlook them. If AA applies, and they are prenominally modified, then they become noun-phrasy enough to meet the requirements for PASSIVE.

It would appear that AA itself must be sensitive to information about degree of noun-phrasiness, for there are many idioms containing NP_2's of such low noun-phrasiness that they do not tolerate prenominal modification. Cf. the sentences in (79).

(79a)   The Sureté has gotten (*frequent) wind of plots to burn down the Eiffel Tower.

(79b)   He let (*smooth) go of the trapeze.

(79c)   They got (*effortless) hold of their attorneys.

(79d)   We lost (*rapid) sight of Mt. Concavity.

The hypothesis that the applicability of AA is conditional upon sufficient noun-phrasiness in the N to be adjoined to in it gains further support from the fact that no nonmodifiable NP_2--such as those in (79)--can ever be passivized, as far as I know.

To recapitulate: I have postulated that idioms must be entered in the lexicon with some (presumably numerical) indication of how

noun-phrasy (= nonfake) NP_2 is. The rule of ADVERB TO ADJECTIVE
requires a minimum degree of noun-phrasiness to apply, and increases the amount of noun-phrasiness of the NP_2 to which the ex-
adverb is attached. The rule of PASSIVE also has threshhold values.
If it overlooks a constituent with a high degree of noun-phrasiness,
bad sentences like (74c), (75c), and (76c) result. For constituents
of intermediate nouniness, like advantage, PASSIVE can produce
either inner passives or outer passives [cf. (69)], but if AA has upped
the nouniness of NP_2, outer passives are disfavored [cf. (70b)].
Finally, for pretty fake NP's like tabs and heed, passivization is
not possible unless AA applies to boost their noun-phrasiness.[25, 26]

3. What It All Means

So where are we? Where do facts such as those in section 2
leave us?

One thing is clear: they leave us without a theory. Only the out-
lines of the quantitative theory that is suggested in the discussion of
PASSIVE and ADVERB TO ADJECTIVE can be seen at present. Even
if there were not seventeen vertically ill-behaved cells and twenty-
five horizontally ill-behaved cells in (9), cells whose ill-behavior we
can only hope will disappear when other factors we can ascribe their
perturbations to emerge (deus ex futura), it would seem premature to
attempt to quantify categories until a far wider range of squishes is
available for comparison.

And so much of (9) is unexplained. The ordering from top to
bottom is not such a problem: in Navaho, such hierarchies as that
among the first four rows of (9) are well documented, [27] and the fact
that some idioms are more frozen than others[28] is also well known. [29]
But why should the syntactic processes that head the columns be
arranged in just the way they are? Why, for example, should get-
passives be choosier than be-passives, rather than vice versa?
Why should the pronouns that appear in tags be less choosy about the
noun-phrasiness of their antecedents than other pronouns? Why
should Being DELETION be so much choosier than To Be DELETION,
when they often produce identical output sequences? And why should
PROMOTION be so much choosier than RAISING, when they seem to
be so similar in function?

A final point. Suppose future research does in fact reveal to be
correct the hunch that I voiced at the start of section 2, to the effect
that no other speaker will share all the judgments in (9), even relative ones; that it might even be the case that no two speakers will
have exactly the same matrix. Are we then to conclude that we are
dealing here with something peripheral? Or with something nonlinguistic, like performance?

To take up these questions in reverse order, if this is performance, it is performance of a quite different nature than what has
been called performance in the past, when the attempt was made to
trace the unacceptability of certain types of constructions--center-
embeddings, to take an example--to certain properties of a hypothesized general human processing algorithm. But in our case, the unacceptabilities are not invariant from speaker to speaker. What
would have to be assumed to account for the variation among speakers
is what we might term a 'performance idiolect'. Each speaker would
have his own way of performing linguistically, from which certain
inferences could be drawn, and which could be used as a basis for
explaining the observed variation. Note that descriptions of such
performance idiolects would necessarily have to refer to language-
particular rules, and even worse, to particular lexical items, like
pay heed to. Clearly, this is a far cry from a general processing
algorithm.

Assuming that some empirical basis could be found for distinguishing such speaker-specific performance from speaker-specific
competence--a very large assumption--then it would still be necessary to study types of performance idiolect. What is an impossible
performance idiolect? Are there implications from one type of
idiolect to another? Can performance idiolects change through
time? And so on. To rename the serious problems raised by the
multitude of variants of (9) is not to remove them.

Now let me return to the question as to whether we are dealing
here with something peripheral. The answer that seems to me to be
most likely here is 'no'. I think that we must confront squarely, as
some investigators, most notably Guy Carden, have done, the fact
that variation is central. There are, to be sure, many sequences
which all speakers will star, and many others which all will accept
fully. But we linguists, as psychologists, cannot be influenced by
such a fact; for we are not interested in the sentences per se, but
rather in the processes which we hypothesize to be involved in their
use, and on the basis of which we seek to explain various features of
the sentences themselves. And while we may achieve some success
in isolating sentences from speakers, how can we do this with processes? If our description of the processes is based only on inferences drawn from the tests of clearly acceptable and clearly unacceptable sequences, we will have descriptions no single one of
which will probably be accurate for even one speaker.

For example, let us consider the process which forms passive
sentences. If the data on which we base our statement of this process consists only of those sequences which rate, across idiolects,
a universal 'yes', or a universal 'no', how will this statement rule

in sentences like (69)-(73), where there is no universal agreement, as is shown compellingly in Coleman (1972)?

Suppose that such phenomena as 'increasing the noun-phrasiness of an NP_2' do exist, but that they are so weak that they cannot ever convert a universal 'yes' into a universal 'no', or vice versa? If this is ever the case, insisting that the grammar be based on clear cases, where the unclear cases are settled by 'letting the grammar decide', as Chomsky suggests (cf. Chomsky 1957:13-14), may have the effect of making such delicate phenomena invisible to our scrutiny. In other words, the research strategy of dealing with clear cases only, valuable though this may be heuristically, in the initial stages of studying a language, cannot be viewed as being a theoretically neutral strategy. For in effect, such a strategy makes an empirical claim: that such incremental, or delicate, processes do not exist.

My own feeling is that they do exist, and that they are of central importance in understanding how squishes arise and change. I fear that the hunt for clear cases which has characterized much of generative grammar in the past has had an unfortunate effect on what we view as being 'the facts'. For what typically happens, when syntax is being done, and a dispute arises as to the acceptability of some example? Too often, a majority of those present will scoff at, or urge to reconsider, speakers who maintain that some unpopular sentence is for them grammatical, or that some popular sentence is ungrammatical. Probably most readers will have participated in syntactic 'votes'--'How many of you get this?' But of what use are the results of such votes, where it is almost never the case that exactly the same partitioning results from votes on any two questions?[30]

In an extremely important and challenging paper, Jerry Morgan (Morgan 1972), in studying the process of VERB AGREEMENT, discusses, among other things, such examples as (80).

(80a)   Either Tom or the girls was responsible.

(80b)   Either Tom or the girls were responsible.

He reports that some speakers he has checked with accept only (80a), some only (80b), some both, and some neither, and that some are unsure. What to do?

Morgan's suggestion is the following: that we distinguish between a 'core' system of rules, and a system of 'patches'. The core system would contain a rule which correctly assigned the ungrammaticalities for simple sentences like (81),

(81a)   The dog $\left\{\begin{array}{l} \text{is} \\ \text{*are} \end{array}\right\}$ barking.

(81b)   The dogs $\left\{\begin{array}{l} \text{*is} \\ \text{are} \end{array}\right\}$ barking.

but it would not make any prediction about sentences with a disjunction in subject position, like (80). Such sentences would 'fall between the cracks of' the core system, which would simply not cover them, and speakers, when confronted with them, would invent some new rule to 'patch up' their grammar. [31]

What linguists would then have to do is to study the kinds of patches that particular speakers invent, as well as the cores that the patches are appended to. Of importance would be questions like these: Are there impossible patches? Impossible cores? Can cores be different for different speakers? Are there generalizations about the areas in which patches are necessary? And, most important of all, how can it be decided whether a particular fact bears on a core rule or a patch rule?

While it is too early to hope for answers to any of these questions, I think Morgan's proposal is the most promising line of research to follow in the immediate future. To see why, let me contrast it with the 'clear cases' approach, to show that it is not merely old wine in a new bottle. First of all, there is nothing in the proposal which would force the core system to be binary. Core rules would assign a variety of levels of grammaticality, and incremental processes and squishes would also be explicitly provided for. Secondly, the core system might make predictions about particular instances which are not universally valid, because they might be overridden by patch rules.

But most important, perhaps, is a difference in emphasis. In the 'clear cases' approach, votes will continue to be necessary, when the going gets sticky. The goal of research in this approach is the Standard Language, with individual variation being seen as incidental.

In the core-patch approach, however, attention will focus upon particular idiolects. No assumptions need to be made to the effect that a core will emerge which underlies every idiolect. Such a core may emerge, of course, but we should not let our methodology prejudge this important issue.

We are now faced with mounting evidence of deep-running syntactic variation everywhere. It is not at all evident that the fact which I take it such concepts as <u>dialect</u> were invented to cover, namely, the fact of mutual comprehensibility, is to be explained by postulating the existence of some 'same dialect' between every two speakers who can in fact communicate. Possibly, if speaker cores (and maybe patches too) are <u>similar</u> enough, in some sense which will require vast amounts of research to make precise, mutual intelligibility will result.

While these remarks are problematic and speculative in the extreme, it is primarily for this last reason, the difference in emphasis, that I am in favor of Morgan's proposal. Much of recent work in syntax has been turning up staggering amounts of variation. I think it is time for syntacticians to take this variation far more seriously than has been the case, of late.

To return to squishes, and things that will hopefully one day become them, like (9). Are they part of the (Ultimately to Become Visible) Core, or are they just possible patches? Only time will tell. And maybe even <u>it</u> won't.

NOTES

The research for this paper was supported in part by a National Science Foundation grant (GS-3202) to the Language Research Foundation and by a grant from the National Institute of Mental Health (5-PO1-MH13390-06), whose support is gratefully acknowledged.

In addition, I would like to thank Lloyd Anderson, Bruce Fraser, Larry Horn, Ed Klima, George Lakoff, Paul Postal, and Arnold Zwicky for letting themselves in for discussions about these matters and even blurrier ones. My indebtedness to P. G. Wodehouse is apparent throughout.

All factual and theoretical claims have been checked on the Accutron to within a tolerance of 0.001 Microzetz. No errors remain.

[1]TAG FORMATION is a merely expository label for whatever process(es?) is (are?) responsible for such tags as <u>isn't it?</u>, <u>were they?</u> etc. (cf. 2.19, for further discussion).

TOUGH MOVEMENT converts (i) to (ii), and LEFT DISLOCATION converts (iii) to (iv).

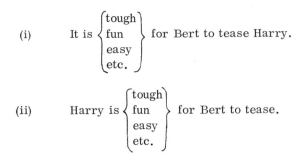

(i)   It is $\begin{Bmatrix} \text{tough} \\ \text{fun} \\ \text{easy} \\ \text{etc.} \end{Bmatrix}$ for Bert to tease Harry.

(ii)   Harry is $\begin{Bmatrix} \text{tough} \\ \text{fun} \\ \text{easy} \\ \text{etc.} \end{Bmatrix}$ for Bert to tease.

(iii)   You can't buy this kind of shells anymore.

(iv)   This kind of shells, you can't buy them anymore.

[2]I will not attempt to justify here my contention that either of the rankings in (4) or (5) is even roughly correct--this I will undertake in section 2. My present concern is to illustrate a more general point.
[3]This fact was first pointed out by William Cantrall.
[4]This sentence is only weak on the reading suggested by the bracketing in (i)

(i)   It seems [that he was in Boston for that reason].

[5]It is quite likely that a contributing factor in this example's badness is the fact that <u>headway</u> must be indefinite, while these <u>what . . . doing</u> S's seem to favor, if not require, definite subjects, cf. (19a).
[6]This sentence is presumably converted to (i)

(i)   No more Schlitz is a funny thought.

by an independent rule which deletes <u>there</u> under some conditions. This has interesting consequences, if true, for it would mean that <u>Being</u> DELETION should not be constrained in such a way as to prohibit the derivation of such NP's as <u>there no more Schlitz</u>. It would seem that such NP's are only to be excluded at the level of surface structure, presumably by an output condition.
[7]While there is little evidence in English which argues that the S's in (28) and (29) cannot be basic, and must be derived by a copying rule, as I have proposed, a strong argument can be imported from German, via universal grammar.

The facts are these: in German, the dislocated NP takes along its case. Thus we find (ii) paralleling (i), and (iv) paralleling (iii).

(i)   Sie lobten $\left\{ \begin{array}{l} \text{den} \\ \text{*dem} \end{array} \right\}$ Professor.

They praised $\left\{ \begin{array}{l} \text{the (acc.)} \\ \text{*the (dat.)} \end{array} \right\}$ professor.

(ii) $\left\{\begin{array}{c} \text{Den} \\ \text{*Dem} \end{array}\right\}$ Professor, sie lobten ihn.

The professor, they praised him (acc.).

(iii)   Sie schmeichelten $\left\{\begin{array}{c} \text{*den} \\ \text{dem} \end{array}\right\}$ Professor.

They flattered the professor.

(iv) $\left\{\begin{array}{c} \text{*Den} \\ \text{Dem} \end{array}\right\}$ Professor, sie schmeichelten ihn.

Since idiosyncratically assigned case must accompany the dislocated NP, a copying rule seems necessary.

[8]Apparently, passivizing this tack lessens its fakeness, at least in this case. If this is so, it is a phenomenon of the utmost importance, for it suggests that no mere lexical marking of idiom chunks for their noun-phrasiness will suffice: rather, noun-phrasiness would have to be in part a derivational property. Cf. section 2.20 for a similar case.

I have not yet had the time to give this matter the serious study it merits.

[9]It is possible that the any-version of (30e) should be produced by LEFT DISLOCATION. If so, its high degree of grammaticality would make it an unexplained ill-behaved cell. I do not doubt, however, that this problem is connected with the abovementioned requirement that headway be indefinite. The idiom make inroads on, another idiom with this requirement, seems to be located in the squish of (9) at about the same height as make headway on. I have not yet found evidence that would indicate whether or not this dual parallelism is accidental.

[10]The badness of this sentence cannot be attributed to the fact that it is a pronoun that has been dislocated, for (i) and (ii) are grammatical.

(i)   Him, he's loopy.

(ii)   ?It, I couldn't find another like it in 10 years.

Probably, dislocation requires that the NP to be copied must be a possible locus of contrastive stress, a condition that seems to be only formulable as a transderivational constraint.

[11]RIGHT NODE RAISING thus provides one more argument in the growing body of evidence pointing toward the conclusion that prepositional phrases and NP's are not deeply different. Another argument, unreported in the literature, to the best of my knowledge, is the fact that there are some circumstances under which prepositional phrases can actually undergo RAISING.

To see this, consider first the effects of the very general rule I will refer to as COPULA SWITCH, which permutes the two NP's of a pseudo-cleft sentence around the intervening copula.

(i) $\begin{Bmatrix} \text{What he found was a banana.} \\ \text{Where she slept was under the bed.} \end{Bmatrix}$

$\Downarrow$ COPULA SWITCH

(ii) $\begin{Bmatrix} \text{A banana was what he found.} \\ \text{Under the bed was where she slept.} \end{Bmatrix}$

This permulation must be effected in the cycle, for if such structures as those in (ii) appear in the complement of a verb which allows RAISING [cf. (iii)], this rule will raise their initial constituents to become the derived objects of the matrix verb.

(iii) It seems that $\begin{Bmatrix} \text{a banana was what he found} \\ \text{under the bed was where she slept} \end{Bmatrix}$.

$\Downarrow$ RAISING

(iv) $\begin{Bmatrix} \text{A banana} \\ \text{Under the bed} \end{Bmatrix}_1$ seems to be $\begin{Bmatrix} \text{what he found} \\ \text{where she slept} \end{Bmatrix}_1$.

Thus both RAISING and RIGHT NODE RAISING support the identification of NP and PP.

[12]It is, admittedly, difficult to topicalize the pronoun it even when it is a nonexpletive definite pronoun--that is generally preferred (and it has often been suggested, though never proved, that it is merely the stressless form of that). However, though the sentence ?? It I detest, in which this has happened, is weak, it is nowhere near as weak as the sentences in (39b), (40b), and (41b), which I would attribute to the fakeness of the it's in these examples.

[13]I am starring this example only when the it which is the superficial subject has become one through TOUGH MOVEMENT, i.e. when this sentence has arisen from (i).

(i) It_1 is difficult to consider it_2 fair that they absconded.

Unfortunately, the remote structure of (i) can also produce (ii), which by <u>To Be</u> DELETION (cf. section 2.15) and NP SHIFT could result in (40a).

(ii) It_1 is difficult to consider [that they absconded]$_{NP}$
        to be fair.

In order to 'hear' the star on (40a), it is necessary to mentally try to apply TOUGH MOVEMENT to the $\underline{it}_2$ of (i) and replace $\underline{it}_1$ with it.

In order to construct an example which paralleled (40a), but in which the conversion from (i) via TOUGH MOVEMENT was the only source, it would be necessary to find some other predicate for which EXTRAPOSITION was possible, but not NP SHIFT. Since NP SHIFT cannot be lexically governed, and appears to be subject only to structural conditions, I am dubious that such an example can be found.

[14]I have indicated, both in (9) and by the prefix on (44b), that I believe that TOPICALIZATION cannot apply to the idiom <u>pay heed to</u> at all. What then of such sentences as (i)?

(i)   No heed did he pay to my imprecations.

My present inclination is to hypothesize that some other, at present totally unknown, fronting rule produces such sentences. Though this rule does (hélas!) exactly duplicate the function of TOPICALIZATION, it does seem to be restricted so that it can only move NP's to the front of the first S up. That is, while TOPICALIZATION is unbounded [cf. (ii)], even with negative constituents [cf. (iii)], this rule seems to be bounded.

(ii)   Jack I think that everybody must realize that Billy
        thinks that we should get rid of.

(iii)   No one do I think you should invite who doesn't know
        how to play Rackmaster.

(iv)   ?*No heed do I think we should pay to his importunings.

If I am wrong in my conjecture that there are two different rules involved here, the column discussed as one in section 2.9 in the text will have split into two, and the bottom cell of the resulting TOPI-CALIZATION columns, which will contain 'OK's' will be both horizontally and vertically ill-behaved.

I will leave this problem for future research.

[15]I assume that some other process obliterates <u>the fact</u> here.

[16]Since PROMINALIZATION concerns only the constraints on linkages between full and pronominal NP's, I have marked 'DNA' in those cells of (9) which correspond to the expletive pronouns it and there, which obviously cannot serve as nonpronominal anaphors.

[17]The splendid ungrammaticality of this sentence is probably attributable to some more general morphological condition--cf. (i)-(iv).

(i)   *Oats's nutritional value is unquestioned.

(ii)   ?Hobbs's inability to write postcards is legion.

(iii)   ?Bubs's house is really nice.

(iv)   Tums's taste is wall-to-wall Yucksville.

If so, it will not be necessary to designate the corresponding cell of (9) as horizontally and vertically ill-behaved.

[18]I use this traditional term here solely as an expository device. I believe that the correct way to regard the conjoined elements of (54b) is as sentence partials, whose subjects have been lost by the operation of SUBJECT FORMATION. Cf. McCawley (1970) and Postal (in press) for details.

[19]Even such hardy souls, however, are unlikely to find respectively-constructions palatable. These are unspeakably vile when they involve idiom chunks and expletives, as in (i)-(iv).

(i)   This tack would be taken on Case 1, and your suggestion would apply in Case 2.

$$\Downarrow \text{ Respectively FORMATION}$$

(ii)   **This tack and your suggestion would be taken on Case 1 and apply in Case 2, respectively.

(iii)   **It and there rained and $\left\{\begin{array}{l}\text{was}\\\text{were}\end{array}\right\}$ puddles, respectively.

(iv)   **Significant headway and accurate tabs were made on resurfacing and kept on the legislators, respectively.

[20]The notation A(*B)C means: AC is grammatical, and ABC ungrammatical. The notation A*(B)C means: ABC is grammatical, and AC ungrammatical. Thus the first means that the parenthesized

element cannot be added, and the second, that it cannot be omitted.

[21]Cf. Lakoff (1970) for discussion of this type of rule.

[22]For some reason, though the rule of To Be DELETION is happy to apply to the passive be after want and would like (cf. They wanted this checked into), the class of verbs in (62) blocks the deletion of this be. Cf. (i)–(iii).

    (i)   ?*I considered the matter checked into adequately.

    (ii)   *Francine seems arrested every day.

    (iii)   *I judged Mort believed to be a Venusian.

It is for this reason that more complicated examples such as those in (62e), (62f), (62k), and (62l) must be checked to see in what way fakeness interacts with To Be DELETION in this class of verbs.

[23]There are no sentences corresponding to the expletives in (71), for pronouns can no more be prenominally modified than they can have a relative clause modifying them.

[24]Patrick Brogan (personal communication) has pointed out to me a compelling argument for the correctness of this rule. The verb dress requires an adverb, cf. (i).

    (i)   He is one who dresses *(snazzily).

And when (i) is nominalized to form the agentive noun dresser in (ii), we find that this noun requires an adjective.

    (ii)   He is a *(snazzy) dresser.

[25]As mentioned in note 8, it appears that application of PASSIVE can also have the effect of increasing noun-phrasiness.

[26]This account provides no explanation for the weakness of outside passives with keep tabs on and pay heed to. [Cf. ?*(72c) and ?(72d)]. I do not understand this phenomenon.

For a detailed and insightful treatment of other problems pertaining to inner and outer passives, and to various dialects based on these, cf. Coleman (1972).

[27]Cf. Hale (to appear) and also Wall (1968).

[28]Cf. Fraser (1970) for an important study of the way a discrete theory of grammar might attempt to describe this fact.

[29]Mysteries do remain, of course. Why, for instance, should weather-it with copular predicates be more noun-phrasy than weather-it with true verbs?

[30]Notice that we cannot escape this bind by retreating to describing only the clear cases of a particular idiolect. For in my idiolect, (70b) is an unclear case. The only evidence that I can imagine having any bearing on it is the grammaticality of (69b), and the ungrammaticality of (72a), (74c), (75c), and (76c), where my judgments are clear. But what do they allow us to conclude about (70b)? That it is fully grammatical? Fully ungrammatical? Either of these runs afoul of my intuition, and if the clear cases are somehow to serve as input to some algorithm that will compute the intuitively correct valence, namely '??', then some advocate of the clear cases approach must spell out in detail some of the properties of this algorithm.

[31]Fillmore makes essentially the same suggestion, in a broader context (cf. Fillmore 1972) which is very relevant to the issues I am discussing here.

REFERENCES

Chomsky, Noam. 1957. Syntactic structures. The Hague, Mouton and Company.

Coleman, Linda. 1972. Keeping track of the tabs we are keeping on our ability to take advantage of the use we are making of various tests we are taking charge of in order to lay claim to the discovery of four syntactic dialects on the construction V + NP + PP. Unpublished paper. Ann Arbor, University of Michigan.

Fillmore, Charles. 1972. On generativity. In: Goals of linguistic theory. Ed. by Stanley Peters. Englewood Cliffs, New Jersey, Prentice-Hall. 1-19.

Fraser, Bruce. 1970. Idioms within a transformational grammar. Foundations of Language. 6(1).22-42.

Hale, Kenneth. A note on subject-object inversion in Navaho. (To appear.)

Lakoff, George. 1970. Global rules. Language. 46(3).627-39.

McCawley, James. 1970. English as a VSO language. Language. 46(2).286-99.

Morgan, Jerry. 1972. Verb agreement as a rule of English. In: Papers from the Eighth Regional Meeting of the Chicago Linguistic Society. Ed. by Paul Peranteau et al. Chicago, Linguistic Department, University of Chicago. 278-86.

Postal, Paul. 1970. On coreferential complement subject deletions. Linguistic Inquiry. 1(4).439-500.

_____. (In press) On raising. Cambridge, MIT Press.

Wall, Robert. 1968. Selectional restrictions on subjects and objects of transitive verbs. Unpublished paper. Bloomington, Indiana University Linguistics Club.

Wodehouse, P. G. (n. d.) Something squishy. In: Mr. Mulliner Speaking. London, Herbert Jenkins. 208–44.

WHAT DO IMPLICATIONAL SCALES IMPLY?

DAVID DeCAMP

The University of Texas

In this paper I will develop two hypotheses about implications which, if validated, would remove the two most cogent objections which critics have raised against implicational analysis of language variation.[1] I will report how I have already tentatively verified the empirical claims of the first hypothesis by means of experimental data, and how I propose to test the claims of the second.

The first objection to implicational scales is that they cut across established categories of linguistics (i. e. phonological, syntactic, and lexical variables are all mixed together along the scale), and so the scales seem only peripheral or irrelevant to the study of formal linguistics. The second objection is that in addition to the inter-informant variation for which Guttmann scaling was originally designed, there is often also a residue of intra-informant variation which cannot be factored out in terms of linguistic contexts or style shifts, so that an informant whose usage varies unpredictably even within one sentence, can hardly be assigned the clear-cut value of 1 or 0 which implicational analysis seems to call for. Until now I have not had convincing answers to either objection.

Labov and others have demanded that implicational scales be more than an empirical accident. This is not a charge that they are only coincidental. The possibility of obtaining by random chance a reasonably clear-cut scale for an adequate sample of speakers is remote. Labov's objection, as I understand it, is far more cogent than that. If the results of scaling are incommensurable with those of formal linguistics, how then can a scale be meaningful to a linguist? For example, in a study of formality of usage among university undergraduates, I found that the choice between the modals can and may,

141

meaning permission, appeared at two nonadjacent points on the continuum, with the question May he go? closer to the ultraformal end of the scale than May I go? A lexical-phonological variable, the pronunciation vahz for vase, intervened between the two uses of may. This discontinuous scaling of the permissive may might be relevant to some theory of social behavior in speech, but it certainly seems incompatible with any familiar theory of English syntax.

The same objection could be made to Stolz and Bills and to most other implicational studies. Some researchers have arbitrarily confined their scales to linguistically related variables, e.g. Bickerton implicationally compared one pronoun variable with another but not with, say, a vowel neutralization. Yet it seemed that using implicational data when they fit the assumed linguistic structure but arbitrarily rejecting them when they did not, only confused the question of whether implicational scales really imply anything or are only an ad hoc device for getting two grammars into one 'polygrammar'.

One could think of general scales like mine, which mix different kinds of variables, as complexes of simpler scales, each confined to one kind of variable. Thus a complex scale could be only the empirical consequence of several simple scales applying simultaneously. I visualize this as looking down through a stack of transparent plastic rulers, whose ends are staggered so that the lines on all of them are simultaneously visible. If this conception could be confirmed, then the objection could be met, for each underlying simple scale would then relate only linguistically comparable features. The scaling phenomena would then support the quite reasonable interpretation that in his rapid and almost continual process of style adjustment and style shift by means of choosing between alternative forms, the speaker does indeed operate within the structure of his grammar, but that several such selection processes may be going on simultaneously.

Together with Mr. Nick Sobin, a graduate student at the University of Texas, I developed a strategy for the experimental verification of this conception of underlying simple scales. One of those transparent plastic rulers could easily be shifted to the left or to the right, relative to the other rulers in the stack, but it would be very difficult to interchange the relative positions of any two lines on the same ruler. If style shifting is indeed the simultaneous operation of several mental task forces, each assigned to a relatively coherent component of the grammar, then the internal consistency with which any one such task force makes its choices between alternatives may be expected to be greater than the external consistency between such task forces. Thus the hypothesis makes the following claim: the implicational relationship between two variable features will be more clear-cut (i.e. fewer exceptions in the data) and will be more replicable if the two features are closely related in the grammar.

Sobin and I then submitted to a sample of 116 university undergraduates a questionnaire on their usage of fifteen sentences containing variables suspected of being implicationally related on a formality-prestige scale. The results were not entirely conclusive but they tend to confirm the hypothesis. The most clear-cut relations held between the three variables which characterize the four 'Klima dialects', the four varieties which Klima (1964) attributed to successive extension and lower ordering of the case assignment rule: Whom could she see? vs. Who could she see?, It was I vs. It was me, and We two left vs. Us two left. As predicted, speakers who combined Who could she see? with It was I outnumbered those with the converse combination, the empty cell, by more than seven to one. Similarly with It was I and We two left, the empty cell was outnumbered by its converse by ten to one. These three variables did not occupy adjacent points on the scale, but ranked fourth, eighth, and eleventh among the fifteen variables scaled. As predicted, the relations between these three variables and the other twelve were generally messy, some of them provoking real doubt as to whether the relations were genuinely implicational at all.

As predicted, permissive may he was clearly scaled as more formal than may I, with the empty cell (i. e. cooccurrence of may he with can I) outnumbered by its converse by eight to one. This replicated the ordering in my earlier study, whereas the pronunciation vahz for vase, which had intervened between may I and may he in the earlier study, was here scaled as more pretentious than either of them. Although this also seems to support our claim, we can say very little about replicability at this time, partly because the three case-assignment variables had not all been included in my earlier study, but primarily because the sampling in that study, which had been intended only as a demonstration of scaling, was anything but rigorous; I had merely polled the members of my own class. I do intend to repeat this 1972 study in order to determine whether, as claimed, the scaling of grammatically similar variables indeed replicates better.

We had expected that the three pronunciation items (vahz for vase, tomahto for tomato, and eyether for either) would form a third coherent subgroup within which the implicational relations would be relatively clear cut, but they did not. Yes, they sort of scaled, in the order eyether, vahz, tomahto, but the vahz-either cell, supposedly 'empty', was outnumbered only two-to-one by its converse--hardly better than pure chance--and both vahz and tomahto were accepted by so few informants that there was no valid way to determine the significance of their relation. This may be a contradiction to our claim, but I believe that there are alternative explanations. First, we were confronting our subjects with written rather than auditory stimuli (i.e. they saw the spelling v-a-h-z on the questionnaire). The sight of funny spellings may exaggerate the deviance of a pronunciation and induce a subject to reject it, thus shifting all such pronunciation features toward the extreme end of the scale, where significance is statistically less determinable. Vahz and tomahto ranked twelfth and fifteenth among the fifteen variables scaled, with only three out of the 116 subjects accepting tomahto. Furthermore, vahz-vase and either-eyether are not really rule-related variables at all, only independent variations in underlying phonological representations, which have in common only the fact they both occur in the lexicon. There is no reason to hold that our hypothesis would necessarily predict that they would form an implicationally coherent group.

Therefore I made a quick and informal search of my Jamaican data for a pair of phonological variables that are indeed related within the phonology. Some Jamaicans maintain a contrast between voiced dental fricatives and voiced alveolar stops, but most do not, so the words then and den fall together as den. The voiceless fricatives do the same, so that thin and tin fall together as tin. Some Jamaicans say both then and thin, many pronounce these as den and tin, and some combine den and thin; but the converse combination, then and tin, is rare. My count of a sample of my data indicates that the empty cell here is outnumbered by more than sixteen-to-one, an implicational relation considerably more clear cut than those between these two variables and any others.

Further verification is needed, of course, and will be provided. But I consider this hypothesis to be tentatively confirmed, and I now think of general scales as surface composites resulting from simultaneous operation of simple grammatically-relevant underlying scales. What implicational scales then imply are sets of hierarchical priorities for control of variables, each set relevant to a certain area of the grammar. Their function is to produce redundancy and thus simplify the speaker's staggering task of making all the decisions necessary for control of style. If we are to claim that a grammar is psychologically 'real', then we must account for the fact that a speaker with only a finite mental apparatus can not only generate an infinite variety of sentences but can also control an infinite variety of combinations of stylistic variables. If implicational scales do indeed represent a technique employed by the speaker to reduce this task to a level where he can manage it, they will have an explanatory as well as a descriptive significance.

I turn now to the other major objection to implicational scaling. Fasold, Labov, and others have pointed out that even after we carefully control the linguistic environments in which variables occur (e. g. to make sure that a speaker's 50 per cent probability of r-dropping does not simply result from his always dropping r's in unstressed syllables but never dropping them in stressed), there is still usually a residue of inconsistency within each speaker's behavior. Until recently, I assumed that the data to be scaled had to be encoded in terms of two-valued judgments, either 1 or 0. Like Stolz and Bills and almost everyone else working with implications, I established scales by positing an arbitrary threshold for each speaker's behavior: above a certain frequency he was assigned a value of 1, below that frequency a value of 0. This technique perhaps yields meaningful results for the group of speakers as a whole, but it certainly is not an accurate description of any one speaker--sort of like that man who has two and three-eighths children. This discrepancy between an individual's inconsistent behavior and his neatly binary representation on the scale I attributed whenever possible to style shift (i. e. the speaker temporarily shifted to a different point on the scale and began speaking a different dialect). Otherwise I dismissed it as merely linguistic 'performance', the failure of empirical observations ever to fit exactly with predictions from theory--especially when the theory is about one thing and the observations are of something else.

It is sometimes difficult to explain inconsistency as style shift, however, especially when there is no other independent evidence of it, when no event has taken place which could have caused such a shift, and when inconsistencies occur even within the same sentence. And like many other linguists, I am tired of using the word perfor-mance as a convenient rug under which I can sweep everything I don't yet have an explanation for. Besides, if these inconsistencies were only performance deviations, we would expect a speaker to be about equally inconsistent on all variables, whereas anyone who has worked with implications must have noticed that any given speaker is considerably more inconsistent on some variables than on others. I claim that he is especially inconsistent on precisely those variables which are located close to the speaker's own cutting point on the scale. At least a good part of speaker inconsistency then is non-random. The question is: can it be rule-predictable?

The assumption that implicational scales have to be formulated in terms of exclusively binary judgments is an unfortunate holdover from the days when all linguistics and nearly all logic were two-valued. Recent studies in nondiscrete syntax, however, have argued convincingly that linguists have too long paid obeisance to the law of the excluded middle. Many if not all of the binary oppositions in syntax can better be thought of as continuous variables. In their grammaticality judgments, linguists must now consider degrees intermediate between starred and unstarred. Thus we now see question marks, percent signs, and other typographical devices for indicating degrees of grammaticality.

Ross's 'squishes' are formally the same as implicational scales. The dimension being scaled is a grammatical attribute such as nouniness (i. e. the degree to which a form behaves like a true, hard-core noun as opposed to a true verb) rather than a sociolinguistic attribute such as formality, ethnicity, or socioeconomic level. But these are only different applications of the same formal device. It should be possible to analogize from one to the other.

Ross has pointed out that when we attempt to apply a rule or constraint to forms having different values for the feature [α Nouny], i. e. forms located at different points along a scale of nouniness, the applicability is by no means equally clear-cut for all values of α. Toward the ends of the scale, i. e. for very high and very low values of α, the applicability is clear, and the test sentences are simply starred or unstarred. The applicability becomes less certain, however, and question marks start to appear alongside or instead of the stars when we try to apply the rule or constraint to forms whose positions on the scale approach one particular point which is crucial to that rule or constraint. Ross calls this point the 'threshold'; most of us, following Guttmann and Torgerson, have been calling it the 'cutting point'. At or near to this cutting point, speakers are often unsure about the absolute applicability of the rule, i. e. the acceptability of the sentences resulting from application, but, Ross claims, they are usually fairly certain of the 'relative' acceptability of these sentences. Thus the feature of nouniness can be scaled even though the degree of acceptability does not abruptly jump from 1 to 0 when the cutting point is reached, but rather has intermediate values within a transitional zone centering on the cutting point. The curve is S-shaped rather than square.

I suggest that this view of nondiscrete acceptability may be true for all implicational scales and that the speaker's ability to make relative judgments, even if not absolute judgments, of acceptability still permits us to scale without first arbitrarily reducing all judgments to values of 1 or 0. The cutting point for a speaker would then be located at that point on the scale where his curve of acceptability judgments crosses the .5 level, ordinarily also the point of greatest slope of the curve. If this hypothesis can be verified, it should satisfy the Fasold-Labov objection and it would still preserve the principal advantages of implicational scales.

One technique of verification is obvious: construct a scale based on a recorded sample of a considerable number of speakers, but instead of scoring each speaker 1 or 0 for each variable, enter each speaker's observed frequencies for each variable, then add up these frequencies, rather than 1's and 0's, when determining whether a genuine implication exists and where its cutting point is located. If the scale implies an empty cell for the cooccurrent pronunciations vahz and either, then a speaker who consistently used these prohibited pronunciations would count for twice as much of an exception as a speaker who used them only half the time. The hypothesis predicts that a coherent scale would result, with a discernible cutting point despite the introduction of variables.

Half of this prediction has already been partially confirmed, by Labov and Fasold. Labov (1968) experimented with a three-valued scale: 1, 0, and * (for variable). Although the familiar implicational matrix emerged (1's and 0's in opposite corners, separated by a diagonal band of *'s), the intermediate value was too broad to establish whether cutting points could be determined with any precision; the majority of all the data apparently fell into this category. Fasold (1970) presented some of Wolfram's data with actual frequencies replacing 1's and 0's, but he, like Labov, was scaling dialects rather than individual speakers, so the limited number of varieties--only four dialects were scaled--again proved only that the distribution was indeed implicational.

The scaling by frequencies of a large number of individual speakers based on free-recorded speech behavior would be an enormous task, involving many hours of listening to tapes and counting. It should indeed be done. Since observation of free speech behavior is only one source of evidence about a speaker's linguistic intuitions, however, I propose the following more economical scheme for verification by questionnaire: define the nonverbal context, e. g. conversation with a work associate of equal rank, and elicit acceptability judgments on a scale of 0 to 10. These are to be used instead of just 1's and 0's in attempting to scale the data. After the subject has completed this questionnaire, then inform him what dimension feature you believe the test variables to illustrate (e. g. formal-informal) and ask him to rank the variables according to that feature. If Ross's observation that the speaker is capable of making consistent relative judgments does indeed hold for other implicational scales, then the cutting points on the resulting scale should be discernible, and the rankings should recapitulate the scale.

I intend to proceed with these testing procedures and hope that others will do the same. If we can verify these two hypotheses, we will be removing two of the major obstacles which now divide some of us. If instead we refute the hypotheses, we will at least have cleared the air and can begin looking for alternatives.

NOTE

[1]On implicational scales, see David DeCamp, Toward a generative analysis of a post-creole speech continuum. In: Pidginization and creolization of languages. Ed. by Dell Hymes. London, Cambridge University Press, 1971, 349-70; and Implicational scales and sociolinguistic linearity. Linguistics. 73.30-43 (1971). The research reported in this paper was supported by a grant from the Institute of Latin American Studies, Austin, Texas.

REFERENCES

Fasold, Ralph. 1970. Two models of socially significant linguistic variation. Language. 46.551-63.
Klima, Edward S. 1964. Relatedness between grammatical systems. Language. 40.1-20.
Labov, William. 1968. Negative attraction and negative concord in various English dialects. Unpublished paper delivered at the Linguistic Society of America Annual Meeting; reported by Fasold (1970).
Stolz, Walter, and Garland Bills. 1968. An investigation of the standard-nonstandard dimension of Central Texas English. Final report to the U.S. Office of Economic Opportunity. Austin, Child Development Evaluation and Research Center, University of Texas.

PHONOLOGICAL RULES AND SOCIOLINGUISTIC VARIATION IN NORWICH ENGLISH

PETER TRUDGILL

University of Reading

This paper is based on a sociolinguistic urban dialect survey carried out in the city of Norwich, England (and reported in detail in Trudgill, forthcoming), and represents an attempt to apply empirical data obtained in the speech community to certain theoretical problems. [1] As one would expect, the English spoken in the city of Norwich is far from being homogeneous. There are still, however, a number of reasons for regarding all the forms of English indigenous to the city as manifestations of a single system, and, therefore, for attempting to develop a single grammar that will account for all these varieties. Norwich speakers, for example, like New York City speakers (Labov 1966) share a common set of subjective attitudes toward linguistic varieties, and they are also capable of assigning fine sociological meanings to different varieties of Norwich English in a way that outsiders cannot. For example, Norwich speakers will evaluate room /rʉːm/ as less statusful than /r ʊ m/, although the former is in fact a possible RP or near-RP pronunciation. There are a number of linguistic characteristics shared by all Norwich speakers which do not occur elsewhere, even in the rural areas surrounding the city, and, although Norwich English does come in many different forms, there are no discrete Norwich varieties, but rather many different interlocking continua. Norwich speakers are also, and this is not without some significance, able to imitate without error types of Norwich English, other than those they normally use, for humorous or other similar purposes. Norwich, then, is a single

149

speech community: it comprises a large number of individuals, some 150,000, who have all internalized the same grammar, although they employ this grammar in different ways. The system of Norwich English I have called a 'diasystem', in order to suggest that (unlike, say, 'British English' or 'East Anglian English', which are collections of systems) it is a single system which nevertheless incorporates many different varieties, and I have attempted to construct a (partial) model of this diasystem (Trudgill, forthcoming). We must be able to develop such a model, it seems, in order correctly and fully to describe the native Norwich speaker's linguistic competence. We have, that is, to provide a model of the linguistic competence of the individual as a native speaker of Norwich English, and as a member of the Norwich speech community.

This, in fact, defines the community as a 'speech community': that the members share not a similar but the 'same' grammar. By the term 'diasystem', in other words, I simply mean the grammar shared by a single speech community. It seems to me that this is the only legitimate form of diasystem. Since Weinreich's usage of the term 'diasystem', a number of linguists, whether or not they have actually used this term themselves, have attempted to compare, relate, or incorporate different varieties in some kind of single system. Generative phonologists have pointed out that dialects can be 'related' to each other by the addition, deletion, or permutation of rules. This is an interesting fact, and an attractive intellectual exercise, but not one, in most cases, that can accurately reflect any kind of 'reality' if attempts are made to incorporate these comparisons in single systems. There are reasons for believing, in fact, that many writers have gone too far in attempting to derive different dialects from a common system. (A good example of this is Brown (1972), who writes that she derives the southern dialects of Lumasaaba from northern dialect forms by extra rules, not because 'the southern dialects derive historically from any existing northern dialect', nor because this 'provides a reasonable framework for a synchronic description of any one of the southern dialects' (p. 171), but because of 'the more economical and revealing statement which this derivation allows' (p. 169), and because her intention is 'simply to demonstrate that the dialects can be shown to be related to each other by a small number of quite general rules' (p. 171).) It does not seem to be possible that speakers internalize rules of the type that relate one dialect to another in any grammar that underlies their own competence. As James Harris says (1969:5):

> The point is . . . that the motivation and justification of a
> grammar of a particular dialect must be based on data from

that dialect and no other if the grammar is to have any
intelligible relation to the linguistic competence of speakers
of the dialect of which the grammar is a theory.

It is not reasonable, that is, to set up, as a single system, at whatever level of abstraction, a diasystem for just any pair or group of
mutually intelligible varieties (pace Bailey 1972b and cf. Labov
1973, for empirical evidence on this point). It is not only unreasonable, moreover. In many cases it is impossible. It is true, of
course, that the phonological systems of most types of American,
Canadian, Australian, New Zealand, and South African
English are closely related to each other, and to the accents of the
south of England, and Wales. In these cases linguists can write
rules which relate these varieties to each other in a coherent way,
and which may have some relationship to the way in which speakers
of these varieties understand each other (cf. Bailey 1972b). We have
to consider, however, that it just is not possible to set up common
underlying forms for or to relate in any coherent way many of the
varieties of English spoken in Northern Ireland, southern Scotland,
and the North and Midlands of England, in spite of the fact that they
are mutually intelligible. Consider the difficulties of incorporating
the following two varieties into a single system:

	R. P.	Glenoe, N. Ireland (see Gregg 1964)
have	/hæv/	/he:/
home	/houm/	/he:m/
move	/mu:v/	/me:v/
none	/nʌn/	/ne:n/
straw	/strɔ:/	/stre:/

The same problem would arise with many other varieties from the
British Isles: the correspondences are not regular enough to permit
incorporation into a single system. Intelligibility is the result of
similarity of grammars, not identity.

The fact remains, however, that within the Norwich speech community, and within the single system, a large amount of variation
does take place, both between and within the speech of individuals,
and we are therefore confronted with the problem of exactly how to
handle this variation. In what follows I shall confine myself to a
study of the variation that takes place in the phonology and phonetics
of Norwich English, although the syntactic variation is in many ways
equally interesting. In order to accommodate this phonological variation I have used the two familiar levels of 'systematic phonemics'

and 'systematic phonetics', and, in addition, a third level I have
called the 'phonetic realization level'. I am aware that this is somewhat controversial, but, since it is not crucial to the present argument, I shall not attempt to define here exactly what is meant by
'level', or to justify this decision at very great length. Briefly, the
systematic phonemic level performs all its usual tasks, and also
handles certain types of variation. The systematic phonetic level,
on the other hand, is somewhat reduced in function. It has been said
that the systematic phonetic level indicates 'the way the physical
system of articulation is to perform' (Postal 1968:273). However,
anyone who has compared the systematic phonetic outputs of phonological grammars as they are usually presented, insofar as there
are any, with normal casual speech as it is actually spoken, will
surely have noted that there is a large discrepancy between the two.
Consider the following perfectly typical Norwich utterance transcribed
fairly narrowly, omitting suprasegmentals, from a tape-recorded
interview:

[nɐ̈ ə ẹ̈ʔ   ‚b ‚dæ̈   lɛ̌   læ̣̈iʔlẹ̈i]

No I haven't been down there lately

This does not, as far as I know, resemble any systematic phonetic
representation that has appeared in the literature. Since this is a
typically Norwich utterance, it is the task of our grammar to produce this kind of utterance as output, and it is the phonetic realization level which makes this possible. (There is not space here,
since it is not strictly relevant, to justify further the setting up of
three levels rather than two (but cf. the three types of notation in
Labov 1972).) It is perhaps worth noting, though, that the systematic phonetic level, which now deals with ideal rather than actual
articulations, remains necessary in order to handle surface contrasts and, amongst other things, to explain those linguistic changes
which are due to pressures in phonological or phonetic space. The
systematic phonetic level comprises units equivalent to extrinsic
allophones, whereas the phonetic realization level deals with units
equivalent to intrinsic allophones. The point is, however, that the
'intrinsic' allophones are due to processes which, although natural,
are not universal. Rather they are particular to the Norwich system.
Variation occurs at all three levels.

   1. Within the Norwich system there are six main types of variation we need to consider. The first of these, although it is concerned with surface contrasts, is handled at the level of systematic
phonemics. Many Norwich speakers consistently make a surface

contrast which other speakers consistently do not make. Pairs of items, roughly those which were distinct in Middle English as long vowels and diphthongs, for example:

gate : gait
daze : days
pale : pail

are distinguished as /ge:t/ and /gæit/ respectively by some, and merged under /gæit/ by others (cf. Table 1). We can best handle

TABLE 1. A Norwich vowel system: Long vowels and diphthongs.

/i:/	bee	/ʉ:/	news	/ɛ:/	peer, pear
/æi/	bay, bake	/u:/	nose	/ɔ:/	poor, pore, paw
/ai/	buy	/ou/	knows	/a:/	pa, par
/oi/	boy	/æʉ/	now	/ɜ:/	purr, pure

this by postulating a difference in lexical entries: there is no reason to suppose that those who never make the distinction have different underlying representations for the two sets of items. This does mean, however, that we are faced with the problem of incorporating within a single grammar two different systematic phonemic vowel systems. This is done by means of a 'diasystemic inventory rule', rule 1, which I believe has some kind of reality, and which relates the one vowel system to the other:

(1) $\left. \begin{array}{c} // \bar{a} // \\ // \text{ai} // \end{array} \right\} \longrightarrow // \text{ai} //$

This is a representation of the fact that some speakers have distinct lexical entries of the type //gāt// and //gait// whereas others simply have //gait//: the element //ā// does not appear in their underlying representations. This is not a normal type of optional or variable rule. All speakers have internalized this rule, but some always apply it in their speech-production, while others never do. This must appear somewhat paradoxical: a rule that is internalized but never used (in production, that is, cf. Bailey 1972b). There are two main justifications for this. One is that we must assume that individuals do employ rules of this type in the comprehension of utterances made by speakers with different underlying systems, so that the selection of //gāt// on the part of the speaker can induce selection of //gait// on the part of the hearer. Now it is true, of course, that speakers from outside Norwich will be able to perform the same sort of operation, in order to comprehend certain types of Norwich pronunciation. I would suggest, however, that outsiders will develop this kind of ability in a rather ad hoc way, by relying on nonphonological clues. They do not have a rule of this form in their grammars, as Norwich speakers do. It does not seem to me, that is, that speakers ever acquire anything approaching a 'panlectal grammar' of the type that Bailey (1972b) has suggested. It is also the case that Norwich speakers are capable, as it were, of reversing the direction of application of this rule. Speakers who never normally make the distinction are capable of doing so, without error, if they wish to for humorous or other purposes. A speaker who habitually says gate, face /gæit/, /fæis/ may say /ge:t/, /fe:s/ for a joke, but would never do the same thing, as an outsider might, with day. This rule, then, is an attempt to reflect the fact that, while there is no reason to suppose on the basis of their own normal speech that certain speakers have contrasting underlying forms, these speakers nevertheless know that other speakers within the system do have different underlying forms and, what is more, they know what these underlying forms are. The evidence for this is as follows. During the survey a small number of younger informants who did not have the /æi/-/e:/ contrast were asked, at the end of the interview, to read out the reading passage again as they thought older speakers would have said it (the /æi/-/e:/ distinction being one that is mainly made in Norwich by older speakers). These informants then consistently made the distinction correctly, demonstrating their knowledge of the other vowel system and the other underlying forms.

2. The major source of variation in Norwich English is also best handled at the systematic phonemic level. This variation concerns the variable distribution of phonological units over lexical items, and takes the following form (cited for convenience at the systematic phonetic level):

(i) Items such as boat, road can have two pronunciations:
  (a) /bu:t/, /ru:d/, in which case boat and boot may be homophonous;
  (b) /bUt/, /rUd/, in which case boat and put, road and hood will be perfect rhymes.

(ii) Items such as spoon and boot can have three pronunciations:
  (a) /spʉ:n/, /bʉ:t/, in which case boot and Bute may be homophonous (since many forms of Norwich English have no [j] in items such as music, tune, cue);

(b) /spuːn/, /buːt/, in which case <u>boot</u> and <u>boat</u> may be homophonous;

(c) /spƱn/, /bƱt/, in which case <u>boot</u> and <u>boat</u> may again be homophonous, and <u>boot</u> and <u>put</u> will be perfect rhymes.

It is not possible to handle this variation by means of implicational scales, since all combinations of possibilities occur. Variation takes place between speakers, within the speech of individual speakers, and from lexical item to lexical item (see Chen and Hsieh 1971). In no case does the selection of one particular pronunciation imply the selection of any other pronunciation. The Norwich data, that is, supports, at this point, the position taken by Fasold (1970) rather than that of DeCamp (1971).

This sort of variation could be handled simply by listing alternative forms in the lexicon. We could, for example, give the phonological entry for <u>boat</u> as both //bōt// and //but// and so on. This, however, would miss a significant generalization that can and should be made at this point. It would suggest that the alternative pronunciations were entirely unmotivated, and would fail to reveal the underlying regularity that these alternations affect whole lexical sets in exactly the same way. It would indicate that the fact that alternations such as <u>home</u> /huːm/-/hƱm/, <u>stone</u> /stuːn/-/stƱn/ are identical is entirely accidental. I propose, however, that the relationships exemplified here between the pronunciations of these lexical sets is not accidental, and that the variation is so large and determined that it cannot be handled satisfactorily simply by listing alternatives in the lexicon. Rather, we are dealing with alternations that are subject to rule, and must be accounted for in a phonological grammar. In fact, we write <u>boot</u> and <u>spoon</u> with underlying //ū// and <u>boat</u> and <u>road</u> with underlying //ō//, and then develop a set of 'diasystemic incidence rules' to handle the alternations. These are of the form:

(2) //ū// ⟶ //ō//

(3) //ō// ⟶ //u//   /___ C

It is not possible to handle this variation at a lower level. We cannot, for example, write, at the systematic phonetic level

/ʉː/ ⟶ /uː/

in order to produce <u>boot</u> /buːt/ rather than /bʉːt/, since this would also produce <u>Bute</u> */buːt/, which does not occur.

Bickerton (1971) has suggested that variation should be handled, not by means of variable rules, but rather in terms of the speaker's choice between two optional categorical rules. The situation portrayed here may appear to support Bickerton's position, since Norwich speakers choose, as with all optional rules, either to apply these incidence rules, or not. The incidence rules portrayed above, moreover, are not variable rules as this term is normally employed, since they contain no variables. The actual data, however, in fact runs counter to Bickerton's argument, and supports the position taken by Labov (e.g. 1969). In the first place, the true, more detailed version of rule 3 does contain variables, since it operates more frequently in some phonological contexts than others. (For example, <u>roof</u> /rʊf/ tends to be more frequent than <u>spoon</u> (spʊn/, which in turn is more frequent than <u>boot</u> /bʊt/.) Secondly, we have to note that the application of these rules is variable. Selection or nonselection of the rules is closely related to sociological factors. As Bickerton has suggested, variation is produced by choice: apply the rule or do not apply the rule. But the choice itself is determined by sociological variables. That is, a fuller form of rule 2 is:

(2)   x $//\bar{u}// \longrightarrow //\bar{o}//$
      x (rule 2) = f (Class, Age, Style).

Rule 2 is, in other words, a variable rule, where x represents a probability that the rule will be selected (details are available elsewhere: Trudgill, forthcoming) which varies from individual to individual, but which is likely, although not certain in individual cases, to show a close relationship with social class and other sociological parameters, to the extent that, on the average, middle-class speakers will operate this rule more frequently than working-class speakers. From this it should be clear that I consider the evidence suggests that Norwich speakers have internalized, as part of their competence as members of the speech community, some quantitative knowledge. They 'know', as individuals, the probability of operation of this rule in particular social contexts. Butters (1971) and Bickerton (1971) believe that this is unreasonable. I do not. Human beings have other knowledge, both linguistic and nonlinguistic, which is clearly quantitative. In writing this paper, for example, I know how often I can use a particular word for a particular stylistic effect, and at what intervals it is acceptable to repeat a particular expression, although of course I am totally unable, consciously, to express this knowledge in figures. Similarly, speakers also know how often and at what intervals they should use particular address forms, endearments, insults, and oaths to achieve particular effects. If I know that if I say <u>bloody</u> more than a certain number of times, a certain type of person will consider me uncouth, then there is no reason to suppose that I should not also know that a certain number of pronunciations home /hʊm/ will have the same effect.[2]

Rules 2 and 3 are not the only incidence rules in Norwich English. For example, the inventory rule, rule 1, is for many speakers in fact an incidence rule. There are some speakers who alternate gate /geːt/ with /gæit/. For these speakers we need rule 4:

(4) $//\bar{a}// \longrightarrow //ai//$

To summarize this point: some (mainly older) speakers have distinct lexical entries for gate and gait, and consistently distinguish them; other (mainly middle-aged) speakers also have distinct underlying representations, but effect a merger, variably, by means of rule 4; other (mainly younger) speakers always operate rule 1 and therefore consistently have the merger. When, finally, at some later stage, the application of the inventory rule has become generalized to the entire community, then the systematic phonemic unit $//\bar{a}//$ will be lost from the system, together, of course, with the inventory rule itself.

3. Other sources of variation in Norwich English are to be found at lower levels. At the systematic phonetic level, for instance, there are a number of variable rules of assimilation which produce variation within the community. Consider rules 5 and 6.

(5) x /iː/ $\longrightarrow$ /ɛː/ $/\_\_\_$ /ə/
     x (rule 5) = f (Class, Age, Style)

(6) x /ə/ $\longrightarrow$ ∅ $/$ /ɛː/ $\_\_\_$
     x(rule 6) = f (Age)

Because these rules are variable in their application, the following pronunciations all occur in Norwich English:

beer	/biːə/	/bɛːə/	/bɛː/
seeing	/siːən/	/sɛːən/	/sɛːn/
he have	/hiːə/	/hɛːə/	/hɛː/

The justification for treating this variation at the systematic phonetic level is that units such as /ɛː/ and /ə/ do not occur at the higher level.

4. The remaining forms of variation we shall discuss here occur at the phonetic realization level, i.e. at the level of actual

articulations. The first type is that which occurs as the result of
rules that realize systematic phonetic elements at the lowest level.
The rules that follow are presented in a somewhat simplified form.
For a more adequate presentation of variable rules see Cedergren
and Sankoff (MS). For example:

(7) $/t/ \longrightarrow x < [t] \sim [\mathfrak{t}\mathfrak{?}] \sim [\mathfrak{?}] >$
     x = f (Age, Class, Sex, Style).

This produces actual articulations such as <u>better</u> [b'ɛtə ~ b'ɛtʔə ~
b'ɛʔə] which are all used in varying degrees by nearly all Norwich
speakers.

A similar rule is:

(8) $/h/ \longrightarrow x < [h] \sim \emptyset >$
     x = f (Class, Style).

This rule is particularly interesting since Bickerton (1971) has suggested that variability is never in fact really 'inherent'. Rather,
Bickerton has claimed, it is simply due to linguistic change, a
'developmental phase': at certain times speakers will begin to
switch from one categorical rule, in this case:

$/h/ \longrightarrow [h]$

to another:

$/h/ \longrightarrow \emptyset$

This change is effected in such a way that at any given point a majority
of speakers approach 100 per cent application of either one rule or
the other, with only a minority hovering around the 50-50 mark.
Bickerton further suggests that the inherent variability claimed by
Labov only emerges as the result of averaging out group scores, and
is not an accurate reflection of the grammars of individuals. Bailey
(1972a) has also argued for this s-curve thesis of linguistic change
and variability. The Norwich data concerning rule 8 provides some
counter-evidence, and supports Labov's thesis. First, the variation
really does appear to be inherent, since there is no sign whatsoever
of any linguistic change taking place. If we divide the Norwich informants into three groups by age, we obtain the following figures for
h-deletion:

Younger than 30 : 51%
30-49   : 54%
50 or over   : 51%

Thus, groups of Norwich speakers of whatever age use approximately 50 per cent /h/-deletion. These group scores, moreover, do not obscure figures for individuals which are predominantly close to 0 per cent or 100 per cent, as Table 2 shows.

TABLE 2. Per cent Norwich informants in different /h/-deletion categories: Lower-middle and working-class.

h-deletion %	% informants	N = 50
0-9	14	
10-19	18	
20-29	16	
30-39	10	
40-49	10	
50-59	6	
60-69	16	
70-79	6	
80-89	0	
90-100	2	

For vowels, realization rules at this level are of the following form:

(9)   /u:/ ⟶ x <[u:-u̜:-öu-ɵu]>   <u>road</u>
              x = f (Style, Class)

(10) /ou/ ⟶ x <[ʌu-ɔ̈u-ɵu]>   <u>rowed</u>
              x = f (Style, Class)

Rules 9 and 10 are somewhat different from rule 8. In rule 8 the output to the rule is variably selected from two discrete alternatives. In rules 9 and 10, on the other hand, the output is to be selected from a continuous area within phonological or phonetic space. The symbolization employed, with the phonetic symbols linked by hyphens rather than tildes, is intended to indicate that the symbols represent, not alternative pronunciations, but rather the outer limits of the area of phonetic space within which realization is possible. The variation that occurs at this level in Norwich English is therefore the result, not of the application of the rule being variable, nor of the rule

selecting from a number of discrete outputs, but rather of the fact
that the output consists of a phonetic area, with the particular point
in the area in any given instance being selected in accordance with x.
Distinctive features are not employed in the outputs to these rules
since they are not precise enough to indicate the fine shades of
phonetic distinction involved. Rules 9 and 10 are an attempt to account for the fact that a given Norwich speaker will move on average,
from, say, the general area of [ṳu] to the general area of [ọ̈u] if the
social context becomes more formal.

It should also be noted that the outputs of the two rules given above
overlap phonetically. This accounts for the fact that some (mainly
middle-class) speakers sometimes lose this surface contrast, or
make a smaller phonetic distinction, in some stylistic (mainly formal)
contexts, under the influence of the British prestige accent R. P.
which does not have the contrast. Note, however, that the failure
by these speakers to contrast, say, nose and knows is not of the same
type as the failure to distinguish gate and gait. All Norwich speakers
have different underlying forms for items like nose and knows, and
speakers who appear to have a merger can always be induced to make
a distinction by, say, asking them to read a pair of items of this type
one after the other in a pairs test. In the case of gate and gait this
does not happen. It is, however, possible that a diasystemic incidence rule:

$$//ɔ̃// \longrightarrow //ou//$$

could develop from this phonetic merger at some later stage: we
might assume that the gate/gait merger started life in this way.

5. A further type of variation is due to processes which actually
take place at the phonetic realization level. All rules at this level
are both optional and variable, and in some types of careful, formal
speech none of them will operate at all. They are necessary, however, in order to produce casual speech of the type illustrated above.
Rules of this type are:

(11) x [n] $\longrightarrow$ <∅>/ [e-ɛ-ɛ̆-ë] ____ [ʔ]
      x (rule 11) = f (Style, Class)

There are two sources of variation here. One is that this deletion is
related to social class and contextual style. The other is due to the
phonetic context for the deletion. The symbolization of this rule is
intended to indicate that deletion can take place after any vowel that
falls into the phonetic area indicated. This means, for example,
that plenty can be [plɛ̣ʔIi]. It also means, though, that where

speakers realize /I/ within this same area, as they may do as the
result of the rule:

(12)   /I/⟶ x<[ị̆-ë̤-ë]>

then the same thing can happen with items such as int (the Norwich
equivalent of ain't), which can be [ë?]--but only in the case of those
speakers who have an open variant of /I/. Variability in one rule
can therefore give rise to variability in another. Other rules at this
level--and there are very many--are:

(13)   x [n] + [ð]⟶ [l] (in certain contexts)
       x (rule 13) = f (Style)

(14)   x [n]⟶ ∅ / ___ #
       x (rule 14) = f (Style)

Further rules at this level delete various segments, notably [ə], lower
and centralize short vowels, delete glides from diphthongs, and so on.
The variable application of these numerous rules results in much of
the variation to be found in Norwich English.

6. The final source of variation I would like to discuss is variation in articulatory setting (see Honikman 1964, Laver 1968).
Working-class and middle-class speech is often differentiated as
much as anything by setting, including voice quality. Often, working-
class speech may be characterized by raised larynx voice and other
features such as blade articulated alveolar stops and pharyngeal tension. This suggests that it might be possible, with more investigation, to simplify many of the at present rather complicated rules
involving the phonetic realization level. We might, for instance,
have general setting rules of the type:

(15)   Vocal Organs ⟶ x<Setting 1 ~ Setting 2>
                        x = f (Class)

(16)   Setting 2 ⟶ High Muscular Tension

(17)   High Muscular Tension ⟶ x<Raised Larynx
                                 Tense Vocal Tract >
                                 x = f (Class, Sex, Style)

(18)   Tongue ⟶ Fronted and Lowered / Raised Larynx

If something of this sort were possible, then we could replace complex rules involving variables of the type:

(12) $/I/ \longrightarrow x<[\overset{r}{\underset{L}{i}}\text{-}\overset{..}{e}\text{-}\overset{..}{e}]>$

by the rule:

(12) $/I/ \longrightarrow [\overset{r}{\underset{L}{i}}]$

and allow the setting rules to produce the more open vowel where appropriate. This would greatly simplify the handling of this type of variation. A possible mechanism for this kind of filtering effect of the articulatory setting might be something like the following:

if   Tongue $\longrightarrow$ Lowered

then $/I/ \longrightarrow [\overset{r}{\underset{L}{i}}]$
                    $\Downarrow$
        $/I/ \longrightarrow [\overset{..}{\underset{.}{e}}]$

NOTES

[1]I am very grateful to William Labov for his helpful comments on this paper, and to Henrietta Cedergren, Michael Garman, and David Sankoff for their help with a number of points.

[2]Variation of this type is therefore the result of differential probabilities of application of incidence rules due to three factors: (a) lexical diffusion--rule features in lexical entries; (b) variably weighted phonological environments--variables in rules; (c) sociological factors such as style and social class--variables on rules.

REFERENCES

Bailey, C.-J. N. 1972a. How the wave model explains what it explains.

_____. 1972b. The integration of linguistic theory: Internal reconstruction and the comparative method in descriptive analysis. In Stockwell and Macaulay, eds.

Bickerton, D. 1971. Inherent variability and variable rules. FL7. 457-92.

Brown, G. 1972. Phonological rules and dialect variation: A study of the phonology of Lumasaaba. Cambridge, Cambridge University Press.

Butters, R. R. 1971. On the notion 'rule of grammar' in dialect-ology. Papers from the Seventh Regional Meeting, Chicago Linguistic Society. Chicago, University of Chicago.

Cedergren, H. and D. Sankoff. MS. Variable rules: Performance as a statistical reflection of competence.

Chen, M. and H. Hsieh. 1971. The time variable in phonological change. JL7. 1-13.

DeCamp, D. 1971. Toward a generative analysis of a post-creole speech continuum. In: D. H. Hymes, ed. Pidginization and creolization of languages. Cambridge, Cambridge University Press.

Fasold, R. W. 1970. Two models of socially significant linguistic variation. Language. 46.551-63.

Gregg, R. J. 1964. Scotch-Irish urban speech in Ulster. In: Ulster Dialects. Holywood.

Harris, J. W. 1969. Spanish phonology. Cambridge, MIT Press.

Honikman, B. 1964. Articulatory settings. In: In honour of Daniel Jones. Ed. by D. Abercrombie et al. London, Longmans.

Labov, W. 1966. The social stratification of English in New York City. Washington, Center for Applied Linguistics.

_____. 1969. Contraction, deletion, and inherent variability of the English copula. Language. 45.715-62.

_____. 1972. The internal evolution of linguistic rules. In: Stockwell and Macaulay, eds.

_____. 1973. Where do grammars stop? Georgetown University Monograph Series on Languages and Linguistics, Monograph 25. Washington, D.C., Georgetown University Press.

Laver, J. 1968. Voice quality and indexical information. British Journal of Disorders of Communication. 3.43-54.

Postal, P. 1968. Aspects of phonological theory. New York, Harper and Row.

Stockwell, R. and R. Macaulay, eds. 1972. Historical linguistics and generative theory. Bloomington, Indiana University Press.

Trudgill, P. J. 1973, forthcoming. The social differentiation of English in Norwich. Cambridge, Cambridge University Press.

PAN-LECTAL GRAMMARS
AND ADULT LANGUAGE CHANGE

BARBARA ROBSON

University of Wisconsin

In this paper, I will be dealing with variation within the individual, and will be talking mainly about changes in adult language. I will describe a particular type of stylistic variation, and then will speculate as to what its linguistic significance is, from the point of view of the individual who exhibits it, and from the point of view of the community language which was the source of the variation. The purpose of the paper is to suggest that we have not the foggiest idea how the individual fits into the linguistic community; although we have a reasonably good idea as to how the individual organizes his language, and although we are able to discern and describe the patterns of variation present in the language of the community, these linguistic advances have furnished us with no insights into the direct relationship between the individual and his community, insights which are crucial if we are ever going to find out how one person communicates with another, which is presumably what variation studies are all about in the first place.

The data with which I will illustrate the preceding suggestions are from Jamaican English, in particular the speech of Jenepher Campbell, who, at the time I was doing field work, was a fourteen-year-old schoolgirl in Irishtown, a village some fifteen miles up into the Blue Mountains from Kingston. Like other Jamaicans, Jenepher has quite distinct styles, and she switches from one to another depending on the social situation. As is usual in Jamaica, the style she speaks in formal situations is noticeably closer to Standard English--whatever it means to say that--than the style she speaks in informal situations; in other words, she is a bona fide member of the Jamaican 'speech continuum' that has been described often in the literature.

I am concerned here with Jenepher's behavior with regard to the segments [Θ] and [ð]. In her informal style, these segments don't occur; she has [t] in words where Standard English has [Θ], and [d] in words where Standard English has [ð]. [Θ] and [ð] do occur in her formal style, however; they alternate with [t] and [d] in most of the words where Standard English has [Θ] and [ð], and also alternate with [s] and [z] in some words where Standard English has [s] or [z]. On the other hand, there are some words in which Standard English has [Θ] and [ð], for which Jenepher has only [t] or [d] in her formal style. Examples of these alternations are the following:

St. E.	Jenepher's formal	Jenepher's informal
think	Θıŋk, tıŋk	tıŋk
farther	farða, farda	fada
with	wıΘ, wıt	wıt
there	ðɛr, dɛr	dɛr, dɛ
some	Θam, sam	sam
so	Θo, so	so
is	ıð, ız	ız
maths	mats	mats
they	dey	dey
thief	tif	tif
them	dɛm, dɛ	dɛm

This type of alternation is characteristic of the segment [ɔ], also. Jenepher has only [a] in her informal style; in her formal style, [ɔ] alternates with [a], apparently at random in words which in Standard English have either [a] or [ɔ]:

St. E.	Jenepher's formal	Jenepher's informal
not	nɔt, nat	nat
dog	dɔg, dag	dag
because	bıkɔ, bıka	bıka
off	ɔf, af	af
water	wɔta, wata	wata

The crucial point in these cases is the inconsistency with which Jenepher alternates the segments in her formal style. This type of wobbly alternation is one that I've run across dozens of times in teaching English as a foreign language, and in casual observation of myself and others trying to pass off as native a contrast we don't have down quite pat. I think it's a common phenomenon among adults; that it's a stable kind of behavior; and that it is a kind of hypercorrection.

Jenepher's wobbling with regard to [Θ], [đ], and [ɔ] is not at all characteristic of her stylistic variation in general: consider, for example, the alternation between [ʔ] and Ø in words which in Standard English have [h]:

St. E.	Jenepher's formal	Jenepher's informal
house	ʔous	ous
hole	ʔuol	uol
happy	ʔapi	api
behind	bɪʔain	bɪain

Consider also the consistency with which Jenepher retains [r]'s in formal style, and drops them in informal:

St. E.	Jenepher's formal	Jenepher's informal
thirty	Θɨrti	toti
garden	gardɨn	gya·dɨn
hard	ʔard	a·d
chair	čiɛr	čiɛr#ɪ, čiɛ#d
hear	ʔiər	iər#ɪ, iə#d

It's perfectly clear what's going on in the real world with respect to Jenepher's [Θ]'s and [đ]'s and [ɔ]'s, especially if you're aware of what goes on at the school she attended. She has picked up the notion that formal, correct English has [Θ]'s, [đ]'s, and [ɔ]'s in it; she has just not completely mastered where the [Θ]'s, [đ]'s, and [ɔ]'s go. She is aware of the existence of these segments in 'English', as opposed to their nonexistence in 'the Patois' (her name for her informal style); she referred to them in discussions with me about language, speaking correctly, and so on.

On the other hand, her style-shifting with regard to [ʔ] and [r] doesn't seem to be something she's been formally taught. First, she would surely have been taught to say [h] instead of [ʔ], and to drop [r]'s before consonants instead of retaining them; [h] and dropped [r]'s occur in the kind of English theoretically taught in Jamaican schools. Second, although she corrected herself in both styles when she made mistakes with one or the other of these segments, she couldn't verbalize about them, as she would have been able to if she had had them discussed in school. Third, she seemed satisfied with her [ʔ]'s as repetitions of my [h]'s, in much the same way that people who speak a different dialect from mine will be satisfied that they are reproducing my pronunciation when in fact they aren't.

From consideration of such matters, I have theorized that style-shifting has been part of Jenepher's language since early childhood, and that her [ʔ]'s and [r]-retaining are features of a formal style that she has had at her command since she learned to talk, whereas her [Θ]'s and [ɖ]'s and [ɔ]'s are features superimposed on her formal style as a result of formal (although not very good) instruction.

I don't know what has happened, or what is going to happen, to her [Θ]'s, [ɖ]'s, and [ɔ]'s; it's possible that by now she's learned where they go and don't go, and that her behavior with regard to them is indistinguishable from her behavior with regard to [ʔ] and [r]. If this is the case, then I happened to catch her in a transitional stage, and there is nothing more I can say about it. It seems more likely, however, that such wobbling is part of her adult language, and is there to stay.

At any rate, the wobbling was there at one time, and the question is its grammatical description. First, [Θ] and [ɖ]: there are several ways to incorporate the [Θ]-[ɖ], [t]-[d] alternation into a grammar of Jenepher's competence. One way is to set up underlying /Θ/'s and /ɖ/'s in words like think and brother and so, and then to posit a rule which says that interdental fricatives become alveolar stops in some words, and alveolar fricatives in others. This rule would be optional in formal style, obligatory in informal style.

Another way is to set up underlying /Θ/'s and /ɖ/'s in words like think and brother, to collapse them with /t/ and /d/ by rule, and say that Jenepher's occurrences of [Θo], [Θam], and [ɪɖ] for so, some, and is are performance errors of the random sort.

Another way, and this is my favorite because it seems simplest, and most in accord with what I think is going on, is to have no underlying /Θ/'s and /ɖ/'s, but to set up a rule to the effect that alveolar obstruents become interdental fricatives in certain words, and then to suggest that the specification of lexical items with respect to this rule is haphazard.

The same sort of analysis can be suggested for Jenepher's [a]-[ɔ] alternation: underlying /a/ becomes [ɔ] in certain words, with Jenepher's apparent uncertainty as to where [ɔ] occurs reflected in the haphazard specification of lexical items.

Whatever the details of the lexical specifications are, I would maintain that Jenepher's [Θ], [đ], and [ɔ] are better described as arising from the operation of rules, rather than as occurrences of distinct segments; the occurrences of [Θ], [đ], and [ɔ] seem to be far more dependent on the phonological identity of the segments they alternate with (i. e. [t, d, s, z] and [a]) than on the particular words in which they occur.

In a panlectal or community grammar of English, the occurrences of [Θ] and [đ] and [t] and [d] are presumably dealt with as occurrences of distinct segments. There should also be a statement or rule to the effect that the contrast between [Θ] and [t], and [đ] and [d], is neutralized, so that the fact that many speakers of English have no [Θ]'s and [đ]'s but only [t]'s and [d]'s is expressed.

[a] and [ɔ] are presumably dealt with in a parallel way in a pan-lectal English grammar: as distinct segments, with a statement to the effect that the contrast between them is neutralized, to reflect the pronunciation of people like Jenepher (before her English teacher entered her life), and, incidentally, western Americans like the author.

A problem arises when we try to express what seems to be going on in Jenepher's speech in terms of a formal relationship between Jenepher's grammar and a panlectal grammar of English.

At least one variationist--Derek Bickerton--has characterized a competence grammar as consisting of 'just those rules, etc., that a given individual must have out of [the panlectal grammar] to pro-duce what he produces' (Lectological Newsletter 1972a). I think that most variationists would agree with his general notion that a panlectal grammar of, say, English, covers everything that goes on in English, whereas a competence grammar covers just those parts of English which the individual controls.

Jenepher has been made aware of a contrast that exists in some varieties of English, and she is trying to incorporate that contrast into her own speech. The best description of that incorporation, in a grammar of her competence, is in terms of a rule. It would be very nice if we could say that she got that rule, in some sense, from the panlectal grammar of English; but we can't, not literally, because that particular rule, i. e. [t] and [d] become [Θ] and [đ], doesn't occur in the panlectal grammar of English.

There is no way that we can formally express what's happened to Jenepher in terms of competence and panlectal grammars unless we deal with outputs, and say that Jenepher has incorporated the surface occurrences of [Ɵ] and [ᴅ] and [t] and [d], which are the outputs of the panlectal grammar, as a rule-produced contrast instead of as a lexical contrast. If we are forced to deal with outputs alone, however, then the panlectal grammar of English becomes simply an inventory of surface forms to which Jenepher has access, and which she can interpret any way which is most conducive to her purposes.

The point that the preceding example was chosen to illustrate is that, given what I believe to be the current notions of panlectal and competence grammars, there is no formal way of relating the two.[1] If this is the case, then there is no way of expressing such facts as the one that the adult draws upon the panlectal grammar as a source for changes in his speech, as it seems obvious that he does in cases like Jenepher's, and in cases of hypercorrection in general. Along broader lines, it seems to me that without principled relationships between panlectal and competence grammars, we can't express, or begin to explain, the interdependence between the language of the individual, and the language of the community with all its inherent variation; and if we can't do that, then we're missing the basic point of variation studies, which is to discover why individuals who don't talk the same way can communicate nonetheless.

NOTE

[1]Note that the problem exists whether a panlectal grammar is held to be outside the individual (my view) or within the individual by virtue of the fact that he understands many more varieties of his language than he produces (the view held in Bailey 1972). Adherents of the latter view must still explain how Jenepher gets the [Ɵ-t, ᴅ-d] contrast out of the rules which handle what she understands, and into the rules which handle what she produces.

REFERENCES

Bailey, C.-J. N. 1972. The integration of linguistic theory: Internal reconstruction and the comparative method in descriptive analysis. In: Stockwell and Macaulay 1972.
_____. 1972b. The patterning of language variation. Unpublished paper.
Bickerton, Derek. 1971. Inherent variability and variable rules. Foundations of Language. 7.457-92.
DeCamp, David. 1972. Iteratives, ideophones, and the locus of a language. Unpublished paper.
Lectological Newsletter, I, 1972a.
_____, II, 1972b.
_____, III, 1972c.

Robson, Barbara B. 1971. A linguistic study of variation in spoken styles within the individual. Unpublished Doctoral dissertation, University of Texas.

DISAMBIGUATION, FAVORED READINGS, AND VARIABLE RULES*

GUY CARDEN

Yale University

1. Introduction. Standard theories of semantics in the tradition of Katz and Fodor (1963) have two apparently unrelated properties. First, they operate by disambiguation, so that the readings of any constituent in context are a subset of its readings in isolation. Second, they idealize away from data about favored readings and assume that, whenever a sentence is ambiguous, all its readings are equally strong.

In this paper I attack both these assumptions, using evidence from linguistic variation and a methodology that requires us to seek a 'unified analysis' for mutually comprehensible dialects. [1] In one case, we find a continuum of informant reactions: starting with informants for whom (1) has two equally strong readings, we find informants for whom one reading is progressively stronger until at last we find informants for whom only one reading is possible.

(1) All the boys didn't arrive.

In the standard model, these informants would have to be treated as forming two distinct dialects; the unified-analysis methodology, however, requires us to treat the unambiguous dialect as the endpoint of the continuum of informants in the ambiguous dialect. This in turn requires some formal means of handling favored readings.

In the second case, we find two sets of informants (totaling eight out of forty) for whom (1) has a reading in context that it does not have in isolation. In the standard model, these 'switch-dialects' might be ignored as insignificant; alternatively, one might propose

171

that the disambiguation hypothesis held for all dialects except the
switch dialects, so that the switch dialects differed from the others
in a crucial aspect of their semantics. Neither approach is appealing. If we are to account for all the dialects with a unified analysis--
for it is clear that the same processes are at work in the switch dialects as in the others--we shall have to abandon the disambiguation
hypothesis for all the dialects.

If my arguments are accepted, what changes will we need to make
in our models for semantics? The continuum of favored readings
seems to require a model in which the probability of a given reading
can vary continuously; the switch dialects seem to show inherently
discontinuous jumps from one reading to another, suggesting difficulties with a purely probabalistic model. My best guess is that
rules of both types will be needed, as is the case in phonology, where
we need both variable and categorical rules. While it will clearly be
a major job to develop an appropriate mechanism, it seems reasonable to hope that Labov's notion of variable rule could be applied in
semantics to handle the favored-reading data with a minimum of
interference with the categorical rules--global or transderivational--
that remain necessary to handle the switch dialects.

2. The disambiguation hypothesis. Standard theories of semantics
adopt a model in which semantic interpretation proceeds by succes-
sive disambiguation: A constituent $\underline{A}$ has $\underline{n}$ readings in isolation; the
context ___B rules out some of these readings, so that the readings
of $\underline{A}$ in context are a subset of its readings in isolation. For example,
(2a) has the familiar copula/progressive ambiguity in isolation, but
the addition of the adverb skillfully in (2b) disambiguates in favor of
the progressive reading.

(2a) They are flying planes.
(2b) They are flying planes skillfully.

According to this 'disambiguation hypothesis', a context can sub-
tract readings but never add them. Turning this around, we can see
that, if $\underline{A}$ has reading $\underline{x}$ in the context ___B, $\underline{A}$ will also have reading $\underline{x}$ in isolation. The added linguistic context ___B only serves to
make the informant notice a reading that was there all along.

Linguists have treated the disambiguation hypothesis as firmly
established and used it as a basis for further argument. I shall give
two examples in outline form.

Example 1: Katz and Postal (1964:72f)

Form of argument: If A̲ has reading x̲ in context, then A̲ must have reading x̲ in isolation.

(KP-1) everyone in the room knows two languages
(KP-2) two languages are known by everyone in the room
(KP-3) There are two languages which everyone in the
        room knows

Katz and Postal's theory predicts that the passive transformation does not change meaning, and they are considering the claim that (KP-1) and (KP-2) are counter-examples because (KP-2) has a reading x̲ [in which 'it is the same two languages for each person' (1964: 72)] that (KP-1) does not share. Their counter argument goes like this:

Step 1: (KP-3) contains (KP-1) as a deep structure constituent.
Step 2: (KP-3) has reading x̲.
Step 3: The disambiguation hypothesis: '. . . it is clear from
        the character of the semantic component that a par-
        ticular constituent cannot have a given reading in a
        sentence context unless that reading is one of that
        constituent's readings in isolation' (1964:73).
Conclusion: Therefore (KP-1) must have reading x̲, apparently
        no matter what informants might say.

Example 2: Chomsky (1970:66f)

Form of Argument: If A̲ does not have reading x̲ in isolation, then A̲ cannot have reading x̲ in context.

(C-92) (Bill) has been here for a month.
(C-93) John hasn't been here for a month, but Bill has.
(C-94) John hasn't been here for a month, but Bill has been
        here for a month.

Chomsky is concerned with deciding whether there is a deletion rule that would derive (C-93) from the same structure that underlies (C-94). In his dialect, the second conjunct of (C-93) has a possible reading x̲ 'Bill has been here at some time during the month', while (C-92) does not have that reading. His argument, if I have understood him correctly, goes like this:

Step 1: If (C-93) is derived from (C-94) by a deletion rule,
'then the second conjunct of (94) has an interpretation
which it cannot have in isolation' (1970:67).
Tacit Step 2: But that would violate the disambiguation
hypothesis.
Conclusion: Therefore (C-93) is not derived from (C-94) by
a deletion rule.

Despite the long history of the disambiguation hypothesis, there
do seem to be cases where additional linguistic context adds a reading. Consider opaque contexts:[2]

(3a) John saw the man who murdered Smith.
(3b) Bill said that John saw the man who murdered Smith.

(3b) appears to be formed by embedding (3a) under <u>Bill said . . .</u>;
but the constituent <u>the man who murdered Smith</u> has two readings in
(3b) (speaker's description vs. Bill's description) and only one reading in (3a) (speaker's description). The additional context has added
a reading.

It might be argued that the ambiguity in (3b) is a special sort, and
that the disambiguation hypothesis only applies to 'real' ambiguities
like those in (2a) and in the Chomsky and Katz-Postal arguments.
In section 4, however, I show counter-examples to the disambiguation hypothesis that involve substantially the same sort of scope
ambiguity that we saw in the Chomsky and Katz-Postal examples.

3. The all-readings-are-equal hypothesis. Standard theories of
semantics have the additional property that a constituent either has a
given reading or it doesn't; no intermediate degrees are possible.
Such a model makes the implicit prediction that, whenever a sentence
has two readings, both readings are equally strong. Of course this
prediction is false in general, since informants regularly report that
one reading is favored--'stronger', 'more likely', or 'more natural'--
even when two readings are possible and the addition of context can
force either reading.

Still, one could plausibly argue that this was a fine point, and that
linguistic theory could profitably idealize away from this inconvenient
data about favored readings. One might, for example, say that a case
where one reading is favored is to be accounted for by 'perceptual
strategies' or by 'performance', while a case where one reading is
required is to be accounted for by 'competence'. In section 4, I consider an example where a favored reading becomes by gradual degrees the required reading. If we are to account for this data, the

same mechanism must handle both the case where the reading is favored and the case where the reading is required.

4. The data: Favored readings.

(4) All the boys didn't arrive.

NEG -Q Reading: $\sim[(\forall x \; \varepsilon \; \text{the boys})(\text{arrive}(x))]$
'Not all the boys arrived.'

NEG-V Reading: $(\forall x \; \varepsilon \; \text{the boys}) \; [\sim(\text{arrive}(x))]$
'All the boys (failed to arrive).'

Informants report two possible readings for sentences like (4): a NEG-Q reading in which the negative is semantically associated with the quantifier, and a NEG-V reading, in which the negative is semantically incorporated with the verb. In a series of interviews, sixteen informants reported that only the NEG-Q reading was possible, twenty reported that (4) was ambiguous between NEG-Q and NEG-V readings, and four reported that only the NEG-V reading was possible. In the standard model, therefore, we have distinct NEG-Q, NEG-V, and Ambiguous (AMB) dialects.

Let us look at these informant reactions in a bit more detail. Among the informants who found (4) ambiguous, only a minority found the NEG-Q and NEG-V readings equally strong. Most favored the Q reading, some slightly, some substantially, some to the point that the NEG-V reading was only marginally possible. It was, in fact, sometimes a difficult coding problem to decide whether to assign a given informant to the AMB or the NEG-Q dialect. The AMB and NEG-Q reading became gradually stronger and the NEG-V reading became gradually weaker until at last it disappeared. Figure 1 gives a schematic representation of the data.[3]

FIGURE 1. Informant reactions. Probability of NEG-V reading for (4) with no context.

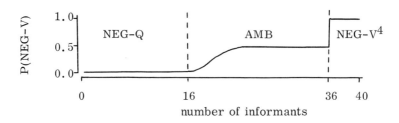

number of informants

In the standard model, we must treat NEG-Q and AMB as discrete dialects, and invent some mechanism D̲ that accounts for the fact that (4) is ambiguous in one dialect but not in the other. Favored readings are ignored, or treated outside of competence. The standard model thus makes the implicit prediction that the AMB dialect is distinguished from the NEG-Q dialect by some discrete mechanism D̲, while the continuum of favored readings within the AMB dialect is to be accounted for by some distinct (presumably noncompetence) mechanism C̲. But it seems clear from the data that the same process is at work in both the cases where the NEG-Q reading is favored and the cases where the NEG-Q reading is required. The NEG-Q dialect is simply the end-point of the continuum in the AMB dialect.

To handle this, we must change the standard model so that the same mechanism can be used to account for the favored readings in the AMB dialect and for the eventual disambiguation in the NEG-Q dialect. Such a model could handle favored readings by continuously varying the 'strength' or 'probability' of a given reading. [5] When the probability reaches 1.0 or 0.0, we have a disambiguation.

It is important to notice that this argument depends crucially on our adopting a mechdology in which we examine all the dialects at once and attempt to account consistently for the observed variation. If we had adopted instead the usual methodology of examining each dialect independently and analyzing it 'on its own terms', we should not have needed to account for the favored readings. In any single dialect, (4) is either ambiguous or it isn't; you can only see the continuum when you look at the whole range of dialects.

5. The data: Switch dialects. For many informants, the meaning of sentences like (4) is affected by polarity-sensitive contexts like until and positive tag questions.

(5a) *John arrived until midnight.
(5b)   John didn't arrive until midnight.

(6a)   John arrived, didn't he?
(6b)   John didn't arrive, did he?
(6c) *John arrived, did he? (question reading)
(6d) *John didn't arrive, didn't he? (question reading)

Until cannot modify a positive point-action verb like arrive; the question tag takes the opposite polarity to that of the sentence it modifies.

The constraints on until and on tag questions interact with the underlying structure of quantifiers[6] in such a way that many

informants who find (4) ambiguous find that (7) has only the NEG-Q
reading and (8) has only the NEG-V reading:[7]

(7) All the boys didn't arrive, did they?
(8) All the boys didn't leave until midnight.

Let us look at the data in more detail; consider Figure 2.

FIGURE 2. Dialects.

Sentence	NEG-Q		NEG-V		AMB	
	A	Switch-Q	A	Switch-V	A	B
(4)	NEG-Q	NEG-Q	NEG-V	NEG-V	NEG-Q NEG-V	NEG-Q NEG-V
(7)	NEG-Q	NEG-Q	*	NEG-Q	NEG-Q	NEG-Q NEG-V
(8)	*	NEG-V	NEG-V	NEG-V	NEG-V	NEG-V
Number of informants	10	6	2	2	13	7
	16		4		20	
Total:	40 informants (Carden interviews)					

In the three subdialects labeled A, everything goes as predicted by
the disambiguation hypothesis. In the AMB-A dialect, the tag disambiguates in favor of NEG-Q and the <u>until</u> disambiguates in favor of
NEG-V. In the NEG-Q-A dialect, (8) is starred: this is in accord
with the disambiguation hypothesis--if your dialect permits only a
NEG-Q reading, and the context permits only a NEG-V reading, then
the resulting S should be ungrammatical. Some informants in fact
report that (8) has the NEG-V reading, but that it is ungrammatical
with that reading. The NEG-V-A dialect works in the same way.
    The AMB-B dialect is also consistent with the disambiguation
hypothesis. The addition of the <u>did they?</u> tag does not affect the
meaning of (4), but this can be accounted for by an analysis in which
AMB-A and AMB-B differ in the relative order of the Tag-Question
and Quantifier-Lowering rules. [8]
    The problem comes with the Switch dialects. In the Switch-Q
dialect (8) has only the NEG-V reading, though (4) without context
had only the NEG-Q reading. In the Switch-V dialect, (7) has only
the NEG-Q reading, though (4) without context has only the NEG-V
reading. In both these dialects the polarity-sensitive context can

force a reading that is not found in isolation; the prediction made by the disambiguation hypothesis fails.[9]

Since the accuracy of the data is crucial here, and many readers may doubt the existence of dialects like Switch-Q and Switch-V, I should emphasize that the interview structure was strongly biased in the direction of finding (4) ambiguous between the NEG-Q and NEG-V readings. After the initial presentation of (4) with 'neutral' stress and intonation, the informant heard the sentence (or sentences of parallel structure) repeated with contexts like (7) and (8) and with stress and intonation patterns known to enforce one reading or the other for other informants. His attention was also called to a 'missing' reading by structured questions of the form 'Could it mean that none of the boys arrived?' The informants who stuck to a switch dialect through such an interview were saying, in effect, 'Yes, I know it has that reading in context; but without the context it has only the other reading.'[10]

How are the switch dialects to be accounted for? It is clear that the same thing is going on in all the dialects, with the polarity-sensitive context determining the relative scope of the quantifier and negative. We must therefore reject any solution that treats the switch dialects independently of the others. Given a sufficiently powerful model, we can attempt to work out a unified solution for all the dialects--George Lakoff (personal communication) has suggested an appealing solution using global and transderivational rules. The crucial thing to notice about any such unified solution, however, is that, once it explicitly abandons the disambiguation hypothesis for the switch dialects, it implicitly abandons the disambiguation hypothesis for all the dialects.

6. Conclusion and speculation. The evidence I have given suggests that we need to make two changes in the standard theory of semantics. First, we need to account for favored readings. Second, we must abandon the disambiguation hypothesis.

The abandonment of the disambiguation hypothesis is not a big change in our theory, since existing models with global or surface-interpretation rules already include more powerful means for controlling meaning.[11] It is, however, a significant change in methodology, and requires a reevaluation of earlier arguments that explicitly or implicitly depended on the hypothesis.

Accounting for favored readings will require a significant change in our theory. The informant reactions to (4) seem to form in part a continuum, suggesting the need for a continuous, probabalistic model of semantics. The same data, however, show one discontinuity, between NEG-V and AMB; and the switch-dialect data seem to be inherently discontinuous, with dialects jumping from

NEG-Q to NEG-V with no intermediate ambiguous stage. This suggests that discrete mechanisms are needed in addition to continuous ones.

The situation is reminiscent of that in phonology, where both variable (continuous) and categorical (discrete) rules are needed. This suggests a promising, though speculative, approach. If we adopt a formalism for semantics like that of Labov's variable phonological rules, [12] we could have the probability $\underline{P}$ of a given reading determined by a number k_i associated with each relevant context $\underline{i}$. The continuum in Figure 1 would then be represented as continuous variation in the value of the appropriate k_i, with the discontinuity at NEG-V resulting from an interaction with a categorical rule.

Such a formalism, in addition to handling the immediate problem with (4), would account for the wide range of favored-reading data, refining and extending the notion of 'ambiguity' in much the same way that Labov's original variable rules refined and extended the notion of 'free variation'.

NOTES

[*]An earlier version of this paper was presented at the Yale Linguistics Workshop; I thank the following for useful comments and suggestions: Clifford Abbott, William Christie, Thomas Dieterich, William Labov, George Lakoff, Andrea Levitt, and Rulon Wells.

[1]For discussion of this methodology, see Carden (1970a, b, 1972).

[2]This example was suggested by Thomas Dieterich.

[3]Two warnings about Figure 1: first, my coding of informant responses is not fine enough for the details of the shape of the curve to have any significance. Second, I am inferring a continuum from thirty-six discrete points; and I therefore cannot rule out entirely the hypothesis that my continuum is actually a step-function resulting from the interaction of a number of categorical rules.

[4]It is interesting that I have found no informants who find both readings possible but favor the NEG-V reading. This discontinuity in the data may be an accident caused by the relatively small number of NEG-V speakers; but, if it is not an accident, it suggests that two different types of process are at work: (1) a continuous process, favoring the NEG-Q reading, (2) a discrete process, favoring the NEG-V reading.

[5]It might be objected that 'statistical' rules like those I suggest could not possibly be part of a speaker's competence; Ross (1970), however, has shown that even more complex statistical notions (specifically, standard deviation, or some equivalent measure of the shape of a distribution) must be part of any complete semantic description.

[6]See Carden (1970a, b) for discussion.

[7](8) causes difficulty in informant work, since it is necessary to distinguish the NEG-Q reading from an irrelevant reading in which the <u>until</u> is construed with the quantifier:

NEG-V Reading: All the boys failed to arrive until midnight; zero arrived before midnight.

NEG-Q Reading: At least one boy didn't arrive until midnight; others may have arrived before or after midnight.

<u>until</u>-with-<u>all</u> Reading: It wasn't until midnight that the number of boys totaled <u>all</u>; the last boy arrived at midnight.

Other polarity sensitive items avoid this problem, but cause difficulties because of dialect variation; many informants, for example, find <u>John budged</u> a perfectly acceptable sentence.

[8]See Carden (1970b), Chapter 4.

[9]If we wished to save the disambiguation hypothesis in the face of this evidence, we could argue that (4) was actually in a context, a 'null' or zero context, and that this null context could disambiguate like any other. There are two arguments against this proposal: (1) If a null context can disambiguate, then no empirical test of the disambiguation hypothesis is possible--any counter-example can be explained away as the effect of the null context. (2) In the data at hand, the context <u>until midnight</u> favors the NEG-V reading in all dialects; the context <u>did they?</u> favors the NEG-Q reading in all dialects except AMB-B, where it has no effect. The generalization appears to be that a given non-null context disambiguates in the same direction in all dialects. The proposed 'null context', however, disambiguates in opposite directions in the switch dialects: it favors the NEG-V reading in Switch-V and the NEG-Q reading in Switch-Q. At least for this data, the null context appears to work significantly differently from non-null contexts. Unless we can find cases where a non-null context disambiguates in opposite directions in different dialects, we must be suspicious of the proposal that the null context plays the same role in disambiguation that non-null contexts do.

[10]I recorded the informants' intuitions about their active dialects; thus some of the Switch-Q informants reported that other people might use (4) with the NEG-V reading but that they would not. Several stress and intonation patterns were presented; the informants listed in the NEG-Q and NEG-V dialects found (4) unambiguous with the same reading for all patterns. (Several informants found various stress and intonation patterns unacceptable.)

While I believe that the interview methodology I used is preferable to any questionnaire methodology I have seen, (cf. Heringer 1970 and my comment following), skeptics will be interested to compare the proportion of switch dialects in two independent studies using questionnaires:

FIGURE F-1. Comparison with questionnaire studies.

Study	Number of informants Switch-Q	Switch-V	Total informants	Per cent switch
Carden (interviews)	6	2	40	20%
Heringer 1970 (questionnaires)	9	1	53	19%
Carden (questionnaires)	13	1	47	30%

[11]Notice that my evidence does not bear on the question of whether some part of the semantics operates by disambiguation; it merely shows that the semantics cannot operate exclusively by disambiguation.

[12]See for example, Labov (1969). I would hope and expect that the same formalism would work for semantic, syntactic, and phonological cases, but a great deal more work is needed before any such proposal can be taken seriously.

REFERENCES

Carden, G. 1970a. A note on conflicting idiolects. Linguistic Inquiry. 1.281-90.

_____. 1970b. Logical predicates and idiolect variation in English. Report NSF 25. Computation Laboratory of Harvard University, Cambridge.

_____. 1972. Dialect variation and abstract syntax. In: New Directions in Linguistics. Ed. by Roger W. Shuy. Washington, D.C., Georgetown University Press.

Chomsky, Noam. 1972. Some empirical issues in the theory of transformational grammar. In: Goals of linguistic theory. Ed. by Stanley Peters. Englewood Cliffs, Prentice-Hall, Inc. 63-130.

Heringer, J. T. 1970. Research on quantifier-negative idiolects. In: Papers from the Sixth Regional Meeting, Chicago Linguistics Society. Chicago, University of Chicago, Department of Linguistics.

Katz, J. J. and J. A. Fodor. 1963. The structure of a semantic theory. Language. 39.170-210.

Katz, J. J. and P. M. Postal. 1964. An integrated theory of linguistic descriptions. Cambridge, MIT Press.

Labov, W. 1969. Contraction, deletion, and inherent variability of the English copula. Language. 45.715-62.

Ross, J. R. 1970. A note on implicit comparatives. Linguistic Inquiry. 1.363-66.

THE CONCEPT OF 'EARLIER-LATER': MORE OR LESS CORRECT

RALPH W. FASOLD

Georgetown University

A cornerstone of the new variation theoretical approach to linguistic analysis is implicational ordering within and among rules. Since David DeCamp (1971) first (to my knowledge) applied implicational analysis to linguistic data, numerous cases have been discovered in which the application of some rules imply the application of others in a single overall pattern. Such a pattern is exemplified in Figure 1.

FIGURE 1. Implicational pattern.

Lects	Rules A	B	C	D
1	1	1	1	1
2	1	1	1	0
3	1	1	0	0
4	1	0	0	0
5	0	0	0	0

A given lect may have all four rules, none of them or some subset of them, but not just any subset. If a lect lacks Rule D but has Rule C, it can be guaranteed that it will also have Rules A and B. If it lacks Rule C and has Rule B, it certainly also lacks Rule D and has Rule A, and so on. The notion of implicational ordering can be expanded to include rules which apply variably in certain lects. One such possible pattern would be the one in Figure 2.

183

FIGURE 2. Implicational pattern with variation.

Lects	Rules A	B	C	D
1	1	1	1	1
2	1	1	1	x
3	1	1	x	x
4	1	x	x	0
5	x	x	0	0
6	x	0	0	0
7	0	0	0	0

In this case (where x means variable application of the rule), only those lects are possible in which rules with variable outputs intervene on the scale between categorically applicable rules and absent rules. There is an abundance of language data that indicates that there is a relationship among the outputs of rules indicated as having variable outputs. Specifically, any x in Figure 2 indicates an output which is larger than the output represented by the x either below or to the right of it. Put another way, the closer you get to a 1 either by moving up in the figure or to the left, the higher the value of the x. Thus, a pattern like the one in Figure 3 is possible, where the letters N indicate numerical frequencies such that $\underline{N}$ is greater than N which is greater than $\underline{n}$ which is greater than n, and 1 indicates categorical output and 0 indicates no output (i. e. the absence of the rule).

FIGURE 3. Frequency pattern.

Lects	Rules A	B	C
1	1	$\underline{N}$	N
2	$\underline{N}$	N	$\underline{n}$
3	N	$\underline{n}$	n
4	$\underline{n}$	n	0
5	n	0	0
6	0	0	0

The numerical values of the upper and lower case Ns are measured in decimals or percentages, but the numerical values are not fixed. The numerical value of a letter does not even have to be exactly the same as the numerical value of the same letter elsewhere in the chart. The two instances of $\underline{N}$ in Figure 3 need not be equal as long as their value is less than 1 and greater than the value of the Ns below and to the right of them. The pattern indicated in Figure 3 is equally well satisfied by the hypothetical numbers in Figure 4a or 4b, or any of a potentially infinite number of other numerical patterns.

FIGURE 4. Hypothetical examples of frequency patterns.

4a. Lects	Rules A	B	C	4b. Lects	Rules A	B	C
1	1.00	.95	.90	1	1.00	.95	.89
2	.93	.88	.82	2	.82	.76	.64
3	.32	.28	.23	3	.57	.43	.35
4	.18	.10	.00	4	.24	.12	.00
5	.12	.00	.00	5	.15	.00	.00
6	.00	.00	.00	6	.00	.00	.00

The same principle applies within a single rule, where the scale is governed by the hierarchy of constraints on variable rules. Implicational patterns within single rules can be read directly from variable rules. One version of the final stop deletion rule in English, for example, is Rule 1:

$$\text{Rule 1:} \begin{bmatrix} +\text{cons} \\ -\text{strd} \\ \alpha\text{voi} \\ <-\text{cor}> \end{bmatrix} \longrightarrow (\emptyset) \quad / \quad \begin{bmatrix} +\text{cons} \\ \alpha\text{voi} \\ <+\text{strd}> \end{bmatrix} \text{B}\sim([-\text{seg}])\_\#\#\text{A}\sim([+\text{syl}])$$

That is, a nonstrident consonant at the end of a word can be variably deleted if preceded by a consonant with the same voicing specification, provided that if the consonant to be deleted is not coronal (in this environment this amounts to saying that it is not [t] or [d]), then the preceding consonant must be strident (in this environment this specifies [s]). The two variable constraints are indicated by upper case Greek letters. The absence of a [+syllabic] segment (i.e. a vowel) favors the operation of the rule as does the absence of a [-segmental] item (i.e. a boundary) between the two consonants. Of the two, the effect of the vowel absence exceeds the effect of the boundary absence. The existence of such a rule predicts the possibility of lect distributions like those in Figures 5-7, among others.

FIGURE 5. Implicational pattern predicted by Rule 1.

	Environments			
	AB	A	B	
Lects	~V, ~#	~V, #	V, ~#	V̄, #
1	1	1	1	1
2	1	1	1	0
3	1	1	0	0
4	1	0	0	0
5	0	0	0	0

FIGURE 6. Implicational with variation pattern predicted by Rule 1.

	Environments			
	AB	A	B	
Lects	~V, ~#	~V, #	V, ~#	V̄, #
1	1	1	1	1
2	1	1	1	x
3	1	1	x	x
4	1	x	x	0
5	x	x	0	0
6	x	0	0	0
7	0	0	0	0

FIGURE 7. Frequency pattern predicted by Rule 1 (data from Wolfram 1969:62, 68).

	Environments			
	AB	A	B	
Lects	~V, ~#	~V, #	V, ~#	V̄, #
1	.79	.49	.23	.07
2	.87	.62	.43	.13
3	.94	.73	.65	.24
4	.97	.76	.72	.34

Figure 7, as a matter of fact, represents real data, where the four lects represent the interview style of the black upper middle through lower-working classes in Detroit, reading from top to bottom (Wolfram 1969:62, 68).[1]

The discovery of patterns like the above can be used to make predictions about the direction of change. Ordinarily, one would expect that the patterns in Figures 1 and 5 would tell us that Lect 1 in each figure is the most advanced historically and Lect 4 is the least advanced. Furthermore, it is possible, usually, to infer that Rule A is the oldest rule and that environment AB is the first one in which the variable rule, Rule 1, began to operate. Similarly, Rule D is likely to be the most recent rule and the absence of both the A and B parts of the environment is likely to be the last set of conditions in which Rule 1 began to operate. Rule A can be expected to be the first one to become categorical in any lect and Rule D the last. The AB environment similarly can be expected to be the first environment in which Rule 1 will become categorical in any lect and the absence of both the A and B environments, the last.

The establishment of these patterns leads to the problem of how to account for the competence of speakers to produce data which fit the patterns. If one were to poll all the practicing American linguists today, most would probably say that we are not required to account for the patterns at all, because they are due to performance or to a kind of competence which is not linguistic. Since patterns of the kind described here are far from rare and since they involve only linguistic elements, it seems unreasonable to ascribe them to nonlinguistic competence or to performance, if performance is defined, as seems reasonable, as competence plus intrusion of nonlanguage factors.

If we take it that it is necessary to account for such patterns in competence, as I do, then it is necessary to decide what principle makes the competence possible. In the first issue of Charles-James Bailey's Lectological Newsletter can be found the results of a questionnaire in which there appeared the following question:

Do you believe that inter-rule relations exist in a single system such that earlier rules are implied by and--while still variable--have greater statistical representations than later rules?

Two of the respondents--Bailey himself and Derek Bickerton--indicated that their opinions were favorable to the hypothesis expressed by the question. While the question itself does not make reference to competence, one could propose that a speaker's knowledge of which rules are earlier and which are later leads to the implication and to the differential output quantities of variable rules.

It is my purpose to show that the notion of 'earlier-later' is not the correct competence principle but that the concept of 'more-less' is. I shall attempt this by showing that there are at least three special cases in which the earlier phenomenon actually produces a lower quantity of output than the later one, but that the 'more-less' principle covers these special cases as well as the more common situations in which the 'earlier-later' principle makes the correct predictions.

The first--and most involved--case of this kind is the case of rule acceleration. Suppose there are two rules, Rule A and Rule B which are moving into some language. Rule A is the older rule while Rule B is the newer. Under these conditions we would anticipate that the implication-cum-variation chart would be consistent with the frequency chart, as they are in Figure 8. Capital N indicates a higher frequency of application than lower-case n.

FIGURE 8. Frequency and implicational patterns before acceleration.

| 8a. Frequency pattern | | | 8b. Implicational pattern | | |
| | Rule | | | Rule | |
Lects	A	B	Lects	A	B
1	1	N	1	1	x
2	N	n	2	x	x
3	n	0	3	x	0
4	0	0	4	0	0

Suppose, however, that in Lect 2, in which both rules are still variable, Rule B accelerates past Rule A, a not uncommon phenomenon. The acceleration is too late to have any effect on Lect 1, in which one rule is already categorical, and is too early to affect Lects 3 and 4, in which one or both rules have yet to appear. At this stage, there would be a conflict between the frequency chart, Figure 9a, and the implicational chart, Figure 9b. At this stage, the implicational pattern, Figure 9b, is still neat, but the frequency table, Figure 9a, is out of order in Lect 2. A situation like this could well be taken as an indication that frequency patterns are not relevant to linguistic analysis, but nothing could be further from the truth. The slightly messy pattern in Figure 9a is the harbinger of things to come. Eventually, the two tables will be in harmony again. Lect 1 will develop a categorical version of Rule B, Rule B will

FIGURE 9.   Frequency and implicational patterns at incipient acceleration.

9a. Frequency pattern	Rule		9b. Implicational pattern	Rule	
Lects	A	B	Lects	A	B
1	1	<u>N</u>	1	1	x
2	N	<u>N</u>	2	x	x
3	<u>n</u>	0	3	x	0
4	0	0	4	0	0

become categorical before Rule A in Lect 2, Lect 3 will gain Rule B at a greater output frequency than it has for Rule A and Lect 4 will gain the newer rule, Rule B <u>before</u> the older rule, Rule A. At that time, the situation will be as in Figure 10.

FIGURE 10.   Frequency and implicational patterns after acceleration.

10a. Frequency pattern	Rule		10b. Implicational pattern	Rule	
Lects	B	A	Lects	B	A
1	1	1	1	1	1
2	1	N	2	1	x
3	N	n	3	x	x
4	n	0	4	x	0
5	0	0	5	0	0

A totally analogous pattern can be discovered within rules. In this instance, we have available a documented case of environmental feature acceleration (called 'reweighting' by Bailey Ms) which we can use to illustrate the pattern. In a number of American English lects, the vowel of <u>bad</u> is being raised to the level of <u>bed</u>, and simultaneously acquiring a pronounced centering off-glide, differentially according to linguistic environment. In New York City, the change apparently started before obstruents and then spread to position before nasals (Labov 1972:140-64). That is, the vowel in <u>pad</u> and <u>pass</u> was raised prior to the vowel in <u>pan</u>. At this point, one would expect the situation to be as in Figure 11.

FIGURE 11. Frequency and implicational patterns before intra-
rule acceleration (reweighting).

| 11a. | Frequency pattern | | 11b. | Implicational pattern | |
| | Foll. Env. | | | Foll. Env. | |
Lects	Ob	N	Lects	Ob	N
1	1	N	1	1	x
2	N	n	2	x	x
3	n	0	3	x	0
4	0	0	4	0	0

Here, the frequency chart and the implicational chart are in harmony.
At some point in time, however, the nasal environment accelerated,
or reweighted, past the obstruent environment.[2] At first, this
acceleration is only relevant for Lect 2, in which the raising rule
is variable in both environments. The acceleration comes too late
for Lect 1, which has categorical raising before obstruents and too
early for Lects 3 and 4, which do not yet have raising before nasals.
At this point, the frequency chart and the implicational chart are in
disharmony, with the disorder in Lect 2 the indication of things to
come, as in Figure 12.

FIGURE 12. Frequency and implicational patterns at incipient
intra-rule acceleration (reweighting).

| 12a. | Frequency pattern | | 12b. | Implicational pattern | |
| | Foll. Env. | | | Foll. Env. | |
Lects	Ob	N	Lects	Ob	N
1	1	<u>N</u>	1	1	x
2	N	<u>N</u>	2	x	x
3	<u>n</u>	0	3	x	0
4	<u>0</u>	0	4	0	0

At this stage, vowel raising has greater output in all environments
than it had in Figure 11, but in Lect 2 before nasals, the output is
phenomenally greater (indicated in Figure 12a by a change from n to
<u>N</u>) and outstrips the increase in output before obstruents (we retain
the symbol N in Figure 12a, but understand that it has somewhat
higher numerical value in 12a than in 11a).

The strict implicational chart in Figure 12b, since it is not designed to handle frequency differences, cannot reflect the incipient
acceleration and still shows the older situation. As in the inter-rule
case, the disharmony between the two displays will disappear as the
acceleration takes hold. Eventually, Lect 1 will develop a categorical rule in both environments, the rule will become categorical in
Lect 2 before nasals while remaining variable before obstruents,
vowel raising will begin in Lect 3 before nasals, but at <u>higher</u> frequency levels than before obstruents, and Lect 4 will gain the rule
before nasals prior to gaining it before obstruents. The situation
is illustrated in Figure 13.

FIGURE 13. Frequency and implicational patterns after intra-
rule acceleration (reweighting).

13a. Frequency pattern Foll. Env.			13b. Implicational pattern Foll. Env.		
Lects	N	Ob	Lects	N	Ob
1	1	1	1	1	1
2	1	<u>N</u>	2	1	x
3	N	n	3	x	x
4	n	0	4	x	0
5	0	0	5	0	0

During the reweighting process, output frequencies will run
counter to what would be predicted by the lateness of the rule.
Later this will rectify itself, since the raising rule will move on to
new lects before nasals prior to before obstruents, in harmony with
the new output frequency differences. But throughout the whole
process, the concept of more or less, which we propose is in competence, will give the correct results. In Figure 9a, speakers of Lect
2 perceive Rule B as more favored (in some sense) than Rule A,
hence will produce a higher output of Rule B in spite of its recency.
In Figure 8a, Rule A was more favored than Rule B in Lect 2. In
Lect 1, Rule A is categorical, so presumably it has lost social significance. In the case of the vowel raising rule, Lect 2 in Figure 11a
has a variable rule with obstruent as the alpha constraint and nasal
as the beta constraint. In Figure 12a, the lect has nasal as the alpha
constraint and obstruent as the beta. Since speakers of the lect are
competent to produce higher outputs when alpha constraints are present than when they are not, no matter what the alpha constraint is
nor what its historical provenience, the concept of more or less
handles the situation at all stages with no trouble at all.

In summary, we assume that acceleration, on either an inter-
rule or intra-rule basis, proceeds according to the general pattern
of Figures 14-16. In these figures, we have introduced hypothetical
numbers into the frequency tables in the hope that this will make the
point clearer.

FIGURE 14. Hypothetical frequency and implication patterns
before acceleration.

14a. Frequency pattern			14b. Implicational pattern		
Lects	Old rule/env	New rule/env	Lects	Old rule/env	New rule/env
1	1.00	.80	1	1	x
2	.60	.40	2	x	x
3	.20	.00	3	x	0
4	.00	.00	4	0	0

FIGURE 15. Hypothetical frequency and implicational patterns
at incipient acceleration.

15a. Frequency pattern			15b. Implicational pattern		
Lects	Old rule/env	Accelerating new rule/env	Lects	Old rule/env	Accelerating new rule/env
1	1.00	.85	1	1	x
2	.65	.75	2	x	x
3	.25	.00	3	x	0
4	.00	.00	4	0	0

FIGURE 16. Frequency and implicational patterns after acceleration.

16a. Frequency pattern			16b. Implicational pattern		
Lects	Accelerated new rule/env	Old rule/env	Lects	Accelerated new rule/env	Old rule/env
1	1.00	1.00	1	1	1
2	1.00	.70	2	1	x
3	.40	.25	3	x	x
4	.20	.00	4	x	0
5	.00	.00	5	0	0

Another situation--one related in a sense to acceleration--in
which the concept of earlier-later proves inadequate as a competence
principle, is the case of stagnant variable rules. Stagnant rules are
rules which become arrested at the variable stage. They are significant social markers, but are not significant as indicators of change.
There are several celebrated cases of stagnant rules in English.
Perhaps the best known one is the variation among the fricative, stop
and affricative pronunciations of the dental fricatives spelled th. This
variability, with the same social significance which it bears today,
has been in American English for not less than three-quarters of a
century and probably much longer. The intra-rule variation of th
can be neatly captured by a variable rule with its attendant assumption
of more or less in competence, but the question of in which environment the rule began is surely irrelevant for present-day English lects.
With respect to inter-rule relationships, as would be the case with a
man running on a treadmill on a track during the running of a 1,000
meter race; the variable th rule must have been passed by many variable rules that were really going someplace. Viewed from the intra-
rule perspective and inter-rule one, the concept of more or less is
far more plausible than the concept of earlier or later in accounting
for stagnant rules.

In a third situation newer rules typically have larger outputs than
older rules. This is the case of rule inhibition, in which the forces
of language change are leading to the inhibition of a rule in the variable stage. Labov (1966) has shown that the desulcalization ('deletion') of post-vocalic /r/ began to become inhibited after World
War II in New York City. Before then, desulcalization was favored
and advancing. Since then, desulcalization has been undergoing
inhibition with the result that the sulcal pronunciation is becoming
more frequent. Deletion rules in decreolization in which a creole
gradually merges with one of the languages of its admixture is an
interesting and typical example of rule inhibition. In such cases, a
creole basilect which has, in some environments, categorical deletion of an item which is never deleted in the standard acrolect,
can be expected to replace the categorical deletion with a variable
deletion rule as decreolization begins. At first, the new variable
rule will have a very large output, i.e. a large proportion of deletions. As decreolization proceeds, the variable rule will have
ever smaller outputs until, as the creole merges with the acrolect,
the rule is lost altogether. Something of the sort must have happened
in the decreolization of the North American slave creole in contact
with standard American English with respect to the deletion of is.
Figure 17 shows the putative creole basilect as the first lect, the
post-creole mesolects in the middle, and the standard acrolect at
the bottom. [3] It is probably possible to find all the mesolects (as

well as the acrolect and possibly even the basilect) in the American black community. Lect 2 would be quite conceivable as the casual style of pre-adolescent street culture members, while Lect 6 is believable as the moderately casual style of lower middle-class adults. The others fall in between. The point is that the historically earliest lects have the highest output level, measured in frequency of deletion, while the most recent ones have the lowest output level. This is the reverse of what would be predicted by the hypothesis in the Lectological Newsletter question. Nevertheless, if more and less is assumed to be a competence principle, Figure 17 would be predicted quite neatly on the basis of a variable deletion rule in which the progressive verb environment outranks the noun phrase environment.

FIGURE 17. Decreolization of is absence: North American Slave Creole via Black English to Standard English.

Lects		Environments	
		__Ving	__NP
1	basilect	1	1
2		1	N
3		N	N
4	mesolects	N	n
5		n	n
6		n	0
7	acrolect	0	0

There is an apparent problem in connection with replacing earlier-later with more-less, however. Suppose two rules have variable outputs, one 5 per cent and the other 95 per cent. One could not always conclude that the 95 per cent rule was the older one and the 5 per cent one the newer. If both the rules are undergoing inhibition, the reverse would be true. If the 95 per cent rule were undergoing inhibition but the 5 per cent rule was moving into the language, then both are new rules; if expansion and inhibition were associated with the two rules in the reverse order, they are both old rules. Unless the members of the speech community knew which was older and which was newer, or at least which were expanding and which were undergoing inhibition, they would have no way of knowing how the change was to be carried on. Since changes commonly take place over several generations, presumably new members of the community move into awareness of changes while rules are in variable stages with no personal recollection of which ones started before which others. But it really is not necessary to assume that speakers have earlier-later or inhibition-expansion knowledge about rules directly. As Labov (1965) has proposed, it seems that language changes in progress are 'embedded' in a social milieu. The lects identified by numbers in the figures in this paper are not distributed randomly; they are associated with age, class, ethnicity, style, and other social factors. An individual speaker will thus unconsciously expand or inhibit a variable rule in his speech based on what the members of the group he is or wishes to be identified with are doing with the rule. For example, if an individual is a young adult, white, middle-class male and he perceives that the highest outputs of a certain rule are to be observed in the formal style of the older members of the more privileged classes and his own age, sex, and class group have much lower outputs, he will tend to inhibit the rule in his own casual speech in accordance of the practices of his own group. On the other hand, if he notices that the feature has been until recently associated with lower classes than his own or with an oppressed ethnic minority but that members of his age and class are adopting and increasing their use of the feature in casual speech although it is avoided by members of higher classes than his own, by older and female members of his own class, and even by his peers in formal styles, he will adopt and increase the usage in his own casual speech. The motivation, in other words, for increasing or inhibiting a rule does not come from a knowledge of earlier-later, but from a knowledge of who in the society is expanding or inhibiting the rule.

It is also quite possible to argue that the notion that more and less as a competence principle is only a rather slight extension of what all linguists already accept as part of competence. The categorical rule, Rule 2, predicts the operation of a linguistic rule on the basis of an environment:

Rule 2: $C \rightarrow \emptyset \ / \ C\_\_$

The rule says that a consonant will always be deleted if and only if it follows a consonant. Looked at in another way, the preceding consonant environment promotes the operation of the rule to the ultimate degree, i.e. categorically. A preceding vowel favors operation of the rule to a lesser degree; in fact, to the ultimately lesser degree; it inhibits the rule completely. But the variable rule, Rule 3, is very similar, except that always and never have been replaced by more and less:

Rule 3: $C \longrightarrow (\emptyset) \ / \ A \ (C)$
                              $B \ (V)\_\_$

This variable rule says, similarly to the categorical rule, that a preceding consonant promotes the operation of the rule more than does the vowel, but not to the ultimate degree. The presence of a preceding vowel favors the rule less than does the preceding consonant, but not ultimately less. Put in slightly different terms, always is simply the limiting case of more frequent and never is similarly the limiting case of less frequent. Since everyone agrees that always and never are part of competence anyway, the extension to more and less frequent seems a rather slight one. In any event, it is not an entirely new principle as the earlier-later principle would be, even if it worked.

NOTES

[1]I have taken some liberties with the formulation of the constraints compared with the way in which Wolfram originally formulated them. I am convinced that my version of the constraints would produce the same pattern that Wolfram found.

[2]Actually the situation is considerably more complicated than this. Originally, the obstruent environment was further differentiated between following voiced stop and following fricative, with raising occurring before fricatives prior to before voiced stops. Voiced stops accelerated over fricatives at the same time that nasals accelerated over both kinds of obstruents, so that the situation goes from fricatives over voiced stops over nasals to nasals over voiced stops over fricatives. Later the order between fricatives and voiced stops reweights again so that the final stage has nasals over fricatives over voiced stops (Labov 1972:150).

[3]There are many more factors entering into the decreolization of is deletion than are mentioned here. There are several environments, not just two, that affected deletion. Furthermore, the decreolization of is deletion intersected with other decreolization factors such as the acquisition of tense, the acquisition of person-number concord forms of to be, and the acquisition of the acrolectal contraction rule. The contraction rule, at one late mesolect stage, reordered with the creole deletion rule at which point the deletion rule became phonological instead of syntactic. For further discussion, see Fasold Ms and also Bickerton (1973).

REFERENCES

Bailey, Charles-James N. (To appear.) Variation and linguistic theory.

Bickerton, Derek. 1973. The structure of polylectal grammars. In: Georgetown University Monograph Series in Languages and Linguistics, Monograph 25. Ed. by Roger W. Shuy. Washington, D. C., Georgetown University Press.

DeCamp, David. 1971. Toward a generative analysis of a post-creole speech continuum. In: Pidginization and creolization of languages. Ed. by Dell Hymes. Cambridge, Cambridge University Press.

Fasold, Ralph. Ms. Decreolization and autonomous language change. To appear in: Black dialect and the history of English. Ed. by William A. Stewart. Special anthology issue of the Florida FL Reporter.

Labov, William. 1965. On the mechanism of linguistic change. In: Georgetown University Monograph Series in Languages and Linguistics, Monograph 18. Washington, D. C., Georgetown University Press.

_____. 1966. The social stratification of English in New York City. Washington, D. C., Center for Applied Linguistics.

_____. 1972. The internal evolution of linguistic rules. In: Linguistic change and generative theory. Ed. by Robert Stockwell and R. K. S. MacCaulay. Bloomington, Indiana University Press.

Lectological Newsletter, No. 1. 1972. Washington, D. C., Georgetown University Sociolinguistics Program.

Wolfram, Walter A. 1969. A sociolinguistic description of Detroit Negro speech. Washington, D. C., Center for Applied Linguistics.

A STUDY IN DIALECT:
INDIVIDUAL VARIATION
AND DIALECT RULES

LYN KYPRIOTAKI

Temple University

1. Introduction. The purpose of this study is to expose the in-adequacy of the term 'dialect' when it is interpreted to mean a select set of features.

The specification of any one feature is questionable on two grounds: (1) if individuals vary on one feature in a rule-governed way, as Labov (1969) has demonstrated, neither their competence nor their performance is being accounted for should this variation arise from the application of differing rules; and (2) the rules themselves are questionable in form, because they obscure differences in individual behaviors and thus fail to reflect or predict the actual behavior of a real speaker.

2. The experiment.[1] Eighty native Philadelphia speakers of varying age, sex, race, and education were tested for their pattern of syllable dropping when forming adverbs and adjectives of the shape /iy/ after roots ending in unstressed /Cul/, where C stands for any English consonant. The probe sought to determine whether the in-formant, given the form /éybul/, would produce /éybɨliy/ (no syllable dropping) or /éybliy/ (syllable dropping). Given the form /páršul/, would the subject produce /páršɨliy/ (no syllable dropping) or /páršliy/ (syllable dropping)? The biggest question was, how would the results relate to current models of variation within dialect?

3. The theory. My earlier studies dealing with Black English plural formations in Philadelphia suggested the presence of a staggering amount of variation. This variation had not been taken into account in other descriptions of this dialect which have appeared in the literature, such as those by McDavid (1967), Labov (1968), Baratz (1969), Wolfram (1969), Fickett (1970), and Fasold and Wolfram (1970). Rather than plunge into an emotionally charged issue such as Black English, I sought to explore the phenomenon of variation in a feature of speech to which speaker/hearers are indifferent. I deliberately selected for study a feature which carries no social significance whatsoever, yet indicates patterns which reappear in other morphological formations such as the comparative /éybul/, /éybɨlər/ or /éyblər/). The assumption was that speakers would be less self-conscious about such a feature, and more easily misled as to the real aspect of language being studied.

In contrast to present models of dialect, that at best allow for individual variation which is statistically predictable for one feature in a given environment, such as Labov (1969), I expected wide variation among my speakers: variation which would not correlate with age, sex, education, or race. I predicted, furthermore, that in order to describe the behavior of each speaker, different rules would have to be written (or a different ordering of the same rules). If syllable dropping proved to be systematic, as I hypothesized, rather than random, it would be awkward to attribute these differences in rule to idiolect. Finally, I predicted that if I took the body of eighty speakers as a community or dialect and drew up rules to represent their pattern as a whole for syllable dropping, the resulting rules would not correspond to the actual rules of any single speaker.[2]

Syllable dropping, for most speakers, is an option, a possible but not obligatory variation of the full form. These variations, as will be shown, occur in patterns within the speech of the individual. For example, a speaker may frequently drop syllables after voiceless stops, but sometimes drop them and sometimes retain them after voiced stops. These patterns of variation must also be accounted for in a description of the language community as a whole, yet current theory provides no way to do so.

4. The method. The first step in the study was to determine whether a written test could be used to explore syllable dropping without distorting the resulting data. In fourteen probe tests oral and graphic forms were tried. Since no apparent distortion emerged when a written test was employed, the present form was selected for its economy and ease of use.

A list was drawn up of fifty-one words, selected so as to contain final syllables commencing with each of the English consonants, to vary in terms of stress, and to differ in the placement of morpheme boundary. Where no real words existed that fit the patterns required, invented words were used, such as antiboastally and mentholly.

The words were controlled for three types of stress pattern: (1) two syllable stems of the shape stress followed by unstress, as in able, evil; (2) stems of three or more syllables ending with a stress followed by unstress, as in unregal, abysmal; and (3) stems of three or more syllables ending with two minimal stresses, as in impossible, wonderful. It developed in the course of the study that the first two types pattern identically.

Morpheme boundary placement proved a difficult concept and represents an area where further study is needed. Proceeding along the lines of traditional morphemic analysis, as in Hill (1958) or Gleason (1961), I considered the 'ible' in impossible as different from the 'le' in drizzle, in that the former has a clear meaning whereas the latter does not. Problems arose immediately. Is the 'al' in illegal a morpheme? It seems to depend upon one's competence in Latin. I shall return to this question below.

The words were then divided and ordered at random into two tests, Test A and Test B, in an attempt to control for ordering effects. Each of our subjects took one of the two tests. Subjects were presented with an instruction sheet (naturally, as misleading as possible), which read as follows:

> This questionnaire is being given to determine the acceptability and unacceptability of certain English sentence patterns. All you are requested to do is to read both sentences in each set and to read them aloud. Then please reread the sentence you prefer. You may prefer any sentence for any reason you want. However, you must choose in each case. In order to eliminate any interference on the part of the interviewer, he or she may not answer any questions.

The subject was then handed one of the two tests. The sentences contained the same words, but the /iy/ form appeared in different positions in the sentences. For example:

Cinderella had prickly hair.
Cinderella had hair that was prickly. (Test A, number 15)

Immorally sexy people seem happy.
Sexy people seem immorally happy. (Test B, number 3)

The untruthfully judging judge judged Laura's fudge.
The judging judge judged untruthfully Laura's fudge. (Test B,
   number 6)

Wiggly walking women are noticed.
Women walking wiggly are noticed. (Test B, number 15)

The informant read these two sentences aloud, then read aloud the
version he preferred. Thus the interviewer heard the /iy/ form three
times. Whenever variation was observed, after the subject had completed the test he was asked to repeat that item. On the score sheets,
we recorded a plus for a maintained syllable and a minus for a dropped
syllable. The occurrence of both versions, a maintained and a
dropped syllable for the same lexical item, was noted as a variation
in the later tabulations.

Not one subject discovered our actual purpose, though several
chortled over some of the sentences or responded negatively to the
invented words. Unfutilely caused particular resentment.

When all subjects had been tested, rules were drawn up to account
for the deletion behavior displayed by each. Then the fifty-one words
were transcribed onto three-by-five cards and the totals for each
word recorded on the card: how many speakers kept, deleted, or
varied with that particular word. From these results rules were
drawn up for the total community. The words were listed in a descending arrangement of syllable retention. Percentages for syllable
retention, drop, and variation for each lexical item are shown in
Table 1 (pp. 205-06). The table proved most confusing when compared with the rules created to describe the behavior of the individual
speakers. It is very revealing, however, for a description of English as a language in the process of change.

5. The results. Our first problem arose in recording the results.
After hours of listening together and comparing our results, Bob
Hobbs and I still sometimes disagreed on the presence or absence of
the syllable. Repeated listening did not alter our firm but differing
convictions. Nevertheless, we believe that this difficulty did not
significantly skew the results of the experiment, because the greatest
variation occurs in precisely those words where determining the
presence of the schwa was most uncertain. Furthermore, since
deletions and variations were finally tabulated together, our differences of opinion made no difference either to the rules for the individual or to those for the language community.

Of the eighty speakers tested, no two individuals displayed
identical behavior, though in drawing up rules to describe the deletions observed, this fact is obscured. For example, speaker B220

deleted in the forms examply, ably, and bemuddly, and varied on prickly, and was therefore assigned rule R5 (deletion occurs after stops). Speaker B33 deleted in examply, and tittly (made-up words), and varied in his pronunciation of ably, wobbly, bemuddly, unfickly, squiggly, and wiggly. The same rule R5 expresses the generality of his behavior, while not taking into account his differences from speaker B220. An extreme example of how the rules fail to represent behavioral differences is provided by speaker B204, who in all instances deleted after stops (but, unfortunately, found unfickly unacceptable and refused to read it at all). These three speakers, whose realized behaviors are so different, are grouped together as instances of rule R5.

Several other major problems were encountered in writing the rules. One difficulty arose when considering speakers who not only failed to conform to patterns that had appeared in looking at the entire community, but who contradicted those patterns. For example, all speakers displayed syllable deletion after voiceless stops, and an implicational rule emerged that if voiced stops allowed deletion, voiceless stops did also. A similar pattern emerged for the sibilants: a speaker who deleted after /z/ also allowed deletion after /s/. However, implicational rules involving place of articulation were less wieldy. The alveolar sibilants /s/ and /z/ clearly favored deletion above other fricatives, but there were six speakers who deleted the vowel in //FULL// in such words as carefully and untruthfully, but who did not delete after other fricatives. The scorings for the community showed how unusual this was: forty-one of our eighty speakers deleted after the alveolar sibilants but not after the other fricatives. (The remaining thirty-three speakers either deleted only after stops or after both slit and groove fricatives.)

An even clearer case of how a few speakers may deviate from widely held rules appears with rule G4, which restricts deletion after alveolar stops. There is outside justification for this rule, since /t/ and /d/ are exceptional elsewhere in English, as in the past tense of regular verbs, where they alone require the addition of an extra syllable. Forty speakers, or half our community, clearly applied rule G4. Of the remaining forty, thirty-seven deleted after fricatives as well as after all stops, indicating that their deletion rule had become considerably generalized. Only three speakers deleted after all stops (thus indicating that they did not have rule G4) but never after any other consonants.

The evidence clearly suggests that most speakers first generalize the option to delete to include deletion after some fricatives as well as stops, while retaining rule G4. Only when deletion has become possible after consonants widely disparate in terms of place and manner of articulation is the generalization extended to the alveolar stops. The three deviant speakers attach less importance to rule G4; they have generalized the deletion option to all stops before extending it to the fricatives. This suggests that in some sense these speakers possess a different competence from the rest. At present, there is no way to provide for discrepancies like this in rules for the community.

The fact that half our speakers lacked rule G4 means that this rule must be interpreted as plus or minus present: a fact which, as will be shown, has a considerable effect on the rules if they are formulated mathematically.

It was not always obvious which rules were operating. For example, speaker A8 deleted in <u>impossibly</u> and <u>prickly</u>, but not in <u>purply</u>, <u>amply</u>, <u>unstably</u>, <u>unfutilely</u>, <u>unboastally</u>, <u>cuddly</u>, <u>locally</u>, <u>unregally</u>, or <u>illegally</u>. Given the limited evidence, should rule G4 be considered present or absent?

One of the most interesting findings proved to be that linguistic rules do not equal logical rules. Several speakers deleted only after labial stops; several speakers deleted only after velar stops. Logically, but not linguistically, this is equivalent to the combination of rules in which all stops allow deletion and alveolars restrict deletion (rule G4). This point will be mentioned again when I try to account for the possibilities available to individuals, given the dialect of the community.

6. The rules of the community.

6.1. General community rules. With an eye towards making the situation readily understandable and a fine disregard for linguistic conventions of rule writing, the overall rules can be expressed by the following generalizations:

G1. <u>Finally</u>, as a single lexical item, contains deletion
G2. There is no deletion after resonants
G3. Stems of stress type three delete the final syllable
G4. Deletion is blocked after the alveolar stops

These generalities, a mixture of yes's and no's, are intended to be ordered. Not one speaker deleted in <u>unfunctionally</u>, even though the stem is stress type three, because deletion after resonants is blocked by rule G2. Rules G1 through G4 might be said to reflect the competence of the speakers in this dialect community, but they in fact do not correspond to the rules or the orderings held by individual speakers, as was exemplified in the discussion of the three speakers who reversed the ordering of rules G4 and G2.

6.2. Linguistic community rules. The following is an attempt to present the possibilities for the community as discovered from studying the language behavior of the individual speakers who comprise its dialect membership. Multiple difficulties encumber this description; I shall discuss them below:

R1. Finally, as a single lexical item, permits deletion
R2. Deletion occurs after labial stops
R3. Deletion occurs after velar stops
R4. Deletion occurs after voiceless stops
R5. Deletion occurs after stops
R6. Deletion occurs after /s/
R7. Deletion occurs after /z/
R8. Deletion occurs after the alveolar sibilants
R9. Deletion occurs after voiceless sibilants
R10. Deletion occurs after sibilants
R11. Deletion occurs after voiceless fricatives
R12. Deletion occurs after stops and fricatives
R13. Deletion occurs in the final syllable of stems of stress type three
R14. The vowel may be deleted in all unstressed syllables of the shape /Cul/

Notice that rule R1 depends on the individual lexical item rather than on its phonological shape; lexical dependence has been shown elsewhere in other, more general studies of syllable deletion (Kypriotaki 1972a, b). Rule R13 relates to stress pattern rather than to consonant type.

While these rules accurately represent the possibilities for all speakers, they in no way show which set of rules the individual speaker selects.

6.3. Mathematical community rules. If we take the fourteen R rules listed above to represent the possibilities for speakers of this community, or this dialect, and assume the rules to be independent (which is not precisely the case), the total possibilities for different rule-governed behavior would be 3×2^{13}. This number is so large that we have neither a predictive nor a descriptive analysis of syllable dropping for this group. Since some of the rules are mathematically equivalent (for example, the presence of both R6 and R7 in any one speaker is the same as the presence of R8), the above analysis is suggestive rather than exact.

While the precise number of possible behaviors is not important here, it is clear that given this system of analysis, the number of alternate conforming behaviors is too vast to be meaningful in any consideration of dialect.

6.4. Implicational community rules. Because no speakers were noted who deleted after fricatives but not after stops, or who deleted after voiced consonants of a general type but not after the corresponding voiceless consonants, implicational rules may be usefully considered. The information to be gleaned from implicational rules in this case corresponds neatly to the implications observed when the words tested are arranged in descending statistical order of syllable retention (Table 1). The figures represent percentages.

TABLE 1.

	Plus	Minus	Vary
Group I Predominant keep			
Illegal	100.0		
Unfunctional	100.0		
Rival	100.0		
Unregal	100.0		
Unfutile	100.0		
Dismal	100.0		
Camel	100.0		
Immoral	100.0		
Oral	97.6		2.4
Menthol	97.6		2.4
Local	97.6		2.4
Abysmal	97.6		2.4
Unboastal	97.6	2.4	
Lethal	97.4		2.6
Atonal	97.4		2.6
Universal	97.4		2.6
Evil	97.4	2.6	
Trustful	95.2		4.8
Bedevil	95.2	2.4	2.4
Hostile	94.8	5.2	
Group II Language trend towards drop			
Commercial	88.1	7.1	4.8
Antiberthal	86.9	2.6	10.5
Reversal	84.2	5.3	10.5

TABLE 1. Continued

	Plus	Minus	Vary
Group II Continued			
Untruthful	81.6	5.3	13.1
Partial	78.6	9.5	11.9
Careful	69.1	11.9	19.0
Drizzle	66.7	21.4	11.9
Bemuddle	65.8	13.1	21.1
Bedazzle	61.9	16.7	21.4
Tittle	60.5	26.3	13.2
Group III Predominant vary			
Purple	52.4	13.2	33.4
Cuddle	50.5	28.6	20.4
Wobble	47.3	31.6	21.1
Unstable	45.2	26.2	28.6
Impossible	42.9	47.6	9.5
Ample	42.9	45.2	11.9
Wiggle	42.1	23.7	34.2
Unfickle	42.1	23.7	34.2
Able	39.5	34.2	26.3
Final	38.1	42.8	19.1
Squiggle	34.2	36.8	29.0
Whistle	32.4	50.0	16.6
Group IV Predominant drop			
Wonderful	23.7	50.0	26.3
Journalistic	21.1	68.4	10.5
Bristle	16.7	64.3	19.0
Example	10.5	57.9	31.6
Prickle	4.8	73.8	21.4

All instances of nasal and lateral tested, with the single exception of the lexical item finally, fall into Group I, in which syllables are always or nearly always kept. Three of the six stems containing final syllables beginning with alveolar stops also appear. Two of the three remaining instances of alveolar stops and most of the slit fricatives are found in Group II, in which syllables are usually kept. The voiced stops, a number of voiceless stops, and finally are found in Group III, which tends strongly towards variation. The voiceless alveolar sibilant /s/ and further instances of voiceless stops appear in Group IV, in which syllables are predominantly dropped.

The most awkward discrepancy in this table involves the words universal (Group I), reversal (Group II), and whistle and bristle (Groups III and IV respectively). Why are these syllables with /s/ treated so differently? Of the four speakers who dropped the syllable in reversally, two were asked to identify the stem. Both subjects replied that reverse was the base form. In fact it was reversal. The test sentence

First 'yes' then 'no' she answered reversally.
First 'yes' then 'no' she reversally answered. (Test B, number 21)

did not make sense, and possibly this example should be eliminated. The difficulty remains: what is the difference between universally and bristly? Or why, when Group IV is bursting with voiceless stops, does locally appear in Group I?

Two explanations present themselves and at the present time I do not see a way to formulate a test that will discriminate between them. It was mentioned at the outset of this paper that the morphemic boundary analysis proved too complex to resolve. Notice that, with the exception of finally, a lexical item, only those words which are spelled with final 'al' appear in Groups I and II, whereas in the last two groups the sounds in question are followed by spelled 'le'. Does the statistical grouping result from a spelling fact or from a morphological one? The final 'al' of local and illegal are perhaps felt to be more strongly present because of such forms as locality and illegality; drizzle and bristle have no corresponding forms *drizzelity or *bristelity. The spelling convention here mirrors a historical fact in English, and I do not see how to establish whether spelling or the underlying morphology is the controlling factor.

Another question which arises from a study of Table 1 involves stems ending in //FULL//. Four words of this type were tested: trustful, untruthful, careful, and wonderful. Of these, trustful retains the schwa 95.2 per cent of the time, untruthful 81.6 per cent, careful 69.1 per cent, and wonderful 23.7 per cent. The high frequency of deletion in wonderfully is readily accounted for in that wonderful belongs to stress type three and is thus subject to rule R13. The difference in treatment of the other three words is a mystery. Perhaps certain consonant clusters block deletion, such as the -stf- in trustfully.

The display in Table 1 strongly suggests that syllable dropping started with the voiceless stops, spread to the voiced stops, and is proceeding to the fricatives by way of the voiceless sibilants. What we have here is a picture of a language in process, language in a state of change. However, this is not a description of dialect. It describes neither the speech of any individual, nor the patterned variance which might be said to comprise the dialect of the community as a whole.

6.5. Foreigners' rules. In addition to our eighty native speakers, thirteen foreigners were tested for their pattern of syllable dropping, on the hypothesis that their rules would substantially differ. Of the thirteen, three lacked rule G4, eight lacked rule R13, and one (who had been here only two months and had never studied English) lacked rule G2 (the widespread rule which blocks deletion after resonants). The remaining two speakers were indistinguishable from native Americans. One, a twenty-seven-year-old Ukranian, had studied English for twenty-three years and been in this country for sixteen years. The other, a twenty-six-year-old Italian, never studied English, but had spoken English for fifteen and a half years and come here as a ten-year-old.

Thus the expected result was obtained: foreigners with little experience in English failed to use the rules commonly found for English speakers. Furthermore, the implicational rules discussed above did not apply; eleven of the foreigners clearly contradicted them.

7. Conclusions. The data from this experiment support what observers of child language have long claimed (for example, Bellugi and Brown 1964): speakers arrive at similar forms through the application of differing rules. If enough instances of a particular feature are observed, two speakers will, as a result of their differing grammars, produce dissimilar forms. In a feature such as the /ly/ formation, to which no status markers are attached, speakers are normally unaware of the discrepancies and simply do not hear that they are pronouncing the same word differently. However, if we extrapolate from the results of this experiment and assume that (1) individual speakers vary in a rule-governed way as to which forms they produce; and (2) speakers in a language community differ among themselves in many grammatical as well as phonological forms; then two results follow.

First, the term 'dialect' as it is presently employed is inadequate in that it fails to account for the extensive, patterned variations which occur both within the speech of an individual and within that of a language community. Dialect as a concept must be expanded to include the patterned variations a speaker produces and the even wider range of such variations which he accepts as part of the same dialect.

Second, before using Dialect Readers such as those advocated by Baratz, Stewart, and others for Black English speakers, which are based on a specific set of features, we need a much closer definition of 'dialect' and of 'feature'. Also, bilingual reading and testing programs such as those presently being employed in New York City and California are based upon a fictional set of features, which will not correspond to the actual speech behavior of most of the individual students most of the time, and may in fact not correspond to the behavior of a single one of them at any time.

NOTES

[1] In conducting this experiment, I had the creative and tireless assistance of Robert Hobbs, a senior in Linguistics at Temple University. He invented most of our test sentences and interviewed well over half the informants.

[2] A study of this type dealing with two speakers was presented by Barbara Robson in a paper entitled 'Community versus individual competence: English /h/ in Jamaican Creole', at the Linguistic Society of America Meeting, St. Louis, December 1971.

REFERENCES

Baratz, Joan. 1969. Language and cognitive assessment of Negro children: Assumptions and research needs. ASHA.

Bellugi, Ursula and Roger Brown. 1964. Three processes in the child's acquisition of syntax. HER. 34(2).133-51.

Butters, Ronald. 1971. Dialect variants and linguistic deviance. FL.200-19.

_____. 1971. On the notion 'rule of grammar' in dialectology. Papers from the Seventh Regional Meeting. Chicago, Chicago Linguistic Society. 307-15.

DeCamp, David. 1969. Is a sociolinguistic theory possible? Georgetown University Monograph Series on Languages and Linguistics, Number 22. Washington, D.C., Georgetown University Press. 157-83.

Fasold, Ralph and Walter Wolfram. 1970. Some linguistic features of Negro dialect. In: Teaching Standard English in the inner city. Ed. by Fasold and Shuy. Washington, D.C., Center for Applied Linguistics. 41-86.

Fickett, Joan G. 1970. Aspects of morphemics, syntax, and semology of an inner-city dialect: Merican. New York, Meadowood Publications.

Friends. 1970. Washington, D. C., Education Study Center.
Gleason, Henry A. 1961. An introduction to descriptive linguistics.
Rev. ed. New York, Holt, Rinehart and Winston.
Hill, Archibald A. 1958. Introduction to linguistic structures.
New York, Harcourt, Brace and World.
Houston, Susan. 1970. Competence and performance in Child Black
English. Language Sciences. 12.9-14.
Kypriotaki, Lyn. 1972a. Initial syllable deletion in rapid English
speech. Paper presented at the Kentucky Foreign Language Con-
ference. Lexington, April.
_____. 1972b. Aphaeresis in rapid speech. Forthcoming in
American Speech.
Labov, William. 1969. Contraction, deletion, and inherent vari-
ability of the English copula. Language. 45.715-62.
_____, Paul Cohen, Clarence Robins, and John Lewis. 1968. A
study of the non-standard English of Negro and Puerto Rican
speakers in New York City. Vol. I. New York, Columbia Uni-
versity.
McDavid, Raven I., Jr. 1967. A checklist of significant features
for discriminating social dialects. In: Dimensions of dialect.
Ed. by E. L. Evertts. NCTE. 9.
Old Tales. 1970. Washington, D. C., Education Study Center.
Ollie. 1970. Washington, D. C., Education Study Center.
Robson, Barbara. 1971. Community versus individual competence:
English /h/ in Jamaican Creole. Paper presented at the Lin-
guistic Society of America Meeting. St. Louis, December.
Weinreich, Uriel, William Labov, and Marvin Herzog. 1968.
Empirical foundations for a theory of language change. In:
Directions for historical linguistics. Ed. by Winfred Lehmann
and Yakov Malkiel. Austin, University of Texas Press. 95-188.
Wolfram, Walter. 1969. A sociolinguistic description of Detroit
Negro speech. Washington, D. C., Center for Applied Lin-
guistics.

VARIATION RESULTING
FROM DIFFERENT RULE ORDERINGS
IN ENGLISH PHONOLOGY

CHARLES-JAMES N. BAILEY

Georgetown University

1. Introduction. It is not necessary to ransack the data of foreign
languages to come up with examples of phenomena that many phonologists seem disposed to regard as rather exotic, and therefore excit-
ing. We need only look at the low-level phonology of the unleveled
varieties of English to find complexities that rival those of any other
language. Nowhere is this statement more true than in the realm of
rule-reordering. But the purpose of the present treatment is not to
demonstrate this except in an incidental manner. The main purpose
of this paper is to provide evidence that will bear on the much-mooted
theoretical issue as to whether rules can occur in only one order or
in no order.[1] Claims of this general sort have been made by Theo
Vennemann (1972) and more specifically by those scholars who have
taken their lead from Koutsoudas, Sanders, and Noll (MS), viz.
Koutsoudas (1971, MS), Ringen (1972, MS), Norman (1972), and
Lehmann (1972). The position of this latter group of writers is that
there is 'no extrinsic ordering', i.e. ordering other than what can
be predicted on the basis of universal principles that refer to the
formal characteristics of each pair of rules. This is a strong claim
which is admirably vulnerable to empirical data and can be falsified
by adducing sure instances of variant orderings of the same pair of
rules, especially if these are identical in the way that rules from
different varieties of a given language often are, or if different words
in the same variety of a language have different orderings (see Bailey
1968b).

In adducing a large number of examples which falsify the claim just mentioned, it is not my intention to challenge the worth of the clever principles of ordering which have been turned up in the findings of those who maintain that there is no extrinsic ordering. I think that these principles can be added to those discussed in King MS (see note 1) as definitions or principles of orderings that are unmarked. Since, however, some of these principles conflict, such conflicts will have to be resolved before my position would be established. That is beyond the scope of the present effort, which is simply to provide evidence bearing on the main claim under discussion. But I fully expect that in the end we shall be able to obviate all instances of a pair of rules in a mutually marked or unmarked ordering.

Practically all of the cases discussed below have to do with rule pairs having either a more general ordering (Kiparsky's unmarked order) in which both apply or a less general ordering (Kiparsky's marked order) in which only one applies. Change proceeds from marked to unmarked order. Part 2 sets up the rules in their marked orders, unless these do not occur in any variety of English; see Bailey (MSd) for the justification and organization of polylectal grammars. Part 3 discusses the reorderings themselves. All fifty-five instances are from English. The rules in part 2 make no pretense to being all the rules of English. (Also see Chapter 10 of SSP for the intonational rules.) In part 4, a suggestion is made for an additional characterization of unmarked order.

In what follows, there is perhaps one instance of the phenomenon first discussed in Anderson (1969) (and reanalyzed in Norman 1972): despite a marked-order relationship in a pair of rules in many words, the order is reversed when a third rule is applicable and intervenes between them in the unmarked relation to both. See the end of part 4.

2. The rules. (1) Certain heavy ('tense') vowels are lightened ('laxed') in given morphological environments; e.g. $//+\bar{a}t+\bar{i}v//$ ⟶ $/+\breve{a}t+\breve{i}v/$ in generating the pronunciation of, e.g. remunerative and communicative, when the penultimate syllable is unaccented. Note that $//+\bar{a}t+//$ does not undergo rule (1) in these words (and many others; e.g. operative) when the penult is mid-accented. The same morpheme may or may not undergo rule (1) compensatory and revelatory, depending on the variety of English concerned. But in all varieties of the language, certain lexical items will be marked one way or the other; e.g. temperature always undergoes rule (1). Trissyllabic words like formative always undergo rule (1). (Grammatize and similar forms in -atize do not contain underlying $//\bar{a}t//$, but rather $//\breve{a}t//$; that the formative $//\bar{a}t//$ does indeed contain a heavy vowel is evident from the reduction to $/\iota/$, not to $/\eta/$, in

delegate (n.) and advocate in lects which distinguish these reduced vowels in the environments shown.)

(2) The bloc of accent rules follows next.

(3) The segment //g// is deleted before a nasal followed by an (internal or external) word boundary, while a preceding //i// vowel is simultaneously made heavy ('tense'); e. g. design#ing (cf. [g] present in designate), paradigm (cf. [g] in paradigmatic). In other clusters not permitted beside an external word boundary, the obstruent which is nearest that boundary is deleted; cf. gnostic and column with agnostic and columnist.

(4) An internal word boundary (/#/) is deleted (in effect is replaced by the /+/ that alone remains) before -ing in nouns and adjectives for some speakers (but not in verbs ending in -ing) in lento tempos, and in long#er, long#est, strong#er, and strong#est for most speakers of English. In allegro tempos the replacement of /#/ before -ing in verbs, nouns, and adjectives is heard in everyone's pronunciation. Rule (4) has to operate prior to (14) for all who say centring, settling, bottling, and burgling--all verb forms--with nonnuclear [r] and [l] in lento tempos. Some speakers make a difference between dai+ly and gay#ly. For various speakers of English there seems to be some inconsistency regarding the agent formative -er; e. g. settl+er, sweeten#er (for the effects of rule [14] on which, see that rule below).

(5) Unaccented /e/ is inserted before inflectional /d/ following apical stops and before inflectional /z/ following sibilants; e. g. raided, matches. This rule has to precede the rule (for those who have it) that changes unaccented /i/ to /ə/ in this environment; see rule (19). Planted ['phlaenɪd] shows that rule (5) has to precede the rule that deletes the underlying //t// here; see rule (20).

(6) Ungeminate //s// is changed to /z/ between two nuclei (syllabic nasals do not exist at this stage); cf. gymnasium and preserve (containing [z]) with gymnastic and conserve (with [s]). The same rule changes /θ/ to /ð/ before word-final //e//, as in wreathe and breathe. Conservation shows that rule (6) has to precede the rule that deletes nasals in the environment found here (see rule [39]), since that rule would otherwise have deleted the nasal which precedes //s// and made it intervocalic so as to be affected by rule (6). But for problems connected with this rule and rule (36), see the Excursus below; see also item 54 in part 3.

(7) After a tautosyllabic vowel, a liquid or glide in the underlying representation is changed into a diphthongal satellite, and in particular //r l// become /ᵊ ˡ/ in this environment. But the change does not operate where [r] is trilled; nor is the lateral affected in North Ireland, for example. Rule (7) has to apply iteratively, first to //r// and then to //l// in snarl, curl, and whorl. The lateral is not affected

in Southern States English after the nuclei heard in <u>school, gule, mule, stole, drawl, cowl</u>; see rule (28) for /ł/ in <u>accrual, dual, bestowal, withdrawal, boil, towel</u>. Contrary to what is heard in most other varieties of English, Northern States English syllabifies intervocalic underlying liquids and glides with the preceding nucleus, thus effecting the merger of the accented vowels in <u>Mary, marry, merry</u> (and <u>Murray</u>) when rule (24) operates. For the reordering of rule (36) before (7) in <u>brilliant</u> and <u>million</u> and of (11) before (7) in <u>value</u>, see items 18 and 17 in part 3. For length in lateral-final nuclei, see rule (42). See item 54 in part 3 for another reordering.

[For the exceptional lexical entries <u>-ion</u> //iɔn// and //ie//, as in <u>piracy</u> and in <u>-ence, -ency, -ance, -ancy</u> //ent+ie ant+ie//, the rule that changes sonorants to non-nuclear segments before unaccented (in rapid tempo, also accented) nuclei--viz. rule (36)--is moved to its unmarked order here. This creates the proper inputs to the rule assibilating apical stops--rule (8). But see the Excursus at the end of part 2 for further discussion. The formatives, <u>-ence, -ency, -ance, -ancy</u>, are generated by rules (36), (9), (18) (reordered prior to [14])-- to which must be added (14) (reordered prior to [12]) for <u>-ency</u> and <u>-ancy</u>, but not for <u>-ence</u> and <u>-ance</u>, which require rule (40g). Rule (36) is also moved to this position so as to have an unmarked order relatively to the palatalization rule (rule [12]); this then may affect <u>bestial, valiant,</u> and the noun <u>associate</u> (where /i/ precedes an unaccented vowel) and in very rapid tempos <u>association</u> (where /i/ precedes an accented vowel). The reordering of rule (36) to here is apparently obligatory where an unaccented vowel that reduces to /ɪ/ follows, since the result is a single /ɪ/ in <u>carriage, marriage, foliage, Isaac, associate</u> (noun). (For some speakers this unaccented /ɪ/ will be changed to /ə/ by rule [19].) When the word <u>gymnasium</u> has [ž], it is clear that rule [36] is reordered to a position following rule (6) and preceding the palatalization rule, (12). Speakers having [š] in <u>Asia</u> appear to have rule (36) reordered to a place before (6).[2] See further item 54 in part 3. The words <u>sufficient, crucial,</u> and <u>vicious</u> can be treated like <u>ignition</u>, where rule (36) reordered to the present position creates an environment for //t// to be assibilated by rule (9); the resulting /sy/ are changed to [š] subsequently by the palatalization rule. If rule (36) is reordered to here, there will be created a closed syllable in <u>valiant,</u> so that rule (15a) below will lighten the //ā// (cf. <u>prevail</u>) in the first syllable. However, it is probable that <u>valiant,</u> like <u>valor</u> and <u>value,</u>

has underlying light //ă//, perhaps as the result of a historical change in a tightly closed syllable.]

(8) At some point before the vowel-shift rules (rule [16]) and before rule (9), velar stops in the Romance part of the vocabulary have to be 'softened', i. e. changed to /dᶻ tˢ/ before //ī ē//. Examples from the light order are analogical and regent; cf. analogue and regal. In the heavy order, /tˢ/ is further changed to /tˢ/ by the (b) part of rule (8); after undergoing rule (9), it ends up as /s/ in opacity (cf. opaque). That regale has [g] before the phonetic output of /ē/ and that electricity has [s] before [ə] show that (8) must precede not only the vowel-shift rule but also the vowel-reduction rule (rule [19]). Rule (8) must also precede the rule that deletes //e// before /#/, viz. rule (18), as purge (cf. purgative) shows. Given the alternations heard in the non-Romance items kirk : church, caff : chaff, rig : ridge, brig : bridge, etc., in parts of the English-speaking world, the scope of rule (8) probably extends beyond the Romance vocabulary and to postnuclear environments.

(9) The (a) part of this rule changes the apical stops //d t// to dᶻ tˢ/, respectively, before /y/. The (b) part of the rule changes these apical affricates--and the /tˢ/ output of (8b)--to /z/ and /s/, as in piracy and democracy (cf. pirate, democratic). These outputs are combined with a following /y/ in the palatalization rule (rule [12]) to yield /ž š/ in explosion, persuasion, promotion, ignition (cf. explode, persuade, promote, ignite). The (c) part of the rule deletes //d// and //t// before the variant of -tive (viz. /sīv/) which follows these segments, as in explosive and responsive. (Note that -sive occurs, somewhat irregularly, also in permissive and expressive; following vowels and consonants other than //d//, -tive is normal, as in emotive, retentive, and elective.)

(10) Sibilant fricatives (and //ss// in tissue, issue, and -pression) are changed to palatals before a boundary followed by a palatal; e. g. horše#shoe. This is only an allegro rule for some speakers. See part 3 below for the results of reordering rule (11) with rule (10) in misuse, etc., and for the results of reordering rule (12) with (10) in question, bestial, moisture, etc.

(11) When light or lax //u// is followed by a light cluster[3] and preceded by /#/, and when it is followed by a light cluster and is unaccented, /y/ is inserted immediately before the vowel.[4] (Some speakers make this change following /#h/, as in human; see also rule [40a].) The change occurs in mis#use, but not in ab+use (see rule [17]). Rule (11) has to follow (6) and (9), but precede (12). If it did not follow (9), culture would have instead of [tˢ] (for //t//, cf. cult) either [s] or, given the operation of rule [12] subsequently, [š]; rule (12) creates [tˢ] in culture, legislature, betcha, etc. The change of

noninitial unaccented //u// is differently restricted in different kinds
of English, particularly after //s n l// in word-initial syllables,
following //r//, and following clustered //l//. Some speakers who
have /sy/ in tissue, /y/ in value, and /ny/ in tenure may disallow
/y/ in the initial syllables of superb, lucidity, and neurotic. Many
speakers disallow /y/ after unclustered //r// even in internal syllables, as in erudite, virulent, and querulous. Rule (11) has to follow
(10) for those speakers who have unpalatalized [s] preceding /y/ in
misuse--an ordering that does not occur in allegro pronunciation.
It is instructive to contrast /yə/ in augury, sulfuric, lemurine, and
conducive with a nucleus lacking /y/ in augur, sulfur, lemur, and
conduction; cf. also fabulous and circular with fable and circle (see
note 6), and communal (accented on the first syllable) with common.

(12) Apical obstruents other than interdental fricatives, also
laminopalatal sibilants and //n//, combine with a following tautosyllabic /y/ to generate the palatals /dž tš ž š ɲ/;[5] see rule
(40e) for the change of /ly/ to /y/ before an unaccented vowel. Rule
(10) has already changed the outputs of rule (9) to palatals; these
now combine with /y/ from rule (11) if no syllabic boundary
intervenes. For perhaps most speakers of English, the present rule
changes //t// to /š/ (not /tš/) when /p k/ precede (e.g. actual,
fracture, rupture, capture) in allegro tempo. After a fricative, the
change is always to /tš/, however, as in fixture, bestial, question.
Closure demonstrates the order (6, 11, 12); essential demonstrates
the order (36, 9, [10,] 12). Where just yet and last year are pronounced with [tšh] instead of deleted //t// following //s//, (12) is
ordered before (13); see item 49 in part 3.

(13) This rule deletes //t// clustered with a preceding obstruent
and //d// clustered with a preceding //n// or lateral, when the apical
stop is followed by an obstruent, nasal, or lateral; when it is followed
by a heterosyllabic //w r//; and (rarely in standard pronunciation)
when it is followed by /h/ or a vowel, or by #, a phonological phrase
boundary. The cluster may not be preceded by a boundary; a vowel
must precede. Examples are mostly, beastly, costly, exactly,
wastepaper, last night, best man, left lane, goldmine, landmark,
old-line, and landlord; contrast lefthand with //t// retained in standard speech, except in very rapid speech (where even just a second
may show deleted //t//). Although the rule frequently operates to
delete the clustered apical stops before //w r// that are not in the
same syllable as themselves (e.g. best win, trustworthy, old widow,
sand walk, last rights, gold rights, end run), the deletion does not
occur before these segments when they are tautosyllabic with the
apical stops (as in vestry, Eldridge, laundry). This rule operates
more frequently at the end of unaccented syllables, as in forest,
dentist, latest, husband, ribald, perfect. In standard speech, the

rule is inhibited if the apical stop in question is immediately preceded by /#/, as in passed or missed, but not if it is preceded by //+//, as in past, or by no boundary, as in mist. This constraint is relaxed in BVE, where also the rule may (much less frequently) operate on clustered apical stops before vowels. When //t// is deleted between a preceding //p// or //k// and a following /#s/, the preceding stop is lengthened at least in the lento speech of many Americans; thus, [k:] is longer in acts and sects than [k] in axe and sex, and [p:] is longer in Copts than [p] in cops. And [f] is similarly lengthened when //t// is deleted in rafts and lifts. Rule (13) has to precede the rule that generates syllabic sonorants out of the corresponding non-nuclear segments between a consonant and /#/ (rule [14]), as explained in connection with the rule in question. Some speakers order rule (13) before rule (5) in tests ['thɛsɪz]; see part 3. Rule (33d) handles word-final clusters like /sts sps sks/ in standard pronunciation; but non-standard speech simplifies such clusters in a variety of other ways on both sides of the Atlantic, either inserting /ɪ/ after the stop or dropping the last /s/. After //d// has been deleted in handler by the present rule, it may be restored by the epenthesis rule ([29]).

In Black Vernacular English, rule (13) deletes //k p// when clustered with a preceding //s// under conditions similar to the deletion of //t// in that environment. Note unmonitored standard asteris(k), especially when followed by a consonant. BVE also deletes word-final postvocalic apical stops, especially following unaccented vowels, under similar conditions.

The explanation for the deletion of clustered apical stops in standard English and of unclustered apical stops in Black Vernacular English, apparently lies in the theory that rule (33a) should precede (13), instead of being placed as late as it has been here. This rule changes word-final apical stops to velar or labial stops before the same. A crazy rule (Bach and Harms 1972) would then be generalized to operate in other environments and, in BVE, to extend the rule's operation to //sk sp// clusters. Rule (41) would subsequently simplify the geminates, thus creating preceding opener syllables lacking the underlying consonants; rule (41) might have to be made more general to cover all the instances covered by rule (13).

Given the reordering of rule (33a), it might be that it could actually replace rule (13) at this position, since (13) may do no more than (33a) and (41) combined.

See item 14 in part 3 for the reordering found in arres(ted) me.

(14) Between a non-nuclear segment and a following nonsyllabic segment or boundary (/#(#)/), a sonorant becomes syllabic; e.g. meter (//mētr//, with final //tr// as in metric), Bible (final //bl// as in biblical), winter (with //tr// as in wintry), table (with //bl// as in tablet), cycle (with //kl// in cyclic), black+n, bitt+n, has(t)e+n,

mois(t)+n, the last of which show that (13) has to precede (14). Contrast sweeten#er and the lento verb center#ing, where rule (14) operates, with the adjective centr+ing and the adjective centr+al, where rule (14) cannot operate. In lento speech, the rule is restricted to prohibit syllabic nasals except after unclustered homorganic stops and various homorganic fricatives, particularly /z s/ (even if clustered, as in Hudson). (See further rule [27a].) Otherwise, rule (38) inserts /ə/, as in swollen. The absence of the vowel lightening in meter, Bible, cycle, table which is heard in metric, biblical, cyclic, and tablet shows that rule (14) has to precede rule (15a).[6] For the ordering of (14) with respect to the rule changing //t// to [d] in certain positions, see item 7 in part 3. The deletion of //t// in center, but not in central, is proof that rule (14) precedes rule (20). Nonstandard 'r-ful' English deletes unaccented /ə/ after //r// in apron, hundred, introduction, etc., by a reordering of rules (19) and (27b) before (14), so that interconsonantal /r/ becomes /ə́/ by the present rule; e.g. [ˈɛɪpə́n ˈhəndə́d ˌɪnə́ˈdəkšən] (whence hypercorrected modren and prespiration).

(15) Part (a) makes vowels light (lax) before heavy clusters (see note 3) in which /#/ does not follow the first consonant (as in metric, biblical, and tablet), but they are made heavy before /ndž/ (see below). (b) Accented vowels become light if followed by two or more syllables, as in Angela, divinity, serenity, natural, and granary. (Both [a] and [b] can be generalized under the rubric of 'tight' syllabic closure, since both [a] and [b] effectively shorten the length of the nucleus which gets lightened.) Part (c) makes a non-high accented nucleus a heavy one when it is followed by /i/ and another vowel, as in managerial, gymnasium, automation. A high vowel is made light in the same environment (e.g. ignition, vicious, sufficient); but see rule (17) for the vowel in furious and curious, and also item 22 in part 3. For problems with (c), cf. the Excursus below. Part (d) makes accented vowels heavy before other vowels, as in variety (unaccented //i// is unaffected in various and variable; contrast compliant, defiant, and reliant with ambient, and science with prescient). There is evidence that part (c) follows the preceding parts of the rule in that Marian, nation, and ration have /ā/, though there has been a reordering in national and rational, if not in denominational (except in Australia) and in one pronunciation of rational.[7] While -arian is regular, -ary and -arily have an exceptional /ɛ/.

Ranger, danger, angel show that velar softening (rule [8]) follows part (a), so that the accented nucleus is made heavy in these examples. Angela shows that (b) may not precede (a); and hydrangea shows that (c) must follow (b). See part 3 for Greenwich. Angle is //angul// (cf. angular).

(16) Here follow the vowel-shift rules. My view on the shift of both the heavy and light vowels differs greatly from Chomsky and Halle (1968; see, for example, Bailey 1970, MSa). The fact that separate rules for heavy vowels are distinguished is due to reorderings of the middle rule with the third and first in various kinds of English; see parts 3 and 4 for comments, and note the pronunciation of geese as ['gəⁱs] in eight locales in the North of England (Kolb 1966: 175), item (3) in part 3.

(a) $\bar{\text{i}}$ (mice) → ε^i, ^{8} ∂^i → a^e → a (nonstandard in some environments)

$\bar{\bar{\text{u}}}$ (voice) → θ^i, ∂^i → $\jmath^e$; a^e (nonstandard)

$\bar{\text{u}}$ (mouse) → θ^u, ∂^u → a^o → a (nonstandard in most environments)

(The change to [a] may be a separate rule; see rule [34] and note 26; see also further changes by rule [43].)

(b) $\bar{\text{e}}$ → i and $\bar{\text{o}}$ → u

(c) $\bar{\text{a}}$, $\bar{\varepsilon}$ → e (but see part 4 of this paper) and $\bar{\jmath}$ → o

The environments for the various outputs of (a) differ in different lects (cf. Bailey MSd). For many lects which have different outputs in different environments, the later ones appear before tautosyllabic voiced non-velars; but different tempo factors affect the results in many lects, as does the presence of /#/ in some. See further, items [34] and [35] in part 3. If there is any variety of English which has a later output in pint (as in pine) than in spite, then it would be necessary to conclude that the rule that nasalizes a vowel and deletes a nasal consonant before a tautosyllabic heavy obstruent (rule [39]) has been reordered before rule (16). But since all lects known to the present writer which differentiate the vowels in spite and find have the former in pint, it is simpler to add this environment, as well as that preceding tautosyllabic voiced velars, to the voiceless environments as environments delaying the changes--i.e. having older outputs. For complications before [t] in mid-accented syllables, see Bailey (MSc). Note that later outputs appear before syllable boundaries (contrast cyclone and bicycle with cyclic and icicle) and before nasals plus syllable boundaries (as in rhinestone and pinetree); this last fact suggests a relationship with rule (39).

After rule (16), or the bloc of rules ordered there, the light accented vowels are /ı ɛ a ɒ/ and /ɯ/ or (except in North Britain)

/ө/ from light /u/, when this vowel is not followed by a light cluster
(cf. rules [11, 17]); /ө/ eventually gets unrounded. Contrast /ɯ/
(changed in some environments in some lects to /ɨ/) in could, book,
look, cushion, and bush with /ө/ in bulb and pulp ['bʌˡ:b 'phʌˡp];
note /ɯˡ:/ (changed by rule [42] to /ɫ/) in bull, pull, wool --but not
in all lects in bully, pulley, woolly. The only unaccented vowel that
has a different representation at this point is unaccented /i/; see
further rule (19). For further developments of the light vowels, see
rule (43). Note that /a/ becomes /æ/ by rule (25), except in a few
lects (e.g. Scots); see later developments of /ɒ/ in rules (24) and
(43).

(17) Light or lax /u/ is changed to /ū/ when it is followed by a
light cluster plus a vowel. See rules (18) and (19) also. The accented
outputs are treated differently in different varieties of English according to the environment that immediately precedes. In certain environments the accented output of /ū/ is merged (except for some
lects in Norwich, England) with the output of //ō// in food and
school, viz. in those environments not preceded by //w y r// or
clustered //l//, as in woo, youth, rude, and flute. In America, the
same is true when //z s ɓ// precede (but the mid-accented syllable
of Matthew is treated as unaccented here; cf. nephew) or when unclustered //l// precedes in the same syllable; many 'r-ful' speakers
add to these the environments preceded by //d t n //. Following
velars, palatals, and //ɟ t n//, Southerners have /iü/ (but cf. rule
[34]). Most Americans seem to have /üᵘ/ after labials; many
Northerners have the same nucleus after velars. Curious and
furious show that (17) follows (15c); but see on these words in part 3
below. Fuschia shows that rule (17) precedes (36).

(18) This rule deletes //e// before /#/. For the exceptional
morpheme //ie// (as in piracy and following //ent// in emergency)--
which reordered rule (36) has already changed to /ye/--it is necessary for rule (18) to be reordered to its unmarked position preceding
(9) and (14), so that /y/ will now be final and get changed to /i/ by
that rule. The verbs abuse and amuse show that (18) has to follow
both (6) and (17). (Apparently nouns in //use// like abuse are
exempt from rule [6].)

(19) This rule reduces unaccented vowels to weak vowels.
(Rule [27]--which must follow rule [19]--is required to produce unaccented /ɘ̇ ɨ/; see rule [27c].) Part (a) changes unaccented low
vowels and light back vowels to /ə/, heavy round back vowels to /ө/,
and non-low front vowels to /ı/, including the output of rule (5). 9
Given that unaccented /yū/ everywhere goes the same route as the
accented segments in woo, youth, rude, and flute, we get the correct /yө/. The unaccented /ө/ here and elsewhere may be changed
to /ə/ in various environments; see below. Part (b) of this rule

changes unaccented /ĭ/ to /ɪ/ in most environments (including the word-final environment in 'r-less' but not 'r-ful' English) except when preceding /ng/ and except when preceding vowels other than /i/, whether or not //x// intervenes: [i], as in archaistic, vehicular, comprehend, Bethlehem, and recreation, but [ɪ] where the following /i/ is close, as it is in 'r-less' readying if //g// has not been deleted by reordered rule [22]. The remaining parts of this rule change unaccented /ɪ/ and less often unaccented /i/ to /ə/ in different environments in different lects of English--in perhaps all environments of /ɪ/, except at the end of a word. The change is rarest for the unaccented high front vowels followed by //ng// and next-most rare when they are followed by //x// or a vowel, and is most frequent and indeed normal before //r//, //l//, [10] //nt// (as in moment, sentence, and residence), and in -ible and -acle quite generally. In America, the change is common in non-final syllables, though less common before /#/, as in be#cause, de#ceive, where it occurs for many speakers and in allegro tempos for most. The change to /ə/ is also normal in America between apical obstruents and //n//, as in satin, mountain. [11] Southerners, but not Northerners, generally keep /ɪ/ in syllables followed by /#/ (as in rapid, the noun delegate, basket, challenge, etc.) except in the most rapid pronunciation. The /ii/ or /yi/ in carriage, foliage, marriage, Isaac, and the noun associate may become /ə/ in Northern States English; but older speakers in the South have [ˈmaᵉkyɫ] for Michael.

Apparently, the treatment of the gemination rule ([31]) with regard to the part of the present rule which changes /ɵ/ to /ə/ in allegro tempo cannot be handled by rule ordering, as might seem possible at first sight. Therefore this part of the reduction rule will have to be constrained so that the change to schwa is not permitted when a vowel immediately follows. Then rule (31) will insert /w/, as in gradual /ˈgraedžɵwɫ/. Possibly /ɵ/ has to be changed to /ə/ before liquid consonants, except in very monitored speech, so that (27c) will operate in fabulous and augury (note 4).

(20) When //t// is followed by an unaccented vowel and at the same time preceded by (tautosyllabic) //n// preceded by an accented vowel, the apical stop is deleted; e.g. twen(t)y, plen(t)y, cen(t)er, en(t)er, win(t)er (but not in central, entry, wintry, nor when //nt// follows an unaccented vowel, as in talented, or an unaccented syllabic nasal--after /n̩/ in patented and /m̩/ in carpenter, where rule (45) changes //t// to /d/.) Note wan(t) it. Planted shows that rule (20) has to follow (5); if not, this word would sound like planned. See part 3 for reorderings connected with sentence and elementary.

(21) (Non-nuclear) //n// is assimilated to the place of articulation of a following tautosyllabic obstruent. Since tempo differences affect the syllabication, one will hear both [n] and [ŋ] in mongoose, [12] and

in fast tempos both [n] and [m] in in between and one [ˈwʌm] moment.
(A morphological rule changes //n// at the end of a Latin prefix like
con- to /m/ across a syllabic boundary, as in commute and immuta-
ble; but cf. [n] in congressional and converse with [ŋ] in congress
and [ŋ] in conversational as a result of rule [21].) See item 24 in
part 3 for some discussion. The labial //m// does not assimilate
but causes the epenthesis rule (rule [29]) to operate. See part 3 for
ordering in cap'm.
    (22) Following /ŋ/, //g// is deleted when /#/ follows immediately,
as in sing#ing##, but not in hunger and finger. (See rule [4] for
stronger, -est, and longer, -est.) In rapid tempos, rule (22) is
reordered before rules (19) and (21), as in nothin(g) and Washin(g)ton;
see item 5 in part 3.
    (23) The satellite lateral (/ɫ/) is deleted before labials (and, if
this rule occurs after the neutralization rule [(24)], as in standard
pronunciation, the preceding nucleus is lengthened). The chief examples are words in -alm (but not calmative, palmary); e.g. calm,
palm. In standard speech, one does not hear [æᵊ] in these words
(this was standard within living memory in some areas) because of
the reordering of rule (24); hypercorrections are blocking rule (23)
sometimes today. See item 20 in part 3. Half, calf, and their
plurals (and the corresponding verb forms) are also affected by rule
(23);[13] but there is no underlying lateral in walk, talk, folk, and
yolk. In the South, the deletion of the lateral in self, help, shelf,
gulf, and golf is hardly fully standard (but British RP may delete
the lateral in the last word), though the deletion is standard in the
noun (not verb) salve, where the lateral is probably not present in
the underlying representation.
    (24) This rule neutralizes various nuclei before /ð/ and precedes
rule (28), which diphthongizes unaccented weak vowels following
accented vowels, and (35), which truncates or abbreviates words by
dropping unaccented syllables after the accented one. The results
are different in different lects, though in one way or another all but
Scots English merge the nuclei in hair and hare (see rule [28] for
mayor and rule [35] for e'er)--and also here in some lects. (The
merger also occurs in Mary, marry, and merry in lects where the
//r// is geminated--because of its having been syllabified with the
preceding accented vowel.) See part 3 for reorderings. Many lects
merge the nuclei of poor with that of pore, though the semantics of
the name may keep Moor and Moore apart from the verb moor when
the latter is like more; conversely, speakers who distinguish poor
and moor from pore and more may pronounce the names Moore and
Poore like the latter. Outside the Southern States, /oᵊ/ (in hoarse)
is often merged with /ɔᵊ/ (in horse). Some Northern States lects

neutralize heavy and light pairs of nuclei before /ł/ also, as in
seal : sill and sailing : selling (if the lateral is geminated).

Two subneutralizations are subordered: (a) changes /ɒ/ in wall,
war, song, log, taught and taut, toss, cloth, and soft to /ɔ/, though
only before the liquids and //x// (in taught, taut, and paw)[14] for some
speakers and in no environments for others;[15] (b) changes /a/ to /ɒ/
(in some lects no change occurs before //r//) before the liquids and
//x//, as in car and bar (cf. carriage, barrister), doll and balsam,
in yacht, and in pa (with underlying //x//). If (a) and (b) are not reordered, /ɒ/ usually unrounds to /a/ before /ð/, /ł/, and //x//. The
(b) change does not occur in many borrowings from the classical
languages (altitude, formaldehyde, canal, etc.; see chapter 8 of SSP),
nor in some names, like Calvin and Alfred. (See rule [35] for Al,
Sal, Poll, Moll, etc. And see part iii for the reorderings in doll
when it rhymes with ball; for falcon and alternate; for reorderings
in for'est, Warr'n, or'nge, and Hor'ce; and also for the ordering
that makes seer ['one who sees'] rhyme with seer ['prophet'], doer
and suer ['one who sues'] with poor, and sewer and ewer with these,
layer and mayor with lair and mare, higher with hire, real with
reel, betrayal with trail, etc.) Note that in the Southeastern States,
where internuclear //r// is syllable-initial /r/ in the phonetic output, Lawrence, Warren, quarrel, etc., have [ɐ], not [ɔ], though [ɐ]
may be slightly retracted when the unaccented vowel of the next
syllable is a non-front vowel, as in Lawrence and quarrel, but not
in Warren. There is a merger of light vowels before tautosyllabic
//r//, except in the North of England and in Scotland, where //r//
may be a vibrant; cf. deter and err with deterrent and error, and
restressed your in the Northern States. (See part 3 for courier,
furious, and curious.) With the reordering discussed in part 3,
betrayal could end up rhyming with sell in the speech of some of
these speakers. (See also note 20.)

(25) At this point /a/ becomes /æ/ except in North English
and Scots. There follow rules to create in-glided and up-glided
light front accented vowels and (in some areas) to raise /ǣ ɔ̄/
('tensed' by a rule preceding [25], but not listed here); note that
rule (25) has to follow the rule creating /ɔ/ itself, viz. rule (24).
In-gliding (to /ə/) and raising occur in word-final accented syllables.
(See the reordering of rule [35] in part 3.) In-gliding (with retraction of the nucleus before labials by rule [43]) occurs before labials
in the Southern States and--for all but the oldest speakers--before
apicals in the Northern and Southern States. Though differently constrained in different locales, in-gliding is least likely before /k/
everywhere; and /ɪ/ is usually unglided before palatals. Before
/g ŋ š/ and progressively less so before other types of consonants,
Southern States /æ/ is changed to /æᶦ/, and not only in word-final

accented syllables, but generally in the appropriate consonantal environments, provided only that the vowel is accented. In various
regions light /ɛ ɪ/ undergo various changes when followed by
/ŋ g ž/, except that /ɪ/ is unchanged before /g/. The changes
before /ž/ require that this consonant should have been created by
an earlier rule--viz. (12). Some Southerners make /ɪ/ closer before /ɲ/ (later deleted by rule [39]) in pinch and inch. Perhaps rule
(25) is the one that changes /e/ to /ɪ/ before /m n/ in many varieties
(though only in some styles in some varieties) of American English;
as a result of this change, /ɪ ə/ is heard before /n/ and /ɨ ə/ before
/m/, always assuming rule (21) to have preceded. These changes
have to precede the rule that deletes nasal consonants in certain environments (rule [39]) and also the rule that changes //t// to /p/ to
/m/ in lemme (= let me) (viz. rule [33a, g]), at least for those that
would otherwise say limme (see item 8 in part 3).

Note that Northern States speakers who do not have the glides in
Pam, Jan, Mass. (abbreviation of Massachusetts), and Ave. which
they do have in ham, tan, class, and calve clearly must have rule
(25) (inoperative in Pamela, etc., before truncation because it normally operates only in word-final accented syllables) prior to
(35), the truncation rule. For the Southern States pronunciation with
the unmarked order of these two rules, see part 3. There is some
question as to whether any variety of English has the marked order
(39, 25), in which (25) is inoperative in bank. The evidence is unclear. Most lects have (25) before (39), which deletes the nasal and
nasalizes the vowel.

(25a) [This rule does not exist where there is postulated //h//
instead of //x//.] After (12, 25) and before (26, 30, 40), //x// has
to be changed to /h/.

(26) Syllable-initial heavy stops are aspirated; except when
word-initial, the aspiration is optional for some speakers before
unaccented nuclei, as in active. Since this rule precedes (27b),
s(e)curity begins with [ˈskh]-, not with [ˈsk]- (Gaberell Drachman,
p.c.). Deep Southern States light consonants are fortis in the same
environments where heavy consonants are fortis (e.g. [b] in Alabama),
though Black speakers and a few Whites have injectives here instead
of an egressive air stream. An implicational series exists such that
speakers who have injective glides have injective liquids; the presence of these in one's speech implies injective nasals; and these
imply injective light obstruents (William Stewart, p.c., who cau-
tions me that the few White speakers having injectives avoid the
labial stop, which is first to appear and most obvious in Black pronunciation).

(27) The (a) part of this rule affects the sequence of unaccented
/ə/ (see rule [19]) plus /n/--also plus /m/ in allegro tempo--so that

the vowel is deleted and the nasal becomes syllabic, subject to various output restrictions on environments where syllabic nasals are tolerated. (But note that rule [32], which assimilates syllabic /n̩/ to other articulatory positions, intervenes before the phonetic output representation.) In general, the creation of syllabic /n̩/ or /m̩/ is permitted after a stop which ends the preceding syllable; but this is much more frequent when apical stops precede than when labials do, and infrequent when velars precede--though more frequent in rapid tempos than otherwise. Syllabic /n̩/ is permitted after syllable-initial /s/ or /z/, as in <u>sonata, Hudson, Watson,</u> and <u>absent,</u> and syllabic /m̩/ is sometimes permitted after /s/, but not /z/ (as in <u>prism;</u> /m̩/ is more likely in <u>handsome,</u> unaccented <u>some,</u> and <u>yes'm</u> than in <u>possum</u> and <u>blossom</u>). Following unaccented syllables, [n̩] exists in <u>Robertson,</u> but never in <u>residence.</u> In the order (27b, a) [n̩] is possible in <u>skel'ton, pur'tan,</u> and (in lects with final /ən/) <u>bull'tin.</u> British RP permits syllabic nasals after the laminopalatal sibilants and also after the other fricatives (with [n̩] in <u>motion, vision, often, heaven,</u> and even <u>question</u> and <u>cavern</u>).[16] The word <u>piston</u> (with [tən]) shows that rule (26) follows the rule which deletes //t// in <u>fast+n</u> (rule [13]). Note that there is no syllabic nasal in <u>London</u> and one in <u>sentence</u> and <u>mountain</u> only where the rule deleting //n// in some environments (rule [39]) is operative. (But see further on <u>sentence</u> in part 3.) Contrast these two lectal pronunciations of <u>golden:</u> mainly Southern States ['goᵘldən], Northern ['goˡ:dn̩]. But <u>molten,</u> even in pronunciations having [1], has [n̩] no less than <u>Milton</u> and <u>resultant,</u> both of which have [ˡ] before (therefore unclustered) /t/. Only in a very rapid tempo does rule (27) operate after velars, as in <u>reckon</u> and 'n (= <u>and</u>), for usually rule (38) below inserts /ə/ after //k// in <u>beacon</u> and <u>black+n</u>. (<u>Beacon</u> may contain an underlying vowel in the second syllable.) Rule (32) assimilates /n̩/ to [ŋ̩] immediately after //k// in these words. Unless rule (19) in a given lect has changed /ɪ/ to /ə/--which may occur in very rapid pronunciation in any lect--one does not end up with a syllabic nasal in <u>cabin</u> (though there may be one in the internal syllable, as in <u>cabinet</u> and <u>cardinal</u>) or <u>bargain</u>. The ending <u>-in(g)</u> is unlikely to have /ə/, but in rapid speech <u>breathin'</u> and <u>missin'</u> may end in [n̩]. (See item 37 in part 3 for the reordering that yields ['rɛsn̩] for <u>restin'</u>.) That the present rule precedes the late rule changing //t// to [d] under certain conditions (rule [45]) follows the present rule is evident from the [t] or [ʔ], not [d], in <u>remittance</u>. (Cockney may reverse the ordering just demonstrated, changing it to the unmarked one.)

    (b) In rapid tempos, /ə/ may be deleted in most situations, though only in very rapid tempos this rule would be uninhibited where it would result in 'un-English' clusters, as in <u>d'lete, T'ledo, m'rine,</u>

p'tato. (In most tempos, the present rule has to precede the rule that inserts /ə/ in some situations; see rule [38].) The commonest environment for /ə/-deletion is following //r// and also following a lateral when it is preceded by an accented vowel, as in abil'ty, rel'tive, and Phil'delphia. The deletion is common in standard speech in this situation when //r// follows, as in Hil(a)ry, gall(e)ry, cel(e)ry, sal(a)ry, scull(e)ry. The deletion following //r// is seen in veter(a)n and differ(e)nt in nonstandard pronunciation; also in hundred for those having /ə/ instead of /ɪ/ in the second syllable. [17] (For vet'ran and diff'rent in standard speech, cf. the degemination rule--[36].) When //r// follows an accented vowel, /ə/ is often deleted in standard speech in Amer(i)ca; also, for those having /ə/ instead of /ɪ/ in the second syllables of or(a)nge, for(e)st, and Warr(e)n. Such speakers as do not apply the neutralization rule ([24]) in the last four examples have the present rule after that one; but see the reordering discussed in part 3, and also the discussion of foll(o)wer. Where speakers have /ə/ instead of /ɪ/ in the second syllables of started and wanted, the result is [ˈstɒˀd] with /dd/ reduced to [d]) and [ˈwɔnd] (showing the operation of rule [20]). See items 11 and 12 in part 3. See also item 30 in part 3.

(c) Universally /ə/ is deleted before a liquid and the output becomes input to the diphthongization rule ([28]) if an accented vowel precedes. The present rule perhaps also syllabifies the following liquid (so that it becomes /l̩/ or /ɹ̩/), regardless of what precedes or follows. [18] The pronunciation [ˈphædən] for pattern in 'r-less' Southern States English shows that the (c) part of rule (27) follows the (a) part; for reordering, see part 3. If rule (27) did not follow (13), //t// would be wrongly deleted in pistol (it is rightly deleted in nestle, where no /ə/ intervened between //t// and //l//). See part 3 for reordering in apostle and epistle, and for [d] in littler and It'ly.

See item 28 in part 3 for a possible splitting up of rule (27c) into two ordered subrules, so that the sulcal liquid is affected prior to the lateral one. For dissyllabic Charles, see note 19 and note 30.

Rule (27c) has to allow for the deletion of /ə/ from /ɵ/ in tabular. Since /ɵ/ is preserved in gradual [ˈgrædʒɵwl̩] in order for rule (31) to create the following prevocalic [w], it does not seem possible to handle tabular with any kind of reordering of rule (27c) before (27b); rather rule (19) may have to require the change of /ɵ/ to /ə/ in allegro tempo before liquids.

(d) Note that s(u)perior, Ch(i)cago, and (British) S(e)ptember may begin with syllabic sibilants ([s̩] or [š̩]). It is possible that these are created at this point. Note in superb that /ɵ/ must already have become /ə/ in order to be deleted.

(28) This rule, which obviously has to follow (19) and (27c), combines an accented nucleus plus a following unaccented peak vowel (/ɪ ə ɚ ɫ/) into a single compound nucleus by making the unaccented vowel a satellite.[19] Thus, at the point of their derivation where fluid and poet are /ˈfluɪd ˈphoɪt/--or, in the Northern States, /ˈfluəd ˈphoət/--i. e. after the underlying vowels justified for fluidity and poetic have been affected by rule (19), the present rule generates /ˈfluᴵd ˈphoᴵt/ and /ˈfluᵊd ˈphoᵊt/, respectively. Note also [ˈdyuᴸ:] from /ˈdiᵘɫ/, showing the later operation of rule (34b), representing dual (cf. duality)[20] and [ˌkhoᴸˈlɛᵊs] in co-alesce (for which see also the rule that geminates internuclear sonorants, [31]). Some speakers having satellite [ᴵ] in fluid and poet (where the syllables are word-final closed syllables) may nevertheless have /ə/ from unaccented /ɪ/ medially (see rule [19]); in such instances, [ᵁᵊ] is heard in the accented syllables of annuity and Louisville (contrast [ᵁᴵ] in Louis and Louie).[21] Where unaccented /ə/ has been deleted in rule (27b), ruin ends up rhyming with moon, and poet with goat; cf. also sci(e)nce, may(on)naise, di(a)per, qui(e)t, etc.[22]

Rule (28) frequently is inoperative in monitored pronunciation. When fluid, poet, and dual remain dissyllabic, rule (31) causes [w] to be inserted between the nuclei.

(29) This is the epenthesis rule (see chapter 4 of SSP), which inserts a stop in certain consonantal clusters (but not between a syllabic nasal, apparently, and a following consonant). The epenthetic consonant that is inserted agrees in place of articulation with the preceding nasal (rarely other sonorants in nonstandard pronunciation) and in order (heavy or light) with the following obstruent or-- when the preceding nasal is /m/ or /ŋ/, or optionally /n/--lateral (also //r// in nonstandard speech).[23] Cf. [b] in hums, [t] in prince, and [p] in contempt, infant, and comfort. (Since the nasal is deleted in the last two examples by rule [39], it is clear that rule [29] must precede that rule.) Since rule (36), which degeminates sonorants, follows (29), this rule is inoperative in standard fam'ly, though it operates in nonstandard chimbley (for chimney, often chimley in some regions); see part 3 for standard humbly and trembling and for nonstandard fambly and even membry (for memory). Rule (29) must follow the rule assimilating nasals (rule [21]) and the rule deleting //g// (rule [22]) and precede the rule that deletes nasals (rule [39]) in order to generate length /ˈlɛkþ/ (see rule [25] for [ɛ̃ⁱ] in this word and for [æ̃ⁱ] in bank, though not in all lects of course, where the ordering of rule [25] is crucial).

For some reason, epenthesis occurs in Abingdon after /ŋ/, but not in Abington or Washington.

(30) Before rule (32), /h/ must be deleted when it is syllable-final, as in vehicle, exhalation, exhumation, philharmonic (but not

vehicular, exhale, exhume, harmony). For those who omit /h/ in
historical, habitual, and hypothesis (but not, of course, in history,
habit, and hypothetical), rule (30) deletes /h/ before unaccented
vowels (but not before mid-accented vowels, as when the middle
syllable of phiharmonic and the final syllable of Bethlehem are so
accented). This may be the old form of the rule; cf. Durham, shep-
herd. It could have resulted from a generalization of the deletion of
syllable-final glides. Note the deletion of //w// in non-syllable
initial 'll (for will), and of syllable-initial //w// followed by an unaccented vowel in Greenwich and nonstandard forward, awkward, was;
but these phenomena have more historical interest than interest for a
description of present-day English.

(31) Next comes the rule geminating internuclear syllable-final
sonorant nuclear peaks and satellites; see chapter 6 of SSP for details in an extended discussion there (a preliminary version of which
appeared as Bailey 1971). Geminated /y/ is later deleted by rule
[37]. (Note that all internuclear sonorants are syllable-final in
Northern States English, but elsewhere underlying internuclear
sonorant consonants--not generated, for example, from /ī ū ū/
and /u/ in certain environments--are syllable-initial and ungemi-
nated, except when they have become syllabic by rule [27], whether
or not subsequently affected by rule [28]). Note that between a
rounded nuclear segment and a following peak vowel /w/ is automatically inserted by the present rule; e. g. situation [ˌsɪtˢeˈweⁱšən].
Note the comments on [w] in very lento fluid and Owen in the discussion of rule (28) above. Depending on whether rule (4) has reduced /#/ to /+/, rule (31) will operate or not; cf. moor#ing (verb)
['moᵈrɪŋ -ɪn], showing the effects of rule [24], and moor+ing (noun
or adjective) ['mʉᵘrɪŋ -ɪn], and also cf. hair#y ['hæᵈːrɪ] with Harry
['hærɪ].²⁴ The present rule of course has to precede the desulcalization rule ([42]) and the rule that degeminates geminate sonorants
([36]) in allegro speech.

Note that in the lects where //l// is syllable-final in cowling as
well as in cowl and in dowry as well as in sour, cowling rhymes with
toweling (as most English-speakers say it)²⁵ and dowry and floury
rhyme with flowery--but not in other lects. While lawyer is ['lɔyə
'lɒᵒyə -ð] everywhere in the Southern States, some speakers rhyme
loyal and royal with roil ['rɔ(e)ɫː], but others say ['rɔyɫ 'rɒᵒyɫ].
Flōral shows that rule (31) follows (15a).

(32) Syllabic nasals are assimilated to a preceding non-continuant;
e. g. /n̩/ becomes /m̩/ in the verb open#ing and in open#er. If rule
(32) did not follow rule (31), the geminate output of the latter would
be [m] in these words (as sometimes in children's speech; see item
40 in part 3). For speakers who have /n̩/ unassimilated to [ŋ] after
[ʔ] in mountain, rule (32) has to precede (33h). See part 3 for

reordering. Rule (32) has of course to follow (19), which reduces unaccented vowels. For cap'm (= captain), see item 44 in part 3.

(33) Here follow a number of consonantal assimilations, subordered among themselves (for placing [33a] where [13] now is, see
under that rule):

(a) In rapid tempo a word-final apical stop is assimilated to the
place of articulation of a following velar or labial stop beginning the
next word if it is in the same phonological phrase: e.g. goob#bye,
goob##book, righk##corner.

(b) A non-sibilant fricative becomes a stop of the same articulatory position word-initially in emphatic pronunciation (e.g. that,
first, very); a light fricative is so changed when a syllabic
nasal follows. (For a possible reordering of the [b] and [f]
parts of this rule, see part 3.) Southern States speakers have /d/
for /z/ in isn't, doesn't, wasn't, hasn't, and /d/ for /ð/ in heathen.
Especially in lower steps of an intonational tune, [bm̩] is heard instead of /vəm/ (where the syllable is unaccented), as in even them
(contrast the predicate adjective, even) and in seventeen (vs. seven).
See part 3 for gov(ern)ment. Rule (33b) has been generalized to the
underlying voiceless order in nuttin' (for nothing); but compare rapid
standard ['ɪ̃ʔ'm̩məs] for infamous. See item 5 in part 3 for nuttin'.

(c) Some speakers have the historic [t] (instead of [Þ]) at the end
of fifth and sixth, where word final underlying //Þ// is clustered
with a preceding fricative. Cf. drift (and height and drought). Most
speakers seem to have [t] for //Þ// in months ['mɔ̃ts] (see rule [29]
for the ordering of epenthesis).

(d) Before /s/, //t// becomes /s/ (and is later deleted by the de-
gemination-of-non-nuclear-segments rule ([41]), as in Tha(t)'s why
and lossa ('lots of') in allegro tempo. In non-standard English, this
change may occur in non-word-final syllables and in more word-final
environments than in standard English; in standard pronunciation,
the change is limited to allegro tempos, and would usually occur
even then only before non-nuclear segments at the beginning of the
following word in the same phonological phrase. Standard English,
however, has the change between /s/ and /#s/, as in feasts and
tests (see the non-standard reordering discussed in part 3). Between these sibilants, other stops are similarly fricativized; e.g.
mosques ['mɐsxs], disks ['dɪᵊsçs], lisps ['lɪᵊsps] (Michael Brame,
personal communication).

(e) In allegro speech, //Þ// often becomes /s/ at the end of a
word when a word beginning with //s// follows in the same phonological phrase; e.g. bath salts. (Data from Walt Wolfram.) But
it is //Þ// that is deleted in fif(th) floor, where /f/ follows.

(f) Non-standard speech changes /d/ (including the output of part [b] of this rule) to /t/; e.g. couldn't [ˈkhɨ ʔn̩t] (showing also the effects of [33h]).

(g) Labial stops produced in parts (a) and (b) of this rule may be assimilated to /m/ in frequent words if /m/ begins the next word in the same phonological phrase, especially in allegro tempo; e.g. lemme, gimme. (For speakers having limme for lemme, see part 3; for other speakers, it is clear that [33g] must follow [25].)

(h) Stops of the heavy order are glottalized when unreleased, especially when word-final (see chapter 4 of SSP). The same heavy stops may also be glottalized before syllabic nasals, /t/ becoming simply [ʔ], including the /t/ output of (33f). Glottalization may affect /t/ in other environments, as before /ɫ/ in bottle (showing that [33h] follows [27c] and precedes [45]).

(i) Sporadically throughout the United States, even among standard speakers, syllable-initial apical stops are assimilated to the sulcal articulation of a following //r// and are palatalized, as in chrain (for train) and jrain (for drain).

(j) Between a preceding //Ꝥ// and a following grave vowel, //r// is deleted in non-standard throw, through, etc., in some regions. The same deletion occurs after /t^{š} d^{ž}/ in Hawaiian English, where jop is heard for drop and chy for try. Since /t/ is heard for //Ꝥ// in Hawaiian English, bathroom is heard as bachroom (data from William Peet, Jr., and Carol Odo).

(k) After /s/, //v// may be heard as /f/, as in Knoxville [ˈnɒksfɫ]; cf. also hafta ('have to'). When /v/ represents 've or of, it may become a bilabial fricative (e.g. I've won). The change of [v] to [b] is more general in some varieties of Black Vernacular English. When /v/ representing 've or of is preceded by a consonant, it may be deleted (e.g. lotsa, shoulda, coulda, woulda, musta). But this probably has to be ordered after the rule inserting /ə/ here, viz. rule (38).

(l) Syllable-final postvocalic interdental fricatives are changed to labiodental fricatives in Black Vernacular English, as in muvvah ('mother') and panfah ('panther'), with (33l) after reordered (39). Unattested [ˈbribm̩] ('breathin'') would have (33l) before (33b).

(34) Two sorts of detriphthongization and two species of dediphthongization occur at this point in the rules: (a) Mid-vowel satellites (/^{e} ^{o}/) are deleted before /^{ɫ} ^{ɚ}/, especially in rapid tempos, though more in some lects than in others. The result in Southern States English is [ˈa^{ɚ} ˈa^{ə}:] as the pronunciation of our and [ˈæ^{ɫ}:] for owl. It is well known that this reduction is more likely in lower steps of intonational tunes than in those that follow, i.e. in our more than in (usually accented) hour. Especially in 'r-less'

English in Great Britain and America, [26] one may hear tire ['tha^ə:]
and tile ['tha^ɫ:], Charleston (South Carolina) ['fɑ(^e)^ə: 'fɑ(^e)^ɫ:];
British RP even has the reductions in dial, higher, and power. The
reduction may occur in /ɔ^{eə}:/ but examples (like foyer, when thus
pronounced) are few, and most have a boundary (e. g. coy#er). How-
ever, the reduction of oil ['ɔ(^e)^ɫ:] is common in the Southern States;
it is not fully standard in all regions. [27] (Contrast all ['ɔl 'ɒ^ol], with
a different lateral.) (b) The other kind of detriphthongization (resembling forms of dediphthongization) has the same goal as the first,
viz. to obviate triphthongs, but it arrives at this end by making the
first syllabic non-syllabic. When rule (28) creates a triphthong by
adding a weak-vowel satellite to /i^ü/ (as in annuity, dual, Hughey,
or /ü^u/ (in fuel), or when similar triphthongs result from other
rules (as in manure, pure and allegro renewer, renewal), the
syllabic /i/ or /ü/ (both high front vowels) becomes /y/ and the first
satellite becomes the nuclear peak: annuity [ə'nyʊ^ədɪ] (in which /ny/
may become /ɲ/ if in rapid speech rules [34] and [12] have an unmarked ordering), dual ['dyu^ɫ:] (see also item 46 in part 3), fuel
['fyu^ɫ:]. (The vowel peaks have been adjusted by rule [43] for these
phonetic outputs.)[28] (c) Note that some speakers also shift the
diphthongs /i^ü/ and /ü^u/ to /yu/ (which by rule [43] becomes /yʉ^u/),
even when another satellite does not follow (especially after /h/).
This leads to pronunciations like Tuesday ['t^šhi^uzdɪ] and duty
['dži^udɪ], i. e. when rules (34) and (12) are reordered. (d) The
diphthong /ɪ^ə/ is sometimes shifted, as in Southern States fear
['fyɛ^ə:], Southern Mountain ['fyʒ], and British RP ['fyʒ:]; the /y/
thus generated is deleted in Southern clear after clustered /l/, but
is retained in British RP by some speakers (see rule [40f]). For
speakers who do not change /u^ə:/ to /o^ə:/ in ewer but who do make
this change in moor, it is clear that rules (24), which neutralizes
nuclei before the complex satellites, (28), which creates triphthongs,
and (34) have to occur in this ordering. But since the writer knows
of no one having [o^ə:] in moor but not in cure, it seems likely that
the panlectal ordering of these English rules would place (28) and
(34) before (24). On the other hand, since a pronunciation like
newer ['ɲo^ə:] or fewer ['fyo^ə:] would be unlikely except in very rapid
pronunciation, the present ordering is established here. But see
item 4 in part 3. Perhaps the neutralization rule will have to consider /#/ as a relevant part of the environment, in order to clear
up this problem.

(35) A rule truncates Alan to Al, Sally to Sal, Solomon to Sol,
Polly to Poll, Molly to Moll, Jerry to Jer', Pamela to Pam, Samuel
to Sam, Daniel to Dan, Massachusetts Avenue to Mass. Ave., and
mathematics to math. For speakers who do not have the vowel
changes stipulated in rule (24) in the first six examples (so that

Sal does not rhyme with doll, and Moll does not rhyme with ball,
and so that Jer' does not rhyme with err or air, but does rhyme
with e'er), it is clear that (35) follows (24). For speakers in the
Northern States who do not have the changes specified in rule (25) in
the other truncated examples (so that Pam and math do not rhyme
with ham and path), it is clear that (35) follows (24); but Southern
States speakers reorder (35) to a position prior to (24) (see part 3).

(36) This rule deletes syllabic sonorants (but not satellite sonorants) before their geminates in allegro tempo--this rule operates
on the sequence /m̩n/ where /m̩/ results from (32)--but in most
tempos the rule is inoperative where it would produce clusters not
tolerated in normal English (e.g. t'mato, T'ledo, pist'ling).[29] The
undeleted [t] in West(o)ner is evidence that rule (13) precedes (36);
but reordering may occur (see part iii). The rule is more likely to
operate as the nucleus following the geminate sonorant consonant is
less accented; thus premium becomes dissyllabic before as'soci,ate
(verb) loses the syllable spelled 'i', and the reduction is more likely
in interest when the final syllable is unaccented than when it is mid-
accented. Only in very rapid tempo would assoc(i)ation or c(ol)lide
(rhyming with Clyde) show the operation of rule (36). Only in tempos
sufficiently rapid to cause the reduction of /#/ to /+/ would rule (36)
operate to make the verbs open#ing and bottl#ing sound like the corresponding nouns or adjectives for speakers who differentiate such lento
pairs. In ev(e)ry, rule (36) appears to be obligatory. It frequently
operates in examples like hist(o)ry, myst(e)ry, quand(a)ry,
bot(a)ny, vet(e)ran, batt(e)ry (contrast batter#y, 'batter-like'; but
the crime of batter+y is usually like the electrical device), summ(a)ry
(contrast summer#y), scen(e)ry, choc(o)late. Rule (36) appears to
be one that applies iteratively from left to right. Only one application is possible where a sequence of two possible environments
are preceded by a consonant; thus, standard personally [ˈphɹ̩s(n̩)n̩łɪ]
and generally [ˈdᶻɛn(ɟ)r̩łɪ], beside nonstandard [ˈphɹ̩sn̩lɪ 'dᶻɛn̩łɪ]--
and compare standard different [ˈdɪf(ɟ)rɜt], beside nonstandard
[ˈdɪfɜ̃t] (note in both that the potential change of unaccented /ən/ to
/n̩/ is ruled out after the sonorant /r/). Note the loss of final /ə/
in nonstandard borough and Barbara; cf. standard temperature
[ˈthɛp(ɟ)rə,tˢhoᵊ:] (also final syllable unaccented: [tˢ(h)ə]) with nonstandard [ˈthɛ̃pɟ,tˢhɟ]. That the present rule follows (15) is shown by
the fact that met'ring does not have the vowel-lightening of metric;
although perhaps a reordering of (36) prior to (15) causes the light
vowel in the accented syllable of national and (some pronunciations
of) rational; but see problems with this which are discussed below.
The standard pronunciations of the verb opening [ˈoᵘp(m̩)nɪŋ -ɪn]
and of cabinet [ˈkhæb(m̩)nɪt] show that (36) follows (32); but see part
3 for the unmarked ordering of these rules, as in open it. The

orderings and reorderings of other rules and rule (36) in <u>fam(i)ly</u> and
<u>mem(o)ry</u>, as well as in <u>sentence</u> and <u>elementary</u>, are discussed in
part 3; but the lack of epenthesis in standard <u>fam'ly</u> shows that rule
(36) follows (30). The nonstandard pronunciations of <u>hundred</u> as
['həndəd] and of <u>apron</u> as ['ɛⁱpən] are discussed in connection with
rule (14); cf. note 17.

(37) The segment /y/ is deleted after a non-low front-vowel
geminate nuclear segment. Even the 'r-less' lects which ordinarily
retain //y// as [y] in the phonetic output may have [y] absent after
[ᵉ] generated from a single underlying heavy nucleus, as in <u>Maya</u>
['maᵉ(y)ə]. But note that rule (37) is inoperative in exaggeratedly
drawled pronunciations, where [y] may be heard in a dissyllabic
<u>square</u>. Ordinarily, however, <u>premium</u> ['phrimɪəm] and <u>labial</u>
['leⁱbɪɫ] lack [y] following [ɪ].

(38) Unaccented /ə/ is inserted between a non-liquid non-nuclear
segment and a nasal standing before an external word boundary in
those environments where a syllabic nasal is not allowed; e.g. <u>prism</u>
(cf. <u>prismatic</u>), <u>organism</u>, <u>barren</u>, <u>swollen</u>, and lento <u>blacken</u> and
<u>blosom</u>. The insertion in <u>elm</u>, <u>film</u>, <u>arm</u>, etc., where a postvocalic
liquid consonant precedes, it not standard. The reduced form of <u>not</u>
written <u>n't</u> also gets unaccented /ə/ inserted before the nasal segment when <u>may</u> precedes;[30] contrast also the presence of /ə/ in
<u>may' ve</u>, but not in <u>they've</u>, as well as in <u>they'd</u> (for <u>they would</u>), but
not in <u>they'd</u> (for <u>they had</u>). Whether these latter phenomena are
handled by rule (38) or not is unclear. The absence of [t] in <u>moisten</u>,
<u>hasten</u>, and <u>Christen</u> shows that rule (38) follows (13), assuming
underlying /mūst+n/, etc. If one does not assume a vowel-free
suffix, one would expect final [ɪn] (with the same nucleus as in the
final syllable of <u>Helen</u> and <u>pollen</u>) in <u>blacken</u> and <u>swollen</u>, which
actually have the same nucleus as <u>lemon</u>. (See note 35.)

(39) When a nasal consonant precedes a tautosyllabic obstruent
of the underlying voiceless order, most Americans delete the nasal
consonant and nasalize the vowel preceding it. This rule follows
(25) for most, if not all speakers (the counterevidence is rare and
doubtful); e.g. <u>crank</u> (Southern States) ['khrǣⁱk]. The epenthesis
rule ([30]) precedes rule (39), as in <u>prince</u> ['phrĩ̃əts], <u>once</u>, <u>contempt</u>
(cf. <u>contemn</u>), and similar examples. <u>Instance</u> may be ['ĩsthə̃ts] or
['ĩstə̃ts]. In <u>handkerchief</u> ['hǣⁱkətˢɪf], rule (13) deletes //d// (if
it is in the underlying representation of this word), (21) assimilates
//n// to /ŋ/, (25) affects the preceding vowel and makes it up-gliding,
and then (39) deletes the /ŋ/, while simultaneously nasalizing the
nucleus preceding. In <u>length</u> and <u>strength</u>, after rule (21) assimilates
the nasal to a velar, rule (23) affects the nucleus in some lects
(changing it to /ɛⁱ/ in the Southern States), after which epenthesis
(rule [29]) introduces /k/, and finally (39) generates ['lɛ̃ⁱkɫ 'strɛ̃ⁱkɫ].

Note that non-apical nasals trigger epenthesis, and do not assimilate, while the apical nasal assimilates but does not cause epenthesis so readily. Thus [ˈlɛ̃ᵊtᵽ] (like punkin for pumpkin) appears to assume a form with underlying //g// (or //p//) absent. The ordering of rule (39) with respect to several other rules is discussed in part 3 in connection with the examples sentence and elementary. Note in the former word that if the first vowel is affected by rule (39) (viz. [ˈsɛ̃ʔn̩s]), the second will be excluded, so that /ən/ can become /n̩/; how this is to be managed is a puzzle. In the other pronunciation (viz. [ˈsɛn̄ᵊts], where rule (20) first deletes //t//), the problem does not arise. For reordering with the vowel-shift rule ([16]) in ninety-nine, but not in ninety, see part 3.

(40) Several late rules affect sonorants. (a) /hy hw/ become /h̯ ḥ/ (with the combined length of two glides). Where speakers have Hugh as [ˈhiᵘ] rather than as [ˈh̯ɥᵘ], they will still have Hughey as [ˈh̯ɥⁱ]. This is important for rule (40b). Note that rule (40) affects the /h/ from aspiration (see rule [26]), no less than /h/ from other sources. (b) /h̯ ḥ/ are replaced by /y/ and /w/, respectively. (c) Before /ɫ/, /y/ is deleted in nonstandard pronunciation; e.g. calculate [ˈkhaeɫ:k(y)ɫˌlɛⁱt]. Cf. deputy [ˈdɛp(y)ədɪ] and regular [ˈreg((y)ɫ)lə]. This rule has to follow the rule creating /yə/ and the rule creating /ɫ/, i.e. (11, 27). Note nonstandard Dan'el, etc. (d) Before /y/, /ɫ/ becomes /ə/, as in double-u (the letter of the alphabet) [ˈdəbəyə], which in fast speech loses the second [ə] by rule (27) when (40d) is reordered ahead of that rule. (e) In all but very monitored Southern States English, /l/ preceded by an accented vowel and followed by /y/ plus an unaccented vowel is deleted; e.g. million [ˈmɪ(l)yən]; cf. will you [ˈwɪyə]. (f) /y/ generated from rule (11) or (34) is deleted after clustered /l/, but only in the former case in British RP. (g) The word-final /sy/ in -ence, -ance loses its /y/, and the word-final /ɲ/ in Dan is changed to [n]. The (g) part of rule (48) probably should precede rule (25). (h) Intervocalic /h/ is given a murmured pronunciation. This rule has to follow (30).

(41) Geminate consonants are reduced to single consonants when adjacent to an external word boundary or another consonant. Internuclear geminate obstruents and sonorants standing before the main accent of a word are simplified (as in command, but not in meanness); but only in very rapid speech are sonorants affected, as in illegal, irremedial. The /#/ must have been reduced by rule (4) for rule (41) to operate on the output of (28a) in good+bye, etc. Cf. usta for 'used to'.

(42) The (a) part of this rule changes /əʳ/ to /ʒ/, as in bird, and /ɯɫ/ to /ɫ:/, as in full. Note that in lects where the underlying liquid consonants in these examples are not syllable-final, as in hurry and bully, the change cannot occur; i.e. the rule does not

affect /ər ɯl/. (b) Then the grooved articulation of the sulcals /ð̣/ may become ungrooved /ə ə:/ and that of the sulcal /ǯ/ becomes-- according to the lect or the environment in the lect--ungrooved /ɵ: ɜ: ʌ:/ (note the length in all these). The /ə/ may be deleted after /ɑ ɔ/. (c) Length is subsequently added at the end of all nuclei ending in the lateral satellite /ł/, except those in which this segment is preceded by a lengthened nucleus generated in part (b) of the rule; e.g. <u>snarl</u> ['snɑ:ł] (contrast <u>doll</u> ['dɑł:]), <u>furl</u> ['fɜ:ł 'fʌ:ł], etc. (contrast <u>dull</u> ['dʌł:] and <u>full</u> ['fł:]), and <u>whorl</u> ['hɔ:ł] (contrast semistandard Southern States <u>boil</u> ['bɔ:ł], which is also the pronunciation of Northern States <u>ball</u>). Length is absent between geminates: [ə̣r ł:]. (See further note 24.)

Finally, unaccented /ə/ is changed to /ɵ ǯ ł/, respectively, before /r/, /l/, and /w/, as in <u>Lackawanna</u> [ˌlæke'wanə], <u>saturate</u> ['sætˢǯˌrɛit], and <u>tabulate</u> ['thæbył,lɛit]--in the last two cases, when rule (27) has not effected the same result. In allegro pronunciation, /ə/ is rounded to /ɵ/ when adjacent to a labial obstruent.

(43) This rule adjusts the nuclear peaks of various monophthongal and compound nuclei. Thus it makes /u ɯ/ into /ʉu ɨ/ in the Southern States except before grave segments in the same syllable. Note <u>good book</u> ['gɨb 'bʉk]. Various lects raise the nuclear peak of /aᵒ/ to /æ/, while others retract the nuclear peak of this diphthong and of /aᵉ/ to /ɑ/, and other minor adjustments occur. Some lects change the vowel in <u>cot</u> to an unrounded back [ɑ] or central [ɐ] vowel, and some 'r-less' lects round (or leave fronted) the vowel in <u>car</u>. Front vowels are otherwise somewhat centralized and central vowels are made back vowels before the complex (liquid) satellites and in some lects before grave consonants, after velars (including /w/), etc. In some Southern States lects, a less drastic retraction occurs before apicals (esp. liquids) when followed by an unaccented non-front 'dark' peak, as Sledd (1966) has shown. Most standard varieties of English diphthongize /e/ to /ɛⁱ/ and /o/ to /oᵘ/ (or /ɵᵘ ɔᵘ/, etc.) when not followed by a satellite (note Deep Southern States over-rounded [ɯ] or [ɯᵘ] in <u>road</u>, etc). This rule therefore has to follow (28). And note Norwich, England's [ʉ] from /ō/, /u/ from /ɯ̄/ (in <u>wrote</u> and <u>road</u>), and /o/ from the diphthongal base of <u>grow</u>, etc. (data are Peter Trudgill's). Some speakers in Norwich distinguish the nuclei in <u>make</u> and <u>day</u>. Various lects have /ɵⁱ: əⁱ:/ from /ɵ: ɜ:/ when not standing immediately before #; some have /ǯ/ from /ɵⁱ/ in <u>joint</u>. Note /ʉⁱ/ from /uⁱ/, /ʉ/ from /u/ in most kinds of English when /y/ precedes, and /ə/ getting rounded when adjacent to a labial. Accented /ɪ/ becomes a central output ([ɨ]) in <u>hit</u>, etc., in New Zealand. In some Southern States lects the low back vowels acquire an /ᵉ/ front glide before palatals;

e.g. push, large, wash, gorge. This rule has to follow (42), as
the examples with 'r' show.

Note that rule (43) affects only accented vowels.

(44) Several late vowel shifts occur here. In Southern Mountain
speech, peaks are moved counterclockwise around the vowel triangle
when followed by /ᵊ/: Fair ['faeᵊ] then sounds like fire ['faᵊ], which
in turn comes to sound like far ['fɤᵊ], which moves on to ['fɤᵊ 'fɔᵊ]
(which does not merge with fore ['foᵊ]). Some lects neutralize cord
and card as ['kh ɤᵊd]; others switch them. Before /ə:/ from /ᵊ/, New
England pronunciation may move clockwise around the vowel triangle.
Even when not before the sulcal satellite, the same movement or
shift is heard in many Northern cities, while the shift in the reverse
direction characterizes Cockney.

(45) Underlying //t// is changed to /d/ if preceded by a lateral
and/or a nuclear segment (which may have to be accented for some
speakers, as in formative and parentage; see Bailey MSa) and also
followed by a vowel; it must also be a syllable-final //t//, which will
be the case if it is followed by an unaccented vowel, and in allegro
tempo even when followed by a mid-accented or fully accented vowel,
as in Plato, pinto (with rule [39] before [45]), tantology, and at all.
Note that the change does not occur for some speakers after /l/, as
in Walter and voltage, or occurs only in allegro tempo for them. On
the other hand, Cockney has the change even before syllabic nasals,
where it is generally ruled out in America. Note [d] for //t// after
[ɬ] in faculty, after [m̩] in carpenter, after [n̩] in patented. This rule
has to follow rule (36), which degeminates sonorants, in order for
vet'ran to have [t] and veteran ['vɛdɚrən] to have [d]. But see the reordering heard in liddler and Id'ly in part 3. Rule (46) must follow
the vowel-shift rule ([16]) for most lects, as united (with the variant
of the accented vowel heard in night) shows; but see item 34 in part 3
for the complex reorderings in United States, etc.

Perhaps as part of this rule is the rule found in some, especially
older and more formal, British RP pronunciation, which changes /r/
to a tap in the same environments as those in which American //t//
becomes /d/. (See also note 24.) Southern States /r/ gets deleted
in the same environment in nonstandard pronunciation. This could
possibly be due to a syllabication in which syllable-final //r// is
changed to /ᵊ/, then to /ə/, and finally is deleted.

(46) Consonants are rounded when tautosyllabic with rounded
nuclear segments adjacent to them or separated from them by another
consonant, as in stroked, pull. Note that /r/ is rounded, as are the
British laminopalatal sibilant continuants and occlusives, whether
adjacent to a rounded or unrounded vowel. The apical sibilants are
rounded in most lects when adjacent to a labial, as in split and grabs
(also in lisps, where //p// has been spirantized by rule [33d]).

At this point also velars are adjusted to the frontness of tautosyllabic front vowels--more as the vowel itself is more fronted--
and before /l/ or /š/, whether tautosyllabic or not. In Charleston
and in Tidewater Virginia, the fronting is extreme before all front
vowels, including /a/ in card, garden. See details in SSP.

Among other consonantal adjustments made at this point is the
retroflexion of all apicals (but less so of interdentals than of alveolars) adjacent to /r/, retroflex apical sibilants in lects where these
exist, and the sulcal vowels /ɝ ɝ ɚ/ in lects where they exist. Note
that the satellite /ɫ/ is retroflex in Melrose, gall'ry, etc.

(47) This rule either shortens nuclei before heavy or underlying
voiceless obstruents or lengthens them before the other order of
obstruents and sonorants. Where nuclei have already been lengthened
by rule (42), the operation of rule (47) leaves the following four-way
differentiation: bird [ə·], bud [ə:], Burt [ə·], but [ə]. But in some
lects, length is neutralized in low vowels not followed by a heavy
obstruent, so that the nuclei of cod and card or laud and lord are
alike (but shorter than the nucleus of car and law), while cot and cart
and taut and tort remain distinct. Finally, the (b) part of rule (47)
devoices consonants and consonant clusters adjacent to an external
word boundary. Note that consonantal liquids and nasals are also
devoiced before a tautosyllabic voiceless segment. As for how this
rule handles the inflections -s and -ed automatically, see the writer's
squib, 'Motivating an alternative analysis of the English inflections'
(Bailey MSb).

Excursus. A few problems may be mentioned here. It seems
that (6) and (12) do have to precede (35), as ordered above, but the
examples are hard to find (Mitchell and Mitch are hardly probative)
and Dan (cf. Daniel with [ɲ]) almost seems to be a counterexample
(but see rule [40g]).

There seems to be a problem with rule (36), which degeminates
nuclear sonorants in rapid speech before vowels (especially
unaccented ones), at least insofar as /iy/ are concerned. Apparently
the rule affecting this cluster can be reordered to different earlier
positions, in contradiction to the theory that when a rule becomes
unordered (stands in the unmarked ordering) it does so with regard,
not just to one other rule, but to all other rules; otherwise, it may
be that this is an anywhere rule. Thus, to prevent the operation of
rule (6) in Asia, as well as to allow rule (6) to operate in vision,
rule (36) must precede (6) in the one instance and follow it in the
other, while being moved up prior to the palatalization rule [12]) in
the lexical exception -ion (but not, for example, in median or medium).
See further item 54 in part 3. Note that rule (36) must precede rule
(15) in national (and some pronunciations of rational) to ensure that

the first vowel will be made light. See for a further reordering of rule (36) before (7) under 18 in part 3; see also item 22. For the suffix //ie//, see under rule (7).

A serious problem in connection with the ordering of rule (36), is that in an item like <u>motion</u> (cf. <u>demote</u> : <u>demotion</u>) the rule has to occur before (12) to cause the palatalization, and yet not have operated before (15a)--so that /o/ does not get made light--or at least before (15c), for the vowel would not be made heavy before /sy/ (from /ty/ by rule [9]). To get around this, however, rule (15c) could be made to operate before a cluster ending in prevocalic /y/; but this would set aside the explanation of <u>national</u> (item 19) below in part 3. It seems clear that rule (17) precedes (36) in <u>fuschia.</u>

Everywhere that rule (36) is moved, rule (31) must be moved along with it and remain prior to it.

It may be that moving these rules ahead of (29) results in <u>low(e)ring</u> and <u>tow(e)ring</u> in some lects; this would be heard only in very rapid enunciation. If this ordering exists, the effect on (34c, d) would be to make this inoperative in <u>dualing,</u> etc.

A problem in the application of rule (39) to <u>either</u> of the pre-nasal underlying vowels in //sentent+ie// is discussed under the rule in question above.

3. Reorderings. Except for a few intrinsic rule orderings, almost every rule can be and is reordered somewhere above. This, along with the hypercorrections that result from inhibiting rules like (20) and (45), produces a great deal of variation in the panlectal grammar of English. Some of the items in the following discussion will merely refer to reorderings already discussed above in part 2.

1. The reordering of (18) before (14) for the ending //+ie// is discussed following rule (7) above.

2. The same discussion deals with the re-reordering of rule (36) for the lexical item just mentioned and for //iɒn//. See also in the preceding Excursus at the end of part 2, where various reorderings of rule (36) in different lexical exceptions are discussed. See further in note 6.

3. Under rule (14) is mentioned the reordering of parts (a) and (b) that generates <u>geese</u> [ˈgəⁱs] from /gɛs/ in some locales in the North of England. (See further discussion in part 4.)

4. In note 20, see the discussion of the ordering and reordering of rules (28) and (24), which generates, for example, [oᵊ] in <u>Stuart</u> and <u>steward</u> and <u>ewer,</u> and makes <u>mayor</u> like <u>mare,</u> <u>layer</u> like <u>lair,</u> etc. See also rule (24).

5. In <u>nuttin'</u> (for <u>nothing;</u> see also [37] below), rule (22) is reordered before (19) and (21). The order of rules in [ˈnəʔn̩] is: (22), (19), inoperative (21), (27a), generalized (33b), and (33h).

6. Af(ter)noon, lacking the second syllable, is generated with
(19), (27c), (42), (27b), and (13), showing several reorderings to
the unmarked order.

7. Possibly the fact that Cockney changes //t// to a light-order
segment before syllabic nasals is due to reordering rule (45) before
(27a) and (33h). At any rate, /d/ in littler and It'ly requires that
(45) operate prior to (33c).

8. Limme for lemme is due to reordering rule (33a) and rule
(33g), which assimilates //t// to /m/ (later degeminated irregularly)
prior to rule (25), which changes //e// to /i/ in the environment preceding /m n/ in some lects, or some styles of some lects. (The
writer is grateful to William Stewart for this example.)

9. Fambly for fam(i)ly results from reordering rule (36), which
changes /H/ to /l/ here, ahead of the epenthesis rule ([29]), creating
an environment in which (29) can operate. The reordering affects
standard humble, humbly, tremble, trembling. In nonstandard English, where rule (29) operates between /m/ and /r/, membry (for
mem[o]ry) is produced by a similar reordering of (36) ahead of this
rule.

10. By reordering (27c) and the desulcalization rule ([42]) ahead
of (27a), pattern will sound like Patton, paten. While this is general
in British RP and in New England, it occurs only for specific lexical
exceptions in some Southern States lects, as in modern ['mɐdn̩].

11. If rule (20), deleting //t// in wanted, occurs before (19) in
lects where the latter rule changes unaccented /ɪ/ to /ə/ in this
word and before (27b), which deletes /ə/ in informal speech, the
phonetic output will sound like wand in the lects in question. (In
BVE, the vowel will be [ɔ] or [ɒᵒ].)

12. Similarly, if rule (45) is ordered ahead of (19) and (27b)
under similar circumstances, started will, after the further operation of (41), sound like starred.

13. If rule (33d) is reordered prior to (5), as in BVE, tesses
will be heard for test. (Data are William Labov's.) White speakers
may be heard saying breakfasses.

14. In BVE sometimes arres' me and similar examples are
found, where final -ted (including the past marker -ed) are absent.
(The data are Ralph Fasold's.) Here we hear a reordering of (41)
before (5), with (13) latest of all.

15. Here we may deal with two pronunciations of sentence. In
the pronunciation ['sɛnɜts], we have the ordering, (20), inoperative
(27a), (29), and (39); the newer pronunciation, ['sɛ̃ʔns], has the
ordering (39), inoperative (20), (27a), (33h), and inoperative (29).
Rule (39) is reordered before the other rules in this latter pronunciation. Both possible orderings of (20) and (39) are marked; see below
in part 4.[31]

16. Let us consider three pronunciations of <u>elementary</u>: (a) [ˈɛləˈmɛnə̩rɪ], (b) [ˌɛləˈmɛnrɪ], (c) [ˌɛləˈmẽtrɪ]. Pronunciation (a) results from the ordering, (20), inoperative (39); (b) is the same, except the optional rule, (36), operates between the two others; and (c) is generated with (36) and (39) before (20), the rule that deletes //t// in the environment /n/ ___ Ṽ. As mentioned in item 15, rules (20) and (39) are marked in either ordering; see part 4.

17. In <u>value</u> or <u>volume</u> and <u>virulent</u> (and similar words like <u>erudite</u> and <u>querulous</u>), rule (11) may be reordered before rule (7), creating pronunciations in which /ɬ ɘ/ precede the /y/ generated in rule (11). In the marked order, these words are [ˈvæ(l)yθ ˈvɪrɬɘt] (where the //l// of the former may be deleted by rule [40e]).

18. A similar development occurs in <u>valiant,</u> <u>billion,</u> and <u>William</u> when (36) is ordered prior to (7).[32]

19. In <u>national</u> and <u>rational,</u> rule (36) appears to be reordered before rule (15a), or else (15c) is reordered prior to (15a), to ensure a light accented nucleus. So also one pronunciation of <u>ration.</u> See part 2, Excursus for further discussion. (Of merely historical interest is the lightening of the accented vowel in <u>Greenwich</u> before //w//-deletion in rule [30].) Perhaps [ˈrɛišənɬ] = <u>ration#al</u>.

20. When <u>calm,</u> <u>palm</u> show the effects of rule (24), this rule has to precede (23). Vowel length is eventually neutralized by rule (47).

21. The reordering of (19, 27b) before (14) in <u>apron,</u> <u>hundred,</u> etc., allows rule (14) to create /ɘ/ out of interconsonantal /r/.

22. When (36) applies before (24), <u>courier,</u> <u>furious,</u> and <u>curious</u> have /ʒ/ or their 'r-less' equivalents in the first syllable. That /yʒ/ appears in <u>curious</u> and <u>furious</u> shows that (36) and (28) follow (11, 19) and precede (7, 24).

23. When (27b) deletes the middle nucleus of <u>caramel</u>, in pronunciations having unaccented final syllable, and this rule applies before (7, 24, 27c), the phonetic output is eventually [ˈkhɑɘmɬ]. Cf. <u>guar(a)ntee</u>. A similar development gives [ʒ] in <u>Amer(i)ca</u>. In lects where unaccented /ɪ/ changes to /ə/ in word-final syllables in rule (19), rule (24) creates /ɔɘ/ in <u>for(e)st,</u> <u>or(a)nge,</u> <u>War(re)n,</u> and <u>Hor(a)ce,</u> making the last two words sound like <u>warn</u> and <u>horse</u>.

24. If any lect has the effects of rule (25) in <u>bang,</u> but not in <u>bank,</u> rule (25) would have had to be in a marked order before (21) in part 2. The only evidence known to the present writer is scanty and uncertain. Therefore, since rule (21) has to precede (25) for most pronunciations of <u>bank,</u> <u>length,</u> and <u>strength</u> (at least where the latter two have /ŋ/ in their derivations), there seems to be no manner in which the change of //ʌ// to /ɔ/ can be prevented in <u>mongoose</u> and <u>congress</u> (where the pronunciations contain /ŋ/), except by constraining this change to occur before /ŋ/ when the vowel occurs in a word-final accented syllable.

25. Where <u>Sol</u> and <u>Poll</u> rhyme with <u>Saul</u> and <u>Paul</u>, truncation (rule [35]) has been reordered ahead of (24). Where <u>volume</u> is ['vɒ^ɫ:yem], the reordering of (11) before (7) mentioned under item 17 above is accompanied by the reordering of (35) ahead of (24). (Cf. item 23 and item 55.)

26. Where <u>foll(o)wing</u> is ['fɔ^ɫ:wɪn], rules (31, 36) precede (7) and (24). The underlying form is presumably //fɒlw//, which has to become /'fɒle/ by rules (2) and (14); note that (14) must precede (31) and the others mentioned just above.

27. Where <u>coral</u> sounds like <u>Karl</u> and <u>Burrel</u> sounds like <u>burl</u> (and <u>mirror</u> like <u>mere</u>), generally heard only in 'r-ful' lects where every intervocalic //r// becomes the satellite /ə̆/, rules (19, 27b, c) have to precede (28), as in part 2, just as when the word pairs are kept distinct in 'r-less' lects, where internuclear //r// in these examples is syllable-initial. (Where very monitored pronunciations keep the word pairs apart in 'r-ful' lects, apparently the marked order with [31] before [7] is 'restored'.) In all of this, there is no reordering to an unmarked order. But such a reordering does occur where <u>choral</u> is pronounced with /ɔ/; the parts of rule (24) that change //a// to /ɒ/ and //ɒ// or /ɒ/ to /ɔ/ are put in this, unmarked ordering, as also when <u>Karl</u> has /ɔ/ or when <u>doll</u> or the last vowel in <u>Panama</u>, <u>ma</u>, <u>Arkansas</u> have the same nucleus. This reordering makes <u>pa</u> //pax// sound like <u>paw</u> //pɒx//. In many lects, this reordering is required for some lexical items, e.g. <u>falcon</u>, <u>alternate</u>, <u>asphalt</u>, and nowadays <u>mall</u>.

28. Where <u>chitt(er)lin's</u> is heard without the parenthesized syllable, the order of rules is (27c) affecting /ər/, (42) (desulcalization of /ə̆/), and (27c) affecting /əl/, plus (36). This looks as though (27c) is recycled; the alternative is to have (27c) divided into two ordered parts affecting /ər/ and /əl/; cf. the iterative ordering of rule (7) discussed above. The alternative appears to be necessary when <u>formerly</u> sounds like <u>formally</u>.

29. For <u>C(aro)lina</u> from //karə̄linV//, rule (2) fails to accent the first syllable with a mid-accent, though it gives a primary accent to the penult. Rule (26) aspirates the first consonant. Then rule (19) reduces all the unaccented vowels to schwa: /kərə'lanə/. Rule (36) reduces /ərə/ to /ə̆/, as in <u>differ'nt</u> and <u>veter'n</u>. Then rule (42) (desulcalization) generates: /khə'lanə/. Rule (27c) creates /ɫ'l/ from /ə'l/, and rules (36) and (46) finally generate the phonetic output: ['chlanə]. In this derivation, rule (42) has to be ordered before (27c), as in item 28 preceding.

30. In <u>cal(o)rie</u>, <u>sal(a)ry</u>, and <u>gall(e)ry</u>, rules (31, 36) are reordered prior to rule (7).

31. In the non-deverbative noun equation, and in some speakers'
pronunciations of transition and circumlocution (with final [žən]),
rule (9) has been moved ahead of (6). See also item 54 below.

32. Where congratulations has [dž] for //t//, rule (45) changing
//t// to /d/ precedes (11, 12). Although this may be a lone lexical
exception at the moment, other words of a similar nature will presumably be heard soon, first in careless speech and then in more
monitored styles.

33. Where persist has [z] at the beginning of the second syllable,
rule (27c) has been ordered before (6), so that //s// is now internuclear. (Note that [z] in absorb and absurd has a different explanation, as does [s] in resource.) Cf. also item 54 below.

34. What amounts to the reordering of (45) and the part of rule
(16) that changes /əi/ to /ae/ or /ae/ to /a/ before /d/, but not
before /t/ in many lects, is heard in some pronunciations of writer
(Joos 1942). In the inland Southern States, this reordering occurs
when the underlying //ĭt// stand in an intonational tune lower than the
next step (on the next accented syllable). Thus, united has [ae], but
United States has [a] in unmonitored pronunciation; for the cause,
see Bailey (MSd). In standard pronunciation both nuclei are [ae] in
typewriter, since here there is a step down.

35. Similar to the preceding is the difference between [ae] in
ninety ['naeni] and [a] in ninety-nine in the same locale. Instead of
reordering rule (45) before (16), here it is rule (20) that is reordered before (16). This is not a lone example.

36. When breathin' ends in [ṇ], whether or not preceded by [d]
for [ð], it has nothing not already found in item 5; nor does [ṇ] at the
end of huntin' have anything not already found here or in sentence
(item 15), where the elimination of the first nasal consonant by rule
(39) reduces the cluster so that [ṇ] can follow /t/ (rule [27a]). But
in restin' (with final [ṇ]), the reordering of rules (22, 19, 27a)
prior to (13) and (21) results in ['rɛsṇ], which like the other forms
in this section is attested.

37. In rapid tempo, throw it in the box can have in reduced to
[ṇ] even in lects which do not allow this syllabic after a preceding
unaccented syllable, if rule (28) is ordered ahead of (27a); rule (28)
changes throw it to ['ꞩroit], which must precede rule (43), which
changes /o/ to /ou/, in those lects where the latter change occurs.

38. Where [ṇ] replaces /n/ following / ʔ/, as in mountain (data
from John Jensen), rule (39) is reordered prior to (27a) and (33h),
which last precedes (32), as in item 38.

39, 40. When (32) precedes (31) in the unmarked ordering,
opener is ['oup(m̩)mə] in child's speech (John Albertini, personal
communication). The ordering, (39, 19, 27a, 33h, 32, 31) and
optional (36) generates ['khə̃ʔ(ṇ)ṇət] for continent and ['mɛ̃iʔ(ṇ)ṇəts]

for <u>maintenance</u>, neither of which the writer has actually heard, but which are probably attested. Note <u>open#it</u> [ˈoᵘpm̩mɪt].

41. When <u>government</u> is pronounced [ˈgəb(m)mə̃t], the rule order is (19, 32, 33b, 31) and optional (36)--with rules (32) and (33b) reordered prior to (31).

42. The pronunciation [ˈɪʔnt] for <u>isn't</u> and [ˈwɑʔnt] for <u>wasn't</u> show the unmarked order of (33b) and (33f), and also (33h); these all operate in the marked order after (32). The unmarked order (33b, f) is set up in part 2, since no instances of speakers who say [ˈkhɨʔn̩t] for <u>couldn't</u> but [ˈɪdn̩t] for <u>isn't</u> are known by the present writer; if any such cases are discovered, the order of (33f) and (33b) will have to be reversed from the order shown in part 2. If (33b, f, h) preceded (32), <u>isn't</u> would be [ˈɪʔn̩t].

43. In <u>cap'm</u> (for <u>captain</u>), (19, 27a) must precede (13) (which deletes //t//), creating an unmarked order between these and (13); (32) remains last.

44. In <u>apostle</u> and <u>epistle</u> (which, no less than <u>pistol</u>, have an underlying vowel intervening between //t// and the following lateral, as heard in <u>apostolic</u> and <u>epistolary</u>) rule (27c) must be reordered prior to rule (13), which deletes //t//. In <u>mustn't</u>, where the //t// of <u>must</u> is absent in the phonetic output, (38) presumably does not insert /ə/ before /nt/ (reduced from //n̩ɒt//) after this special morpheme, <u>must</u>, just as the same rule irregularly does insert /ə/ after <u>may</u> before /nt/.

45. The pronunciations of <u>Tuesday</u> and <u>mature</u> with [tš] from //t// and of <u>duty</u> sounding like <u>Judy</u> reveal a reordering of rules (34b, c) prior to (12). Cf. [ˈdžuˡ:] for <u>dual</u>.

46, 47. Where the cluster [štš] is heard in <u>bestial</u>, <u>question</u>, <u>Christian</u>, and <u>moisture</u> we have rules (36) reordered before (12) (except in <u>moisture</u> and <u>vesture</u>, generated by [11] before [12]); further, rule (12) is here reordered before (10).

48. When <u>misuse</u> is [(ˌ)mɪš'yᵘz], we have rule (11) reordered prior to rule (10).

49. The pronunciations [ˌjəš'tšhɛət] for <u>just yet</u> and [ˌlæ(ⁱ)š'tšhɨə:] <u>last year</u> exhibit the reordering of (12) and (10), as in item 47; the marked order in part 2 would generate <u>jus' yet</u> and <u>las' year</u> when (13) deletes //t//. But <u>juš' yet</u> and <u>laš' year</u> are generated by reordering (13) before (10).

50. When <u>right here</u> is [ˌra(ᵉ)'tšhɛə:], rule (34d) and (40a) create [ˈhᴊɛə:] before (12) operates.

51. Rule (17) has to occur before the accent rules in <u>-ture</u> and <u>-tude</u> (as lexical exceptions), so that the pronounced parts of these endings may act as heavy syllables in the accent rules in <u>solicitude</u> and <u>overture</u>.

52. If <u>science</u> and <u>diaper</u> are not generated from underlying representations lacking the vowel cluster (see note 22, where //ī//

is suggested as the underlying vowel), then rule (28) has to be reordered prior to the vowel-shift rule ([16]), at least in lects where
the output vowel is the one expected before another vowel, not the
one expected before (a nasal plus) a heavy obstruent.

53. If rule (13) deletes //t// in <u>won't go</u> and <u>don't know</u>, the output
will be ['wo^{u}ŋg'o^u 'do^{u}n 'no^u], where, in the former example allegro
syllabication allows rule (21) to operate. Apparently, placing (39)
before (13) generates ['wõ$^{\tilde{u}}$ ɪgo^u 'dõ$^{\tilde{u}}$ 'no^u], also very frequently
heard pronunciations.

54. Where <u>convulsion,</u> <u>dispersion,</u> <u>Persia,</u> and <u>conversion</u> have
[ž], (7) has its unmarked position prior to (6), making //s// internuclear.

55. Where <u>Pam</u> and <u>Dan</u> show the effects of rule (25), rule (35)
has to be reordered before (25); this is general in the Southern, but
not Northern, states.

David Stampe (1969:448) has suggested a reordering of what are
the (a) and (b) parts of rule (47) to their unmarked order, which results in making all word-final obstruents sound like the heavy order.
I have never heard this lect of English, except in <u>Jacob,</u> <u>blessed,</u> etc.

See part 4 for the reordering in <u>break</u> and <u>-tain.</u>

In a section on syllabication in chapter 9 of SSP, there is discussed a reordering which causes mid-accented syllables, treated
like accented syllables in the syllabication of the consonants preceding their nuclei, to be treated like unaccented syllables in faster
tempos. Contrast the two syllabications of <u>Plato</u> and of <u>pinto.</u>

4. Discussion. While it seems likely for many reasons that rule
reorderings begin in rapid tempos, and at first with one or two lexical exceptions, the occurrence of <u>circumlocution</u> (but not <u>locution</u>)
in the reordering numbered 31 in part 3 casts some doubt on this
assumption. (For an alleged example of a rule's moving from a more
general to a less general ordering, cf. Hurford (1972); cf. also the
discussion on the next page.) Some instances of pairs of rules
having both their possible orderings marked or unmarked may be
mentioned. In part 3, items 15 and 40, problematic situations occur.
In 15, <u>sentence</u> involves two rules having mutually marked orders,
although one order allows both the rules to operate in different parts
of the word, viz. in the pronunciation ['sɛnɜ̃ts], where (20) precedes
(39). Since this appears to be the older pronunciation, the rationale
for reordering is unclear; but the order of (20) before (39) has been
set up as the marked one in part 2 because the form in question appears to be the older one. Perhaps one of the many proposals contained in the writings mentioned in part 1 provide the needed principle
for determining the unmarked ordering. As for the two pronunciations of <u>opener,</u> [ɪo^{u}pm̩nə 'o^{u}pm̩mə], both orderings of rules (31)

and (36) are unmarked, in that both rules apply either way. The principle of opacity[33] makes the correct prediction relating to the newer ordering; see Bailey (MSa). But a slight extension of an older principle of Kiparsky's does this also. The present writer believes that the principle of greater generality, which Kiparsky (1968) regards as characterizing unmarked orderings, applies to the example under discussion, since more underlying segments are affected (altered) by the ordering (36)-(31) than by the other ordering. This agrees with the fact that children (some of whom have [36] before [31]) use more unmarked phenomena than adults. This explanation is harder to apply, however, to the two orderings in sentence.

Under rule (16) it might be reckoned that the rule changing underlying $//\bar{\varepsilon}//$ (heard in standard English only in break and -tain; cf. breakfast and retention), which is found in words spelled 'ea' (not necessarily all those spelled 'ear') in Irish, for example, has two orderings with respect to the rule changing $/\bar{e}/$ to $/i/$. The marked order, having $/\bar{e}/$ changed to $/i/$ before $/\bar{\varepsilon}/$ is changed to $/e/$ (or $/\varepsilon^i/$, after rule [43]), is heard in Irish; the other, unmarked order-- (16c), (16b)--is heard in most lects of English. This creates a problem for the lexical exceptions break and -tain (as well as a few other words which historically had $//\bar{\varepsilon}//$, but need not nowadays for most lects, since no alternations give away the possibility that this could be the underlying segment); for they would have to be exceptional in having a marked ordering, whereas lexical exceptions (Bailey 1968b) have the unmarked ordering in all other known instances. The vowel-shift rules have other problems, since the rule which changes $/\bar{i}/$ and other high vowels to $/\partial^i/$ and other diphthongs is known to be later than the rule raising $/\bar{e}/$ to $/i/$. But it has to have been inserted earlier than the last-named rule in geese, standard ['gis]; moreover this traditional pronunciation involves a marked ordering of the two rules. This poses a problem for the theory, generally very strongly supported by other evidence, that new rules are added at the end of the part of the rules to which they belong--at least when they are added in the marked order, since simultaneous reordering to an unmarked order is not precluded by the theory.

Although rule (36) has to follow most of the rules which follow (6), it does seem to be ordered before it when Asia and vision have [š] instead of [ž]. This is the marked order, since (6) is prevented from functioning. Perhaps this is an instance of the sort discussed in Anderson (1969) in which a rule can have a marked relation to another rule unless some other rule intervenes in an order that is mutually unmarked for all three pairs of rules. This possibility will not be explored further here. [34, 35]

NOTES

[1]By mutual consent of everyone, rules which are not in an ordered
relationship with each other (one cannot affect the other) are 'unordered'. Stampe (1969) first claimed that unmarked ordering is
non-order, viz. the order in which rules could repeatedly apply anywhere. The school headed by Koutsoudas and his colleagues advocate
a similar view. Kiparsky (1968) first discussed reordering and
characterized marked and unmarked order (see below). Cf. (contemporary) Chafe (1968) and (slightly later) Wang (1969). A convenient summary of proposals to supplement Kiparsky's original
characterizations of marked and unmarked orderings will be found
in King (MS), which includes Kiparsky's (1971) later views, as well
as several proposals of King's own, but not (in the preliminary version seen by me) Parker and Bailey (1970), Vennemann, or the views
of the school of Koutsoudas, Sanders, et al. The direction of reordering is from marked to unmarked. Where Kiparsky speaks of
reordering, Stampe (1969) would speak of unordering.

[2]This poses a problem for the theory that when a rule changes to
the unmarked order with respect to one rule, it changes to that
order with respect to all other rules too. See the Excursus below.

[3]Light clusters include single consonants, /kw/, and combinations of obstruents plus liquids. Obstruent-plus-lateral clusters
are usually heavy clusters, like all combinations of sonorants, but
occasionally obstruent-plus-lateral clusters are light; the same is
true of /st/ clusters. Light clusters are found in Euclid, Eustace,
nucleus, duplicate, Houston, beast, coast, etc., but a heavy one in
public. Light obstruent clusters merely close a syllable; heavy
clusters of any kind 'tightly' close a syllable; see chapter 9 of SSP.

[4]Rules (19) and (27c) change unaccented /yel yɘr/ to /yɫ yɘ́/, as in
fabulous ['fæbyɫləs], angury ['ɔgyɘ́rɪ]. Cf. rules (31, 40c).

[5]Apparently the rule is inoperative for word-initial /ty dy/ and
word-final /sy/, as in duration, tumultous, and emergence. Note
that the [š] heard in residential, etc., is not heard at the end of
residence, hospice, compliance, and preface (cf. resident, hospital,
compliant, and prefatory for underlying final //t//). In -ency and
-ancy (-//ent+ie -ant+ie//), rule (14) has to precede (12).

[6]Tabloid requires the operation of rule (36). The underlying
representation is //tābul//, as in tabular; cf. //fābul// in fable and
fabulous. Table and fable are derived from these underlying representations by putting rules (19) and (27c) before (11) (so that it will
not operate); after these rules, (15a) makes the //ā// in tablet, tabloid
light, and (15b) makes the same nucleus light in tabular and fabulous
--but (15) does not affect the accented nucleus in table and fable
because the lateral has become /ɫ/ (by [27c]) and no longer forms a

heavy or strong cluster with the preceding /b/. As said before, (36) affects tabloid, and it must be ordered before (15a), so that the accented nucleus will become light in this word. Nobler and abler (contrast nobility and ability) may be amendable to the same treatment.

[7]Contrast /ā/ in Mary with /æ/ in Marilyn, and with /æ/ in Mary+land, but /ā/ in Mary#land. This last example shows that there must be two syllables following the vowel to be lightened before any word boundary intervenes. Parent has the light accented nucleus in the Southern States, but the heavy one in England.

[8]The data from the North of England in Kolb (1966) make it clear that /ī/ first changed to /ɛⁱ/; it changed to /əⁱ/ only after /ū/ began to change to /eᵘ/, frequently changing to /əᵘ/ when /e/ from /u/ before a heavy cluster changed to /ə/. See Bailey (MSd). English also has /eⁱ/ from //ü// in joint, etc. If the peak in this nucleus unrounded and the diphthong lowered, /aᵉ/ is the result (in joint, hoist, poison, etc.); otherwise, it could lower to /ɔᵉ/.

[9]In syllable-timed rhythm as in some poetic recitations and in singing, the inflections at the end of roses and waded are [ɛz ɛd] for speakers who normally have the vowel [ɪ] here in the accent-timed rhythm of ordinary prose /aᵉ/ reduces to /ɪ/.

[10]Older speakers retain /ɪ/ before /l/ in tunnel and vowel, perhaps in -ible, often in satin, perhaps hardly ever any more in -ent or -ence, and then only in rural locales.

[11]Then unaccented /ən/ changes to /n̩/ by rule (27a). Contrast /n̩/ in satin with /ɪn/ in robin, cabin, bargain, and compare /ən/ in organ (cf. organic). Despite /ɪn/ in cabin, cabinet shows in its medial syllable the development, /ɪn/→/ən/→/m̩/ (by rule [32], and similarly for /ŋ/ in allegro organize. See also the discussion of BVE nuttin' (for nothing) under rule (33b).

[12]The assimilation is more likely in foreign words like Bankok and Bengal than in 'native' names like Hancock, Cronkite, and Bancroft, though 'nc' and 'nq' (as in banquet) seem to be spellings that are less prone to be pronounced with the velar nasal--or what is heard as such, since the nasal is deleted by rule (39) when //n// and //k// are tautosyllabic. Despite the tautosyllabicity of //ng// in penguin, one does not always hear the velar nasal in this word, perhaps because of the 'gu' (cf. 'qu' in banquet).

[13]The rule that inserts //r// in some 'r-less' lects before //mp nt s f Þ// in the 'broad-a' words goes here too; cf. popular spellings like 'arsk, marster, carstle'. Cf. 'dorg' for ['dɔᵊg].

[14]Note that //x// is velar like //g ŋ// and a heavy fricative like //s f Þ//, and so belongs to both classes; but it is generally treated like the former by speakers who have /ɔ/ before velars but not before the heavy fricatives--mainly in the far Western States.

[15]Also before a lateral followed by /#/, as in hall and ball, even if the lateral is not a nuclear segment. Some speakers have //ɒ// as the third vowel in alcohol and alcoholic; the former has [ɔ] or [ɒᵒ], while the latter has [ɐ]. But there are of course other pronunciations. Apparently most speakers also limit the change before the non-liquid sequents in which the word operates to oxytonic syllables, since the rule is absent in congress, conquer, mongoose (when this last has /ŋ/), a situation which does not seem to be amenable to different rule orderings, the way certain other nuclear adjustments are handled (by reordering rule [25] with respect to other rules; see later). See item 24 in part 3. See details of rule (a) in SSP.

[16]British RP has syllabic /n̩/ in vision, motion, and even after the cluster in question--in short, after the laminopalatal sibilants. In fact, British RP can have lento pronunciations with syllabic nasals following any of the underlying voiceless fricatives and, perhaps less frequently, following the underlying voiced fricatives. This is heard in America only in very rapid tempos. Pronunciations with /n/ in vision, motion, etc. show that rule (27a) has to follow rule (12).

[17]For hundred, apron, introduction, etc. with [ɟ], see rule (14). Note that //r// has to be changed to /ɘ/, before rule (27a), so that there will be no preceding cluster to prevent the generation of /n̩/ in important. See the discussion of personally later under rule (36).

[18]In English, syllabic nasals (and their geminate consonants) may precede syllabic sonorants (as in seasonal, seasoner), but they may not follow syllabic sonorants, just as they may not follow non-nuclear sonorants. There are a variety of reasons why /ɘ‿ ɫ/ are to be regarded as vowels and why syllabic nasals have to be treated as non-vowels. Besides the restrictions on the occurrence of syllabic nasals after most clusters, which do not apply to the complex vowels, there is the fact that rule (45) changes //t// to [d] under certain prosodic conditions when the complex vowels follow, but not when syllabic nasals follow.

[19]There has to be a subordering in words like snarl, curl, and whorl, such that first /ɘ/ becomes satellite /ɘ̯/, and then /ɫ/ is made a satellite to the entire preceding nucleus. See under rule (7); cf. note 30.

[20]In any event, real = reel, he'll = heel, betrayal rhymes with trail, dial rhymes with file. For roil and royal cf. note 27. As a result of rule (28), the words on the left below have no unaccented syllable following the accented syllable, but they will rhyme with the words on the right only if rule (28) precedes (24), as is usual in allegro tempo for many speakers.

overseer	leer
layer	lair
mayor	mare

betrayer	bare
gayer	glare
higher	hire
Myer	mire
lower ('reduce height	
of')	lore
withdrawer	drawer
bestower	store
tower	sour
pursuer	tour
doer	dour
reviewer	pure

For those lacking the restriction against /ł/ in school, goal, ball, cowl, etc. (see rule [7]), accrual, bestowal, withdrawal, towel, etc. will rhyme with these as a result of the operation of rule (28). (See further comments at end of rule [24].)

[21]A problem arises if any speakers who have /ə/ in the unaccented syllable of rapid, etc. nevertheless have /ɪ/ in fluid, poet, annuity, Louisville. As it does not seem possible to put rule (29) before (19), the only solution would be to restrict the change of unaccented /ɪ/ to /ə/ in rule (19) to environments not preceded immediately by a vowel.

[22]Where diaper and quiet have the same nucleus as ripe and quite in lects which differentiate this nucleus from the one in jibe and ride, the underlying representation must lack the vowels spelled 'a' in diaper and 'e' in quiet. It does not seem possible to reorder (28) prior to (16) in these instances. See also item 52 in part 3.

[23]Nonstandard membry (for memory) will be discussed later; note also the name Hendry for Henry. Rarely does false have epenthesis (to rhyme with faults). Notice that epenthesis is not standard in n__l, as in channel, at least when the lateral is syllabic; for handler, however, see rule (13). It has been claimed that some speakers 'de-epenthesize', as it were, prints, etc. to sound like prince without epenthesis. Epenthesis has occurred more than once in the past history of English, as in timber; cf. pre-Elizabethan ympnal (for hymnal).

[24]British RP speakers who have the tap [ɾ] for syllable-final internuclear //r// have it preceded by /ə/ (not /ᵊ/, as even in 'r-less' lects in America) when the next preceding nucleus is a heavy one. Thus, hairy is BRP / hæᵊɾɪ hɛᵊɾɪ/. The comments that have just been made do not apply to the nuclei in starry, furry, or abhorrent, where /ə/ is not heard. Note that the heavy nuclei of British RP have this /ə/ before internuclear /r/, as in serious, area, fiery, glory, jury, fury, even when no /#/ follows underlying //r//.

[25]For speakers for whom rule (19) does not change unaccented /ɪ/ to /ə/ in word-final syllables before /l/, <u>towel</u> is [ˈthɑ ᵒɫ:] (with variations in the vowel preceding the lateral).

[26]It is possible, but not likely, that the phenomena in (34a) are caused by the vowel-shift rule ([16]) in those regions where /aᵉ/ becomes /a/ before voiced segments other than //g//. However, the treatment of the back vowels in these areas, and the failure of /əⁱ eᵘ eʲ/ to have special developments before the complex satellites suggest that <u>hour</u> and <u>owl</u> be treated under (34a).

[27]Those Southerners who rhyme <u>royal</u> (cf. <u>loyal</u>) with <u>roil</u> may pronounce the former as [ˈrɔɫ:] or [ˈrɔᵉɫ:] (which alone is standard in some areas); but <u>royal</u> and <u>roil</u> do not rhyme in the speech of those who say [ˈrɔyɫ ˈrɔᵒyɫ] for <u>royal</u> (and similarly for <u>loyal</u>). The writer recently heard even <u>employer</u> [ɪmˈphlɔyə] on Washington television.

[28]In the Northern States, <u>mature</u> may be [məˈtˢhuˇᵊ̌]; cf. the palatals everywhere in <u>sure</u> and <u>sugar,</u> and in some areas in <u>sumac</u>-- formerly also in <u>suit,</u> etc.

[29]The cluster [dᶻw] can occur in rapidly pronounced <u>gradually.</u> But [kyl nrl snl] (where all are non-nuclear) are clusters which cannot occur in <u>calculate,</u> <u>generally,</u> and <u>personally.</u> Note [mr] in very rapid <u>marine,</u> [dl] in <u>delete,</u> [wy] in <u>w'yes</u> (for <u>why yes</u>), and [yw] in <u>y'went</u> (for <u>you went</u>).

[30]Rarely is <u>weren't</u> (or <u>Charles</u>) dissyllabic in an exaggerated drawl.

[31]That both orders of these two rules are marked--i. e. in either order one of the rules is inoperative--is true with respect only to the first vowel. When (20) precedes (39), as in the older pronunciation, rule (39) does operate on the second nucleus. The problem is mentioned under rule (39).

[32]If speakers relate <u>valiant</u> (as well as <u>valuable</u> and <u>valid</u>) to <u>prevail,</u> then both words have underlying //ā//, which will have to be shortened the same way as <u>national;</u> see item 19 below, also discussed in the Excursus at the end of part 2.

[33]For this principle, see Kiparsky (1971).

[34]Considerable simplification in rules (2, 11, 15, 17) is possible if the concept of 'open syllable' is available, providing that the syllabication of English internuclear consonants is generally what is termed 'unmarked'; e.g. V-CV, V-CRV (where R is a sonorant). See Theo Vennemann, 'On the theory of syllabic phonology', Linguistische Berichte 18 (1972), 1-18. Rule (8) also presupposes this syllabication. However, syllabication can differ in different tempos, with effects on English rules; e.g. (13). More significantly, rule (20) and later rules imply a surficial syllabication for obstruents which is 'marked'; viz., VC-(R)V. Such a situation--change of syllabication--

has never been noted in the literature, so far as I know. It seems to require a 'rule' between (19) and (20) that changes the syllabication from unmarked to marked. It would, of course, continue to allow for tempo differences like that commented on at the end of part 3 above in connection with <u>Plato</u>, <u>pinto</u>. Between unaccented nuclei, there is contradictory evidence for the syllabication of //t//. Rule (27a) (see p. 225) treats this consonant as syllable-initial, preventing a following syllabic [ŋ]; this is an unmarked syllabication. Rule (45), however, requires that internuclear //t// have a marked syllabication (with the preceding nucleus, unaccented or accented). The latter is stronger evidence.

[35]After this article was in proof, it was realized that the motivation for the ordering of rule (38) at the top of p. 226 is inadequate in not accounting for the change of //s// (cf. <u>spastic</u>) to [z] in <u>spasm</u> ['spæzəm]. For the sibilant in question to be intervocalic in order for rule (6) to operate, (38) would have had to precede.

REFERENCES

Anderson, Stephen R. 1969. West Scandinavian vowel systems and the ordering of phonological rules. Bloomington, Indiana University Linguistics Circle.

Bach, E. and R. T. Harms. 1972. How do languages get crazy rules? In: Linguistic change and generative theory. Ed. by R. P. Stockwell and R. K. S. Macaulay. Bloomington, Indiana University Press. 1-21.

Bailey, Charles-James N. 1968a. Dialectal differences in the syllabification of non-nasal sonorants in American English. General Linguistics. 8.79-91.

_____. 1968b. An untested idea on lexical exceptions to the regular ordering of the phonological rules of a language. Available from ERIC Document Service, PEGS 25/2.

_____. 1970. The English great vowel shift past and present. Papers in Linguistics. 3(1).173-78.

_____. 1971. Vowel reduction and syllabic sonorants in English. University of Hawaii Working Papers in Linguistics. 3(2).36-104. (To appear in rev. form as part of SSP = Bailey MSc.)

_____. MSa. Further observations on unmarked rule order.

_____. MSb. Motivating an alternative analysis of the English inflections.

_____. MSc. [Abbreviated SSP in this writing.] Southern States phonetics.

_____. MSd. Variation and linguistic theory. (To appear.)

Chafe, Wallace L. 1968. The ordering of phonological rules. International Journal of Linguistics. 34.115-36.

Chomsky, Noam and Morris Halle. 1968. The sound pattern of
English. New York, Harper and Row.
Hurford, James R. 1972. The diachronic reordering of phonological
rules. Journal of Linguistics. 8.293-95.
Jones, Daniel. 1964. An outline of English phonetics. 9th ed.
(With minor alterations.) Cambridge, W. Heffer & Sons, Ltd.
Joos, Martin. 1942. A phonological dilemma in Canadian English.
Language. 18.141-44.
King, Robert D. MS. Rule insertion.
Kiparsky, Paul. 1968. Linguistic universals and linguistic change.
In: Universals in linguistic theory. Ed. by E. Bach and R. T.
Harms. New York, Holt, Rinehart, and Winston. 170-202.
_____. 1971. Historical linguistics. In: A survey of linguistic
science. Ed. by W. O. Dingwall. College Park, Linguistics
Program, University of Maryland. 576-642.
Kolb, Eduard. 1966. Phonological atlas of the northern region.
Bern, Francke Verlag.
Koutsoudas, Andreas. 1971. On the non-sufficiency of extrinsic
order. Bloomington, Indiana University Linguistics Circle.
_____. MS. The strict order fallacy.
_____, Gerald Sanders, and Craig Noll. MS. On the application of
phonological rules. Bloomington, Indiana University Linguistics
Circle.
Lehmann, Twila. 1972. Some arguments against ordered rules.
Language. 48.541-50.
Norman, Linda. 1972. The insufficiency of local ordering. CLS(8).
490-503.
Parker, Gary and Charles-James N. Bailey. 1970. Ternary
markedness values? An approach to the measurement of com-
plexity in the operation of phonological rules. University of
Hawaii Working Papers in Linguistics. 2(4).131-42.
Ringen, Catherine. 1972. On arguments for rule ordering.
Foundations of Language. 8.266-73.
_____. MS. Rule order and obligatory rules. (To appear in the
proceedings of the Eleventh International Congress of Linguists,
Bologna, 1972.)
Sledd, James. 1966. Breaking, umlaut, and the southern drawl.
Language. 42.18-41.
Stampe, David. 1969. The acquisition of phonetic representation.
CLS(5).443-54.
Vennemann, Theo. 1972. Phonological uniqueness in natural
generative grammar. Glossa. 6.105-15.
Wang, William S.-Y. 1969. Competing changes as a cause of
residue. Language. 45.9-25.

NATIVIZATION AND VARIATION
IN ENGLISH PHONOLOGY[1]

LARRY NESSLY

University of Michigan

Variationists currently seem to be concerned mainly with two
sources of variation. One involves the spread of an innovation
throughout a language, with differences in form resulting from the
presence, absence, and extent of the change, as correlated with age,
geographical area, linguistic environment, and other categories
through which the innovation can spread. Examples of this kind of
variation can be found in Labov (1972) and Weinreich, Labov, and
Herzog (1968). The other kind of variation involves the adoption of
one general kind of speech by a group of speakers having another
kind of speech. Variants arise from the degree of adoption, which
is generally correlated with the social standing or aspirations of the
speaker. For example, Bickerton (1971a, 1971b) discusses a situation in Guyana, in which the adoptive speech group speaks Guyanese
Creole (Bickerton's 'basilect'), the adopted speech is Standard
Guyanese English (the 'acrolect'), and between these two types of
speech lie the various degrees of adoption (the 'mesolect(s)'). In
addition, Fasold (1970) discusses a number of examples of variation in Black English, which we may view as involving the adoption
of Standard English by a group with a Black English background (like
the lower working-class speech), with degree of adoption of the
Standard English pattern correlated with social class. [2] In this paper
I would like to provide another example of the adoptive type of variation, using nativization in English as the source of variation.

The type of variation that I will be concerned with can be illustrated by the two forms [gəráž]/[gǽriǰ], in which the first form has

final stress, a reduced [ə] in the first syllable, a tense [ā] in the
second syllable, and a final [ž], while the second form has initial
stress, a lax [æ] in the first syllable, a reduced-vowel [i] in the
second syllable, and a final [ǰ]. I claim that these two variants
should be assigned a single underlying form. The way to relate
these forms is to identify more foreign and more native surface
variants of the same underlying structure, and then to arrange these
variant qualities into an implicational hierarchy from more foreign
to less foreign. These variants are all within the speaker's competence. In this analysis the foreignness of the loans is hypothesized
to correlate with the education and social standing of the speaker, so
that educated higher class speakers use the more foreign variants,
while lesser educated lower-class speakers use the more nativized
variants. The parallel with the Guyanese example and the Black
English example should be evident. The major problem with the
nativization material is that the foreign loanwords eventually assimilate to the native pattern, to be replaced with newer loans. In this
way, while the forms can be arranged along a hierarchy of foreignness, eventually any given form will lose its variants and become
nativized. While the hierarchy itself will still be intact, at any given
time a number of loans will still be fairly foreign or will already be
fairly nativized, and many other forms may show only a few of the
possible variants. What is of interest, however, is the general
system of nativization, not the status of any particular loan.

The first step in the treatment is to argue that the variants all
derive from a single underlying form. The current way of treating
variants in generative phonology is to represent them with different
underlying forms, as in /gVræž/ for [gəráž], and /gaerVǰ/ for
[gǽriǰ] (with the 'V' standing for a reduced vowel whose underlying
quality is unrecoverable). The problem with this approach is that
it represents the difference between [gəráž] and [gǽriǰ] as the same
kind of difference between <u>clavicle</u> and <u>collarbone,</u> which have
basically the same meaning but different phonetic shapes. While
speakers recognize [gəráž] and [gǽriǰ] as variants of <u>garage</u>, they
do not recognize <u>clavicle</u> and <u>collarbone</u> as phonological variants of
the same basic form. To represent the variants of <u>garage</u> with
different underlying forms is to suggest that they have nothing to do
with each other phonologically, much as <u>clavicle</u> and <u>collarbone</u>. I
maintain, on the contrary, that the variants of <u>garage</u> can all be related to each other by rule, and will shortly support this contention
with evidence. Current phonological theory relates such forms as
[sēn]/[sǽnəti] phonologically, since they can be related by rule,
both phonologically and morphologically. To fail to relate the
variants of <u>garage</u> in a similar way is to indulge in a capricious
decision about what is phonologically related and what is not.[3] The

first step is to recognize that variants that can be related by phonological rule should be given the same underlying form.

The next step is to establish how the variant qualities of these loans can be related. I will first consider the foreign and native qualities of vowels, then the variants [š]/[č] (for ch) and [ž]/[ǰ] (for ge or gi), and finally variation between final stress and nonfinal stress. This will then lead to a discussion of how these variants can all be placed within a single hierarchy of foreignness.

A discussion of native versus foreign vowel qualities can already be found in Nessly (1971) and in Hill and Nessly (1971) (hereafter H–N). It is argued in H–N that lax vowels are more native than tense vowels, on the basis that tense vowels can often be predicted, and since lax vowels seem to be the unmarked case. Given this assertion we can specify tense vowels as more foreign and lax vowels as more native. [4] Within the tense vowels we can also find more foreign variants and more native variants. For the present discussion I will limit the examples to the front vowels, since these are less complicated. Discussion of the back vowels can be found in H–N. For a we find the variants more foreign [ā] versus more native [ē], as in [təmāto]/[təmēto] (tomato), [dātə]/[dētə] (data), and [swāv]/[swēv] (suave). For e we find the foreign/native variants [ē]/[ī], as in [krēdō]/[krī dō] (credo), [bētə]/[bītə] (beta), and [pēdrō]/[pīdrō] (Pedro). For i we find the foreign/native variants [ī]/[ay], as in [mərīə]/[məráyə] (Maria), [fərīnə]/[fəráynə] (farina), and [vīgō]/[váygō] (Vigo). All of these pronunciations are taken from Kenyon and Knott (1953) (hereafter K–K), with those of Vigo being taken from the Addenda. Anyone who doubts that [fəráynə] is a reasonable pronunciation for farina should see Jones (1956), who gives only that pronunciation for farina. A number of questions arise with respect to these vowel alternants. The first is the question of how we can tell which variant is the more foreign one. One way is to observe which variant occurs with other foreign variants, as in [ī] in [paestīš] (pastiche) (Jones), [ē] in [klīšē] (cliche) or in [rōdēō] (rodeo), and [ā] in [mēnāž] (menage). Another way is to ask speakers which is the more foreign way to pronounce the word. Still another way is to observe which variant ultimately changes into the other variant, that is, to observe the direction of nativization. All of these ways suggest that the more foreign tense vowel qualities are [ī] for i, [ē] for e, and [ā] for a.

Another question that could be raised is whether these vowel alternations are systematic. It is possible that the vowel qualities could vary randomly rather than in some orderly fashion. This question is easily answered. Notice that we do not find such alternations as *[təmāto]/[təmóto] (tomato), *[krēdō]/[krūdō] (credo), and *[fərīnə]/[fərānə] (farina). With the exception of a few extra alternations mentioned in H-N, the kinds of variation that these vowels can participate in are extremely narrow. In fact, foreign [ī] and [ē] are the unshifted equivalents of native [ay] (i̱) and [ī] (e̱), with [ā] replacing unshifted [æ]. The vowel alternations are therefore systematic.

Having observed the systematic relations between the native and foreign variants, we can question whether the native variants are nothing more than spelling pronunciations. To really consider this question we have to look at the premise in some detail. To say that spelling pronunciations are involved, rather than regular phonological processes, is to claim that speakers cannot assign the foreign vowel qualities to the spellings. If speakers can produce foreign qualities for these spellings, then they are aware that the spelling can have either variant, and can choose between the variants. The claim that spelling pronunciations are involved entails that the pronunciation is independent of the spelling, and that contamination is the result when speakers use the spelled form of the word rather than the spoken form. All that is necessary to undermine the spell-- ing pronunciation charge is to show that speakers who are ignorant of other languages can still give foreign values to spellings, showing that both the foreign and native qualities are related to the spelling, so that neither is more of a spelling pronunciation than the other. I have already collected such data, showing that naive speakers can productively assign foreign qualities to spellings, and this data will appear in Nessly (forthcoming) (speakers 4, 8, 9, 19, and 30).[5] The evidence has to do mainly with i̱, with lesser supporting examples for a̱ and e̱ (mainly because of the nature of the word sample).

In summary, then, the tense vowels in English have foreign and native variants, which are systematically related by productive rule.

As another example of foreign versus native qualities, we can observe variation between [š] and [č], and [ž] and [ǰ]. In both cases the variation derives from the French values for native [č] and [ǰ]. We can find such variants as [šéviət]/[čéviət] 'cheviot (cloth)' (K-K), [šæmpén]/[čǽmpēn] (champaign) (K-K), and [šǽnti]/[čǽnti] (chantey) (K-K). The problem now arises as to whether legitimate phonological rules are operating here. It is possible that the [š] is the proper pronunciation in these forms, and that the [č] derives only from pronouncing the spelled ch in the normal way. (I am assuming that everyone agrees that the [š] is more foreign.) Now, however, consider that the following Spanish words can also be pronounced with [š]: machete (K-K), chaparral (in the television program 'High Chaparral'), chicano, and Chavez (both forms pronounced with [š] by some newscasters). Since these words are pronounced with a [č] in Spanish we face two options: there is a phonological rule that changes [č] to [š], or the pronunciation [š] is a

spelling pronunciation. Since the usual spelling pronunciation interpretation would be that the [č] in a word like <u>cheviot</u> is the spelling
pronunciation, it is strange if instead we regard the foreign [š] as a
spelling pronunciation, suggesting that [š] is not a spelling pronunciation in the usual sense of the term. I claim that speakers read <u>ch</u>
as [č] in these forms and then apply a rule changing [č] to [š] if the
form is identified as French or has an appropriate phonological shape.

We also find variation between [ž] and [ǰ] in the forms [prestǐž]/
[préstiǰ] (<u>prestige</u>)(K-K), [žəné]/[ǰənét] (<u>Genest</u>, <u>Genêt</u>) (K-K),
[gəráž]/[gəráǰ] (<u>garage</u>) (K-K), and [gǽráž]/[gǽráǰ] (<u>garage</u>) (Jones).
Again the question arises whether the alternation is based on phonological rule. The evidence that I can cite is quite slight. The
humorous form [gārbáž] (<u>garbage</u>) must be taken from the spelling
since normal [gárbiǰ] would be derived from /gaerbVǰ/, which is an
inadequate base for deriving [gārbáž]. However, this suggests that
final stress, final-vowel tensing, and [ž] for <u>ge</u> (these being derived
from <u>garbage</u>) are spelling pronunciations, which is contrary to its
usual sense of 'independent of the standard pronunciation and conforming to the regular spelling rules'. Instead it seems that speakers
can convert [ǰ] to [ž] in the appropriate circumstances, and that the
variants for <u>ge</u> cited here are phonologically related.

There is a third type of variation yet to be considered. In Nessly
(forthcoming)[5] I argue that final stress is a non-native pattern, and
that final stress nativizes to nonfinal stress. The argument, briefly
summarized, is that final stress comes only from borrowings which
specifically supply this stress pattern, and that final stress commonly
disappears in loans while on the other hand native forms do not
develop final stress variants. Without going into detailed argument
in this discussion I will assume that final stress is foreign while
nonfinal stress is native. Examples of this alternation are [dekéd]/
[déked] (<u>decade</u>) (Jones), [šelǽk]/[šélaek] (<u>shellac</u>) (Jones), [šifán]/
[šífən] (<u>chiffon</u>) (K-K), with vowel reduction in the second variant,
and [hōtél] versus common [hótel] (<u>hotel</u>). In these cases we see
both final-stress variants and nonfinal-stress variants of the same
form, with the final-stress variants expected to disappear eventually.
This is certainly the same process that affected French loans which
entered the language over 400 years ago (as in <u>sólace</u>, <u>chápel,</u>
<u>hómage,</u> and <u>fórtune</u>--see Serjeantson 1935).

Having identified some foreign/native variants in English, I
would now like to discuss how to relate combinations of these qualities in a systematic way. For example, given a hypothetical word
[čǽpīk] (<u>chapique</u>), can we predict both the ultimate nativized form
of the word, as well as the assimilations that the form will go through
on its way to that nativized form? Can we say whether that form is
any more or less nativized than a form like hypothetical [məgás]

(magace)? What I will propose in this part of the paper are general guidelines in the assimilation of foreign loans. These guidelines will take the form that one assimilated state implies an earlier more foreign state and a later more assimilated state, and that a given form can be located as a point within this hierarchy of assimilated forms. First I will discuss the concept more carefully and then give examples as illustration.

First let us observe that nativization is a gradual process. If English borrows a form [məgás] (magace) one year, it will not be [mǽgəs] the next year. Nativization seems to be a gradual process, proceeding from one stage of anglicization to the next. To mirror this progression of nativized forms we need to set up a 'path of anglicization', in which the variants are arranged linearly from the most foreign to the most native. Given an occurring variant, with the notion of path of anglicization we can locate that variant along a continuum of change, determining how far the nativization has advanced, how far it has to go, and what stages it will pass through on the way. Notice that this notion is quite similar to the 'implicational hierarchy' of variation theory (see Bailey 1972a).

While the notion of a path of anglicization is conceptually clear, it is difficult at times to determine a strictly linear progression that fits all forms. There seem to be moderately complex constraints operating on the acceptability of various forms that could be expected along this path. Rather than discuss all the difficulties and possible solutions in this paper I will give some examples to show how forms can in general be arranged along such a progression.[6] I will look at the words banal, pecan, garage, and police.

For banal Jones cites the variant [baenál], which I take to be the most foreign, since [ə] in the first syllable would be more native. Next we find this reduced vowel in [bənál] (Jones, K-K). The tense vowel (which is marked) in the final syllable laxes to give [bənǽl] (K-K). The final stress shifts to the first syllable, and the vowel becomes predictably tense (see H-N), giving [bḗnəl] (Jones, K-K). The initial vowel then becomes lax, giving [bǽnəl] (K-K), the most nativized form. In this fashion we can arrange the variants of banal along a single continuum from more foreign to more native.

For pecan K-K cite [pikán], with a foreign tense vowel in the final syllable. This vowel laxes in the pronunciation [pikǽn] (Jones, K-K). Finally, we find [pī́kaen], with initial stress (K-K). We can eventually expect to see the variants [pī́kən] and [pḗkən].

For garage K-K cite [gərážz], with a final [žz]. This changes to [ǰ] in their citation [gəráǰ]. Next we can place [gǽrāž] (Jones, K-K), with initial stress. The final [žz] changes again in [gǽrāǰ] (Jones). Finally, we find the fully anglicized form [gǽriǰ] (Jones). It is possible that the path bifurcates into separate subpaths at points and later merges into a single hierarchy again. For example, one group of speakers may have the path [gəráž], [gǽráž], [gǽráǰ], etc., while another group has [gəráž], [gəráǰ], [gǽráǰ], etc. There are several cases like this that need to be investigated more fully.

Finally, we consider the variants of police. First we can list Jones' citation [pōlĩs], with a pretonic tense vowel. This laxes in [pəlĩs] (Jones, K-K). We can next list the common but nonstandard American pronunciation [pólĩs], with initial stress. A further nativized form is [póləs], which Daniel Boyle (personal communication) has found to be common throughout large parts of Ireland among more educated speakers with a meaning similar to bogyman and occurring in the sentence 'The police will get you'. This same pronunciation ([póləs]) is the preferred one among working-class speakers in Ireland (Labov, personal communication). Finally, we find the pronunciation [póləs] in the South Durham dialect in northern England reported in Orton (1933:291). This is the most nativized form.

One aspect of the above discussion needs comment. Some people may notice that the examples were chosen from a variety of sources: standard American, nonstandard American, RP (Received Pronunciation--upper-class British speech), Irish English, and the speech of South Durham. To some this may be equivalent to choosing examples from Dutch, Finnish, Basque, Welsh, and Greek and then writing a grammar of 'European'. My reply is that the citations from Jones and K-K both support the notion that there are gradient forms of nativization, and certainly these can be grouped into a path of anglicization. There is little reason to believe that Australian, for example, lacks examples of nativization, or Indian English, or Guyanese English, or even the speech of Bayonne, New Jersey. In fact, it is probable that every language has foreign elements in it, and at least some of these must have forms with different degrees of nativization. I am assuming that all speakers of English have basically the same system of treating these loans, that the system is panlectal within English, and that to choose examples from a variety of sources is merely to fill in the gaps that a single source might have. In this framework the path of anglicization is a constant, regardless of where given forms may be within it for given types of speech. From this viewpoint if RP has only one middle variant for hypothetical magace , while standard American has three more foreign variants, then the grammars of the two types of speech do not necessarily differ. It is possible that the speed of nativization and the variants that a form can take between the end points of the continuum could vary, but the variants from both types of speech would still fit into a single framework. I claim, then, that the treatment of foreign loans throughout English (in the broad sense) is

constant in its general form, and that significant differences between
types of speech arise from different constraints put on aspects
of the process, and do not arise from such differences as one type
of speech having a path of anglicization while another type does not.

So far the discussion has been of the nativization of foreign loans.
One can also ask whether forms along the path of anglicization can
reverse direction and become more foreignized. This does seem
possible. K-K, for example, cite the single pronunciation ˈvælɪt
for valet, and then make the following comment: 'A pseudo-French
ˈvaele, vaeˈle is sometimes heard. Valet, with a t, has been English
for at least 400 years.' Jones cites praːg for Prague, and then has
the following note: 'There existed until recently a pronunciation
preig which is now probably obsolete.' If a form develops more
foreign variants, then it is becoming more foreignized. It is possible for speakers to become more sophisticated in their treatment of
loans, to want to seem more cosmopolitan, to become more educated, to develop greater contact with the lending language, and so
on. This would lead to a foreignization of the form. The prospect
of having both nativization and foreignization operating as dynamic
processes within the same continuum makes the account more complicated. Not only do we have to account for the distribution of forms
along the path of anglicization, but we also have to take account of
the possibility that a given form within that continuum may be moving
either toward nativization or toward foreignization. This tends to
highlight the fact that it is the structure of the continuum that is important, rather than the number of variants, their position, or the
direction of movement for any given form.

With respect to nativization and foreignization, it is possible to
test these ideas through speaker reactions. One way to test nativization is to give speakers a foreign-sounding word and then ask them
what the most native pronunciation would be. Conversely, to test
foreignization it would be possible to give speakers a similar word
and then ask what the most foreign pronunciation would be. The
results would constitute evidence on the extent of these processes
among speakers. Also, it would be possible to present speakers
with two variants of the same form, such as [pōlís] and [pólīs] for
police, and then ask which variant is the more foreign. In this way
it would be possible to test the hierarchy of foreignness in the path
of anglicization. It is likely, of course, that speakers from different social classes would give different answers.

Given the distribution of variants of a single form correlated
with the social class of various speakers, one would expect that the
speakers with higher education and social standing would have the
more foreign variants, would be less likely to nativize the form
quickly, and would be more likely to foreignize the form (under

appropriate circumstances). We could also expect the speakers with higher social and educational standing to have more loans in their lexicon. [7] We can therefore expect the loans into English to give us two sources of variation: one is the variants of a form in the dynamic situation, as it passes from more foreign to less foreign, and the other is the variants of the form as they would correlate with social class, with the higher-class speakers having more foreign variants then the lower-class people. On the one hand we have what would be the stable distribution of variants through the social classes, with the more native variants toward the bottom, and on the other hand we have the dynamic of variants arising from the shift of forms toward the more native end of the spectrum. These two sources of variation compound the problem of describing the phenomena.

At this point I will summarize parts of this discussion. It should first be noted that insofar as the processes of foreignization and nativization apply in English, the synchronic description of them is dynamic. A given form can be placed along the path of anglicization, and both its earlier variants and its later variants can be specified (or predicted) to some extent if it is known whether the form is nativizing or foreignizing. Furthermore, the form can be related to other forms, as variants can be related to other variants, in terms of which form or variant is more nativized or foreign. Both the dynamic and the comparative aspects of the situation are richer than current phonological theory allows.

At the beginning of this paper I distinguished two major sources of variation: the spread of an innovation through a group of speakers, and the adoption of one kind of speech by a group of speakers using a different kind of speech. In the first case we find the innovation spreading dynamically through geographic areas, age groups, and so on. We also expect the innovation eventually to permeate the entire group of speakers. This is variation by language change. In the second case we find a continuum of adoption, especially one which distributes along the lines of social class. This continuum is not necessarily dynamic (it may involve a stable degree of adoption rather than a dynamic process of assimilation), and the adopted speech is not expected to permeate the entire group of speakers (in the sense that the entire group changes its mode of speech completely).

With respect to the static aspect of the adoptive pattern, it is possible that the Guyanese Creole and Black English cases mentioned here are actually dynamic. In print Bickerton (1971a:10, 11, and 1971b:487) strongly hints that both cases are dynamic, in that the Guyanese Creole is 'evolving' toward the English system, with Black English likewise evolving toward its superstrate. In a personal communication, however, Bickerton has hedged both implied

claims in the following way. He now considers the basilect to be
moving toward the acrolect, possibly resting at a point somewhere
within the mesolect(s), since both the acrolect and the basilect are
apparently receding in Guyana. He is also unsure now whether the
Black English situation is dynamic. If it turns out that the Guyanese
and Black English situations are dynamic, then they will share that
dynamicness with the adoptive pattern of nativization in English.
The parallel between these adoptive cases and nativization would be
even stronger. Guyanese Creole and Black English would be dynamic
upwards (toward Standard English) while nativization would be dynamic
downwards (toward native phonology), but both would show the adoptive pattern coupled with a dynamic path of change.

NOTES

[1]I would like to thank Nancy Conklin, Kenneth Hill, and Charles
Pyle for their comments on this paper.
  [2]I do not mean to claim that these two sources are the only
sources of variation, but rather mean to claim that at least until
recently they were the most studied sources. One can also think of
other kinds of sources: some of the examples of implicational
hierarchies in Bailey (1972a) that do not fit clearly into a language
change or adoptive pattern; the variants in Stampe (1972), arising
from the degree to which natural processes may apply; and the 'rule
ordering' variants of Bailey (1972b), which may ultimately be explained in terms of application or nonapplication of natural (Stampe-
like) processes. The dynamic adoptive approach for English in the
present paper can also be found in Hoard and Sloat (1972).
  [3]Variants such as abdómen/ábdomen and sonórous/sónorous
also need to be given a single underlying form. Since we can assume
that historically these had the same underlying form (see Nessly
forthcoming and note 5), to posit synchronically separate forms is
to push the problem one step back, since it is then necessary to
identify the historical process that would have produced the variants.
In my forthcoming dissertation (see note 5) I suggest how these variants are related.
  [4]This identification of tense vowels as more foreign is meant to
apply to loanwords. I do not necessarily claim that the tense vowel
of native bake is more 'foreign' then the lax vowel of native back.
  [5]Any reference to my dissertation ('Nessly forthcoming') involves
an aspect of it that is already written. Until the dissertation is
available in complete form I will be glad to send copies of the
appropriate parts upon request.
  [6]It is possible, of course, that some of these variants do not fit
within a single linear progression. As an initial hypothesis I will

assume such a linearity, and then revise the hypothesis if the data warrants it.

[7]Throughout this paper I am assuming that the upper classes have more contact with foreign languages than the lower classes. In those cases such as reported by Wolfram, Shiels, and Fasold (1971) and by Fishman, Cooper, Ma, et al. (1968), however, where lower classes have strong contact with a foreign language, their speech should be marked by large numbers of loans, foreignness of variants, and the other indicators of such contact.

REFERENCES

Bailey, Charles-James N. 1972a. The patterning of language variation. To appear in: Varieties of present-day American English. Ed. by R. W. Bailey and J. L. Robinson.
_____. 1972b. Variation resulting from different rule orderings in English phonology. Paper presented at the joint meeting of SECOL VIII and the NWAVE Colloquium. To appear in the collected papers from the meeting.
Bickerton, Derek. 1971a. On the nature of a creole continuum. Paper presented at the Caribbean Linguistic Conference, Mona, Jamaica, May 1971.
_____. 1971b. Inherent variability and variable rules. Foundations of Language. 4.457-92.
Fasold, Ralph W. 1970. Two models of socially significant linguistic variation. Language. 46.551-63.
Fishman, Joshua A., Robert L. Cooper, Roxana Ma, et al. 1968. Bilingualism in the barrio: The measurement and description of language dominance in bilinguals. U. S. Department of Health, Education and Welfare. Washington, D. C. OEC-1-7-062817-0297.
Hill, Kenneth C. and Larry Nessly. 1971. Review of: The sound pattern of English by Noam Chomsky and Morris Halle, 1968. New York, Harper and Row. To appear in Linguistics.
Hoard, James E. and Clarence Sloat. 1972. Variation in English stress rules. Paper presented at the joint meeting of SECOL VIII and the NWAVE Colloquium. To appear in the collected papers from the meeting.
Jones, Daniel. 1956. English pronouncing dictionary. Eleventh edition. New York, E. P. Dutton.
Kenyon, John S. and Thomas A. Knott. 1953. A pronouncing dictionary of American English. Springfield, Mass., Merriam.
Labov, William. 1972. The internal evolution of linguistic rules. In: Linguistic change and generative theory. Ed. by Robert P. Stockwell and Ronald K. S. Macaulay. Bloomington, Indiana University Press. 101-71.

Nessly, Larry. 1971. Anglicization in English phonology. In:
Papers from the Seventh Regional Meeting of the Chicago Lin-
guistic Society. 499-510.
_____. Forthcoming. English stress and synchronic descriptions.
University of Michigan dissertation.
Orton, Harold. 1933. The phonology of a South Durham dialect.
London, Kegan Paul, Trench, Trubner.
Serjeantson, Mary S. 1935. A history of foreign words in English.
London, Routledge and Kegan Paul.
Stampe, David. 1972. Divinity fudge. Paper presented at the
joint meeting of SECOL VIII and the NWAVE Colloquium. To
appear in the collected papers from the meeting.
Weinreich, Uriel, William Labov, and Marvin I. Herzog. 1968.
Empirical foundations for a theory of language change. In:
Directions for historical linguistics: A symposium. Ed. by
W. P. Lehmann and Yakov Malkiel. Austin, University of Texas
Press. 95-195.
Wolfram, Walter, Marie Shields, and Ralph W. Fasold. 1971. Over-
lapping influence in the English of second generation Puerto Rican
teenagers in Harlem. Washington, D. C., Center for Applied
Linguistics. OE Grant 3-70-0033(508).

VARIATION IN ENGLISH STRESS PLACEMENT

JAMES E. HOARD AND CLARENCE SLOAT

University of Oregon

0. For the vast majority of English words the location of stress is the same in all dialects and in all styles. Nevertheless, the position of stress for a substantial number of English words differs from dialect to dialect and/or from style to style. It is the purpose of this paper to show that the range of variation in stress placement is strictly limited and reflects very simple kinds of exceptions to the general stress rules or the presence of different types of junctures. The stress rules upon which we base the exposition are refinements of the rules given in Sloat (1972) and Sloat and Hoard (1972).

We take up first some examples which exhibit junctural differences. The stress placement in the words given in columns I and II depends on whether their suffixes are internal or external.

I	II
ádumbr+àte	adúmbr#àte
récond+ìte	recónd#ìte
éxplet+ive	explét#ive
ápplic+able	applíc#able
áspir+ant	aspír#ant
dísput+able	dispút#able
réspir+able	respír#able
réfut+able	refút#able
substánt+ive	súbstant#ive
rèmonstr+átion	remònstr#átion

265

The stress placement for both columns is predictable given the junctures indicated. In fact, quite aside from words such as those in I and II, for which stress placement varies, there are many other words which require us to recognize junctural differences. Consider the words given in III and IV.

III	IV
ádmir+able	desír#able
éxor+able	consúm#able
sépar+àte	elóng#àte
réson+ant	abérr#ant
cónjug+al	refús#al
démonstr+àte	remónstr#àte
réplic+àte	demárc#àte
rélat+ive	collát#ive
polýgam+y	pólypòd#y
photógraph+er	kídnàpp#er

While the words given in III and IV do not have stress variance, it is clear that they reveal a contrast in stress placement that has to be accounted for in some manner. The obvious way, given the fact that there are in general two suffix classes, is to posit a sandhi difference. The choice of external sandhi junctures for words like those given in column IV seems quite natural since the primary stress of desíre, consúme, refúse, kídnàp, and so forth is in the same location as the primary stress of desírable, consúmable, refúsal, and kídnàpper. Conversely, the primary stress of admíre, replý, and phótogràph is in a different location than it is for ádmirable, réplicate, and photó-grapher. It is quite reasonable to suppose that an internal suffix influences stress placement in the latter cases.

1. The Suffix Stress Rule accounts for the location of primary stress for the words in III.

Suffix Stress Rule

(1) $S \rightarrow [+\text{stress}] / \underline{\quad} (S) \quad V \quad C_0(+i)\#(\#)$,
$\qquad\qquad\qquad\quad [+\text{suff}]$

where S = string = VC_0.

The Suffix Rule specifies that the primary stress on a word is most typically two strings to the left of a governing suffix vowel. Where the term (+i) is null and term C_0 is at most a single consonant, examples, in addition to those given in III are:

(1a) súpple+ment, íncre+ment, réfer+ent, résid+ent, critéri+on, critéri+al, áctu+al, hármon+y, harmóni+ous, impérat+ive, týmpan+i, íntegr+al, psychíatr+y, necéss+i+ty, resid+ént+i+al, actu+ál+i+ty, demonstr+át+i+on, compens+át+i+on, demónstr+at+ive, evápor+ate, cónfisc+ate, invéstig+ate, cómpens+ate, philósoph+ize, amýgdal+oid, nítr+ous, nítr+ide.

Where the optional (+i) term is present we have:

(1b) présid+ent+i (présidency), óccup+ant+i (óccupancy), délic+at+i (délicacy).

There are several conditions involving the optional (S) term of the SSR. First, the suffix -ic does not permit the optional term. That is,

(1c) +ic → [-(S) of SSR]

Examples are eléctr+ic, titán+ic, eccéntr+ic, magnét+ic, emphát+ic, psychiátr+ic, and Homér+ic; (lúnatic and pólitic are exceptions). It is quite clear that -ic is generally an internal suffix, since it not only places stress but shortens immediately preceding long vowels, as in hypnót+ic, telescóp+ic, and satír+ic.

Second, internal short vowel suffixes and those containing the diphthong oi permit optional string (S) only if (S) contains at most one consonant.

(1d) $\breve{V}$, oi → [-(S) of SSR] unless S = $VC_0^1(r)$
[+suff] [+suff]

Examples are momént+ous, contént+ment, incidént+al, resíst+ant, cylíndr+oid, mollúsk+oid.

Third, internal short vowel suffixes do not allow optional string (S) if a long vowel immediately precedes.

(1e) $\bar{V}$+ $\breve{V}$ → [-(S) of SSR]
[+suff]

Examples are idé+al, Europé+an, Pythagoré+an, Caribbé+an, pharyngé+al, laryngé+al, epicuré+an. The last four examples have alternatively the stress patterns Caríbbe+an, pharýnge+al, larýnge+al, and epicúre+an indicating an underlying short vowel before the final suffix. This gives these words the short i suffix extender of Shakespéar+i+an, Jeffersón+i+an, Macedón+i+an, and so forth.

Fourth, the suffixes -ive, -ible, -ent, and -ant do not permit optional string (S) if a phonetic s, regardless of its underlying source, precedes.

(1f) -ive, -ible, -ent, -ant →[-(S) of SSR]/ s+___.

Examples are explós+ive, condúc+ive, expréss+ive, abús+ive, adhés+ive, decís+ive, corrós+ive, divís+ible, expréss+ible, obsolésc+ent, reminísc+ent, depréss+ant.

There are a number of morphological rules which enable us to predict, in part, when a suffix is external and, as a result, plays no role in stress placement and no role in other internal sandhi processes.[1] For example, the nominal suffix -al is external, as in arriv#al, perus#al, deni#al, repris#al, dismiss#al, and rebutt#al. The -al adjectival suffix is external after -ion, as in proféssion#al, óption#al, and rátion#al. When it is not lexical, -at(e) is external, as in authoriz#átion, regiment#átion, and thunder#átion. The suffix i is external after ar and or as in ántiqu+ar#i, mígr+at+or#i, nécess+ar#i, and oblíg+at+or#i. A final agentive suffix -or is external after ate as in óper+àt#or, ínhal+àt#or, návig+àt#or, and éduc+àt#or. We also find external sandhi with a short vowel suffix after a root containing h, as in inhér#ent and inhál#ant (cf. ínhal+àt#or with a long vowel suffix ate).

The Suffix Stress Rule and the conditions and morphological rules noted account for the location of primary stress for the words given in I and III.

We need to note also that the direction of change in English is towards regularization of suffix sandhi. Unlike the word ádmir+able, which has able suffixed internally, most words have able suffixed externally, as in desír#able and consúm#able. Any change in the sandhi of able should be in the external direction. This seems to us correct since we find admír#able to be a possible pronunciation, but we find that désir+able and cónsum+able are not. On the other hand, the suffix ate is generally internal and the direction of change seems to be from external to internal. We find rémonstr+àte to be a possible pronunciation (and one which in fact we have heard) but we find demónstr#àte and concéntr#ate impossible.

2. The location of primary stress for the words given in II and IV is not due to the suffixes which are present but is to be accounted for in terms of the Root Stress Rule. The Root Stress Rule places stress on words which have no suffixes and on words which have external suffixes.

Root Stress Rule

(2) $S \rightarrow$ [+stress]/ ([) $[S_0\_\_\_(S_W)(S(\acute{S}S_0))](\#)[S_0]$
    St R   R -R -R

$((\#)[S_0](\#)[S_0])_a)\#(\#)$, where $S_W = VC_0^1(r)$, R = root,
a R R -R -R   St

-R= non-root, and St = stem.

The basic part of the Root Stress Rule is the obligatory term

$[S_0\_\_\_(S_W)(S(\acute{S}S_0))]$.
R   R

This term accounts for the primary stress of such words as ínterest, sátire, Ohío, Óregon, Adiróndack, Monongahéla, Winnepesáukee, shériff, and Póntiac since any final string can be ignored as can one additional weak string.

By a general convention, if the word domain ##___## contains a stress, the application of a rule places a secondary stress. For the basic part of the Root Stress Rule first application places a primary stress on the penultimate syllable of Monongahéla. The rule re-applies since in a root the sequence $\acute{S}S_0$ can be ignored. Reapplication places the secondary stress and results in Monòngahéla. Wìnnepesáukee , Tàtamagóuchi , and Àdiróndack are similar cases.[2]

The general convention also applies to words stressed by the Suffix Stress Rule. The first application of this rule places the primary stress on the ate of author+iz#átion. Reapplication, with the suffix -ize placing a secondary stress gives àuthor+iz#átion. Àrgu+ment#átion and ràti+fic#átion have similar derivations.

Since the Suffix Stress Rule applies before the Root Stress Rule, compounds with an internal suffix affixed to the second root will have reversed stress patterns. Thus, àntipróton and èpicýcyoìd have primary stress placed by SSR and an initial secondary stress placed on epi and anti by RSR.

The optional term a of the Root Stress Rule permits a root to be ignored. For a word like telescope that consists of the two roots tele- and scope, the first application of RSR gives primary stress

on téle. Reapplication places a secondary stress on the root scope
and yields the appropriate stress pattern

[téle]+[scòpe].
R   R R   R

There are many similar English compounds. We also consider the
morphemes con, ab, inter, sub, and re to be roots, as in (the
nouns) cóntràst, ábstràct, íntervìew, súbscrìpt, and réjèct. Again,
the first application of RSR places a primary stress on the first root
and reapplication of RSR gives a secondary stress on the second root.

There are redundancy rules which exempt certain roots from the
Root Stress Rule. For example, the roots ab, sub, ad, and con are
regularly [-RSR] in verbs and adjectives. The final root is therefore
stressed in absúrd, subsúme, admít, and contáin. The morphemes
be, for, re, and de are regularly [-RSR] for nouns, verbs, and adjectives, as in belíef, belíeve, forgét, forbéar, repéal, replý, re-
léase, remárk, recéive, recéipt, desíre, and decéit. There are,
of course, a number of exceptions; for example, re is stressed in
the nouns réjèct and rélày.

There are other exceptions to the RSR. The root stant of ínstant
and cónstant is [-RSR]. Other roots, such as the man of póstman,
wóodsman, and fíreman, are usually [-RSR] in compounds. Compare, however, máilmàn and rágmàn.

The Root Stress Rule, as it is formulated above accounts for the
location of all primary stresses for the words given in IV and of the
secondary stresses on the compounds pólypòdy and kídnàpper. Most
of the words of IV are either verbs or adjectives and we get primary
stress by the root rule only on the second of the two roots. The noun
refúsal has its stress also on the second root since re- is regularly
[-RSR] for both nouns and verbs. We have also accounted for the
location of primary stress for the words given in II. Note particularly, that the root stant in súbstant#ive is not stressed since stant
is [-RSR]. Compare substánt+ive and also substánt+i+al where primary stress is placed by the Suffix Stress Rule.

The redundancy rules concerning roots which are not subject to
the Root Stress Rules are themselves subject to a good deal of variation. Consider the examples in V and VI.

V	VI
contrást-V	cóntràst-V
concréte-NAV	cóncrète-NAV
condígn-A	cóndígn-A
conflíct-V	cónflìct-V

V	VI
connáte-V	cónnàte-V
transpórt-V	tránspòrt-V
transfér-V	tránsfer-V
transmít-V	tránsmìt-V
transplánt-V	tránsplànt-V
expórt-V	éxpòrt-V
excéss-N	éxcèss-N
exhále-V	éxhàle-V
explóit-NV	éxplòit-NV
extráct-V	éxtràct-V
extínct-A	éxtìnct-A
defénse-N	défènse-N
defláte-V	déflàte-V
degráde-V	dégràde-V
demóte-V	démòte-V
detáil-N	détàil-N
permít-N	pérmìt-N
pervérse-A	pérvèrse-A

The examples of VI seem to us indicative of a change in progress toward fewer lexical redundancies which exempt certain items from the Root Stress Rule. This has the obvious effect of reducing stress distinctions between noun, verb, and adjective compounds.

3. Consider now the example of variation given in VII and VIII.

VII	VIII
guitár	guítàr
cigár	cígàr
debút	débùt
perfúme	pérfùme
locáte	lócàte
políce	mígràte
fragmént-V	frágmènt-V
tormént-V	tórmènt-V

To account for the stress variation in VII and VIII we need to introduce the Final Sequence Rule.

Final Sequence Rule

(3) $S_X \rightarrow$ [+stress]/___#(S), where $S_X = \overline{V}C_0$ and a number of
other specified sequences.

The Final Sequence Rule places a stress on final long vowel strings.
It will also place a stress on a number of final short vowel strings.
Many of the short vowel sequences are noted in Ross (1969). The
short vowel sequences include ar, ac, ex, ox, on, ol, oc, ek, acle,
aster, ander, and (m)ent.
Since the Final Sequence Rule follows the Root Stress Rule, FSR
accounts for the secondary stresses of the words in IX. The RSR
applies, then the FSR.

IX

sátìre, Híttìte
Ómàr, Bólivàr, NÁSCÀR
sátisfỳ, elóngàte
démonstràte, frústràte
réalìze, ellípsoìd
Póntiàc, Adiróndàck
Híckòk, kópèk
Kléenèx, Clóròx
árgòn, phénòl
tábernàcle, álabàster
sálamànder, óriènt-V
cómplimènt-V

Now if the RSR does, for whatever reason, fail to apply, the FSR
will place a primary stress. There are, in fact, a number of cases
where RSR is regularly skipped. For many speakers of English
words ending in -oo, -oon, the phonetic sequence [īs], -ee, -esque,
and -ade are regularly [-RSR]. Disyllabic words in -ar with an
initial weak string are also [-RSR] for many speakers. In addition,
many words are idiosyncratically marked [-RSR]. Thus, by either
a regular redundancy rule or by a lexical note, we can account for
the final stress of the words given in X. Only cadét, chiffón, Berlín,
and chagrín require a lexical note, the other examples are [-RSR]
by redundancy rules.

X

shampóo, Magóo
ballóon, salóon
valíse, Deníse
degrée, debrís
arabésque, grotésque
paráde, charáde
catárrh, Lamár
cadét, chiffón
Berlín, chagrín

If we accept the notion that the redundancy rules and lexical exceptions particular speakers and dialects maintain are not identical, we can readily account for the variation between the words given in VII and VIII. Those who say guítàr and cìgàr do not have the redundancy rule for ar. Those who say pólìce either do not have the redundancy rule for [īs] words or exempt certain words from the restriction. Some dialects, especially British dialects, except disyllabic words in ate from RSR; this gives locáte, migráte, etc. Dialects which lack this redundancy rule have instead RSR followed by FSR; this gives lócàte, mígràte, etc. Those who exempt by a redundancy rule two syllable verbs in ment from RSR have fragmént and tormént; those who do not have frágmènt and tórmènt.

Those speakers who mark words like debut and perfume as [-RSR] have the pronunciations debút and perfúme with final syllable primary stress. Those who do not mark these words as exceptions to RSR have débùt and pérfùme by the regular application of RSR followed by FSR.

The words given in VII and X are all of foreign origin. Many such words seem to be changing over to the stress patterns of VIII and IX. It is clear that in our system of stress placement rules, complete nativization involves only the loss of [-RSR] lexical redundancy rules or of [-RSR] lexical notes for individual words. That is, any word which is [-RSR] and has primary stress placed by FSR is a word of foreign origin. The application of FSR rather than RSR preserves the location of stress as it is (or was) in the donor language.

Other cases of complete nativization involve the omission of FSR. We note that many familiar, nontechnical words in on and ol are not subject to FSR. Thus, people who live in the Pacific Northwest say Óregon while outsiders say Óregòn. Other examples are Agamémnon, péntagon, and Ámazon beside Agamémnòn, péntagòn, and Ámazòn. Words such as báron and cárbon are not subject to FSR but words such as árgòn, néòn, and prótòn are. Among ol words, Cárol and Brístol are not subject to FSR; but technical terms such as phénòl and glýcòl do receive a secondary stress by FSR. Whether or not final on or ol receives a stress by FSR depends on whether or not it is deemed to be part of a technical or foreign vocabulary.

5. We have tried to demonstrate in this paper that English stress placement variation can quite easily be treated within the framework of stress rules we have posited. Variation is not due to basic differences in the stress rules from one dialect to another but is due instead to minor differences in sandhi, in lexical notes, and in lexical redundancy rules. The quite plausible and simple account of variation which we are able to provide is, we feel, very strong evidence for our stress rules. Moreover, in every case we have examined, the direction of stress placement changes is precisely in accord with the propositions that (1) sandhi is often regularized, (2) special lexical notes are often dropped, and (3) lexical redundancy rules are subject to change or loss much more readily than are the basic phonological rules themselves. What this means is that changes like débùt from earlier debût, and nonattested but possible sûprème for suprême and réquìre for reqúire are readily understood. However, pronunciations like senténce, syllâble, linguistíc, demónstràte, effórt, and exércìse are hard to fathom even in context. Try the following example:

This senténce is a linguistíc exércìse to demónstràte that placíng stress on impossíble syllâbles réquìres a sûprème effórt.

We conclude by noting that réquìre and sûprème, as given in the example, are quite understandable, even if unusual, and are potential regularizing changes within our system. However, without adding new stress rules, without greatly changing stress rules, or without adding lexical notes to items which do not now have them, our rules will not permit such changes as are represented by effórt and linguistíc. We are thus able to suggest that our rules have an appropriate predictive power when viewed both from a static and from a dynamic perspective.

NOTES

[1]See Sloat and Hoard (1971) and Hoard (1972) for some discussion of a number of internal sandhi processes.
[2]Note that a reapplication of RSR applies only to long roots. Words like recommendation and incrimination receive secondary stresses by the Anacrusis Rule given in Sloat and Hoard (1972).

REFERENCES

Hoard, James E. 1972. Naturalness conditions in phonology, with
particular reference to English vowels. In: Contributions to
generative phonology. Ed. by Michael Brame. Austin, University of Texas Press. 123-54.
Ross, John Robert. 1969. A reanalysis of English word stress,
part I. Mimeographed.
Sloat, Clarence. 1972. Stress in English. Presented to the Graduate
Linguistic Circle, UCLA, February 29.
_____ and James E. Hoard. 1971. The inflectional morphology of
English. Glossa. 5.47-56.
_____. 1972. English stress. Presented at the summer meeting
of the Linguistic Society of America, Chapel Hill, North Carolina.

ACCEPTABILITY JUDGMENTS
FOR DOUBLE MODALS IN SOUTHERN DIALECTS

RONALD R. BUTTERS

Duke University

It is well known that there exists a colloquial use of the phrase
might could meaning 'might be able to' in the speech of the American
South. Atwood (1953:35) finds it a 'typically South and South Midland
form' (especially prevalent in North Carolina) for all but 'cultivated'
speakers.[1] And Eliason (1956:245) finds the expression (though 'but
rarely') in the written English of North Carolina before 1860, citing
one example (I know I might could and should enjoy myself, from a
school boy in Lincoln County in the western piedmont in 1859).

In fact, besides might could, at least three other such double
modal expressions can be observed in actual speech in the South
Midlands and the South: might would, might should, and might ought
to [ɔtə j.[2] Their use is by no means limited to the least prestigious
of speakers nor to the most formal of situations; I have, for example,
actually observed the following:

(1) You might would say that ('It might be that one would say that')
    --Harry K., age twenty, a Duke University English major
    from coastal Georgia, in private, semi-formal conversation
    with his instructor (this writer).

(2) I might should come over there ('Maybe I should come over
    there')--Virginia B., age forty-five, a secretary who
    attended college for two years and who, though she grew up
    in Pennsylvania, has lived most of her life since age
    eighteen in the South; in a semi-formal telephone conver-
    sation with this writer.

(3) <u>You might ought to tie that tree from the other side</u>
('You probably ought to tie that tree from the other
side')--Morris K., about forty-five, who has lived all
his life in the South (primarily in Georgia and North
Carolina). He is the owner of a successful landscaping
business, which brings him into frequent formal conversation with many upper middle-class non-southerners.
However, he is also a friend of this writer, and the
conversation reported was rather less formal than the
other two.

The fact that Atwood's 'cultivated' informants did not, according to
the <u>Linguistic Atlas,</u> use <u>might could,</u> and the fact that the forms
have not generally appeared in writing, suggests that the use--and
perhaps knowledge--of the double modal constructions is subject to
social variability of the sort reported in recent years in numerous
studies of social dialects.

The basic purpose of the present paper is to describe some
aspects of this variation among 'cultivated' Southern speakers. However, the attempt to do so raises immediate methodological problems
which I believe are of a much more general nature. As Labov has
pointed out (1971) and elsewhere, the linguist has three potential
sources of data: (1) introspective judgments concerning synonymity,
acceptability, grammaticalness, formality levels, and the like; (2)
similar judgments garnered from native informants; and (3) the data
of actually occurring speech (especially if that data has been mechani-
cally recorded). Data of the third type is, in Labov's view, generally
superior:

. . . elicitations are normative data that reflect social prestige
and stigma; and the intuitions of the theorist are inevitably
influenced by his theoretical orientation . . . For a large body
of data independent of the activity of the linguist we must draw
upon the conversation of everyday life (1971:454).

Concerning the use of introspection in dialect studies, one might
add that, in addition to running the risk of unconsciously altering the
data to prove himself right, the linguist obviously faces the problem
of validity in attempting to report intuitions about dialects which are
not his own. Having lived my first twenty-seven years in two adjacent counties in east-central Iowa, my intuitions about double modals
are highly suspect; they were learned rather late in life, and they
are based upon what is sociologically rather limited evidence, since
by far the greatest percentage of my contacts with native southerners
has been with relatively sophisticated speakers in fairly formal

situations. Finally, double modals are a rather marginal aspect of the language in question. While one may hear <u>can't</u> pronounced [kent] countless times in the course of a single day, and while the diphthong which I pronounce [ay] will be pronounced [a:] an even greater number of times in a similar time period, the use of the double modals is relatively quite infrequent, simply because the occasions for using them are rather rare. Generalizing from only a few examples, the non-native runs the risk of merely grafting the double modals onto his own linguistic system (as, say, a simple allomorphic alternative to <u>maybe,</u> which they resemble closely), thus missing some of the possible subtleties of the southerner's use of the construction. [3]

Low frequency phenomena, moreover, present special methodological problems for the use of Labov's 'hard data' approach. Because double modals are not very frequent (compared to the phenomena usually examined in variability studies), the amount of data necessary to produce meaningful results concerning speakers' use of them would be many times that needed for the study of copula-deletion, r-dropping, θ-realization, question formation, and the like. Furthermore, while it is perhaps conceivable that a large body of data might practically be used to tell us which of the more common double modal constructions are used by speakers, it seems almost inconceivable that in practice one could amass an amount of data necessary to exclude some possible forms, or even to decide very well about some of the less common ones (e.g. <u>might would</u>).

Perhaps an example drawn from nonvariable syntax will help to clarify this point. There is in English a well-known rule which permits the movement of certain verbal particles to the right of the direct object: <u>He cut up the meat</u> vs. <u>He cut the meat up.</u> According to my intuitions, these alternatives are in free variation for simple objects, although, as is well known, complexity in the object tends to inhibit the transformation in what has classically been called actual 'performance' (<u>He cut the meat which you bought at the store from the beautiful lady butcher with the big brown eyes up</u>; nor does this complexity have to be a matter of sentence length: <u>He can't cut the mustard up anymore</u> would be 'better', I think, left untransformed). Furthermore, the transformation becomes obligatory when the object is a pronoun: <u>He cut it up</u> vs. *<u>He cut up it.</u> These are facts which are readily obtained from introspection. One would, however, need to examine an enormous amount of 'hard' data even to begin to suspect the right grammatical restrictions and performance constraints. Furthermore, errors in utterance--which Labov rightly suggests are of no particular methodological consequence to the sort of phenomena he usually studies (that is, high frequency phenomena)--could make a real difference here; one mistaken utterance of *He cut up it could lead the analyst astray for a very long time indeed.[4] Finally, since there is no a priori reason to rule out intragroup variability with respect to such marginal phenomena--even where social variables are constant[5]--the temptation to treat the data from several speakers as homogeneous would have to be resisted.

In short, the use of a purely objective methodology for investigating double modal constructions would require many hours of recording of the informal speech of many individuals. It seems unlikely that we might develop techniques for eliciting spontaneous productions of the utterances in question (and such techniques in themselves would raise methodological questions). Thus the amount of data necessary would, I think, exhaust our energies and our resources for the sake of information which, however interesting it might be, is rather peripheral to the overall system of speech in the American South. As Labov himself has noted in a recent article (1972:117): 'the rarity of many grammatical forms' suggests that 'it will always be necessary to extend our observations with intuitions.'

And in fact, this situation may not be as bleak as it might seem. Preliminary results suggest that the study of intuitive judgments--the linguist's own, but also especially those of informants--can have very fruitful results. Labov (1971) notes with praise the landmark syntactical study of Elliott, Legum, and Thompson (1969), and the more recent work of Guy Carden (1971, 1972). Such studies have been concerned not with social (or regional) correlates of speech variation, but rather with the lectal variation that arises purely as a result of speakers generalizing slightly different linguistic rules from virtually identical data. There is no reason why such methods cannot be extended to situations where social and regional correlates exist. The results of a preliminary survey by questionnaire of fifty-one persons, supplemented by individual interviews and to some extent the (admittedly questionable) intuitions of the investigator, furnish what seems to me to be a fairly reliable outline of the use of double modal constructions among 'cultivated' speakers, with some suggestions concerning social distribution as well.

Semantically, the constructions denote roughly what might be conveyed in formal Standard English with perhaps, or informally with maybe, e.g. You perhaps should . . . , You maybe could . . . , etc. That is, they carry the force of uncertainty, reticence, deliberation, and/or politeness, depending upon linguistic and situational context.[6] Used with a first person pronoun, the constructions often suggest that the speaker is deliberating: I might could move the pawn, I might should (or ought to) pretend I don't care about her any more, I might would ask her if I didn't think she'd say no. With a second person

pronoun, the meaning is more often that of a mitigating politeness for
a (perhaps gratuitous) suggestion or an oblique command: You might
could move the pawn, You might ought to (should) pretend you don't
care about her any more, I suppose you might would ask her if you
didn't think she'd say no?;[7] in isolation, You might would tends to
mean the impersonal you, i.e. 'One perhaps would . . .' In the
third person, the construction is, in isolation from context, ambiguous between the two readings. He might could kill the chickens
either means 'I suggest that he kill the chickens' (politeness reading)
or else 'He just might kill the chickens' (deliberative). He might
should kill the chickens means either 'The practical course of action
for him might be to kill the chickens' (deliberative) or 'I suggest that
he has a kind of obligation to kill the chickens' (polite). In these ambiguities, the use of the double modals seems to part company
slightly with the standard colloquial use of maybe; at least, He maybe
could kill the chickens doesn't have for me the reading 'He just might
kill the chickens', though He might could kill the chickens seems to.

All but two of the fifty-one informants were Duke University undergraduates aged 18-22, and all correspond generally to Atwood's
'cultivated' informants. Geographically, twenty-five were from the
states of the old confederacy; twenty-six were from elsewhere.[8]
They were asked to rate twenty-four sentences containing double
modals (including used to could) or maybe according to the following scale:

(1) I have never heard this construction used.
(2) I have heard this construction used by others, but it isn't
    a part of my own normal speech patterns.
(3) I've used this construction in informal conversation as a
    part of my own normal speech patterns.
(4) I've used (or might use) this construction generally,
    including in writing, as a part of my own normal speech
    patterns.

Not surprisingly, familiarity with these items was far higher among
southerners than non-southerners. Even though they are now, in
North Carolina, living in a dialect area where double modals are
used, between seventeen and twenty-two of the twenty-six non-
southerners professed never to have heard at all might shouldn't,
might should, might could, and I might ought to; the total for might
would reached twenty-three. No non-southern informant admitted
at all to using any of the forms (response 3 or 4), except that three
of the twenty-six felt that they sometimes used You might ought to
(but not I might ought to) in casual speech (see below). For southern
speakers, on the other hand, the situation is reversed; between

seventeen and nineteen informants out of the twenty-five said that
they were familiar with might should, might could, and might ought
to (responses 2, 3, or 4), though only eleven admitted to using one
or more of the constructions normally in informal speech, and no
more than six admitted use of any one form. Clearly, then, Atwood's
claims concerning the geographical and social distribution of might
could are confirmed--and extend to might should and might ought to
as well. That roughly 25% of these 'cultivated' southern speakers
confess to using such forms is, however, higher than Atwood's discussion would indicate, and in fact it seems certain that the percentage of 'cultivated' users is even higher. Virginia B., for example,
the secretary whose actual utterance of the sentence I might should
come over there was mentioned above, declares on her questionnaire only that she has heard others use such forms (response 2),
but does not admit to using them herself. And Yvonne R., a college
graduate in her early twenties from eastern Tennessee, on the
questionnaire also denied using any of the forms, but readily said
in a follow-up interview that she does certainly use them when she
'goes back home'--and home is the relatively well-to-do family of
a Johnson City physician--although she is 'pretty careful' of what she
'says around Duke'! In short, there appears to have been considerable variation in the ways in which speakers interpreted the phrase
'normal speech patterns'--a problem that also exists in studies which
ask for the 'acceptability' or 'grammaticalness' of sentences.

I conclude, then, that these double modals are thought of among
'cultivated' speakers as informal regionalisms, with at least some
social stigma attached to them. One is also lead to the conclusion
that their use is even greater among 'noncultivated' speakers, though
little data was available on the social backgrounds of the informants.
Whether this stigma is great enough to explain the fact that, for any
given item, roughly one-third of my southern informants claimed
never to have heard them spoken by anyone, is a matter for some
conjecture. In general, individual informants were quite consistent;
either they had 'never heard' of all or nearly all of the items, or
else they had heard of most or all of them. Such informants seem
randomly distributed geographically and by sex, though perhaps some
pattern of this sort might emerge if more data were collected. In
part, I believe that many informants were unaware of what their own
speech patterns are. As Bolinger (1968) has pointed out, judgments
of 'ungrammatical' may stem from the momentary inability to see
the nondeviant interpretation of an utterance, e. g. his example of
It wasn't dark enough to see, which seems deviant, though It wasn't
dark enough to see Venus in the sky is obviously nondeviant; see
also Bever's example The horse raced past the barn fell (Bever and
Langendoen 1972:46), the nondeviant interpretation of which many

speakers fail to see at first glance. In a similar manner, it does not seem too surprising that informants might believe that they have never heard forms uttered which they in fact may even say themselves--especially when the informants are not likely to have seen the forms in print before, as is the case with double modals.

On the basis of the data collected, two other conclusions seem rather strongly indicated. One is that might would is a far less widespread form than the other double modals. Roughly 50 per cent of the southern informants' responses to might would were 'never heard of', and only one informant said he had ever used it (and then only in the second person).

A second conclusion which our data would indicate is that the negated forms of the double modals may be somehow less acceptable than the positive forms. Twice as many of the responses to I might shouldn't were of the 'never heard' category, as compared to I might should (fourteen 'never heard' the negative, but only seven 'never heard' the affirmative), and mightn't should was even more unfamiliar (twenty-two 'never heards').9 The negative form of only might should , however, was tested with these informants. Stronger conclusions must await testing for the other forms as well.

Likewise, other firm conclusions must await the gathering of a larger amount of data. Even within the limitations of the present study, however, certain patterns seem to be emerging. For example, if we look at the data for all of the southern speakers taken as a group, little difference is found in the relative use of might should, might could , and might would. There are, however, eleven speakers who indicated actual use of one or more forms. Nine of these eleven use either I might ought to (4/11) or You might ought to (7/11) or both (2/11); seven of eleven use either I might could (5/11) or You might could (5/11) or both (3/11); five of eleven use either I might should (1/11) or You might should (5/11) or both (1/11); only one of the eleven uses might would (and then only in the second person). This suggests, at least, the possibility of an implicational series: the presence of might would implies the presence of might should; might should implies might could; might could implies might ought to. In fact, for these eleven informants, this turns out nearly always to be the case: only informants 2 and 9 reject might ought but embrace might could, and only 9 embraces might would but rejects might should. Since might ought was also found in the second person in actual use among northerners as well as southerners, and since two of the eleven southern double modal users also rejected almost completely all forms except You might ought to, we may actually be dealing with two different linguistic processes here, with might would, might should, and might could making up an implicational series which is unrelated to might ought to. My own intuitions--though I view them here with considerable suspicion--lead me to believe that might ought to is a marginal colloquial form from my youth in Iowa, whereas the other double modals seem alien indeed.

Again, however, let me stress that such conclusions are for the present highly tentative. It has been my concern primarily to present a preliminary analysis, and to suggest what course future research might take with this and other marginal phenomena. At the same time, of course, I would stress that the limitations of such an approach are obvious. We have uncovered little about the class distribution of variables throughout society, except that we have concluded that they are doubtless more frequent in nonprestigious dialects. As Labov has noted (1971), questionnaire techniques work best with mature, sophisticated speakers--with those who are used to dealing with the written word, with taking tests, and so on. With less sophisticated speakers, other techniques must be found. Nevertheless, I hope that I have demonstrated that variability studies based upon intuitive judgments can be quite revealing about not only nonsocial variability such as Carden and others are studying, but about socially correlated variables as well.

NOTES

[1]Atwood also notes with surprise that the construction is found 'in the German area of Pennsylvania' as well, and that (18) the archaic pronunciation [maut], limited primarily to the geographical South, appears in the phrase might could 'in only about two-thirds as many informants . . . as use it in might have helped'. Traugott (1972: 192-93) believes that the constructions are developments of similar Middle English forms.

[2]A similar regionalism, used to could, has also been observed, but will form little part of this discussion. Atwood discusses only negated used to in the phrase used to be: didn't used to be, used not to be, used to not be, and a few other variants (33-34). It is my impression that might can, might will, and especially might may are also used, though not might shall. Labov, Cohen, Robins, and Lewis (1968:260-63) also found might don't and must didn't among speakers of Black English.

[3]Frank Anshen, Elizabeth Duke, Bruce Fraser, and William Labov all have suggested to me (personal communication) that, like maybe, the use of might in these constructions is essentially adverbial, and that the term 'double modal' is a bit misleading. Their arguments--that unlike true modals, but like adverbs, might in general cannot be negated (*He mightn't could go) nor preposed for questions (*Might he could go?)--seem convincing, but I here will

continue the use of the term 'double modal' anyway, though 'adverbial <u>might</u>' might would be better.

[4]It seems likely, moreover, that it is exactly in the case of such low-frequency phenomena that one might expect to find mistakes and uncertainties in speakers. A speaker might regularly use, for example, <u>might could</u> as a normal part of his informal speech, but extend the construction by analogy to <u>might should</u> once in a while-- even though he might feel, upon reflection, that such an extension were odd or alien. A parallel situation might be the substitution of <u>raise</u> for <u>rise</u> (<u>The bread was raising</u>), though the normative strictures against that substitution are probably not shared by the modal extension.

I have had little success in getting responses to deliberate conversational use of sentences which violate the rule involving obligatory particle movement for pronoun objects, e.g. *<u>Did you make up it</u>?, even though this rule seems fairly strong and fixed. Even so, the fact that mistakes can occur unnoticed doesn't mean they will. The following dialogue did occur, though it doesn't involve a normal particle:

Daughter (age eleven): You have a typewriter in here.
Father: I brought home it from the office.
Daughter: That sounds funny.
Father: What? 'Brought home it?'
Daughter: Brought home it: Brought it home. What is there
to eat?

I can also report the utterance <u>The night before the exam I looked over it</u> (without stress on <u>it</u>) from a nervous student.

[5]It has been argued in several places that such intragroup variability does indeed exist, and that it has been overlooked in several studies dealing with variable data. See Butters (1971a, 1971b) and Bickerton (1971).

[6]All subjects were asked if they could state a meaning difference between <u>You might should move the pawn</u> and <u>You should move the pawn</u>. Of the eleven southern informants who admitted to ever using any of the forms themselves, only one mentioned that <u>might should</u> seemed more polite than <u>should</u> alone. Nine associated <u>might should</u> with doubt or hesitancy, uncertainty, or indecision, 'maybe' vs. 'definitely should', etc. (The eleventh informant could find no meaning difference, even though he said he uses <u>You might should</u>). I suspect, however, that with a less cerebral, more emotional topic, the politeness connotation would be foregrounded, e.g. in <u>You might should pay him back the money you owe him</u>. The only individual interviewed orally to whom the question of connotations was raised

felt that such forms were used 'to be polite'; however, she also felt that she did not use such forms herself, though she had heard them used.

[7]I have no data on the question forms of double modals. I suspect Might should I ask her?, Might shouldn't you ask her? would be acceptable, though William Labov (personal communication) believes that there are no question forms for double modals, and at least two native speakers, Elizabeth Duke and William Neal, agree.

[8]One informant from Miami, Florida, was counted among the northern informants.

[9]Similarly, usedn't to could and used to not could show almost total rejection (nineteen and eighteen respectively), as opposed to used to couldn't (five total rejections). It should be pointed out, however, that used to could and used to couldn't show equal acceptability; apparently, the extension here is generally accepted.

REFERENCES

Atwood, E. Bagby. 1953. A survey of verb forms in the eastern United States. Studies in American English, No. 2. Ann Arbor, University of Michigan Press.

Bever, T. G. and D. T. Langendoen. 1972. The interaction of speech perception and grammatical structure in the evolution of language. In: Linguistic change and generative theory. Ed. by Robert P. Stockwell and Ronald K. S. Macaulay. Bloomington, University of Indiana Press. 32–95.

Bickerton, Derek. 1971. Inherent variability and variable rules. Foundations of Language. 7.457–92.

Bolinger, Dwight. 1968. Judgments of grammaticality. Lingua. 21.34–40.

Butters, Ronald R. 1971a. Black English {-Z}: Some theoretical implications. Paper presented at the Linguistic Society of America Winter Meeting in St. Louis, Missouri, December 1971. Mimeographed.

_____. 1971b. On the notion 'rule of grammar' in dialectology. Papers from the Seventh Regional Meeting, Chicago Linguistic Society. Chicago, Chicago Linguistic Society. 307–15.

Carden, Guy. 1971. A dialect argument for not-transportation. Linguistic Inquiry. 2.423–26.

_____. 1972. Multiple dialects in multiple negation. Papers from the Eighth Regional Meeting, Chicago Linguistic Society. Chicago, Chicago Linguistic Society. 32–40.

Eliason, Norman. 1956. Tar-heel talk. Chapel Hill, North Carolina, University of North Carolina Press.

Elliott, Dale, Stanley Legum, and Sandra Annear Thompson. 1969.
Syntactic variation as linguistic data. Papers from the Fifth
Regional Meeting, Chicago Linguistic Society. Chicago,
Department of Linguistics, University of Chicago. 52-59.
Labov, William. 1971. Methodology. In: A survey of linguistic
science. Ed. by William Orr Dingwall. College Park, Md.,
Linguistics Program, University of Maryland. 412-91.
_____. 1972. Some principles of linguistic methodology. Language
in Society. 1.97-120.
_____, Paul Cohen, Clarence Robins, and John Lewis. 1968. A
study of the non-standard English of Negro and Puerto Rican
speakers in New York City. 2 vols. Philadelphia, The U.S.
Regional Survey.
Traugott, Elizabeth Closs. 1972. The history of English syntax.
New York, Holt, Rinehart and Winston.

CREOLIZATION AND LANGUAGE ONTOGENY: A PRELIMINARY PARADIGM FOR COMPARING LANGUAGE SOCIALIZATION AND LANGUAGE ACCULTURATION

DAVID M. SMITH

Georgetown University

Introduction. While basking in the sunlight of their new-found respectability creolists should go a step farther. They should seize the occasion to press upon linguists the insights their studies offer to a host of contemporarily interesting issues. It is now clear that attempts to account for several features of pidgin-creole languages (here called acculturating languages)[1] have been the impetuses to much recent advance in linguistic theory. For example, traditional inability to cope with the great synchronic and diachronic variation in such languages has spurred the development of variation theory; the sudden appearance and persistence or equally sudden disappearance of pidgins has challenged notions of language genesis and of 'functional equality'; and, finally, the striking formal resemblances in geographically dispersed acculturating languages has led to a renewed interest in the operation of natural, universal factors in language processes.

Today it is widely accepted that adequate linguistic theory will account for synchronic and diachronic variability, that languages do develop (some being better for some things than others) and that any kind of change involves the interplay of universal linguistic forces and culture specific social forces. Creolists have long had to defend these positions. Now that preliminary models and paradigms have been worked out to deal with these facts, it is our contention that acculturating languages provide useful insights into a number of developmental phenomena.

In this vein the present paper makes the following three points. (1) Both language acculturation, phylogenetic development, and language socialization, ontogenetic development, are real, on-going processes which must be conceptually and empirically distinguished from each other and from other types of language change. (2) These processes are parallel with respect to both formal and functional features and, under certain conditions, interpenetrate. (3) The intersection and interpenetration of these processes provides a useful paradigm for analyzing some types of culture contact, particularly modern urbanization.

1. Language socialization and acculturation distinguished. A discussion of development of language must recognize three sets of contrasts (see Figure 1). Development is distinguished from normal change, phylogeny is distinguished from ontogeny, and acculturation is distinguished from enculturation.

FIGURE 1.

1 +DEV	+PHYLO	+ACC	= Language acculturation
2 +DEV	-PHYLO	-ACC	= Language socialization
3 +DEV	-PHYLO	+ACC	= Second language learning
4 +DEV	+PHYLO	-ACC	= Language of children of language community
5 -DEV	+PHYLO	-ACC	= Natural change in language community
6 -DEV	-PHYLO	-ACC	= Natural change in communicative competence of adults

Allowing for internal constraints, these three contrasts, when treated as binary features, yield six empirically possible language change situations. Each one of these sets of contrasts has important implications for an understanding of language acculturation and language socialization.

1.1 Language change vs. development. While all languages change, not all languages are developing. Development, or acculturation, occurs in a speech community where either two different languages or two nondivergent dialects are present and speakers are forced by social pressures to use a lect which is not their native tongue. Examples of situations where languages develop are urban communities with in-migration of different ethnicities or classical pidgin producing contexts. Languages used in these social situations can be plotted on a prepidgin-postcreole continuum and are characterized by ongoing change in formal scale or scope of function (cf. Hymes 1971:65ff).

The same sort of distinction, with an added complication, can be made from an ontogenetic perspective. The language of an individual changes over time. In a homogeneous speech community[2] (that is, one without two nondivergent dialects or two different languages) the change is nearly imperceptible, following normal linguistic constraints in response to changing social contingencies. In other contexts, however, when he is learning a second language or when he is living in an acculturating speech community, for example, his competence may be developing. Furthermore, there is evidence that the development of individual competence in these situations closely parallels acculturation in a phylogenetic sense. That is, in the process of learning a second language, the new lect will undergo changes in formal scale, scope of function, and referential sorting out. While peripheral to this paper, it is worth noting that, the comparison of these two processes, language acculturation and second language learning (which is thus also acculturative), should yield data on marking conventions by adults, useful techniques of language teaching, and a host of other questions.

1.2 Acculturation vs. enculturation. However, even here the changes in an individual's language competence differs significantly from what happens in language socialization. Language socialization refers to the development of communicative competence in an individual as he grows up. Children, obviously, acquire both a set of rules capable of generating the acceptable speech of their community and the rules for using this competence. This total communicative competence develops gradually until at least puberty and is evidently inextricably tied to neuro-physiological maturation. Thus socialization is necessarily a unique event for any individual.

This process of acquiring communicative competence results in the individual developing a functioning cognitive framework for dealing with the world he experiences. It includes a set of perceptual strategies and of conceptual categories. Any new information he encounters as an adult, including a second language, will be processed through it. This is enculturation or acquisition. The difference between enculturation and acculturation or between acquiring and learning is that the former involves the developing of a cognitive framework while the latter involves modifications of a framework in response to contacts with another.

Since acculturation is not directly tied to neuro-physiological maturation, social contingencies can alter or even reverse normal sequences. This, for example, is precisely what happens in pidginization where a language unnaturally becomes unmarked in response to social demands placed upon it.

1.3 Ontogeny vs. phylogeny. Both acculturation and enculturation may be viewed as having a phylogenetic or ontogenetic locus, and it is important to keep them distinct. Phylogenetic acculturation, the concern of most creolists, for example, is, like any aspect of language, an abstraction. As such it is inaccurate to say that it is directly subject to the same pressures or functional demands which influence the development of an individual's language competence.

In summary, the paradigm discussed here serves to set language acculturation and socialization (1 and 2 in Figure 1) in a context amenable to comparison. Both are developmental phenomena, but acculturation is phylogenetic and acculturative while socialization is ontogenetic and enculturative. The next step required in explicating their social significance is a comparison of the two.

2. Language acculturation and socialization as parallel processes. This paper is concerned with processes, not real or putative static phenomena. I am not dealing with pidgin or creole languages but with acculturative processes which will be compared with encultura- tive processes. In taking this approach it is possible to escape the problems inherent in defining and hence the risk of reifying concepts that are primarily heuristic. At the same time a number of signifi- cant relationships viewed as shifting points on continua can be examined.

Taking our clue from Hymes (who himself was acting in keeping with established practice) we can look at three criterial features of developing language to establish comparative baselines. These are formal properties, functional characteristics, and referential quali- ties of language. Pidginization involves simplification of form, re- striction in function, and admixture of vocabulary by comparison to a base language. Creolization involves elaboration in form, expan- sion of function and stabilization and incorporation of the lexicon into the referential framework of the new system. These are well- attested phylogenetic processes and the specific procedures that are followed can be isolated. For example, simplification involves un- marking and generalization; restriction involves the elimination of some or all of the integrative functions of language.

I submit that strikingly parallel processes can be observed in the development of communicative competence of children. Earliest stages exhibit formal simplification involving unmarking and generali- zation. With respect to social functions equally significant parallels can be seen. Early language is used to perform only relatively simple social tasks and as competence increases the uses to which speech is put increases. Evidence for this can be seen in the socio- psychological problems encountered or the functional equivalents developed by children, such as the deaf, with arrested speech development.

Something similar happens with the referential quality of a child's language. Not only does he start with a mixture of social lects which must be sorted out, but his perception of the referential world is significantly different from that of the speech community as a whole.

Thus, in every sense, by comparison to the language of the speech community, a child's language is pidginized. As his development proceeds, it undergoes a transformation not unlike the process of creolization; and once it is formally and referentially adequate to meet all the needs served by adult language, it expands in use to perform those functions, a process similar to that of decreolization. This can be very roughly depicted as follows, remembering that we are dealing with gradatums and not mutually discrete entities.

FIGURE 2.

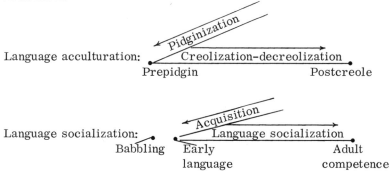

Note: In this diagram language acquisition is considered to be the development of formal linguistic competence and language socialization the development of communicative competence in addition. The former is roughly parallel to pidginization, the latter to creolization and decreolization.

3. The intersection of language acculturation and socialization. With respect to the two continuums, language socialization and language acculturation, we can conceptualize four possible and three empirically demonstrable social situations. They are: (1) a speech community where the language is not acculturating but where children are being socialized into it. (2) A speech community where the language is acculturating but in which there are no children being socialized. (3) A speech community where the language is acculturating and children are being socialized into it at the same time, and (4) the highly improbable situation where the language of the speech community is stable and at the same time there are no children being socialized.

3.1 Homogeneous speech community. Situation 1 is characteristic of a homogeneous speech community. Here there does not
exist a relatively stable acrolect with shared rules for usage against
which the communicative competence of children can be compared at
various points (n') in their development. Since the language is not
developing (not to be confused with changing) it can be depicted
graphically as a point. The child's developing competence can be
shown as a continuum.

FIGURE 3.

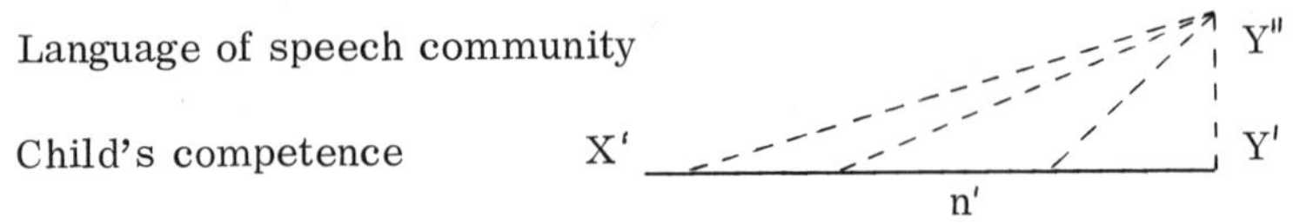

Language of speech community

Child's competence

Note: In Figures 3 through 5 the following conventions are used.
Plain symbols (X, Y, n) are used with reference to an acculturating
language, double primes (X", Y", n") with reference to a base language a developing language is compared with and single primes (X',
Y', n') with reference to a socializing language. Thus, Haitian
Creole would be Y, Haitian French Y", and the language of a single
speaker Y'.

In this situation any point on the X'-Y' continuum (n') can be compared with X' and viewed as developing, i.e. becoming elaborated
in form, expanded in function, and standardized referentially. At
the same time any point can be compared with Y" and viewed as
simplified in form, restricted in function, and anomalous as to
reference.

3.2 Pidgin speech community. Situation 2 would be typical of a
pidgin speech community where people interact for specialized purposes (multilingual sailors on a ship, plantation contexts, etc.).
The language used is not the first language of any of the speakers
and there are no children born into the speech community. Here
again there is only one continuum, but it is phylogenetic. This can
be depicted as in Figure 4.

FIGURE 4.

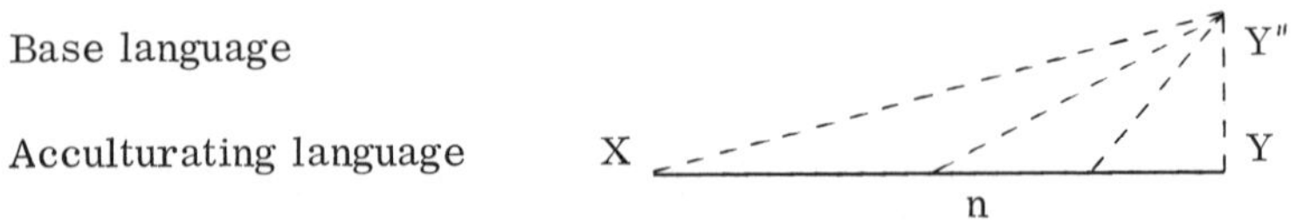

Base language

Acculturating language

In this case the acculturating language can be compared at any point (n) with Y″ (the base language) and will be simplified in form, restricted in function, and referentially, will exhibit lexical features of Y″ mixed with alien features. At the Y point of development it will be formally and functionally equivalent to but referentially distinct from Y″. Examples of such decreolized languages would include Sierra Leone Krio which is formally and functionally equivalent to Standard English but a distinct language and, for those who accept the creole origins of Black English, Black Vernacular English can be viewed as a functionally equivalent nondiverging dialect of Standard English.

At the same time, any point (n) on the X-Y continuum may be compared with X and will exhibit the process of creolization or decreolization.

3.3 Urban speech community. Situation 3 is typical of multi-ethnic urban communities. Here the language of the speech community is developing or acculturating and at the same time there are children being socialized with consequent development of individual communicative competence. This can be depicted as two continuums.

FIGURE 5.

Base language

Acculturating language

Child's competence

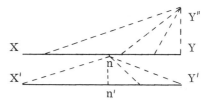

In this case, several points of comparison are possible. Any point on the X-Y continuum can be compared with Y″ and seen as simplified, restricted, and lexically mixed. Any point (n) on the same continuum can be compared with X and viewed as elaborated, expanded, and referentially stabilized. Any point (n′) on the X′-Y′ axis can be compared with n and will exhibit simplification, restriction, and referential anomaly. n′ can also be compared with X′ and will exhibit elaboration, expansion, and referential stability. In this picture n will represent the stage X-Y has reached at a given point in time.

Since n is a point on a developing language it will be pidginized with reference to Y″. This is possible because all of the speakers of n have another language to meet some of their social and psychological needs. This being the case it is probable that Y′, the fully developed language of a socialized young person, will be more elaborated and expanded than n. Thus, in the normal course of events the collective Y'-s, at any point in time, would tend to move n toward a Y. However, this tendency may well be counteracted by continued in-migration which will have the opposite effect of pulling the n of the speech community toward X.

4. Conclusion and application. Language change, and more specifically, language development, must be understood as the interplay of natural linguistic forces and culture specific social forces. The foregoing configurations, especially Figure 5, provide an abstract framework for viewing the normal development of language, both ontogenetically in socialization and phylogenetically in acculturation. What remains, in understanding the processes for any specific contact situation, is to plug in the particular social facts of that speech community. An incomplete illustration from real life will serve to demonstrate the potential utility of this paradigm.

4.1 The Italo-Americans of Boston. The north end of Boston is a geographically isolated enclave of over 11,000 people, 98 per cent of whom are of Italian descent. Intermixed with second- and third-generation Italo-Americans are large numbers of immigrants. By our definition the speech community is heterogeneous since both Italian and English are spoken regularly. While Italian is the first language of many, if not most, of the adults and is itself an acculturating language in some sense and contains elements from several divergent southern Italian dialects, the significant developing language is English. This variety of English is an n in the sense described in Figure 5. At any point it is simplified, restricted, and mixed with reference to Standard English. Furthermore, due to the nature of the community, there are speakers who could be plotted at various points along the continuum from X to Y. Those on the X end would be newly arrived immigrants, those on the Y end either American-born Italo-Americans or early immigrants.

Children, both immigrant and American-born, are constantly being socialized into the community. Not only are they forced to develop competence to some extent in Italian and in Italian English, but their schooling requires competence in Standard English. Thus their finished competence in English Y', while perhaps not identical to that of a native-born speaker in a homogeneous English-speaking community, will be less pidginized than the n of the community. Therefore, the normal tendency would be for the collective competences in English of young people to pull the English of the speech community toward Y, i.e. toward a more standard variety of English.

However, there are a number of countervailing pressures on this development. First, there is constant in-migration of Italians with minimal competence in English. They serve to keep the n pulled toward the X or more pidginized end of the axis. In addition, from an ontogenetic perspective there are complex attitudinal factors working in the community. These are themselves, of course, results of social facts. One example will suffice to illustrate this.

Most of the Italians come from southern Italy with a strong tradition of family-centeredness and patriarchy. Newly arrived families find themselves split attitudinally. Parents view the democratic family structures of the United States as permissive and a threat to their way of life and consequently may become more conservative and withdrawn from social contact than in Italy. They also see learning English as a threat and so have strong attitudes toward maintenance of Italian. Adolescents, on the other hand, see the situation very differently. To them, learning Standard English is seen as a means to escape the oppressive paternalism of home; and they will use it as much as possible. However, since Italian and Italian English are required for survival in the community, they tend to become di- or tri-glossic thereby minimizing their effects on the development of n in the speech community.

4.2 Conclusion. The above represents only a small number of the culture-specific social facts that would have to be fitted into the framework if it were to adequately describe the linguistic behavior of the community. There is no conceptual reason why careful ethnographic endeavor could not do this. Sociolinguistic methodologies and models able to elicit and sort out the kinds of variation present in the community have already been developed and tested. The present acculturative paradigm promises an analytical framework useful in explaining the source of these variations and how they contribute to language development.

NOTES

[1]Acculturating languages is used rather than the awkward and misleading term, Pidgin-Creole languages. The latter is misleading not only because it may carry pejorative connotations and is oversimplistic, but also it reflects a reification of inexact and heuristically problematic concepts. Acculturating, on the other hand, reflects a semantic distinction basic to this paper, namely, the difference between acculturation and enculturation. Acculturation is a learning process. Enculturation or socialization is an acquiring process. The latter involves internalizing a set of perceptual categories and a cognitive framework; the former follows this acquisition and so is in some respects fundamentally distinct.

[2]The notions of homogeneity and heterogeneity are used with caution. I suspect that if it were possible to quantify the variation present in speech communities, the total number of lects (registers, stylistic variations, different languages) would not vary significantly

from one speech community to another. Variations are created or neutralized in response to the social needs of the community. Here a homogeneous is one without the presence of different languages or widely divergent dialects. A heterogeneous community is one with more than one language or widely divergent dialects spoken. By definition acculturating language communities are thus heterogeneous.

REFERENCES

Hymes, Dell, ed. 1971. Pidginization and creolization of languages. Cambridge University Press.
Smith, David M. 1972. Language as social adaptation. In: Languages and Linguistics Working Papers, No. 4. Ed. by Richard J. O'Brien. Washington, D. C., Georgetown University Press.
_____. 1972. Some implications for the social status of pidgin languages. In: Sociolinguistics in cross-cultural analysis. Ed. by David Smith and Roger Shuy. Washington, D. C., Georgetown University Press.
_____. 1973. Language, speech, and ideology: A conceptual framework. In: Language attitudes: Current trends and prospects. Ed. by Roger Shuy and Ralph Fasold. Washington, D. C., Georgetown University Press.

FOCUSING AND DEFOCUSING IN HAWAIIAN ENGLISH[1]

CAROL ODO

Pacific and Asian Linguistics Institute
University of Hawaii

In this paper I will first present an account of primary accent placement in Hawaiian English (HE), and second propose a syntactic rule based on the prosodic shape of a sentence--specifically on the location of primary accent.

Since HE is in a post-creole continuum in the sense of DeCamp, many of the rules are variable and their variability can be correlated with social as well as linguistic factors. This will be a basic assumption even though variability will not be dealt with here. The body of data which provides the basis for rules and underlying forms posited here includes only speakers from age eight through thirty. (It is possible that older speakers may have different rules and underlying forms.) Most of the example sentences below are from our HE data pool initiated two years ago by William Labov.

Location of primary accent. Although HE is syllable-timed, there is a more-or-less rule-determined position for primary accent within the word. The rule is similar to the Standard English Main Stress Rule (Chomsky and Halle 1968). There are no unaccented syllables in HE, however, and the distinctions--if any--between secondary and tertiary accents are difficult to determine. Also, adjustments like the Alternating Stress Rule, Auxiliary Reduction Rules, and Compound Rule do not apply. The tendency is for primary accent to be retained on the final accented syllable of the word; e.g. hurricáne, dog-cátcher.

This tendency is carried over to the sentence level: all final
accented syllables in the sentence usually carry primary accent.
Where SE lowers pitch on all object pronouns, HE does not except
for the pronouns it and om, e.g.

(1) He talk Hawaiian to dém.

(2) He talk Hawaiian tó om.

Contrastive stress, which in SE would shift primary accent from
clause-final position to elsewhere, applies only optionally in HE.
Its use depends on how important the contrasting piece of information
is to the discourse. It is less likely to be used in a simple infor-
mation-giving statement such as:

(3) I gotta help my Hawaiian brothers and my Samoan bróthers.

where there is no contrastive stress on Samoan, but it is more
likely to be used when correcting something said earlier:

(4) A: . . . the guy with the black jéans . . .

(5) B: No, the blúe jeans.

In HE a declarative sentence with normal intonation will have a shape
(using Bolinger's notation) something like:

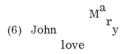

(6) John
love

Sentences with tags have basically the same shape, although the
shape of the tags may be different. One type, the emphatic or
narrative tag has a rising contour and high pitch:

```
          ho    me  eh
(7) I   going        ,        (narrative)
    was
```

```
          ho  me  eh         (emphatic)
(8) John         ,
    wen
```

Translated into SE, the first is simply 'I was going home, you see' and the second is 'John went home, didn't he?'

The other type, <u>or something</u> tags, usually has a low pitch and a falling contour:

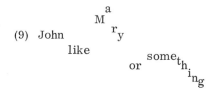

(9)   John

This type of tag can carry varying degrees of emphasis but normally its pitch contour is lower than that of the rest of the sentence. Other <u>or something</u> tags are <u>you see, you know, I think,</u> and <u>like that.</u>

Focusing and defocusing. In HE, topicalization seems to work in ways similar to SE where the phenomenon involves the moving around of sentence material.[2] Given the pair of sentences:

(10a) They never see the shów.

(10b) The shów, they never see.

the immediate problem is to determine which one is basic, if they are in fact related. The comma after (10b) indicates a pause.

It was suggested in the previous section that the unmarked intonation pattern for declarative sentences has its point of primary accent clause-finally. Not only does sentence (10c) below show the unmarked pattern, but (10d) shows that their constituents bear the same accents although their order is different.

(10c) They never see the shów

(10d) The shów they never see[3]

It would be reasonable to claim, then, that (10a) is basic and that constituents have been moved to form (10b). Ross' (1967) Topic Transformation moves an NP to the left of the sentence, and it seems that the same thing could be happening in HE. The following example shows that the VP can also be topicalized:

(11a) (When the kids slide down) the pants come dír[1]ty.

(11b) (When the kids slide down) come dír[1]ty, the pants.

Because of my confusion with terms like 'theme', 'topic', 'focus', and 'topicalization' (for which there are at least two definitions), I have decided to use Fillmore's term 'focusing' and apply it only to cases where the location of a primary-accented constituent has been shifted from its original clause-final position to a clause-initial position in order to draw attention to the particular constituent.

The focusing rule, then, might be the same as Ross' Topicalization rule. It would in (10a) move <u>the show</u> to the left of <u>they never see</u>, because the speaker wishes to focus on, or underscore it; and the remainder of the sentence serves only to provide minimal semantic or structural support. But is the focused element moved to the front, or is the defocused material moved to the end, or are they really the same thing?

The sentences below are further examples of what might be called focusing:

(12) Thirty só[1]mething, he had. <He had thirty só[1]mething.

(13) Dodge bá[1]ll, we play. <We play dodge bá[1]ll.

(14) They wó[1]rse, them kind guys. <Them kind guys wó[1]rse.

(15) She only like plá[1]nts, my grandma. <My grandma only like plá[1]nts.

Ross derives (12) and (13) from Topicalization and (14) and (15) from Right Dislocation. In HE they all have the same intonation pattern and I will try to derive all of them from a single rule.

I will propose two views, one which would move things to the front (Focusing) and the other which would move things to the end (Defocusing). The possibility that things are not moved will also be discussed.

The Focusing Transformation is a rule which fronts the object NP in (12) and (13), and fronts the VP in (14) and (15). The latter two, unlike <u>come dirty, the pants</u> add a subject pronoun. The rule appears to generate correct surface forms for the above. For sentences like (16), (17), (18), and (19), which are similar in prosodic shape, the justification for the rule--that is, to focus or draw attention to an item--is questionable.

(16) We wasn't born that t$\overset{1}{\text{i}}$me, but. <But we wasn't born that t$\overset{1}{\text{i}}$me.

(17) Lemme see your c$\overset{1}{\text{a}}$mera, then. <Then lemme see your c$\overset{1}{\text{a}}$mera.

(18) He sh$\overset{1}{\text{a}}$rp, but. <But he sh$\overset{1}{\text{a}}$rp.

(19) He s$\overset{1}{\text{a}}$w em, already. <He already s$\overset{1}{\text{a}}$w om.

The rule implies that all the sentence elements except for the words but, then, and already are focused and 'moved' to the left. On the surface this may seem unnatural, and in fact, at a deeper level the focusing rule has limitations which the defocusing rule does not have.

The Defocusing Transformation assumes a similar underlying structure--except perhaps for cases where a subject pronoun has been inserted[4]--and moves material to the end of the sentence. Since the permuted elements are de-emphasized, their pitch must be lower than the rest of the sentence, and since they are moved outside the sentence boundary, there is a natural pause before them. So far, both Focusing and Defocusing will generate the correct surface forms. Additional data, however, proves Defocusing to be correct.

In the following:

(20a) They never like g$\overset{1}{\text{o}}$, but, my friends.

(20b) But my friends never like g$\overset{1}{\text{o}}$.

Assuming that (20b) is basic, (20a) cannot be derived from it by applying the focusing rule, which would move never like go to the left. The result of such movement would be an unacceptable intonation pattern, which has no pause or pitch decrement after but:

<pre>
                        g^{o}
(20c)   never like
      They   my friends.
                           but
</pre>

On the other hand, if Defocusing applies, in two stages, first moving but to the end, the derived sentence is:

<pre>
            friends   g^{o}
(20d) My   never like
                              but
</pre>

which is completely acceptable and similar to other but-final sentences. In its second application Defocusing shifts my friends to the end giving (the equivalent of [20a]):

(20e) They never like g^o
but
my friends

The obligatory pause after but is indicated by a pitch decrement between but and my friends. The material moved by Defocusing is de-emphasized, and each successive application of the rule--it probably does not apply more than twice--generates lower and lower pitches.

The defocusing rule, which I have shown to be better than the focusing rule, asserts that things are moved from one position to another. In the following examples none of the items in (a) have been moved to form (b); the meanings are the same and intonation patterns of (a) and (b) are the same as normal intonation, and normal intonation plus defocusing rule, respectively:

(21a) . . . because Robet left.

(21b) . . . Robet left, that's why

(22a) . . . even though you took a bath.

(22b) . . . you took a bath, and then

Since (b) means the same as (a), one could analyze That's why as a clause-final spelling of because, and and then as the clause-final spelling of even though. But then one would have to go even further for the following examples:

(23) Pita never know the guy, was

(24) I wanted to put the noodles in, was

and say that either was is an abstraction of past tense which is defocused (and is also left behind); or that the underlying VP contains two past markers, one of which is was, and this is only realized when it is moved to the end.

The difficulty posed by was-final sentences leads to perhaps another analysis: that the basic structure of a sentence already has defocused material. It appears that the material following primary accent in all the above examples have the same prosodic shape as

or something -type tags, which were described earlier. Like these
tags, which might also be described as afterthoughts, they have
little semantic content, low pitch, and are not really necessary to
the sentence. A systematic study of variation in the use of tags will
probably show that older Japanese--not necessarily bilinguals, but
those who are heavily exposed to the language--will use more tags
than older speakers of other ethnic groups. Tags are frequently
used in Japanese, and the final was in Hawaiian English looks sus-
piciously like Japanese desu, which also has low pitch and little
semantic content. It is both a polite marker and a copula which reflects the tense of the main verb. Compare the HE and Japanese
sentences:

(25) He wanted to see you, was.

(26) Ano hito wa anata ni aitakatta n' desu. [5]
     he   you   wanted to see +past copula

Was whose features are (+past, +copula) in other HE environments
must be a literal translation of desu.

I will not venture to explain how sentences acquire tags, whether
tags are present in underlying structure, or whether a rule of tag-
addition has been adopted by HE.

The main point of my paper was to establish a prosodic base for
syntactic analysis in HE, and I would like to return to it. When
William Labov was at the University of Hawaii in 1970, he generated
interest in the sentences:

(27) Four boards wen take.

(28) The keys lose.

Richard Day (1971) analyzed these as middle verb constructions
similar to the door opened. However, when I checked with several
other native speakers they could not understand the sentences when
read with unmarked intonation as in:

(29) four $^{\mathrm{boards}}$ wen $^{\mathrm{t^a k_e}}$

the same as one would use with other middle verbs; e.g.

(30) The $^{\mathrm{door}}$ wen $^{\mathrm{o^p e_n}}$

When I used Defocused or 'tag' intonation, however,

(31) Four $b^{o^{a^r}d_S}$

   wen t^{a}k$_e$

its meaning was clear: that 'someone took four boards', or 'four boards, someone took'. In this case, intonation can provide a test of whether a verb is middle or not: with normal stress on the verb, it is middle; with tag intonation it is not middle.

   NOTES

[1]My thanks to C.-J. Bailey, Derek Bickerton, Mike Forman, and Greg Lee for their help with earlier drafts of this paper.
[2]As in analyses such as Ross' (Constraints on variables in syntax).
[3]Like or something tags, they never see can have higher pitch contours depending on context, but usually its contour will be lower than that of the focused item.
[4]In cases such as She only like plants, my grandma, where a pronoun has been inserted, the underlying sentence may have been derived from a rule similar to Ross' Left Dislocation:

(a) My grandma only like plánts. ==> (Left Dislocation)

(b) My grandma, she only like plánts. ==> (Defocusing)

(c) She only like plánts, my grandma.

Sentences like (b) are common in HE; e.g.:

(32) Him, he drínk.

(33) Me, I no like Fasi too múch.

(34) Patsy, she okáy.

(35) The mada, she no like om gó, but.

Alternatively, the underlying structure might have the NP dominating both Noun and Pronoun, as suggested by G. Williams.
[5]I am grateful to Hiroshi Sugita for explaining to me the structure of this sentence.

[6]In my speech tags are a basic part of the sentence in certain contexts; for example, when talking about something I'm not too familiar with, or something.

REFERENCES

Bailey, C.-J. (To appear.) Southern states phonetics.

Bolinger, Dwight. 1968. Aspects of language. New York, Harcourt, Brace and World, Inc.

Chomsky, Noam and Morris Halle. 1968. The sound pattern of English. New York, Harper and Row.

Day, Richard. 1971. Middle verbs and linguistic change. Working Papers in Linguistics 3(3).19-28. Honolulu, University of Hawaii.

Fillmore, Charles J. 1968. The case for case. In: Universals in linguistic theory. Ed. by Emmon Bach and Robert T. Harms. New York, Holt, Rinehart and Winston. 1-90.

Ross, John Robert. 1967. Constraints on variables in syntax. Unpublished doctoral dissertation, Massachusetts Institute of Technology.

Williams, George. 1972. Left and right dislocation. Paper read at SECOL, University of Georgia.

TENSE NEUTRALIZATION
IN THE HAWAIIAN POST-CREOLE GRADATUM

RICHARD R. DAY

University of Hawaii, Kamehameha Schools

This paper is concerned with the treatment of the past tense in the Hawaiian post-Creole Gradatum. I hope to provide support for McCawley's 1971 proposal that the past tense is an intransitive verb. I also hope to provide evidence for the correctness of Kiparsky's 1968 claim that the historical present in early Indo-European is an underlying past. I propose that there is a process, widely used in the Gradatum, which I call 'tense neutralization'. By this term I mean the neutralization of the past tense to the unmarked, or present, tense. This occurs in conjunction with another past tense or a past time adverbial in a clause which usually precedes, in the surface structure, the tense which is neutralized.

Before getting too far into the discussion, it is necessary to explain the usages and formation of the present and past tenses in the Gradatum. The present tense in unmarked; its formation requires the simplest form of the verb morphologically, since there is no affixation (or morpheme which might carry tense), even in the third person singular. Its usage, with the exception covered in this paper, is the same as the present tense in Standard English.

The preterit in the Gradatum is formed by placing the past tense marker wɛn before the verb. The past tense copula is waz. The pattern of wɛn + verb is illustrated in (1). These sentences are taken from Labov's 1971 article on tense.

(1a) Oh, I wɛn grab em up.
       'I picked it up.'

(1b) Oh, he wɛn live over twenty years, boy.
      'He lived for twenty years longer.'

(1c) Eh we wɛn enjoy em, boy.
      'We liked him.'

(1d) Yesterday he wɛn start work.
      'He began to work yesterday.'

(1e) They wɛn show us all over the place.
      'They showed us everything.'

(1f) I wɛn tell im for go with me.
      'I asked him to go with me.'

(1g) But then--the wife wɛn come.
      'Then his wife came along.'

These sentences, then, demonstrate the general pattern of past tense
formation. We seen w<u>ɛn</u> used as a past tense marker with verbs
that take <u>ed</u> in Standard English and with the stems of verbs that
show ablaut and other vowel changes in Standard English.

This pattern, however, exhibits variation. There are instances
when the expected past tense, either <u>waz</u> or <u>wɛn</u>, is missing. That
is, the verb apparently is present tense, even though the context is
past. The reason for this follows.

Let us look at (2), which I offer as a typical example of tense
neutralization in the Gradatum. This example comes from a tape
which I was able to transcribe myself, and is given in a somewhat
different format from (1) above.

(2) so hi wɛn da^{o}n de^a æn opɪn da
     'so he went down there and open the

     do^a æn tra^{e}n tə dræg da ga^e a^{o}t
     door and tryin' to drag the guy out'

     'So he went down there and opened the
     door and was trying to drag the guy out.'

None of the verbs in this utterance has the expected pattern of
either <u>wɛn</u> or <u>waz</u>. In the first line, we find a past tense, w<u>ɛn</u>, but
it is not what we should expect to find, which is <u>wɛn go</u>. The explanation for this comes later, but I should point out at this point that
it is not related to tense neutralization. The next verb, <u>opɪn</u>, is not

preceded by wɛn, and the last verb, which is a progressive, does not have waz before it. The Standard English equivalent forms display past tense verbs. The lack of past tense markers in the last two verbs would be a mystery were it not for tense neutralization. I submit that the second verb in (2), although it appears to be present tense, is derived from an underlying past tense structure which has undergone a rule that neutralizes the underlying past to a surface present. Thus we have opɪn instead of the expected wɛn opɪn.

Tense neutralization is also at work with the progressive traᵉn, 'trying'. Given the past tense context, the expected form is the past progressive, waz traᵉn. I claim that through tense neutralization, the past tense has been neutralized or reduced to the present or unmarked tense. Since there is no surface realization of either ste or ɪz (possible forms of the present tense copula), we can assume that the speaker was operating in one of the lects which either variably used ɪz or ste, or that the speaker did not have the spelling rule in his grammar. (For a detailed account of this, see Day 1972.)

What we have in (2), then, is a surface structure with the sequence of verb tenses as past, present, present. I propose that the sequence that underlies this is, at some point in the derivation: past, past, past; and that, through a process called 'tense neutralization', the last two tenses are neutralized to the unmarked or present tense. That is, the underlying sequence of tenses is reduced or neutralized to the unmarked tense, with the exception of the first verb in the sequence, which in the Gradatum is the present tense.

There are cases when tense neutralization can take place without the underlying sequence of past, past. This occurs when there is a past time adverbial in the derivation, as demonstrated in (3).

(3) ɪn doz deⁱz ɪn hana
     'in those days in Hana

     wɛn aᵉ gɛt oni wʌn tu beⁱbi
     when I get only one two baby

     aᵉ go wɪt papa aᵒ ovʌ
     I go with Papa all over'

     'In those days, in Hana, when I had only
     one or two babies, I went with Papa all over.'

Here is an utterance which is obviously in the past tense because of the expression ɪn doz deⁱz. However, none of the verbs has a past tense marker; each verb is unmarked, or in the present tense. It is my claim that the time adverbial ɪn doz deⁱz carries the reference to past time, and allows tense neutralization to take place. That is, the underlying structure sequence of past time adverbial, past, past undergoes tense neutralization to give the surface structure of past time adverbial, present, present.

That tense neutralization can occur with either a preceding past tense verb or a past time adverbial is very significant. It can be proposed that time adverbials and tense belong to the same grammatical category. From this it follows that perhaps we have some evidence for McCawley's 1971 claim that the past tense should be represented as a predicate in the underlying structure.

My proposal offered here of tense neutralization and the representation of adverbials and tense in the same grammatical category corresponds closely to Kiparsky's 1968 claim of what the historical present is in early Indo-European. He does not call the process tense neutralization, since it also neutralizes modes, but refers to it as 'conjunction reduction'. In describing the process, Kiparsky (1968: 35) says:

> . . . the sequence . . . Past and . . . Past . . . is reduced
> to . . . Past . . . and . . . zero . . . , and since it is the
> present which is the zero tense, the reduced structure . . .
> Past . . . and . . . zero . . . is realized morphologically
> as . . . Past . . . and . . . Present . . .

From this it is quite clear that Kiparsky and I are indeed talking about the same phenomenon; tense neutralization is a form of what he calls conjunction reduction.

It is Kiparsky's claim that the historical present in early Indo-European is syntactically past but is realized on the surface as present. He feels that it is an underlying past which has undergone tense neutralization, or, in his term, conjunction reduction. He claims that it optionally reduces occurrences of the past to the present. It is interesting to note here that tense neutralization is also an optional process in the Hawaiian post-Creole Gradatum.

It is important to bear in mind that Kiparsky is discussing early Indo-European. As he remarks (1968:32), 'In general, however, conjunction of past and historical present is quite untypical of modern languages.' To my knowledge, there is nothing in the literature which posits tense neutralization as a fact of present-day English. However, as is demonstrated by (2) and (3), it is alive and well in the Hawaiian post-Creole Gradatum, in which English is one of the major donor languages. [1]

Kiparsky's explanation for why tense (and mood) was subject to, in his term, conjunction reduction, is that it was an adverbial constituent in the underlying structure; tense and time adverbs thus belonged to the same grammatical category and were in complementary distribution. It is from this stage that the ancestors of modern Indo-European languages began copying the features of the referents of time adverbs on the verbs; this was first done optionally, and later became obligatory. The general adverb ended up as the 'augment' on indicative verb forms in Indo-Iranian and Greek. [2]

The very interesting thing here is that the facts from the Hawaiian post-Creole Gradatum presented in this paper apparently substantiate the correctness of Kiparsky's claim. It is as if a partial history of the English language were repeating itself in the Hawaiian post-Creole Gradatum. [3] It appears as though tense and time adverbs in the Gradatum are members of the same grammatical category; past tense is not marked by affixation, but by what can be construed to be an adverb--wɛn. Moreover, there are a few verbs which optionally use either wɛn or mark past tense the same way as they would be in Standard English. These verbs are the so-called strong and the irregular weak verbs. This explains why in (2) above we find wɛn instead of wɛn go. I feel that these facts provide strong support for Kiparsky's proposal.

The treatment of wɛn as a past tense adverb also lends support to McCawley's 1971 argument about tense in English. He refines Ross' 1967 treatment of auxiliaries and proposes that tenses should not be features, as claimed by Chomsky (cf. 1957, 1965), but are in fact underlying verbs. McCawley (1971:111) contends that:

> . . . the past tense morpheme is an intransitive verb, that it is a two-place predicate meaning 'prior to' in the same sense in which she is a predicate meaning 'female', that is that pronouns both stand for things and express presuppositions about the things they stand for.

In closing, I would like to refer to Postal's principle of 'anaphoric islands' and tense neutralization. [4] Postal (1969) proposes that there is a constraint against the formation of anaphoric constructions across word boundaries. This would predict that past tense could be deleted with respect to a preceding occurrence of past tense if past tense is realized as a word, but not if it is part of a word. Thus we have

(4)	[past]		X	[past]		
	word	word		word	word	
	1	2		3		$\Rightarrow$
	1	2		$\emptyset$		

but not

(5)   [. . . past]   X   [. . . past]
   word   word   word   word
    1   2   3   4   5   ⟹
    1   2   3   4   ∅

I would like to mention that here we have an investigation of what some linguists might term a marginal system--a post-Creole gradatum--which has turned up important evidence for linguistic theory.

NOTES

[1]Tense neutralization may also be present in Black Vernacular English to some extent. In a very interesting article on what he terms Negro Non-Standard English, Dillard (1971:397) cites (i) from Stewart (1968): (i) We was eatin'--an' we drinkin', too.

[2]I am grateful to C.-J. Bailey for this observation.

[3]It might be speculated that this is a general process of natural languages.

[4]I would like to thank P. Gregory Lee for pointing out to me the relationship between Postal's anaphoric islands and tense neutralization.

REFERENCES

Chomsky, Noam. 1957. Syntactic structures. The Hague, Mouton and Co.

_____. 1965. Aspects of the theory of syntax. Cambridge, Mass., MIT Press.

Day, Richard R. 1972. Patterns of variation in copula and tense in the Hawaiian post-Creole continuum. Unpublished doctoral dissertation, University of Hawaii.

Dillard, J. L. 1971. The Creolist and the study of Negro non-standard dialects in the continental United States. In: Pidginization and creolization of languages. Ed. by D. Hymes. London, Cambridge University Press. 393-408.

Kiparsky, Paul. 1968. Tense and mood in Indo-European syntax. Foundations of Language. 4(2).30-57.

Labov, William. 1971. On the adequacy of natural languages: I. The development of tense. Unpublished paper.

McCawley, James D. 1971. Tense and time reference in English. In: Studies in linguistic semantics. Ed. by Charles J. Fillmore and D. Terence Langendoen. New York, Holt, Rinehart and Winston. 97-113.

Postal, Paul. 1969. Anaphoric islands. In: Papers from the Fifth
   Regional Meeting of the Chicago Linguistics Society. Ed. by
   Robert I. Binnick, et al. Chicago, University of Chicago, Depart-
   ment of Linguistics. 205-39.
Ross, John R. 1967. Auxiliaries as main verbs. To appear in:
   The structure and psychology of language. Ed. by Thomas G.
   Bever and William Weksel.
Stewart, William. 1968. Continuity and change in American Negro
   dialects. The Florida FL Reporter. 6(1).3-14.

SOME THOUGHTS ON
NATURAL SYNTACTIC PROCESSES

ELIZABETH CLOSS TRAUGOTT

'The fundamental problem of linguistic theory, as I see it at least, is to account for the choice of a particular grammar, given the data available to the language-learner' (Chomsky 1972:125). [1] This famous claim of Chomsky's is a challenging one that must surely give much food for thought to anyone interested in the theory of language. It seems to me particularly unfortunate, then, that Chomsky himself has in fact never really taken up the consequences of his own claim in any serious way. He has taken a narrow view of the problem, restricting himself to the question, what are the limits on the class of grammars that enable a language-learner to choose a particular grammar? Furthermore, he has assumed that this choice is dictated primarily by an evaluation measure, as yet not well understood. Chomsky has explicitly denied the importance of accounting for the competence involved in appropriate language use within his concept of a class of grammars so restrictive and hence rich as to account for language acquisition. Furthermore, he has not, in practice, paid attention to the fact that what is essential in language acquisition is the construction, not simply choice, of models, that is, the child's ability to change from one model to another (Sinclair 1971).

In my view, a theory of language in general (as opposed to a theory of a particular language) must do at least three things: it must account for (1) universals of language, which tell us what a possible language is, (2) perceptual strategies, which are constraints on learnability, and (3) natural processes, which are constraints on expressibility (Traugott 1972a, 1972b).

The universals of language are of two kinds, substantive and formal. The formal ones will tell us what restrictions there are on the class of possible grammars in terms of admissible rules. The

substantive universals will specify possible categories of grammar.
Some will be definitional, such as the claim that all sentences of
natural languages necessarily involve, among other things, pre-
dication, and time-deixis (location of the proposition relative to the
time of the speaker's utterance [Fillmore 1971]). Other universals
will be statements of tendencies. These tendencies include the functional potentials of discourse (gestural, emotive, reactive, referential, poetic, and so forth [Fillmore 1972]); potentials of systematic
variability (conditions under which variability can apply, and conditions on the systematicity of variability); and also potentials for
hierarchic relationships among categories--for example, grammars
may include rules for deriving temporal from locative terms, but
not vice versa (a case in point is Anderson's [1971:12] synchronic
claim that 'the surface markers of tense and aspect have their ulti-
·mate source in temporal locative structures', for example, He is
going is to be interpreted as He is in the state of going). These
tendencies also include statements about potential semantic weighting, such that certain structures are primarily contentive while
others, such as logical connectives, categories specifying time-line,
aspect, mood, and so forth, are primarily grammatical--that is a
notion that Sapir entertained in Language (1921), and one that has
recently been used effectively to account for language change by,
among others, Givón (1971), Kay and Sankoff (1972), and particularly Labov (1971). Furthermore, and most important for the
present discussion, these tendencies are diachronic as well as
synchronic; they include the tendency of locative terms to become
temporal--temporal under and before derive from locatives, not
vice versa. Inclusion of both diachronic and synchronic universals
might provide a solution to the controversy between adherents of
'anti-localistic' theories, who argue that some cases are primarily
semantic or 'concrete' in function (such as the IE instrumental,
ablative, or locative) and others primarily syntactic (indicating
subject, object, or some close connection with another noun, as do
the nominative, accusative, and genitive respectively). Kuryłowicz
has argued that the controversy really 'rests upon a misunderstand-
ing, a confusion of diachrony and synchrony. Though all cases go
back to forms denoting spatial relations, case-forms with grammatical (syntactical) functions are attested at every stage in the history
of a language' (1964:202). Surely a grammar should in its metatheory state what possible functions cases can have synchronically,
how they can arise, and in what ways they can change. This is not
to confuse diachrony and synchrony, but to see them as two distinct
dimensions of the same problem, and hence closely interrelated.
This seems to me to reflect the spirit, though not necessarily the
letter of the dynamic models of language proposed by Greenberg

(1966), Bailey (1970), Bickerton (forthcoming), Weinreich, Labov, and Herzog (1968), and many others.

Secondly, a theory of language must account for tendencies in perceptual strategies--that is, in the constraints on learnability. The importance of these strategies for language acquisition and historical change has been discussed in detail, especially by Slobin (1971), Bever (1970), Bever and Langendoen (1971), and Kiparsky (1971). Space limitations unfortunately prevent me from pursuing them further here, though I think they are as important to a theory of language as universals and natural processes.

Much has been said recently about natural phonological processes, largely inspired by Stampe (1969), who has argued that they are of crucial importance for any attempt to explain language acquisition and language change. Natural phonological processes, he points out, are constraints on expressibility; they are articulatorily motivated, and include such phenomena as devoicing of obstruents (because of the oral constriction), loss of vowels through a voiceless vowel stage, and so forth. Many processes are in conflict, as is, for example, the devoicing of obstruents in intervocalic position, since it contradicts another equally natural process--assimilation in voiced environments. He sees language acquisition as involving the solution of such conflicts by the suppression, limitation, and ordering of natural processes. Children may fail to suppress, limit, or order enough to match the adult language and hence the result may be an apparent simplification of the adult's system; ontogenetically, however, the failure is not simplification. In fact, nothing has happened. Simplification, he argues, is therefore not an explanatory principle in historical linguistics, only a descriptive one.

The concept of natural process is extendable to syntax, although what natural processes might be at this level is less immediately obvious. If we can accept an unordered semantic base, one which is essentially cognitive, and which reflects a kind of semantic weighting such as I proposed at the beginning, then we can argue that a natural syntactic process is one which gives spatio-temporally ordered expression to this unordered cognitive base, in certain restricted ways. I hypothesize, for example, that there are natural tendencies in language to give analytic expression to such grammatical elements as negation, tense, aspect, mood, logical connectives, and so forth. Such syntactic processes are obviously in conflict with phonological ones. This may help explain the tendency of languages to shift from analytic to synthetic structures and back again. In my view the argument about whether there is a cycle or not and whether analysis precedes synthesis is a pseudo-problem. In any time span a cycle may appear to be operating, if we take a descriptive point of view. If we take an explanatory one, however, there are two simultaneous processes, one syntactic and analytic, the other phonological and synthetic, and the cycle is only the apparent result of certain processes. The particular resolution of conflict between phonological and syntactic processes doubtless in part accounts for language-specific, as opposed to universal, variability (Wolfram 1972).

Exactly what motivates the change in the dominance of one process over another is an important question. It can only be answered in terms of the input to the child's grammar-construction processes, some of which is linguistic, some of which is social, and includes prestige-pressures. For children are not battle-grounds in abstracto of conflicting universals, perceptual strategies, and natural processes. They can do nothing without input, their own as well as others, linguistic as well as social. The interplay proposed here is characterized by the Model of Language Acquisition in Figure 1.

FIGURE 1. A model of language acquisition.

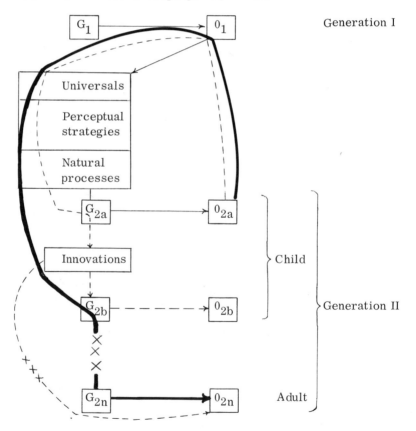

In this model G_1 and 0_1 stand for all the input to the child from
speakers older than himself, whether peers or adults; they are
heterogeneous, and may involve not only multiple lects but also
multiple languages. The child hears 0_1 and on the basis of universals, perceptual strategies, and natural processes he develops the
set of hypotheses G_{2a}, which is expressed as 0_{2a}. Then using his
own output, 0_1 (which is also changing), and his inbuilt linguistic
mechanisms he innovates; these innovations either become integrated
into his grammatical system, in which case they are restructured in
G_{2b}, or else they continue as innovations--rules added at the end of
the grammar which function as cover-up rules to disguise the difference between the child's system and that of adults or other prestige
speakers (Andersen 1972) and may never become fully integrated.
The process of grammar construction is repeated several times
until the adult system G_{2n} is reached, and may continue to a limited
extent throughout the speaker's life.

For the remainder of this paper, I would like to expand on the
notion of natural processes and why it is so important for an understanding of language change. Let us assume that we can accept the
notion of cognitive universals which are hierarchized such that dual
is shown to imply plural, but not vice versa, time is shown to imply
space, and that structures involving time-lines--signalling, for
example, dependence of one event on another and deduction of one
event from another--imply aspect, and so forth. We would expect
syntactic processes to give surface expression to these structures
in the order: plural, then dual; space, then time; aspect, then time-
line. The latter has recently been shown to be true in the acquisition of French (Ferreiro and Sinclair 1971). The implicational relationship I am discussing is tied in with markedness which, as
Stampe (forthcoming) argues, is, like simplification, a descriptive
term accounting for relationships within particular grammars, not
an explanatory one accounting for what actually goes on in language.
It is usually said that changes in the history of languages go from
marked to unmarked; they obviously also go vice versa, since
marked forms that are lost at one stage are often renewed at a later
one. For example, a dual may develop; so may a previously lost
temporal expression. Kuryłowicz (1972) has recently written an
article on time and space deixis, specifically devoted to description
of such renewal. Children, however, start out with the least marked
grammar and acquire marked features. It therefore has often been
suggested that historically languages typically become less marked,
ontogenetically more marked, hence the relation between history and
acquisition seems paradoxical. There is, however, no paradox if
we allow for natural processes. If the input language does not have
a certain category in its surface structure, for example a dual, a

child may fail to suppress the natural process which would give discrete surface manifestation to a potential underlying cognitive category, in this case dual, and so, given the right social conditions for
dispersion of innovations, a dual may develop in the language where
there was none before. In other words, if a language does not have
a certain marked category in its surface structure, it may develop
one because children innately have the capacity to reach down further,
so to speak, into the implicational hierarchies, and give surface expression to them; this will produce renewal of the expression of
marked categories. However, if a language already has many marked
surface categories, it may lose them because the children do not
reach that far down into the implicational hierarchy; it will then appear
that the language has, to that extent, been simplified. It seems that
this situation is the more typical of the two.

Natural syntactic processes are also useful in explaining other
seemingly paradoxical phenomena. It has been claimed by Halle
(1962), Kiparsky (1965, 1968), King (1969), and others that children
typically simplify the language and adults elaborate it, and that children can change grammars in radical ways, adults cannot. To anyone who believes this, pidgins and creoles present an insoluble
problem, since pidgins are non-native languages and are usually
acquired by adults, but they seem to involve gross simplification,
while creoles, being native languages, are acquired by children but
seem to involve gross elaboration. The paradox once more results
from comparing and describing languages instead of trying to explain
them.

Pidgins typically involve simplification of function (Hymes [1971]
calls this 'restriction), and of surface structures (Hymes allows only
this to be called 'simplification'). It is debatable whether they involve simplification of inner structure (what Hymes calls 'reduction')
--if we accept a cognitive basis, surely they do not (Labov 1971).
One of the interesting things about pidgins is that while a new lexicon
is usually learned, the adult's basic grammatical system, or something close to it, is still distinctively present; even more interesting
is the fact that just the kinds of grammatical structure which appear
analytically in language acquisition tend to do so in pidgins, for
example, negatives, logical connectives, aspect and tense. Furthermore, as in language acquisition, tense is most usually expressed,
if at all, by adverbs, aspect by verbs or particles. Is the supposedly
radical linguistic mutation involved in pidgin acquisition perhaps not
so radical after all ? Does it not involve the acquisition of lexical
items so typical of adult innovation, combined with a return to earlier
processes, especially syntactic ones, that have in the speaker's
native language been partially or wholly suppressed? This would
make sense if we wish, as Ferguson (1971) does, to relate pidgin

simplification to the general ability we all have to simplify in various ways in talking to foreigners, babies, --and, I may add, stupid people. Even small children seem to do this--three-year-olds know how to simplify for two-year-olds, and do so largely by reverting to structures similar to their own earlier ones. The pidgin speaker's ability to renew syntactic processes with some ease, but not phonological ones, also seems to be tied in with the tendency for adults to learn the syntax of a foreign language considerably better than the phonology.

The acquisition of creoles is also no problem from the point of view of natural processes. Labov (1971), Kay and Sankoff (1972), Sankoff and Laberge (1971) and others have shown how creoles may involve the rapid development of particles or inflections from adverbs, full verbs, and other such categories: 'Depidginization appears to involve a transfer of grammatical function from free to bound forms, from open class morphemes to closed class morphemes, and from forms with denotative content to forms specializing in grammatical content' (Kay and Sankoff 1972). In other words, phonological processes conflict with the syntactic ones, and this results in more synthetic structures; what's more, the development of these structures follows along the lines of the universal tendencies of language--verbs of finishing give rise to completives, verbs of being or existentials to progressives, desideratives to futures, and so forth. All in all, the elaboration evidenced by creoles is not at all unnatural. It follows along lines generally characteristic of language acquisition. In a sense, first- and second-generation creoles represent the closest thing to 'pure acquisitional principles' that one can find outside of inhumane experimental conditions, since there is little pressure from the input (specifically of the older generation) to suppress or cover up innovations. It is not to be wondered at, then, that first- and second-generation creoles develop surface marked categories with greater rapidity than other languages, or that, given the necessity of expanding the functions of language, they develop systematic variability within a generation or two.

In conclusion, the notion that there are syntactic as well as phonological natural processes seems to be a very important one for explaining how we acquire a language (whether it is our first, second, or fifth), for explaining how and why language changes, and furthermore, though I have only implied this, for the very nature of grammars--why do they contain syntactic rules, why do syntactic rules work the way they do? This latter problem is one that has been the topic of Vennemann's recent studies (Vennemann, forthcoming). We came to the conclusion that natural syntactic processes are a necessary concept independently and from considerably different viewpoints, but both in search of prediction of change rather than post-facto analysis and in search of explanation rather than description.

NOTE

[1]I owe a great debt of gratitude to colleagues and students at Stanford University, especially Naomi Baron, Eve Clark, Charles Ferguson, and Joseph Greenberg, for the impetus they have given me to synthesize disparate ideas; and to Paul Kay and Gillian Sankoff for permitting me to use materials collected for and by their seminar on pidgins and creoles at the University of California, Berkeley, spring 1972.

REFERENCES

Andersen, Henning. 1972. Abductive and deductive change. Paper given at the Stanford Linguistics Colloquium, January 1972.
Anderson, John M. 1971. The grammar of case. London, Cambridge University Press.
Bailey, Charles-James N. 1970. The integration of linguistic theory: Internal reconstruction and the comparative method in descriptive analysis. University of Hawaii, Department of Linguistics. 2.4.
Bever, Thomas. 1970. The cognitive basis for linguistic structure. In: Cognition and the development of language. Ed. by John R. Hayes. New York, Wiley and Sons.
_____ and D. Terence Langendoen. 1971. A dynamic model of the evolution of language. Linguistic Inquiry. 2.433-64.
Bickerton, Derek. Forthcoming. On the nature of a creole continuum.
Chomsky, Noam. 1972. Studies on semantics in generative grammar. The Hague, Mouton.
Ferguson, Charles A. 1971. Absence of copula and the notion of simplicity: A study of normal speech, baby talk, foreigner talk, and pidgins. In: Pidginization and creolization of languages. Ed. by Dell Hymes. London, Cambridge University Press.
Ferreiro, Emilia and Hermine Sinclair. 1971. Temporal relations in language. International Journal of Psychology. 6(1).39-47.
Fillmore, Charles J. 1972. A grammarian looks to sociolinguistics. In: Georgetown University Monograph Series on Languages and Linguistics, Monograph 25. Washington, D.C., Georgetown University Press.
_____. 1971. Lectures on deixis. University of California Santa Cruz. Summer Program in Linguistics.
Givón, Talmy. 1971. Historical syntax and synchronic morphology: An archaeologist's field trip. Papers from the Seventh Regional Chicago Linguistics Society. Chicago, University of Chicago.

Greenberg, Joseph H. 1966. Language universals. The Hague, Mouton.

Halle, Morris. 1962. Phonology in generative grammar. Word. 18.54-72.

Hymes, Dell, ed. 1971. Pidginization and creolization of languages. London, Cambridge University Press.

Kay, Paul and Gillian Sankoff. 1972. A language-universals approach to pidgins and creoles. In: Pidgins and creoles: Current trends and prospects. Ed. by David DeCamp and Ian F. Hancock. Washington, D. C., Georgetown University Press (to appear).

King, Robert D. 1969. Historical linguistics and generative grammar. Englewood Cliffs, N. J., Prentice-Hall.

Kiparsky, Paul. 1965. Phonological change. Unpublished doctoral dissertation, Massachusetts Institute of Technology. (Available from the Indiana Linguistic Society.)

_____. 1968. Linguistic universals and linguistic change. In: Universals in linguistic theory. Ed. by Emmon Bach and Robert T. Harms. New York, Holt, Rinehart and Winston.

_____. 1971. Historical linguistics. In: A survey of linguistic science. Ed. by William O. Dingwall. College Park, Md., University of Maryland, Linguistics Program.

Kuryłowicz, Jerzy. 1964. The inflectional categories of Indo-European. Heidelberg, Winter.

_____. 1972. The role of deictic elements in linguistic evolution. Semiotica. 5.174-83.

Labov, William. 1971. On the adequacy of natural languages: I. The development of tense. Mimeographed.

Sankoff, Gillian and Suzanne Laberge. 1971. On the acquisition of native speakers by a language. Paper given at the Northeastern Linguistic Society, October 1971.

Sapir, Edward. 1921. Language: An introduction to the study of speech. New York, Harcourt, Brace and World.

Sinclair, Hermine. 1971. Acquisition of language, linguistic theory and epistemology. Paper presented at Centre Nationale de Recherche Scientifique, December 1971.

Slobin, Dan I. 1972. Developmental psycholinguistics. In: A survey of linguistic science. Ed. by William O. Dingwall. College Park, Md., University of Maryland, Linguistics Program.

Stampe, David. 1969. The acquisition of phonetic representation. Papers from the Fifth Regional Meeting of the Chicago Linguistic Society. Chicago, University of Chicago.

_____. Forthcoming. Review (with James D. McCawley) of Noam Chomsky and Morris Halle, The sound pattern of English.

Traugott, Elizabeth Closs. 1972a. Lectures on historical linguistics and its relation to studies of language acquisition and pidgins and creoles. University of California at Santa Cruz, Summer Program in Linguistics.

_____. 1972b. On the notion 'restructuring' in historical syntax. Paper given at the XIth International Congress of Linguists, Bologna, August 28-September 2.

Vennemann, Theo. Forthcoming. Explanation in syntax.

Weinreich, Uriel, William Labov, and Marvin Herzog. 1968. Empirical foundations for a theory of language change. In: Directions for historical linguistics. Ed. by W. P. Lehmann and Yakov Malkiel. Austin, University of Texas Press.

Wolfram, Walt. 1973. On what basis variable rules? In: New ways of analyzing variation in English. Ed. by Charles-James N. Bailey and Roger W. Shuy. Washington, D. C., Georgetown University Press.

THE SPANISH CARIBBEAN:
A CREOLE PERSPECTIVE[1]

RICARDO OTHEGUY

City University of New York

The question of substratal influence as a causative factor of dialect differentiation in New World Spanish has had a long and polemic history in the field of Spanish dialectology. Advocates of analyzing at least some dialectal differences in terms of substratum have clashed with adherents of the view that all possible explanations in terms of peninsular origin or internal motivation should be exhausted before invoking the concept of a substratum. This latter position, with its implicit goal of achieving economy of explanation at the possible expense of ascertainable historical facts, has received its most clear and influential formulation in Malmberg 1959 and 1964.[2]

In this paper, substratum will be discussed in relation to the Spanish Caribbean, an area generally regarded as a distinct dialect zone and shown by dialectologists to be definable in terms of uniquely shared linguistic features (Lamb 1969:101-23). I shall focus here on two questions which seem fundamental: what language Spanish was in contact with and what that language was like. Unlike Mexico and the South American mainland, where large segments of the population still speak languages other than Spanish, the Caribbean situation offers no direct evidence for an answer to these two questions.

Possibly for this reason, published references to substratum in the Caribbean usually fall into two categories: they either ignore the question of the substratum language altogether, or they assume that, despite the large numbers of Africans that lived in the area during colonial times, no contact existed between their language(s) and Spanish.[3] This, the argument goes, is because the diverse language background of the Africans caused them to give up their

respective native languages and immediately adopt Spanish, thus pre-
cluding the possibility of language contact.[4] This latter view finds
support in the long-held notion that there are no Creoles in the
Spanish-speaking world today and thus no reason to think that there
ever were any.[5]

The claim made by Granda (1968, 1971) that the Spanish of
Blacks in the Antilles during colonial times was a Creole has, if
shown to be true, important consequences for our elucidation of the
linguistic past of the Caribbean. In addition to implying that a high
degree of linguistic homogeneity existed among the Africans of the
islands, Granda's claim suggests that all through the colonial period
Spanish was in contact with a language which possessed a markedly
West African sound system and grammatical structure and thus could
have had a profound effect on the development of the Spanish of the
area. I will refer to this language, as speakers of Spanish did during
colonial times and folklorists and dialectologists do today, as 'habla
bozal'[6] (henceforth HBA, for 'habla bozal antillana').

In this paper I will reexamine certain aspects of the structure of
HBA for the purpose of establishing its status as an Afro-Caribbean
Creole. I will begin by showing that even though the claim in Granda
(1971) is essentially correct, it is not supported by the data that is
presented,[7] thus leaving the question unsettled. I will then present
additional evidence, showing conclusively that HBA was a Creole.
At the end of the paper, I will discuss the implications of this conclusion for the question of substratum in Caribbean Spanish today.

My analysis, like Granda's, is based on the transcriptions of the
speech of aged Cuban Blacks recorded during the second quarter of
this century by Lydia Cabrera[8] and published in several of her works.
Granda took his data from Cabrera (1969). I took mine from that
work and also from Cabrera (1970a), which contains samples of the
same speech variety.

Granda has based his claim largely on the fact that certain morphemes of Spanish are many times not present in HBA.[10] These are:
articles, copulas, and the particles de, que, and a. These same
items are many times present in HBA. Granda's own examples have
instances where articles and copulas appear, and my corpus shows
many occurrences of de, que, and a. The example in (1) contains
all three.

(1) lo baró quitá to derecho a la mué que fue la río y jallá
    la suete de lo rey Ekoi (1970:259).

    'The men took all privileges away from the woman who
    went to the river and found the good fortune of the kings
    of Ekoi.'

In addition, Granda finds evidence for the Creole status of HBA in
the presence of subject pronouns where they would not appear in
Spanish and in the lack of inflection in nouns[11] and, though less
common, in pronouns as well. As far as the pronouns are concerned,
the value of the observation is difficult to ascertain in a corpus with
very few first and second person utterances, even though, on occasion, the presence of the pronouns does give HBA a certain un-
Spanish flavor.

What we have left as evidence for the Creole status of HBA, then,
is the Creole nature of the noun, which never appears inflected in any
of the attestations. Since this is not enough to support his claim,
Granda points to the cases where articles, copulas, etc. are missing
as additional evidence that HBA was a Creole. But if the sentences
where the items are missing are to serve as evidence that the language is a Creole, then the sentences where they are present can
only be explained as the product of decreolization, which is in fact
what Granda claims.

This then begs the question of why one should claim to begin with
that HBA is a Creole, and leaves us with the problem of having to
choose between alternative classifications (one in term of a Creole,
the other one in terms of a dialect of Spanish) on a purely subjective
basis. If we turn to the vocabulary of HBA, we find that most of its
lexical items are transparent cognates of the corresponding Spanish
items and many times are identical with them. But this too can be
explained, should we prefer the Creole classification, by an appeal
to relexification (Thompson 1961, Stewart 1962) and does not advance
the argument in either direction.

In order to place the discussion on more objective grounds, one
would expect the proponent of a Creole classification to present at
least one aspect of the grammar of the language in question which
functions in a manner similar to that of known Creoles and where the
erosion caused by decreolization has not obscured the evidence to
such an extreme that we are left with the situation described above,
where only personal preferences can swing the argument in one
direction or another. (A discussion of a similar problem along the
lines suggested here can be found in Tsuzaki [1971].) This should
include evidence that at least some of the constructions in the putative
Creole are not possible constructions of the target language.

Such a claim seems to be implicit in the analysis given in Granda
(1971) for the verbal system of HBA, which the author sees as consisting of an uninflected verb stem that may appear either by itself
or preceded by the markers ya, ta, and va. [12] It will be observed
that the verbal markers of the Granda analysis are identical in form
with morphemes of many dialects of Spanish. Furthermore, in the
examples provided by Granda, [13] they function exactly as those forms

do in Spanish. Since the component morphemes are perfectly straightforward Spanish in both form and function, it seems entirely capricious to regard these sentences as relexified Creole constructions
that make use of Spanish morphemes. They could just as well be
regarded as Spanish sentences, with the only non-Spanish feature
being the partial loss of inflection in nouns and verbs. I conclude
that there is nothing in the data offered by Granda that should make
us think that HBA possessed the system of verbal markers that has
been claimed for it. I conclude, furthermore, that the morphemes
ya and va were used in HBA exactly as in Spanish, and that ta, which
I will show below to have functioned in a Creole fashion in HBA, has
not been shown to do so in the sentences offered in Granda, where it
too could be interpreted as having a perfectly straightforward Spanish
use.

From the above it follows that I consider Granda to be right for
the wrong reasons, and that his decision to consider HBA a Creole,
though correct, does not follow from his data. [14] Given the important
implications for both Creole studies and Spanish dialectology that
follow from his conclusion, it seems necessary that it should find
solid support in the data.

The sentences in (2) through (7) below are taken from my corpus
of HBA. None of these sentences can be interpreted through Spanish,
i. e. their morphemes, even when they have a Spanish form, do not
have a Spanish function or meaning. The context in which the sentences appear is provided for the convenience of the reader. The
construction in question is underscored.

(2) ¿ Cómo va sé máno branco, si ta afé, tá prieto yo?
     ¡ Tá jugá! (1970:54).

     'How could I be a brother to the white man, since
     I am dark and black? You must be kidding!

(3) Ya branco ta debaratá cosa. (1970:54).

     'The man is already destroying everything.'

(4) Ikú ese cane na má, pellejo mío sí, se pedé. Pero
     yo ta hí. Uté cuide. Prítu mío ahí. Yo só piera ese
     (1970:108).

     'Only my flesh will die. But I am there. You be
     careful. My spirit is there. I am that stone.'

(5) ¡ Pera un poco muchacho! ¿ No ta mirá palangana allí
con vela prendía? (1969:160).

'Wait a while, young man! Don't you see that
bucket with a candle on it?'

(6) Obon Tanzé e rey mueto que entrá pecao y pasá bongó
(1970:88).

'Obon Tanze is the dead king that got into the fish
and into the drum.'

(7) Divino entonce né mata mué . . . (1970:259).

'Divine then, he kills woman . . . '

Observe that in (1) ta cannot be a phonological reduction of estoy.
We could, however, consider that ta is a reduction of the uninflected
form estar, or that it is itself the invariant form of the Spanish verb.
But if the ta in sentence (2) were a phonological reduction of estar
and (2) a sentence of Spanish, it would be a completely ungrammatical one, since Spanish here uses the verb ser, and not estar. There
is no reason to believe that ta could ever be considered a phonological reduction of any form of ser. In sentence (3) the Spanish interpretation would force us to regard ta debaratá as a phonological reduction of está desbaratando, an unlikely construction in this context.
This can be seen even more clearly in (5), where it would be impossible to consider ta mirá as a phonological reduction of estás
mirando, since the Spanish sentence that would result-- ¿ No estás
mirando esa palangana? --would be ungrammatical on two counts:
(1) the lexical item mirar is inappropriate, and (2) the estar + Vndo
construction could not be used in this context.
    I conclude, therefore, that in (1), (2), and (5), ta (1) does not func-
tion within the system of any known Spanish dialect, and (2) is not,
therefore, a phonological reduction of estar and not a morpheme of
Spanish. The sentences in which ta appears above are, therefore,
not sentences of Spanish.
    In (4), the demonstrative ese does not function as demonstratives
do in Spanish. Demonstrative adjectives in Spanish precede the noun
unless that position is occupied by another modifier, usually an
article. That is, ese piera and la piera ese would have Spanish word
order; they would be anomalous, however, as is (4), because of the
lack of gender agreement. The order of the morphemes would conform to the Spanish system, allowing us to say, at most, that these
are Spanish sentences where the lack of inflection of certain items

has disturbed the concordial pattern. The sequence <u>Yo sô piera ese,</u> however, is ungrammatical in Spanish both because of its morphology and because of its syntax. With regard to the use of <u>allí</u> in (5), we should note that in Spanish this form is never an adjective, which is the function that it performs in this sentence. Even as an adjective, however, it violates the rules of Spanish, as did <u>ese</u> in (4), by its postnominal position in the absence of a prenominal modifier.

Finally, observe that in (6) and (7) there is a double mention of the subject of the sentence, once as a noun and once immediately after it as a coreferential pronoun. Except in very marked contexts, this is an impossible Spanish construction. These sentences, too, are outside the system of Spanish syntax.

Sentences (2) through (7) show that HBA possessed a number of structures which do not conform to the grammar of Spanish. These examples provide crucial evidence for the conclusion that HBA has to be considered as something other than a dialect of Spanish. Having shown this, we are in a position to bring into the discussion the features offered by Granda to prove that HBA was a Creole. Note that it is only after such crucial examples as (2) through (7) have been presented that it makes any sense to entertain such a claim. This is because (1) only after we prove that the language is not Spanish can we say that the Spanish features which alternate with Creole features are there because of decreolization, and (2) because only now do we have a reason to claim that those constructions which fit both a Spanish and a Creole system might be part of a Creole. That is, since, for instance, <u>ta</u> in sentences (2), (3), and (5) cannot be a morpheme of Spanish, then <u>ta</u> in (8) is not necessarily a morpheme of Spanish either, despite the fact that, if taken in isolation, <u>ta creá</u> in (8) could be interpreted as a phonological reduction of <u>está creando.</u>

(8) Uté mira, tó mundo, ripiá, facitó, tó mundo camina sobre tiera. Y cuando uté quié ensuciá, uté ensucia la tiera. Y son deuda que uté ta creá con tiera . . . (1970:263).

'You look, and everyone--the rich and the poor--they all walk on the ground. And when you want to relieve yourself, you do it on the ground. These are debts that you are creating with the ground . . . '

Having established by means of (2) through (7) that HBA was not a dialect of Spanish, and having seen, furthermore, that many of its features point to the likelihood of its being a Creole, the status of constructions like (8) is still unclear. We need more evidence to determine whether in (8) we have a manifestation of an accidental overlap between the European and the Creole grammar, or a case of decreolization. This latter possibility becomes very interesting in cases such as <u>Pavo real ta bucán palo</u> 'The peacock is looking for a branch', where an incipient Spanish morphology, namely <u>n</u>, has sprouted on the verb stem.

In addition to the features presented by Granda to prove that HBA was a Creole, I will add the following. I have already shown in (6) and (7) attestations of coreferential sequences of noun and pronoun, as well as, in (4) and (5), postnominal demonstratives, which are found in Spanish, French, and English Creoles the world over (Taylor 1971). One should also note, particularly with reference to sentence (5), the similarity with the system of demonstratives that exists in Papiamentu, where, exactly as in (5), location is indicated by a postposed determiner, cognate with the Spanish adverbial, as in <u>e buki aki</u>, 'this book', <u>e buki ei</u>, 'that book', and <u>e buki ayá</u>, 'that book yonder' (Goilo 1970:28). Other Creole constructions in the corpus of HBA that I have collected are emphatic duplications, such as <u>Ne murí jayá tiempo tiempo ante</u> (1970:88) 'he died a long time ago', and absence of locative prepositions, as in (9) through (12).

(9) . . . Pa nkamá coge huevo ese, pasa cara, pasa cuerpo, limpia bien . . . (1969:160).

'. . . Pa nkamá(?) take that egg and rub it over your face, your body and clean yourself well . . . '

(10) . . . y píritu di é bobé pecao que mué cogé, né contrá lo río . . . (1970:88).

'. . . and his spirit turned into a fish that the woman took; she found it in the river . . .

(11) . . . la mué que fue la río . . . (1970:259).

'. . . the woman who went to the river . . . '

(12) . . . rey mueto que entrá pecao y pasá bongó . . . (1970:88).

'. . . dead king who entered inside the fish and got into the drum . . . '

Finally, it should be noted that HBA has among its many Creole features the forms <u>né</u> and <u>é</u> for the third person singular personal pronoun. Examples of <u>né</u> have already been seen in sentences (7) and (10). The form is also present in such sentences as <u>ese mimo so</u>

primero saco que né usa pa ñamá 'that is the same sack that he uses to call' (1970:259). Examples of é can be seen in (6) and (10), as well as in (13) and (14).

(13) . . . y con ropa dé, y con cuero dé y pecá hace saco pá sacá é d'ahí . . . (1970:259).

'. . . and with her clothes, her skin, and the skin of a fish, he makes a sack to take her out of there . . . '

(14) . . . To eso son deuda que coge con é pá uté. Pa comé, saca fruta, saca vianda. E dá comé uté tó . . . E sabe que día mañana e te va comé . . . Y día que tú mori e cobra (1970:263).

'. . . all those are debts that you incur with it. In order to eat, you take out fruits and vegetables. It gives you all that you eat. It knows that tomorrow it will eat you, and the day you die, it will collect its debts.'

I have not been able to explain the alternation between né and é, nor to account for the alternation of di é with dé. It is clear, however, that né is used only as a subject and é as both subject and object. Note again in this case the direct correspondence of form and function with Papiamentu, where é is the only third person singular form of the personal pronoun.

The reader should keep in mind that, with the exception of the lack of inflection in nouns and the presence of né and é, which do not seem to compete with inflected nouns or with él and ella from the target language, all the features presented in Granda (1971) in support of the claim that HBA was a Creole as well as those added here existed in the language alongside decreolized constructions. For instance, the corpus contains not only piera ese, palangana allí, and huevo ese, which we have already seen, but also ese otá (1970: 108) 'that stone', where the linear arrangement of the morphemes conforms to the grammar of Spanish rather than to that of a Creole.

For these alternations to be considered evidence of decreolization rather than the sort of imperfect learning that exists in any contact situation, our corpus should include, in addition to utterances that cannot be accounted for through the syntax of the target language, some evidence that these utterances function within a different system, where a fair amount of consistency can still be observed. Having rejected the proposal made in Granda about the use of ya and va as verbal markers, I will suggest that verbs in HBA, while showing some of the elements of the target language and some of the Creole, functioned nevertheless within a consistent system at the time of the recordings in Cabrera.

Verb stems in HBA are uninflected in that they show no alternations in their segmental morphology. There is, however, a regular suprasegmental alternation which can be gleaned from Cabrera's use of accent marks. The regularity and systematicity of this alternation leads me to believe that Cabrera's use of the accent mark was careful and deliberate. However, the nature of the corpus makes it impossible to determine whether Cabrera was marking stress or high tone. Having made this observation, I will write 'stress patterns' and mean whatever suprasegmental alternation is reflected by the shift in the placement of accent marks in the transcription.

The two stress patterns in the verbs of HBA were final stress and penultimate stress. The appearance of one pattern is predictable under certain circumstances. In the situation outlined in (a) below, final stress will always occur. In those cases where stress placement is contrastive, namely (b), it has come to perform the tense- and aspect-marking function which in other Creoles is carried out by preverbal markers. If HBA ever had a full-fledged system of such markers, at the time that we are allowed our first glimpse of the language only one such marker survives, namely the marker ta, which marks present tense. The loss of preverbal markers and the introduction of a tense- and aspect-marking stress alternation similar to that of Spanish characterize the process of decreolization in the HBA verb.

For the purpose of this analysis, the constructions containing verbs in HBA can be divided in two groups: (a) sequences of two verbs, or of a verb preceded by the marker ta, or by pa, ya, or cuando, and (b) all other constructions.

When the verb appears in constructions of type (b) both stress patterns appear. There is not enough evidence to determine whether the major meaning difference is one of tense or aspect. But it seems that penultimate stress signals noncompletive aspect and nonpast tense. Final stress indicates completive aspect.

The following are constructions of type (b), where stress is contrastive. Note that the context indicates that the meaning of the verb is completive, the tense being past in (15) and (17), but apparently projected to a future time in (16).

(15) . . . Cucha canto. To nosotro brincó la mar salá y to
       nosotro son uno . . . (1970:67).

       'Listen to the song. All of us crossed the sea and
       all of us are one.'

(16) . . . Mañana yo ikú. Ikú ese cane na má . . .
(1970:108).

'Tomorrow I will die. Only my flesh will die . . . '

(17) . . . y píritu di é bobé pecao que mué cogé . . .
(1970:88).

' . . . and his spirit turned into the fish that the
woman took'

Verbs with penultimate stress indicate noncompletive aspect.
These include historical presents, as mata in (7); imperatives, as
cucha in (15), and pera in (5); and generics such as coge and sabe
in (14). Note the contrast between cogé and coge in (10) and (9).
    It should be noted that this system held in HBA even in those few
attestations of segmental inflection that are available. Consider the
alternation of bení with viene in (18),

(18) . . . pa ñamá Namanguí, píritu Ekoi que dése bení
religió que quita secreto la mué. Mbanekué morí,
Ekoi viene bucá pa llevá mundo la vedá (1970:259).

' . . . to call Namanguí, spirit of the Ekoi from
which comes the religion that takes the secret
from the woman. Mbanekué died, Ekoi comes to
get him to bring truth to the world. '

where the form bení has kept the stress pattern which marked completive aspect in HBA and which regularly marks past tense in Spanish today, but which in this item runs against the stress pattern of
the target language model vino, which has penultimate stress.
    Finally, the invariant nature of the copula in HBA should be noted.
Even though the nature of copular sentences cannot be fully ascer-
tained from the corpus, cases of zero copula are present (see, e.g.
(6)). The invariant copula so(n) seems to be the prevailing type of
construction. Examples can be seen in (4), (8), and (15).
    I conclude that the crucial cases of impossible Spanish construc-
tions presented in (2) through (7), plus the Creole features discussed
here and in Granda provide strong support for the conclusion that
HBA was a Creole, [15] genetically related to the other Caribbean
Creoles either through a monogenetic development linked to a process of relexification or through a common West African origin
(Alleyne 1971).

Turning now to the Spanish spoken in the Caribbean today, consider the features which are generally regarded as distinguishing of Caribbean phonology, at least at the lowest social strata (Lamb 1969:114-18). They appear listed in (19):

(19a) The merger of /r/ and /l/ and their realization as zero or aspiration in syllable-final position.

(19b) The syllable-final realization as zero of what is an /s/ or an aspiration in other dialects or in higher strata of the same dialect.

(19c) The lenis articulation of all nonsyllabics in syllable-final position.

(19d) The velar realization of /n/ in word-final position.

There are, of course, differences within the Caribbean area in the social and geographic distribution of these phenomena. The point here is that these are the features which characterize, as a whole, the area where Africans lived in the Spanish-speaking world, and where a Creole has been shown to have existed during colonial times.
Since our knowledge of HBA comes from texts using Spanish orthography, we can have direct information on HBA phonology only with regard to those features from (19) which can be captured by variations from the Spanish spelling conventions. These are (a) and (b). Both are shown to have been features of HBA in the examples given here, as well as in the observations on HBA phonology contained in Alvarez Nazario (1961). Given the presence of (d) in Papiamentu today, and given the similarities already observed between these two languages, it seems reasonable to speculate that (d) was also a trait of HBA phonology.
Two of the features in (19)--namely (a) and (d)--are widespread throughout the Creoles and throughout the languages of West Africa as well. Only (a) is found elsewhere in the Hispanic world--in Andalusia--with any degree of geographic continuity (Alonso 1967:239). It is significant that the realization of the merger there is usually [r], whereas the realization of the merger is [1] in Caribbean Spanish, as it is in the Creoles and in the languages of West Africa (Ladefoged 1968:29). Observe, then, that these two distinguishing features of Caribbean Spanish phonology, which have no significant counterparts in the other dialects of Spanish, are also distinguishing features of the Creoles, including HBA.
The close correspondence between West African, Creole, and Caribbean Spanish phonology can be observed not only in the individual

traits that characterize this dialect of Spanish, but also in a single tendency that seems to underlie all of them. As in many other languages, in all dialects of Spanish a number of phonemic contrasts which occur initially or medially are neutralized in syllable-final position. It has been widely accepted since Alonso (1945) and Alonso and Lida (1945) that the number of possible contrasts in several dialects of Spanish is being reduced in what amounts to a drift (Sapir 1921) toward an absolute CV canonic shape. It seems clear from (19) that this drift, with varying degrees within specific subareas, has progressed the most in Caribbean Spanish, in which dialect the least number of contrasts in syllable final position is possible (López Morales 1971:129-30). The distinguishing features of this dialect are in fact all manifestations of the general downgrading of the functional load of the final position within the syllable.

In this respect one should note that the CV canonic shape is one of the outstanding features of the phonology of West African languages and of the Creoles, including HBA. It is significant that the one over-riding difference between Caribbean Spanish phonology and the phonology of other Spanish dialects--namely the considerably greater development in the Caribbean of the open-syllable drift--as well as two of its most important individual distinguishing features--namely (a) and (d) in (19)--are perfectly matched in the phonology of most Creoles.

Finally, a comparison of a syntactic trait which is peculiar to Caribbean Spanish with an equivalent construction in the Creoles will show that the substratal traces left by HBA in the Spanish of the area are not restricted to the phonology but appear in the syntactic level as well. To my knowledge, the most salient distinguishing trait of the syntax of Caribbean Spanish is the preservation of subject-verb order in certain interrogative sentences where other dialects invert. In cases where the interrogative pronoun is non-subject and the subject of the verb is a second person pronoun, Caribbean Spanish shows inversion only as an option where other dialects regard it as obligatory (Kany 1951:125, Andrade 1930:13, Padrón 1948:468). That is, sentences such as ¿Qué ud. quiere? 'What do you want?', ¿Qué tú dices? 'What are you saying?', and ¿De dónde uds. vienen? 'Where are you coming from?' are peculiar to the Caribbean. In light of the considerations made above about Caribbean Spanish phonology, it is significant that in the Creoles inversion of subject and verb in questions never occurs (Hall and Hall 1970). It seems entirely possible that the Creole pattern may account for this partial departure of the Caribbean question formation process from that in the rest of the Spanish dialects.

In summary, the data presented here strongly suggest that the 'habla bozal' spoken in the Spanish Antilles (and possibly throughout the Caribbean) during colonial times was a Creole. This fact requires that studies of Caribbean Spanish be reoriented to include not only considerations of the relationship of this dialect to other Spanish dialects, but also to the closer-by Creoles of the surrounding Caribbean. Specifically, the findings here and in Granda (1968, 1971) force us to discard the argument that the diverse language background of the Africans and their early rejection of their native languages made it impossible for their speech habits to have had any effect on Caribbean Spanish. This is because we have seen that African structures and sound systems survived for centuries in HBA, the single Creole that they all spoke. Given this, the sample points of coincidence presented here between features which are shared by most Creoles but which are peculiar of Caribbean Spanish cannot be discarded as a coincidence and must be taken into account in any explanation of the historical genesis of this major dialect type.

NOTES

[1]I would like to thank J. Dillard for some important references; E. Bendix and B. Hall for substantive suggestions on the analysis of 'habla bozal'; and E. Lattey for reading the manuscript and considerably improving its style. I would also like to acknowledge the help of Z. Malisdorf in all facets of the writing of this paper. Finally, thanks are specially due to R. M. R. Hall for encouraging me to write this paper and for introducing me to the writings of Granda, which have been most valuable. This includes not only the work of which this paper offers a critique, but also Granda's many previous papers on the subject which have appeared in Boletín del Instituto Caro y Cuervo.

[2]The abstracts provided in Solé (1970) of the papers involved in the controversy give an interesting overview of this question.

[3]Examples of the first category abound in the literature, where cursory references are often made to an unidentified substratum of unspecified consequences for Caribbean Spanish. See Isbasescu (1965:594) and Lamb (1969:119-20), to name only two.

[4]The clearest formulation of this position is found in the Introduction to López Morales's quite valuable Estudio sobre el español de Cuba, 1971.

[5]This view is repeated, for instance, as late as Rosenblat (1964). The discovery of Palenquero, a Spanish Creole of the Caribbean coast of Colombia (Escalante 1954, Montes Giraldó 1962, Bickerton and Escalante 1970) did not alter this notion.

[6]That such a language existed is a matter of historical record and the interested reader can check such sources as Alzola (1965). The historical evidence exists in the form of literary attestations

and of contemporary reports. Of particular interest to the Creole hypothesis is Pichardo (1836), where we see 'habla bozal' described as 'disfigured' Spanish, showing the obviously Creole features of a language 'sin concordancia, número, declinación ni conjugación' (liii). Even more important for the Creole claim is Pichardo's observation that 'este lenguaje es común e idéntico en los negros, sean de la nación que fuesen' (liii), where we learn that the often-observed language variation among the slaves was overlaid with a Spanish lingua franca that they all spoke in a similar manner, regardless of their origin.

[7]It is acknowledged in Granda (1971) that the work is of a preliminary sort and this perhaps explains the inconclusive nature of the data.

[8]Cabrera, a well-known student of Afro-Cuban language and folklore, did not use any sort of rigorous transcription method (her main concern in these works was not linguistic) but simply adapted Spanish orthographic conventions for her purposes. This in no way affects the substance of my argument, nor of Granda's, since neither one makes claims concerning phonetic detail. It should be noted that only a handful of Cabrera's informants speak HBA, the rest being recorded as speaking in Spanish.

[9]Cabrera (1969) was originally published in 1954. Granda worked with the 1954 edition. I worked with the 1969 edition. Although I am sure that there is an earlier edition of Cabrera (1970), the copy that I have does not indicate it.

[10]Granda also points to the absence of passive and reflexive sentences.

[11]Number inflection is clearly lacking. Lack of gender inflection must be inferred sometimes from the absence of agreement between nouns and their modifiers, since the shape of the nouns themselves does not always provide enough evidence.

[12]The meanings of the verbal markers according to Granda, translated into the terminology used in Taylor (1960) and Voorhoeve (1957) to express the meaning of verbal markers in Papiamentu and other Creoles, would be as follows: ya: realis, past, completive, durative; ta: realis, present, noncompletive, durative; va: nonrealis, present, completive. Considering these meanings, one clear indication that ya and va are not verbal markers is that in one of the examples provided by Granda (1971:487) Ya va entrá, the sequence of ya and va has not resulted in a sentence meaning 'I should have entered'. This is what one would expect if, as Granda claims, the markers in HBA worked in any way similarly to those of such languages as Papiamentu or Sranan where sequences of the verbal markers with the equivalent meaning to that of ya and va appear.

[13]The examples provided by Granda for the verbal markers of HBA are the following: ya pará arriba tengue; ya pará rriba jagüey; ya para rriba ñangüe; ta bucá palo; de to ese que yo ta nombrá; ya va entrá; cosita yo va hacé (1971:487).

[14]After the oral version of this paper was read at SECOL in October 1972, W. Stewart commented that I had been perhaps too critical of Granda, who may have had access to considerably more data than appears in Granda (1971). This could very well be so. I have simply indicated that based on the data published by Granda the conclusion remains questionable and that a preliminary demonstration of the impossibility of considering some of the utterances as utterances of any dialect of Spanish is a necessary step.

[15]The data presented here are only for Cuba. Data for the rest of the Caribbean are scarce and are often of a literary sort and thus not as suitable for analysis as Cabrera's transcription. However, from the evidence in Alvarez Nazario (1961) and from the statements in Granda (1968), it seems that the conclusions reached for Cuba apply at least to the rest of the Spanish Antillian domains and possibly to the entire Spanish Caribbean.

REFERENCES

Alleyne, Mervyn C. 1971. Acculturation and the cultural matrix of Creolization. Hymes, ed.
Alonso, Amado. 1945. Una ley fonológica del español. Hispanic Review. 13.91-107. (Reprinted in Alonso 1967a.)
_____. 1967a. Estudios lingüísticos: Temas españoles. Madrid, Gredos.
_____. 1967b. Estudios lingüísticos: Temas hispanoamericanos. Madrid, Gredos.
_____ and Raimundo Lida. 1945. De geografía lingüística: l y r implosivas en España y América. Revista de Filología Hispánica. 7.332-42. (Reprinted in Alonso 1967b.)
Alvarez Nazario, Manuel. 1961. El elemento afronegroide en el español de Puerto Rico. San Juan, Instituto de Cultura Puertorriqueña.
Alzola, Concepción. 1965. Habla popular cubana. Revista de Dialectología y Tradiciones Populares. 21.358-70.
Andrade, Manuel. 1930. Folklore de la república dominicana. New York, The American Folklore Society.
Bickerton, Derek and Aquiles Escalante. 1970. Palenquero: A Spanish-based Creole of Northern Colombia. Lingua. 24.254-56.
Cabrera, Lydia. 1969. El Monte. Miami, Ediciones C. R.
_____. 1970. La sociedad secreta Abakuá. Miami, Ediciones C. R.

Escalante, Aquiles. 1954. El Palenque de San Basilio.
Divulgaciones Etnológicas de la Universidad del Atlántico. 3.5.
Goilo, E. R. 1970. Papiamentu textbook. Aruba, N. A., De Wit,
N. V.
Granda, Germán de. 1968. La tipología criolla de dos hablas del
área lingüística hispánica. Boletín del Instituto Caro y Cuervo.
23.193-205.
_____. 1971. Algunos datos sobre la pervivencia del criollo en
Cuba. Boletín de la Real Academia Española. 51.481-91.
Hall, R. M. R. and Beatrice L. Hall. 1970. Some Papiamentu-
general Creole grammatical constraints. Paper read at the
Prome Simposyo Internashonal di Papiamentu.
Hymes, Dell, ed. 1971. Pidginization and creolization of languages.
London, Cambridge University Press.
Isbasescu, Cristina. 1965. Algunas peculiaridades del español
hablado en Cuba. Revue Roumaine de Linguistique. 10.571-94.
Kany, Charles. 1951. Spanish American syntax. Chicago,
University of Chicago.
Ladefoged, Peter. 1968. A phonetic study of West African lan-
guages. London, Cambridge University Press.
Lamb, Anthony. 1969. A phonological study of the Spanish of
Havana, Cuba. Unpublished doctoral dissertation, University
of Kansas.
López Morales, Humberto. 1971. Estudio sobre el español de
Cuba. New York, Las Américas.
Malmberg, Bertil. 1959. L'extension du castillan et le probléme
des substrats. Actes du Colloque International de Civilizations,
Litteratures et Langues Romanes. 249-60.
_____. 1964. Tradición hispánica e influencia indígena en la
fonética hispanoamericana. Presente y Futuro de la Lengua
Española. 2.227-43.
Montes Giraldó, José J. 1962. Sobre el habla de San Basilio de
Palenque. Boletín del Instituto Caro y Cuervo. 17.446-50.
Padrón, Alfredo. 1948. Giros sintácticos corrientes en el habla
popular, culta y semicultas cubanas. Boletín de Filología.
5.467-95.
Pichardo, Esteban. 1836. Diccionario provincial de voces cubanas.
Matanzas.
Rice, Frank, ed. 1962. Study of the role of second languages.
Washington, D.C., Center for Applied Linguistics.
Rosenblat, Angel. 1964. La hispanización de América: El castellano
y las lenguas indígenas desde 1492. Presente y Futuro de la
Lengua Española. 2.189-216.
Sapir, Edward. 1921. Language. New York, Harcourt, Brace
and World.

Solé, Carlos A. 1970. Bibliografía sobre el español en América. 1920-1967. Washington, D. C., Georgetown University Press.
Stewart, William. 1962. Creole languages in the Caribbean. In: Rice, ed. 1962.
Taylor, Douglas. 1960. Language shift or changing relationship. International Journal of American Linguistics. 26.155-61.
_____. 1971. Grammatical and lexical affinities of Creoles. In: Hymes, ed. 1971.
Thompson, R. W. 1961. A note on some possible affinities between the Creole dialects of the Old World and those of the New. Creole Language Studies, 2.
Tsuzaki, Stanley. 1971. Coexistent systems in language variation: The case of Hawaiian English. In: Hymes, ed. 1971.
Voorhoeve, Jan. 1957. The verbal system of Sranan. Lingua. 6.374-96.

THE BOUNDARIES OF WORDS
AND THEIR MEANINGS

WILLIAM LABOV

University of Pennsylvania

If we take seriously the traditional notion that linguistic signs
represent the union of a form and a meaning, there can be no limit
to our interest in the meanings of words. But for a number of reasons,
linguists have concentrated their attention on the forms of words and
their combinations, and the meanings of only a small number of grammatical particles. The description of the meanings of words has
been left to the lexicographers, for better or for worse; and linguists have long contented themselves with glosses which are labels
but not descriptions. Recent activity in combinatorial semantics has
not extended as yet to the meanings of words.

The reason for this neglect is certainly not a lack of interest,
since linguists like any other speakers of a language cannot help
focusing their attention on the word, which is the most central element
in the social system of communication. [1] It is the difficulty of the
problem, and its inaccessibility to the most popular methods of inquiry, which is responsible for this neglect.

We encounter many ordinary objects that are clearly and easily
named, but many more where it is difficult to say exactly what they
are if we confront them directly. In any kitchen, there are many
containers that are obviously bowls, cups, mugs, and dishes. But
there are others that might be called cups, or might not; or might be
a kind of a cup, according to some, but a kind of a dish according to
others. This is a problem of formal description more than a problem
of the language; for the puzzled expressions that we get when we hold
up such an object for naming rarely appear in the everyday use of the
language. The most casual observation suggests that the language has

340

many adroit ways of dealing with the problem, but that has not helped lexicographers when they attempted formal definitions of words.

Words have often been called slippery customers, and many scholars have been distressed by their tendency to shift their meanings and slide out from under any simple definition. A goal of some clear thinkers has been to use words in more precise ways. But though this is an excellent and necessary step for a technical jargon, it is a self-defeating program when applied to ordinary words. It is not only that words are shifters; the objects to which they must be applied shift with even greater rapidity. Words that are bound to simple conjunctive definitions will have little value for application in a world which presents us with an unlimited range of new and variable objects for description. Words as well as the world itself display the 'orderly heterogeneity' which characterizes language as a whole (Weinreich, Labov, and Herzog 1968). Again we would argue that this orderly heterogeneity is functional. Rather than complain about the variable character of the meanings of words, we should recognize the existence of an extraordinary ability of human beings to apply words to the world in a creative way. The problem is no less central than the one which Chomsky has identified in relation to syntax. Just as we employ a finite set of rules to produce an unlimited number of sentences, so we employ a finite set of words to describe an unlimited number of objects in the real world around us.

The ordinary methods of investigation which have been used to define words represent only a part of the methods which might be used to attack this problem. Language can be studied through introspection, formal elicitation, the study of texts, experiment, and/or observation (Labov 1971). But only the first three approaches have been taken to the study of words and their meanings. This paper will report for the first time a series of experimental studies of the use of words which have been carried out over the past ten years.[2] The main focus has been on the denotation of cups and cuplike containers, and the use of words such as <u>cup</u>, <u>bowl</u>, <u>dish</u>, <u>mug</u>, <u>glass</u>, <u>pitcher</u>, etc., and their corresponding terms in other languages. New techniques have been developed for the study of the variable conditions which govern denotation. But there are also invariant components among these conditions, and the entire study must be firmly located as an aspect of the basic categorizing activity of human beings. Before we consider the experiments themselves, it will be necessary to outline the traditional categorical view which attempts to capture this aspect of linguistic behavior and the problem of defining boundary conditions within that view.

1. The categorical view and its limitations

If linguistics can be said to be any one thing it is the study of categories: that is, the study of how language translates meaning into sound through the categorization of reality into discrete units and sets of units. This categorization is such a fundamental and obvious part of linguistic activity that the properties of categories are normally assumed rather than studied. Behind all of the theories of linguistic structure that have been presented in the twentieth century there is a common set of assumptions about the nature of structural units. This set of assumptions can be called the 'categorical view'. It includes the implicit assertions that all linguistic units are categories which are:

(1) discrete
(2) invariant
(3) qualitatively distinct
(4) conjunctively defined
(5) composed of atomic primes

By 'discrete', it is meant that the categories are separated from each other by clear-cut discontinuities of form or function; by 'invariant', that the category as a type recurs as precisely the same in each occurrence, despite the fact that tokens may vary; by 'qualitatively different', that the units are completely different from each other, and not distinguished as homogeneous elements in a linear or ordered sequence; by 'conjunctively defined', that there is a set of properties associated with the unit which are in some way criterial or necessary, essential as opposed to other properties which are unnecessary, accidental, or redundant, and that all of these essential properties must be present for the category to be recognized.

The fifth property may be considered an extension of discreteness: although some categories are compounded of others, there is a limit to any such subdivision, and all categories are ultimately composed of a set of integral categories which cannot be subdivided.

Membership in these categories, and relations of inclusion and exclusion among categories, are established by rules which are obligatory or optional, but optionality cannot be further characterized. No statements can be made as to whether one such rule applies more often than another. [3]

These properties of linguistic categories are far from arbitrary. They appear to correspond well to the basic structure of language as we deal with it everyday. It is sometimes said that man is a categorizing animal; it is equally appropriate to say that language is a categorizing activity. The total abandonment of any one of these properties might be shown to have unfortunate consequences for linguistic analysis. But some modification appears to be necessary, as the present report and other recent work demonstrates.

Scholars have assumed the properties of the categorical view for a wide range of categories: features, phonemes, morphemes, intonation contours, verbs, modals, nouns, nodes, cycles, derivations, styles, languages, manner adverbs, dialects, etc. Because this characterization of language seems to be firmly based on the nature of linguistic activity, it has provided a useful base for a first approximation to grammars and the principles of writing grammars.

But this view of man as a categorizing animal fails if it takes categorizing activity for granted, since it cannot deal with the facts of linguistic change which have been studied over several centuries, nor with the orderly variation within linguistic structure which we have charted in some detail in recent years (Weinreich, Labov, and Herzog 1968).

In the categorical view, the properties of categories are assumed. Scholars then typically argue how many categories exist, and what items are assigned to what categories.[4] This is an important and essential activity: many fields which study human behavior deal with categories which are not firmly enough established to allow the question, one category or two?[5] But in many areas of linguistics, we have extracted as much profit as we can from these debates, and we can turn to the resolution of long-standing questions by examining the correspondence of the categorizing process to linguistic activity. Instead of taking as problematical the existence of categories, we can turn to the nature of the boundaries between them. As linguistics then becomes a form of boundary theory rather than a category theory, we discover that not all linguistic material fits the categorical view: there is greater or lesser success in imposing categories upon the continuous substratum of reality.

There are cases where the categorical nature of a boundary is immediate and obvious, as suggested in a property-item matrix such as Figure 1. Here there are a series of eight items (a-h) which may be thought of variously as languages, dialects, villages, parts of speech, words, phonemes, etc., and seven properties (1-7) detectable in them. The presence of these properties is associated with category X, their absence with category Y. In Figure 1 it is plain that items a-d are X's, and e-h are Y's. Though it is possible to select a single property as the distinctive, or criterial, or essential one, we feel much more confident about categories which are defined by the co-occurrence of a large number of items. Thus it is clear that French and English are different systems, and we use these terms without misgivings. But we are not so happy with such categories as dialects established by the evidence that two speakers disagree with each other on the acceptability of a single sentence type[6] and we are particularly critical of sub-categorizations of parts of speech which are justified by only one property.[7] .

FIGURE 1. Property-item matrix for a clearly categorical boundary.

```
                        Item

                 a  b  c  d  e  f  g  h

            1    +  +  +  + │ -  -  -  -
    ≫       2    +  +  +  + │ -  -  -  -
    t       3    +  +  +  + │ -  -  -  -
    r       4    +  +  +  + │ -  -  -  -
    e       5    +  +  +  + │ -  -  -  -
    p       6    +  +  +  + │ -  -  -  -
    o       7    +  +  +  + │ -  -  -  -
    r
    P            X ←CATEGORY→  Y
```

However, a certain degree of vagueness is often characteristic of boundaries. In the most extreme case, categories can be justified even when no boundaries can be set up between them.

Thus, in Figure 2, any decision to locate the boundary between categories X and Y would obviously be an arbitrary one. Yet the fact that the data on properties (1-7) can be organized in the implicational series shows that there is a structure here, which effectively constrains the data to eliminate at least half of the possible permutations

FIGURE 2. Property-item matrix for the absence of a boundary between two categories.

```
                        Item

                 a  b  c  d  e  f  g  h

            1    +  +  +  +  +  +  +╱-
    ≫       2    +  +  +  +  +  +╱- -
    t       3    +  +  +  +  +╱- - -
    r       4    +  +  +  +╱- - - -
    e       5    +  +  +╱- - - - -
    p       6    +  +╱- - - - - -
    o       7    +╱- - - - - - -
    r
    P            X ←CATEGORY→  Y
```

of items and properties. Given empirical data which resembled
Figure 2, we could not say with any certainty whether any given item
b-g was to be classed as a sonorant or an obstruent, a verb or a
modal, a speaker of the white vernacular or of the black vernacular,
a Romance or a Germanic language, a pidgin or a creole, as the
categories X and Y may variously assign membership. The transition between X and Y occupies the entire property-item space. Such
matrices have been discussed as theoretical possibilities by a number
of recent writers, beginning with Quirk (1965) in regard to grammatical categories, and DeCamp (1971) in regard to sociolinguistic
systems and the Creole continuum. But in regard to geographical
dialects, it has long been argued that such gradient models are
characteristic of the diffusion of linguistic features across a terri-
tory and the challenge has been to establish that boundaries between
dialects are anything but arbitrary (Weinreich 1954, Stankiewicz
1957).

The most vigorous development of the modal of Figure 2, on both
the theoretical and empirical side, is to be found in the work of
Bickerton, who proposes that linguistic structures contain no homogeneous categories at all, but only continuous transitions bound by
implicational series, with no properties showing co-occurrence restrictions at all (1971, 1972). Nevertheless, even in dialect geography, most investigators agree that properties do bundle, and that it
is possible to show boundaries of varying degrees of clarity even when
all variable features are superimposed upon a single map. This type
of bundling or co-occurrence of properties in a variable matrix is
illustrated in Figure 3, where the division between categories X and

FIGURE 3. Discontinuity reflecting co-occurrence restrictions
on properties in a variable matrix.

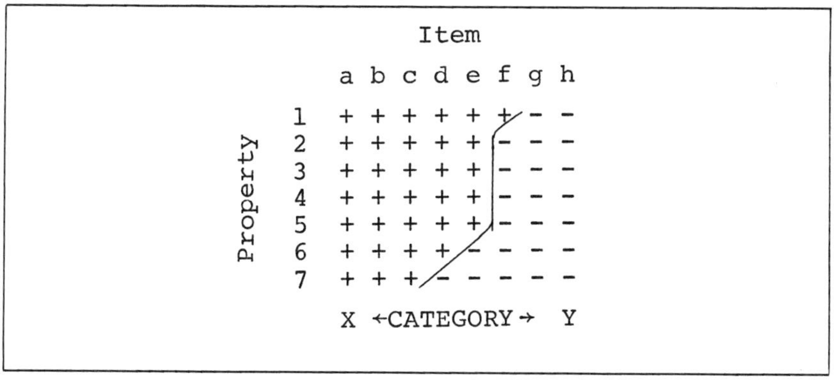

Y appears to be less arbitrary than in Figure 2. Items a, b, c are clearly X, and d and e appear to be X's as well, though a bit defective in relation to properties 6 and 7. Items g and h are clearly Y, and f is again a Y, though imperfect. The important feature of Figure 3 which makes this division possible is the simultaneous shift or co-occurrence restrictions exhibited by properties 2-5. These provide us with evidence of systematicity within the rules which govern property 2 and tie them to those which govern properties 3, 4, and 5. In dialect geography, the discontinuity of Figure 3 would represent a bundle of isoglosses; in an urban speech community, it would represent a subsystem characteristic of a class or ethnic dialect. If Figure 3 represents the distinction between modals and other verbs, the bundling properties might be subject to inversion, reproduction in tag questions, and not contraction. In phonology, we find that initial stops show co-occurrence of initial aspiration, voicing lag, and stronger release of air pressure. Whether or not we choose one of these properties as distinctive, the co-occurrence reinforces our confidence in the existence of the categories.

Another sort of discontinuity in a variable matrix appears in Figure 4. Here there is no co-occurrence of any two properties, but there are items that clump together. Items e-h are all characterized by properties 1-3 but not properties 4-7. This situation

FIGURE 4. Discontinuity reflecting a concentration of homogeneous items in a variable matrix.

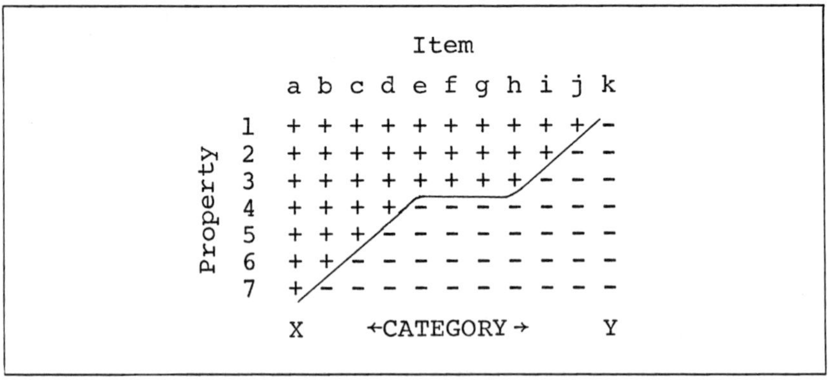

tempts us to redefine our category system, possibly setting up a third category X' which is defined by properties 1-3 only. In dialect geography, this would mean that relatively homogeneous speech communities exist; in phonology, it would mean that some combinations of features were more heavily exploited than others for some functional reason. It is clear that this second type of discontinuity

appears in Bickerton's data, and is one of the main focuses of
Bailey's approach in building rate into models of phonological linguistic description (1971).

In large-scale studies which are accountable to a given population or body of data, we may find no examples of perfect co-
occurrence or perfectly homogeneous groups. But given an empirical approach to the problems of linguistic analysis we can report
the actual discontinuities in transition which exist. Thus if we are
to take seriously the categorical property of language, we must pass
beyond the categorical view which takes it as given, and study the
process of categorization itself by focusing on such discontinuities
directly. By avoiding the categorical view, or some equally rigid
principle of distribution, we are free to study the real properties
of such boundaries, and deduce the higher level properties which
govern the use of language.

This paper will introduce the study of variability in denotation,
systematically displacing the categorical view which has dominated
previous studies in order to discover the regularities which relate
the properties of shape, function, material, etc. as they govern
the conditions for the act of denotation. To do so, we will have to
reject in particular property (d)--the notion that categories are to
be defined conjunctively through their distinctive features. These
distinctive features or essential attributes are the working apparatus
of the scholastic tradition which has dominated almost every school
of linguistic thought until recently, and our pursuit of a secular mode
of inquiry will inevitably bring us into conflict with that tradition.

2. Conditions for denotation

In this study, we will be dealing with the conditions which govern
denotation, that is, the act of naming or reference which associates
a linguistic sign with an element of the extra-linguistic world. Denotation or reference has been especially excluded from some recent
studies of combinatorial semantics, as if this topic were outside of
the proper domain of linguistics (Katz and Fodor 1963). Yet the
fundamental relation of form to meaning in designation is to be seen
only in the conditions which govern the act of reference: that is, the
significatum of the sign.

Though this investigation deals with the application of signs to
concrete objects, it is not a study of the act of reference, and
should not be confused with the point of view that identifies meaning
with use. We are dealing rather with the knowledge of ability to
apply a term to a range of objects in a way that reflects the communicative system utilized by others. Following Weinreich (1962),
we define the significatum or meaning of a sign, as the conditions

which govern denotation. Given a situation in which such conditions are actually fulfilled, so that the sign can be used in reference to the situation, the token of the sign is said to denote. Thus

(1) $L(x)$ if C_1 and C_2 and C_3.

That is, the sign L denotes the object x if all of the conditions C_1, C_2 . . . are fulfilled. These conditions C_1, C_2 . . . are sometimes called criteria, or conditions of criteriality. The relationship here is one of intersection: each of them must be fulfilled, or the sign does not denote. In other words, these are essential conditions, or distinctive features of the designatum. They are quite parallel in this respect to the distinctive features of the Jakobson-Halle framework (1952): essential properties that are always present (except when they are replaced), and the only properties which need to be included in a specification of the phoneme or the sign. All other--redundant-- properties can be discarded from the specification of meaning.

In the present state of semantic investigations, most articles draw upon the intuitions of the theorist in order to isolate these distinctive features and their internal structure. A great deal can be learned through such introspection, especially if intuitions are sharpened, by the use of the right linguistic frames. Let us see how much can be achieved within the categorical view by the use of our linguistic intuitions, beginning with a definition of a cup cast in the model of (1):

(2) The term cup is used for an object which is (a) concrete and (b) inanimate and (c) upwardly concave and (d) a container (e) with a handle (f) made of earthenware or other vitreous material and (g) set on a saucer and (h) used for the consumption of food (i) which is liquid [(j) and hot] . . .

In order to find out which of these ten conditions are criterial, we can apply the test frame proposed by Weinreich, It's an L but C. If the property is essential and expected to be present, the result is absurd since but implies something contrary to expectation. Thus the absurdity of It's a chair but you can sit in it establishes that there is something about the property of seating someone that is essential to chairs. In the test sentences given below, we insert first the property listed as an essential condition in definition (2); on the right, a contrary or opposing property. If the original property cited is essential, criterial, or distinctive, we should have unacceptable or absurd sentences on the left, and acceptable or sensible sentences on the right.

(3)

It's a cup but . . .

a.	*it's concrete.	it's abstract.
b.	*it's inanimate.	it's alive.
c.	*it's concave.	it's convex.
d.	*it holds things.	it doesn't hold anything.
e.	*it has a handle.	it doesn't have a handle.
f.	*it's pottery.	it's made of wax.
g.	*it's on a saucer.	it has no saucer.
h.	*it's used at meal times.	they use it to store things.
i.	*you can drink out of it.	you can eat out of it.
j.	?you can drink hot milk out of it.	?you can drink cold milk out of it.
k.	?it has a stripe on it.	?it doesn't have a stripe on it.

My own reactions to these sentences are indicated by asterisks or question marks; they suggest that properties (a-i) satisfy this approach to essentiality or criteriality. For item (j) we get two sentences that are equally irrelevant or questionable. There is no reason to think it surprising that we can drink hot milk out of a cup; but equally so, it is not surprising that we can drink cold milk out of it. Similarly, if we add a feature which is obviously accidental and not essential, like a stripe (k), we get questionable results on both sides. 8 It is of course the lack of symmetry between the two opposing sentences rather than the absolute judgment which makes the test reasonably precise.

If the study of linguistic intuitions were a satisfactory approach to the defining of terms, it would seem that linguists have a great deal to contribute to the writing of dictionaries. But lexicography as it has been practised is an art of a different kind, where the intuitions of the lexicographer combine with traditional lore (the definitions found in other dictionaries) and a large body of citations from published sources. The dictionary maker does not rely upon his intuitions to cover the full range of applications and meanings which the term cup might have, but tries instead to frame a definition that circumscribes as narrowly as possible the whole range of uses that he can collect. The result is a kind of definition which linguists usually find quite unsatisfactory.

(4) cup, n. 1. A small open bowl-shaped vessel used chiefly
to drink from, with or without a handle or handles, a stem
and foot, or a lid; as a wine cup, a Communion cup; specif.,
a handled vessel of china, earthenware, or the like commonly

> set on a saucer and used for hot liquid foods such as tea,
> coffee, or soup. --Webster's New International Dictionary,
> Second edition.

There are quite a few features of this definition which linguists might
find peculiar, but the most objectionable is the use of qualifying words
like chiefly, commonly, or the like, etc. These are the kinds of
indefinite quantifiers that linguistics has been trying to escape from
since the early days of comparative method. In the current linguistic framework, a property can be optional or obligatory. If it
is optional, then it is in 'free variation'. and nothing more can be
said about its frequency.[9] Even more objectionable is with or without
a handle, or handles. Such a phrase is hardly specific to cups; it
can be applied to any object in the universe. I myself, for example,
come with or without a handle or handles.

Let us ask how a reader is expected to use this definition. Suppose an object is not used to drink from. How does the reader utilize
the expression used chiefly to drink from? Is the object he is examining less of a cup? Should he then call it cuppish, or a thing like a
cup, or can he go ahead and call it a cup just the same? The definition does not help to make the kind of decision which was discussed
in section 1, where the categorizing spirit of language is invoked to
decide if in fact, an object is, or is not, a cup.

Webster's definition goes far beyond this categorizing activity;
it has an encyclopedic quality, which could seemingly expand indefinitely to tell us anything or everything ever known about cups.
There are of course many other entries besides the principal one
that I have quoted. The sixth is the principle generalizing entry
which covers the extended and metaphorical uses of cup most freely:

(5)   6. A thing resembling a cup (sense 1) in shape or use,
       or likened to such a utensil; as (a) a socket or recess in
       which something turns, as the hip bone, the recess
       which a capstan spindle turns, etc. (b) any small
       cavity in the surface of the ground. (c) an annular
       trough, filled with water, at the face of each section
       of a telescopic gas holder, into which fits the grip of
       the section next outside. (d) in turpentine orcharding,
       a receptable shaped like a flowerpot, metal or earthen-
       ware, attached to the tree to collect resin.

We wonder whether the first part of this definition could not be added
to every noun in the dictionary. Is there any term which cannot be
applied to a thing resembling its main referent in shape or use, or
likened to it? Beyond this, we have four uses of dazzling specificity,

which are obviously inserted only to cover some particular three-by-five slips which the dictionary staff happened to have collected. If the reader is not capable of understanding uses (a-d) without help from the dictionary, it seems unlikely that he will be able to survive in everyday life where terms are freely extended in such a way to even more specific objects.

Thus the Webster definition seems to be overly specific in some areas, but terribly vague in others. No current linguistic text would hold it up as a proper model or guide for semantic description. It is true that it will be contradicted far less often by experience than definition (2). But definition (2) can be defended by saying that it covers only the essential or distinctive properties of a cup; the Webster definition seems to be governed only by the need to cover all of the uses of cup that have been accumulated in its files.

The balance of this paper will report experimental studies of the use of the term cup. Surprisingly enough, these studies will show that the Webster definition is superior to the criterial definition (2) in every respect. A first indication of this situation appears when we consider some properties of such criterial statements which raise great difficulties for empirical investigations.

The conditions specified in formula (1) are usually taken to indicate the presence or absence of a given feature: that is, they govern the denotation of L by binary decisions. Thus a cup may or may not be concave, may or may not be used as a container. Similarly, in componential analysis we define a relative as either male or female, either colineal or ablineal. But the generation condition is a linear scale; we must establish some criterial value along that scale, such as first ascending generation, to locate father (Wallace and Atkins 1960). We do find many such cases of simply yes-no conditions, such as whether a tree has cones or not. But we more commonly encounter dimensions which require us to establish criterial values to complete our definition. For L to denote, C_1 must achieve a critical value. Thus we need a formulation such as

(6) $L(x)$ if C_p and D_r and E_t . . .

where C, D, and E each vary along separate dimensions, and L does not denote if the value of C is less than p, etc. Thus a tree is not a white pine unless it has five needles in each fascicle. But again, it is unusual to find such discrete criterial values in empirical work: normally, the criterial condition is a range of values within which L will denote. Thus we must formulate

(7) $L(x)$ if C_p^q and D_r^s and E_t^u . . .

where L does not denote if the value of C is less than p or greater than q, etc. Thus a tree is not a yellow pine if its needles are in bundles of less than two or more than three.

We may note here one further limitation of the traditional, categorical approach to denotative conditions which may cause difficulties: the various conditions C, D, E are normally considered to be independent of each other. It is possible that one condition is dependent on the other in the sense that it is a precondition for the other. Thus the leaves of a pine tree must be needles, implying some maximum of cross-section relative to length. And the needles must be in bundles of a certain number, entailing the existence of needles as a feature superordinate in the taxonomy. But the criterial values for a needle, and the criterial values for numbers of needles in a fascicle, are independent of each other. The number of needles in a bundle required if white pine is to denote are usually independent of the specification of maximum cross-section of the leaves. We do not, for example, say that a white pine is a tree with bundles of five needles if they are thick or three to four when they are thin. [10]

This property of independence of criterial conditions is firmly entrenched in the componential analysis of kinship terms, plant taxonomy, etc., which is the area where the most progress has been made in descriptive semantics. Nevertheless, our empirical investigations will show us that the independence of criterial values is not a fundamental property which governs native competence in the use of words. The formal modifications of (7) necessary to cope with this situation will be developed at the conclusion of our report.

The remaining limitation of the modified categorical formula (7) which we must amend is its discreteness. The criterial conditions C_p^q imply discrete cutting points p and q. Yet in the world of experience all boundaries show some degree of <u>vagueness,</u> and any formal system which is useful for semantic description must allow us to record, or even measure, this property.

3. The measurement of vagueness

When we approach the empirical problems of naming things, we find that vagueness is almost a universal property of the criterial ranges C_p to C^q. In kinship terminology, we have ready-made discreteness: there is no intermediate step in the nuclear family between first and second generation, and no vague borderland or fringe area between them. But the borderline between a tree and a shrub is not discrete. Leaves may be deeply lobed or shallowly lobed, but there is a vague area in-between where we are in doubt. This vagueness is not a property of our perception or the weakness of our instruments, nor the abstractness of our objects. Some of the most concrete data are by nature vague, and some concrete objects are in themselves vague, as for example, fog.

Can we measure vagueness? At first glance, this may seem to be a self-defeating idea. Yet if we follow the reasoning of Max Black (1949), it seems quite feasible to measure the vagueness of terms within a given context. A term's vagueness, following Black, consists of the existence of objects concerning which it is impossible to say either that the term does or does not denote. He constructs a consistency profile upon three fundamental notions: (1) users of a language; (2) a situation in which a user of a language is trying to apply a term L to an object x; and (3) the consistency of application of L to x. The subjective aspect of vagueness may be thought of as the lack of certainty as to whether the term does or does not denote; and this may be transformed into the consistency with which a given sample of speakers does in fact apply the term. The problem of vagueness is seen most clearly when we have a large number of objects which differ by only small degrees from each other, as in Black's example of a series of chairs which gradually become indistinguishable from a series of blocks of wood. At one end of the series, a single term L clearly denotes; at the other end, it does not; and in the middle we are left in doubt. If the consistency of application of L to x for each of these objects is measured, we obtain a consistency profile. Measurements are not of course comparable except in a given situation, but we can distinguish various types of gradients and opposing relations within that situation and regular transformations of it. A precise symbol will show a sharp gradient, while a vague term will show a very slight one. But more importantly, we will be able to use this mechanism to demonstrate the effect of changes in various properties upon the application of the term, and their mutual interaction.

The present series of studies is based upon the series of cup-like objects shown in Figure 5. The first four cups across the top show increasing ratios of width to depth. If the proportional width of the cup at upper left is taken as 1, then the widths of the cups 1, 2, 3, 4 increase in the ratios of 1.2, 1.5, and 1.9 to 1, all with constant depth. [11] A fifth decrease in width (No. 20, not shown here) gives us a ratio of 2.5 to 1. Proceeding downward along the left margin, we have five increments of depth with constant width; the depth is increased in the ratios of 1.2, 1.5, 1.9, 2.4, and 3.0 to 1. In the center of the diagram are cups which depart from the concave shape of 1-4 and 5-9. Cups 10, 11, 12 are cylindrical, with increasing depth; and cups 13, 14, 15 show the same increments for the tapering pattern of a truncated cone. In the lower right we have forms that depart maximally from the modal cup at upper left. The short- and long-stemmed cups show variation in the form of the base, and

FIGURE 5. Series of cup-like objects.

the square and triangular objects show variation in the contour of the perimeter. The drawings of cups are presented to subjects one at a time, in two different randomized orders; the subjects are simply asked to name them. They are then shown the same series of drawings again, and this time asked to imagine in each case that they saw someone with the object in his hand, stirring in sugar with a spoon, and drinking coffee from it (or in some languages, tea), and to name them in this context. In a third series, they are asked to imagine that they came to dinner at someone's house and saw this object sitting on the dinner table, filled with mashed potatoes (rice for some languages). In a fourth series, they are asked to conceive of each of these objects standing on a shelf, each with cut flowers in it. We will refer to these four contexts as the 'Neutral', 'Coffee', 'Food', and 'Flower' contexts.

There is another set of diagrams with no handles, and a third with two handles, which are used in a more limited series of namings. In other series, we specify the material of these cups as china, glass, paper, and metal.

The responses to these tests are in the form of noun phrases, often with a wide range of modifiers. In our present analyses, we consider only the head noun. That is, we do not care whether the object is called a long cup, a funny cup with a stem, or a kind of a cup; as long as the head noun is cup, it will be classed here as 'cup'. We have carried out these tests in a fair range of languages, and recently extended this study to contrast bilingual and monolingual speakers of Spanish and English, in various degrees of proficiency. But the material reported here will be drawn from a series of eight investigations of speakers of English, with sample sizes ranging from eleven to twenty-four subjects. The fundamental relations to be discussed here are confirmed with great consistency in each of these tests. The first series was drawn from exploratory interviews in the speech community, but most of the others from classes or series of individual students at Columbia University and at the University of Pennsylvania. [12]

Figures 6 and 7 show a series of consistency profiles for the application of cup to a series of objects of increasing width. Figure 6 is for Group A of eleven subjects from the first series in 1964 (without cup No. 20), and Figure 7 is an immediately following series with Group B, also with eleven subjects. The solid lines show the consistency profiles for cup and bowl in the first, Neutral context. For Group A, the applicability of cup is 100 per cent for the first two cups, drops slightly for a ratio of 1.5 to 1, and then plunges sharply to less that 25 per cent for the wider objects. The line crossing from lower left shows the percentage of applications of bowl to the same objects. At about the width of 2.2 to 1, the

FIGURE 6. Consistency profiles for <u>cup</u> and <u>bowl</u> in Neutral and Food contexts, Group A, N = 11.

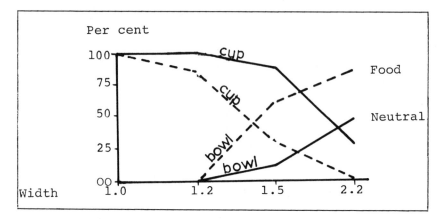

FIGURE 7. Consistency profiles denoted as <u>cup</u> and <u>bowl</u> in Neutral and Food contexts, Group B, N = 11.

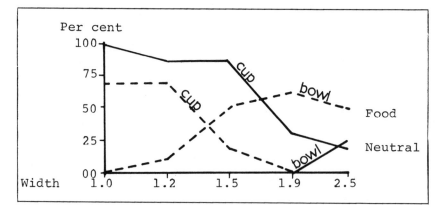

likelihood of the object being called a bowl is roughly equal to the likelihood of its being called a cup. This is the fringe area, in which it is possible to assert with equal truth that the object is a cup and that it is not a cup.

The same relations for the Neutral context appear again in Figure 7, this time with five degrees of width. Again the fringe area cross-over point is at a width ratio of 2.2 to 1.

The dotted lines show the effect of switching the context of de-notation to Food--that is, containing mashed potatoes. The pattern is the same as for Neutral, but it is shifted to the left. Now the abrupt drop in the cup pattern is after cup No. 2, and the cross-over point is between 2 and 3, that is between the width ratios of 1.2 and 1.5. The same phenomenon appears in both Figures 6 and 7. The term bowl is applied more frequently in the transitional area than cup, although the modal values are immune from the shift.

Figure 8 shows consistency profiles for objects of increasing depth. Only Group A is shown here; Group B gives similar results. The term mug is shown superimposed on instances of cup, since as all informants agree that cup is a superordinate term for mug: that is, mug is a kind of cup.[13] On the other hand, vases are not kinds of cups. The number of items named as vase in the Neutral context is shown by the solid line at the lower right of Figure 8. In Figure 9,

FIGURE 8. Consistency profiles for cup, mug, and vase in Neutral context, by depth for Group A, N = 11.

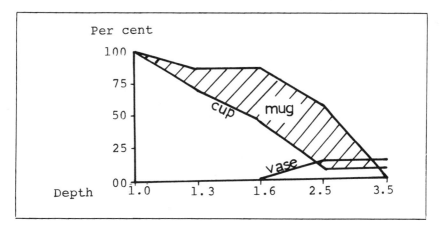

the same series of objects are shown in the Flower context; more favorable to vase, and less favorable to cup and mug. In fact, mug does not appear in the Flower context at all. Here again we see a regular shift of consistency profiles, so that now the crossover area lies between depths of 1.3 and 1.6, rather than at 3.5.

4. The interdependence of conditions for denotation

Many different dimensions and sub-tests within these series confirm the general pattern of Figures 5 and 6: the consistency profiles for any given term are radically shifted as the subjects conceive of the objects in different functional settings.[14] The consistency profiles are regularly elevated for cup by the Coffee context, depressed by Food, and even further depressed by the Flower context. The

FIGURE 9. Consistency profiles for cup and vase in Flower
context, by depth, for Group A, N = 11.

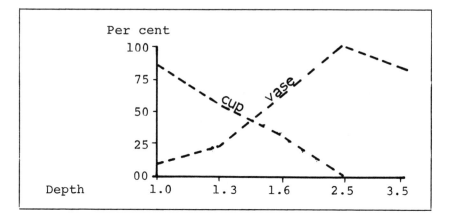
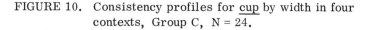

clarity and strength of the effect is illustrated by the fact that it
emerges consistently with groups of less than ten subjects. Figure
10 shows the effect of all four contexts on the application of cup to

FIGURE 10. Consistency profiles for cup by width in four
contexts, Group C, N = 24.

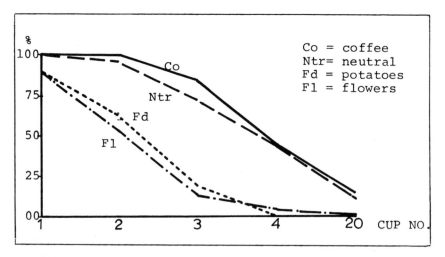

containers of increasing width, and Figure 11 the effect on containers
of increasing depth. This was a series carried out in 1968 on Group
C, with twenty-four subjects. The increment of Coffee over the
Neutral context is a slight one in Figure 10, and for these shallow
containers the Flower context decreases the use of the term only a

FIGURE 11. Consistency profiles for cup and mug (Neutral) by
depth in Group C, N = 24.

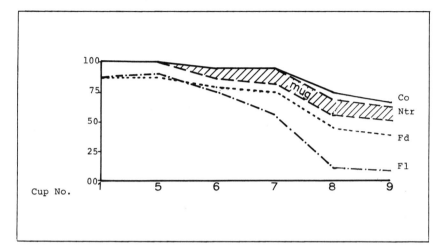

little more than Food. In Figure 11 this effect is much greater, as
bowl competes with cup less in the Food context and vase competes
more with cup. The effect contributed by mug to cup is shown here
for the Neutral context only; in the others, mug is added to cup, but
not shown separately.

Formal representations. It is normally assumed, as we noted
above, that the criteria for denotation are established and selected
independently of each other. The relations of form and function
would therefore appear on a two-dimensional graph as a rectangular
block bounded by the straight lines C = p and C = q, as in Figure 12.
This is the pattern which we normally find in the schematic representations of componential analysis (Wallace and Atkins 1960, Figure 1).
If we take condition C as referring to form (e.g. ratio of width to
depth), and condition D as referring to use (e.g. function as a container), then the term always denotes if C lies between p and q, and
D lies between r and s. This is the categorical view of denotation,
corresponding to formula (1).
    The data we derive from our studies of cup, bowl, vase, etc.,
corresponds to a very different model. Figure 13 shows a linear
model which approximates the data. Instead of locating the outer
and inner limits of the conditions C and D, we locate at the origin
the modal values of C and D, p_0 and r_0. The values of p and r
which depart in various ways from this modal value will be located
along the ordinate and abscissa respectively. The diagonal line
shown in Figure 13 is merely one of many that connect points of

FIGURE 12.   Orthogonal model for independent conditions for
denotation.

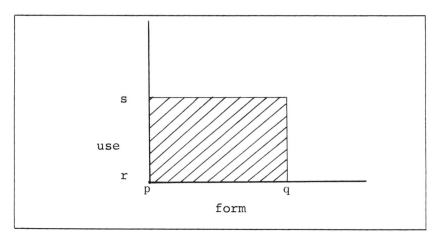

FIGURE 13.   Linear model for relations between conditions
for denotation.

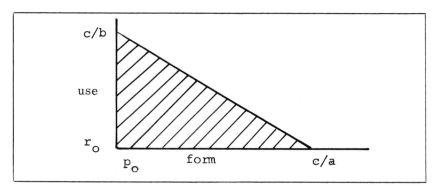

equal probability of the term L denoting. To express a quantitative
relationship between the values of form and function presupposes that
function has been quantified, and in our present state of knowledge
this does not seem likely. If that could be done, however, the relationship between form and function might appear as

(8) $a \cdot (p - p_0) + b \cdot (r - r_0) = c$

If the diagonal line of Figure 13 is taken to represent the outer limits
of all cases where the probability of L denoting is more than zero,
then it will show two specific limits of form and function for cup.

When p is equal to the modal value for form p_0, then $(r_0 - r) = c/b$, and similarly, when r is equal to the modal value for form r_0, then the outer limits of $(p_0 - p)$ will be equal to a quantity c/a. This means that under no circumstances will any object with a form beyond c/a be called a cup.

If this is not the case, and if there is no outer limit of shape or function which limits the use of cup, then we would have a hyperbolic model such as Figure 14. Here there are no outer limits. When

FIGURE 14. Hyperbolic model for relations between two conditions for denotation.

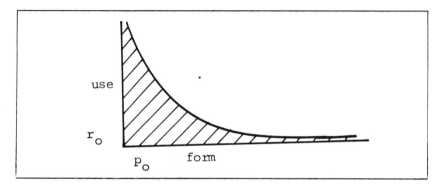

$p = p_0$, then almost any value of r will permit the application of the term cup, and when $r = r_0$, then any value of the shape p will permit the term to denote. In this case, the relations of use and form would appear as

(9) $(p - p_0) \cdot (r - r_0) = c$

Thus as $(p - p_0)$ approaches zero, $(r - r_0)$ becomes indefinitely large.

We do not yet have a wide enough range of data to test these models, although the evidence of Figures 6, 8, 9, 10, and 11 argues for an approximation to the linear model of Figure 13. The linearity is most evident in the slopes for cup, especially in Neutral and Coffee contexts. In some arrays, we note sudden discontinuities when vase, for example, begins to compete actively with cup and mug in the deepest containers. There are further interrelationships between the invariant core or modal values of one term and the variable skirt of another which must be explored if the model is to be refined.

The location of a subordinate term. Figure 10 showed combined figures for cup and mug, based on the notion that mug is included within the superordinate cup. This claim can be supported by examining responses to the cylindrical series of cups 10, 11, and 12, where mug is most strongly favored. Figure 15 shows that in the Coffee and Neutral contexts, mug expands to its maximum extent with No. 11; in the Coffee context it denotes in over three-quarters of the total responses. Note that the most sensitive index of the

FIGURE 15. Consistency profiles for cup, mug, and vase for cylindrical cups of increasing depth in three contexts, Group C, N = 24.

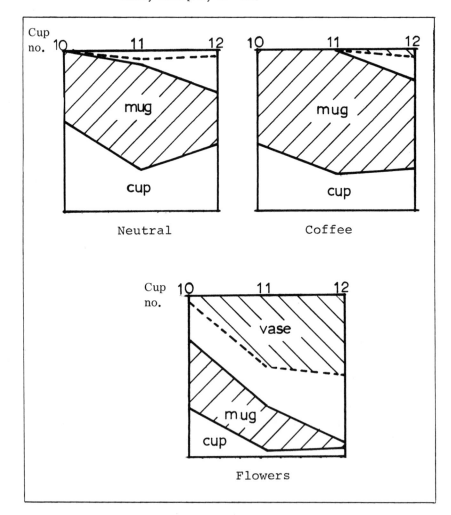

predominance of <u>mug</u> is its relation to <u>cup</u>, for No. 11, the
ratio of <u>mug</u> to <u>cup</u> is quite high, but in No. 10, it represents
only about half of the combined category, and in the longer cylinder
of No. 12, the proportion of <u>mug</u> to <u>cup</u> again recedes. The fact
that <u>mug</u> reaches a maximum at a certain depth, and then recedes,
flanked by greater proportions of <u>cup</u> on both sides, indicates that
<u>cup</u> is the residual or unmarked category out of which <u>mug</u> is speci-
fied. Thus in the most favored Coffee and Neutral contexts, we observe the following pattern in the ratios of mug to cup:

	Mug/Cup		
	No. 10	No. 11	No. 12
Coffee context	1.4	2.4	1.5
Neutral context	.8	1.8	.8

It appears that the empirical study of denotation can offer us further
insight into the superordinate/subordinate relationship through the
study of such regular patterns.

Further articulation of function and form. In recent tests we
have explored the possibility of further subdividing the functional
scale, in order to show more delicate shifting, and looking forward
to ordering the functional contests by more exact criteria. Figure
16 shows the consistency profile for <u>cup</u> in a recent test with the

FIGURE 16. Consistency profiles for <u>cup</u> in four contexts,
Group D, N = 15.

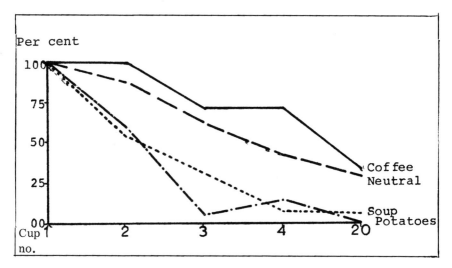

fifteen subjects of Group D, where the Food context was subdivided into Soup and Potatoes. Soup is normally a hot liquid, like coffee, but it is eaten rather than drunk, and is often served in a bowl. Potatoes, as a solid food, is regularly served in a bowl and never in a cup, and we would thus expect that Potatoes favors <u>cup</u> even less than Soup. Figure 16 does not bear out this expectation, however. Again, the largest break is between Coffee and Neutral contexts, on the one hand, and the food contexts on the other. But Soup and Potatoes are evidently not distinguished. This may be due to the fact that both of these contexts favor <u>bowl</u> strongly at the expense of <u>cup</u>, except in the modal values of <u>cup</u>.

Figure 17 shows the same contexts in a range of cups of increasing depth, with some additional details. Here the role of Soup is

FIGURE 17. Consistency profiles for <u>cup</u> in five contexts by depth, and <u>bowl</u> and <u>glass</u> in one context (Neutral, no handle). Group D, N = 15.

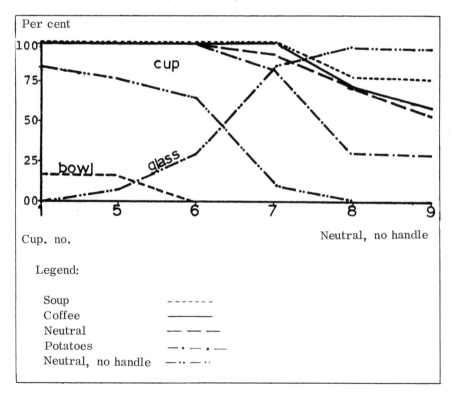

Per cent

Cup. no.   Neutral, no handle

Legend:

Soup	- - - - - - -
Coffee	————
Neutral	— — —
Potatoes	— · — · —
Neutral, no handle	— ·· — ··

suddenly reversed. Instead of being confounded with the Potato context, it now appears to be the context which favors <u>cup</u> more strongly than any other, even coffee. This must be because <u>cup</u> is not now competing with <u>bowl</u> in the Soup context, since the deeper containers are less like bowls than the modal cup container No. 1. Again, we note that the largest difference between contexts is that which separates Food (potatoes) from the others.

Below the Potatoes profile, there is one in which <u>cup</u> is even more disfavored. This is the series of diagrams of cup without handles (see Figure 17). Even in the neutral context, the effect of removing the handle appears to be greater than the shifting context with the handle. Here we can see how strongly <u>glass</u> competes with <u>cup</u> in this handle-less condition, with a cross-over point between Nos. 6 and 7. The effect of removing the handle from the containers is seen even more clearly in Figure 18, which shows the application of <u>cup</u> to objects of increasing width, with and without a handle.

FIGURE 18. Consistency profiles for cup with and without a handle in Neutral context, for Group D, N = 15.

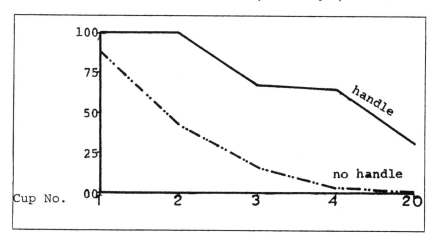

5. Redefining <u>cup</u>

We may now attempt to utilize our new information about the conditions for denotation of cup in reconstructing the definition of this term. Returning to the two definitions presented in section 2, we find that (2) is even less attractive than ever, but Webster's second edition definition (4) does not look quite as bad as it did at first. The expression <u>with or without a handle</u> can now be read as <u>usually with a handle, sometimes without,</u> in line with the findings presented in Figure 18. Expressions such as <u>used chiefly to drink</u>

from, commonly set on a saucer, used for hot liquid foods, etc.,
express the regularities which were brought out in Figures 6-11.
The writers of the definition seemed to anticipate by one means or
another many of the findings of our more objective procedures, and
they have resolutely adhered to terms which may appear uselessly
vague to less experienced lexicographers. This should not be surprising, as we have found similar tendencies in the treatment of
variability by practicing phonologists, who have undertaken the task
of describing new languages (Labov 1971). Though the theory they
are operating under strongly forbids them to characterize the frequency of free variants, they regularly insist on inserting such informal qualifiers after they have stated the principal allophonic
distributions. Thus we find Bucca and Lesser writing about Kitsai
voiceless I:

> It is in free variation with i. The free variation is less
> frequent in final position where i is more used; and in medial
> position before the consonantal groups ts, st, sk, sn, tjk,
> where I is predominant (1969:11).

Such statements about relations or more or less express informally the variable constraints which are formalized in recent
direct studies of variability (Labov 1969, Cedergren and Sankoff
to appear). In the same way, good lexicographers make an informal
attempt to capture the variable properties which reflect the deep and
subtle competence of the native speaker, a competence he must have
to name the wide variety of new and intermediate objects in the
world.

But the Webster definition still fails to capture the most systematic
and intricate aspect of variability in the use of cup. On the one hand,
there seems to be a wide range of objects that we call cup without
hesitation. But the size of that invariant range fluctuates systematically according to function, material, and other properties. As we
examine the figures given above, there appears beyond the invariant
range a systematic decline, almost linear, in the probability of an
object being called a cup. Though a hyperbolic, asymptotic model
like Figure 14 may be possible, most of our data is linear, and whenever we actually observe a terminal point, it is quite sharp. We can
therefore construct a definition which reflects this double variability:
the invariant core is itself variable in extent, controlled by the
interrelation of a number of factors, while the variable skirt follows
a relatively simple downward slope.[15]

> The term cup is regularly used to denote round containers
> with a ratio of width to depth of $1 \pm r$ where $r \leq r_b$, and

$r_b = \alpha_1 + \alpha_2 + \ldots \alpha_\nu$ and α_i is a positive quantity when the feature $\underline{i}$ is present and O otherwise.

feature 1 = with one handle
      2 = made of opaque vitreous material
      3 = used for consumption of food
      4 = used for consumption of liquid food
      5 = used for consumption of hot liquid food
      6 = with a saucer
      7 = tapering
      8 = circular in cross-section

Cup is used variably to denote such containers with ratios of width to depth of $1 \pm r$ where $r_b \leq r \leq r_t$ with a probability of $r_t - r/r_t - r_b$. The quantity $1 \pm r_b$ expresses the distance from the modal value of width to height.[16]

The various factors controlling the invariant core are ordered in accordance with the data presented here, rather than the dictionary definition itself, but there is no contradiction between them. The expression regularly used is intended to capture the fact that there are objects which in the range of contexts indicated will be called cups by practically all speakers.

The second half of the definition reflects the general fact that the vagueness profile of cup is approximately linear, so that the probability of applying cup to an object is proportional to the distance one has moved from the outer limit of the invariant core and the cut-off point r_t. The quantity $(r_t - r_b)$ may vary considerably, and so alter the slope of the variable skirt or fringe of cup-like objects.

This definition is thus designed to register the categorical character of our lexicon along with its flexibility and adaptability for application to a wide range of objects. We can schematize this relation by Figure 19, which shows the two aspects of variability superimposed upon an item-speaker matrix similar to the item-property matrices of section 1.

The model of Figure 19 is an elaboration of Figure 3: it reflects the categorical nature of the phenomenon by delineating an invariant core; but it also specifies the variable location of the boundary which marks the limits of categories and the limitations of the categorizing process.

The study of variability is the obverse of the study of invariance; one without the other has little significance, and a linguistic study devoted to only one or the other misses the richness of the phenomenon. It is not true that everything varies, anymore than it is true that everything remains distinct and discrete. We must locate the boundary between the invariant and variable areas of language with

FIGURE 19. Invariant core and variable range for denotation of
items by speakers.

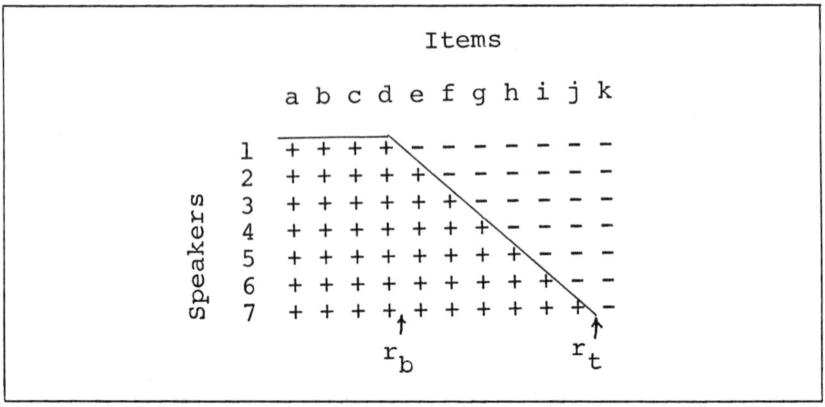

Items

a b c d e f g h i j k

```
            a  b  c  d  e  f  g  h  i  j  k
        1   +  +  +  +  -  -  -  -  -  -  -
        2   +  +  +  +  +  -  -  -  -  -  -
   S    3   +  +  +  +  +  +  -  -  -  -  -
   p    4   +  +  +  +  +  +  +  -  -  -  -
   e    5   +  +  +  +  +  +  +  +  -  -  -
   a    6   +  +  +  +  +  +  +  +  +  -  -
   k    7   +  +  +  +  +  +  +  +  +  +  -
   e
   r                  r                 r
   s                   b                 t
```

the same precision that we have learned to use in studying the variable elements themselves (Labov 1972b). We cannot escape the
overall implications of section 1: that language is essentially a
categorical device. If we want to understand it, we have to do more
than count the categories; we have to measure them, weigh them,
and eventually record them at work.

5. How an object is not known per se

A review of the linguistic literature on distinctive features reinforces our conviction that there is no significant difference between
the distinctive/redundant opposition and the Aristotelian notion of
essence and accident. A search for distinctive features is fundamentally a search for the Aristotelian essence, through which the
thing itself is to be known.

The essence (τὸ τί ἦν) of each thing is that which it
is said to be per se (καθ᾽ αὐτό).

Metaphysics VII. IV. 4

Essence is opposed to accident, and reflects the way things really
are, intrinsically, and cannot help being. One's essence is identical
with one's own nature, as Aristotle points out, continuing the above
passage:

'To be you' is not 'to be cultured', because you are
not of your own nature cultured. Your essence, then, is
that which you are said to be of your own nature.

Furthermore, it is clear that for Aristotle, the essence of a substance is identical with and inseparable from the thing itself. But essence is somehow the verbalizable aspect of substance:

It is obvious, then, that the definition is the formula (λόγος) of the essence. VII. V. 7

The definition we have presented in section 4 is obviously not the essence of a cup, nor limited to essential attributes. There is no question of a handle or a saucer being an essential attribute of a cup, anymore than 'white' is an essential part of the essence of 'man' (to use Aristotle's favorite example). One cannot separate an essential attribute from the object, and cups without handles are common enough. In our definition, properties such as these play an important role in circumscribing the outer range of regular usage, which varies with their presence or absence. Our ability to recognize a cup depends upon our ability to recognize such accidents, contrary to the opinion of Aristotle:

That each individual thing is one and the same thing with its essence, and not merely accidentally so, is apparent, not only from the foregoing considerations, but because to have knowledge of the individual is to have knowledge of its essence. VII. VI. 9.

These quotations from the philosopher should make it quite evident that scholastic linguistic theory is quite in harmony with Aristotle's categorical viewpoint, which is in almost every detail the categorical view sketched in section 1. It is not uncommon for linguists to insist that one or the other aspect of property of an object is the essential property for the naming of it; as for example, the claim that function is the essential thing in naming objects while form is accidental. [18] The empirical evidence presented here will serve to underline the interrelation of form and function, and their symmetry in the process of denotation. A secular approach to further research in semantic description will necessarily carry us outside of the schools, beyond the limitations of scholastic intuitions, and beyond the categorical view which survives intact in the doctrines of the schoolmen.

The experimental studies reported here represent only one step outward from this scholastic setting. Further research will carry us towards experimentation in a more natural setting (Labov 1971). But the results so far are encouraging enough to suggest that semantic theory, like phonological theory, can find firm ground if we take even one step away from the intuition of the theorist and towards the observation of language in use.

NOTES

[1]One of the classic problems of defining the boundaries of a category is that of defining the word in English (Hockett 1958:166). The difficulties of providing a categorical definition are so great that many linguists have abandoned word as a technical term and substituted lexeme, formative, etc. But the word seems to be the linguistic unit of greatest social significance in our own and many other cultures. The problem of defining the category word can be taken as one of the important issues to be attacked as linguistics shifts from being a theory of category to a theory of limits and boundaries (see section 1).

[2]The first report of this work was to the Linguistic Society of America at the Annual Meeting in New York City on December 28, 1964, entitled 'Interdependent conditions for denotation'. The present report incorporates results from a number of further studies carried out at Columbia University, and recent work at the University of Pennsylvania in 1972 with the help of Franklin Jones.

[3]The analysis of the categorical view presented here is based upon Labov (1965); for the additional consideration of the prohibition on constraining free variation, see Labov (1971).

[4]See for example Martinet 'Un ou deux phonèmes' (1939) and countless other discussions of category assignment in the literature.

[5]Several other fields concerned with human behavior have not yet been able to formulate questions precisely enough to answer such questions. For example, it is very difficult to argue in role theory whether certain small differences in rights, duties, and obligations represent one role or two; there seems to be no principled way of deciding whether being the father of a five-year-old child is a different role from being the father of an eight-year-old child.

[6]On the questionable status of such idiosyncratic dialects, see Labov (1972a).

[7]Such ad hoc categories are regularly criticized in syntax as having no explanatory adequacy. But when a category can be shown to have two relatively independent properties, one property at least is said to be 'explained'; that is, the overall rule statements can then be simplified by the use of the category in question. The distinction of count-nouns vs. mass nouns, for example, is associated with differences in co-occurrence with the plural, with the indefinite article, and partitive quantifiers like some.

[8]Of course one can construct contexts in which it is reasonable to say either form of (k). For example, 'All of the cups in this

store have stripes on them. This is a cup but it doesn't have a stripe on it. ' But such contexts can be constructed with equal facility for both the positive and negative forms.

[9]This is a property associated with the categorical view, as discussed in section 1 above; for further discussion, see Labov 1971.

[10]There are a few disjunctive statements of this sort in plant taxonomy, but they are rare. As a plant grows, its leaves may become thicker, develop more lobes, and its bark may develop an entirely different form. The difficulties of recognizing immature specimens may require such interdependence of the criterial properties. The fact that the formal taxonomy usually does not reflect such interdependence does not mean that people do not utilize more sophisticated models when they actually recognize trees.

[11]The actual ratio of width to depth in the drawings is not immediately obvious, since they are slightly foreshortened in depth. The figures used throughout this discussion are the relation of the width or depth of a given cup to the width and depth of cup No. 1. I am indebted to Felix Cooper, the well-known illustrator of scientific texts, for the precise execution of this series of drawings.

[12]I am indebted to Franklin Jones of the University of Pennsylvania, who carried out an extensive series of studies of the denotation of cups and other objects in connection with a study of differences in Spanish and English bilingualism, and to Beatriz Lavandera who completed a comparable series in Buenos Aires.

[13]For more objective evidence on this point, see below.

[14]The subjects show an extraordinary ability to register the effect of different contexts through verbal instructions. Some preliminary tests with more concrete instances of contextual shifting did not show any clearer results, although this is an area to be explored further.

[15]The basic form of the rule presented here is due to David Sankoff of the Centre des Recherches Mathématiques in Montreal.

[16]The slope of the variable area is itself quite variable, but it cannot be specified as long as function is not a quantified linear scale.

[17]In actual fact, the ratio of width to height which is most typical of coffee cups in American households is considerably less than 1, reflected in the way we have located cup No. 1. Cup No. 5 exhibits in perspective this 1:1 ratio, and a glance at the various representations of increasing depth shows that it is in fact favored as strongly as No. 1.

[18]From an oral presentation of Noam Chomsky in Los Angeles, 1966, developing a point of view based upon thought experiments performed by Philippa Foot.

REFERENCES

Aristotle. 1933. The metaphysics. With translation by H. Treden-
nick. Cambridge, Harvard University Press.
Bailey, Charles-James N. 1971. Building rate into a dynamic
theory of linguistic description. Working Papers in Linguistics.
Honolulu, University of Hawaii.
Bickerton, Derek. 1971. Inherent variability and variable rules.
Foundations of Language. 7.457-92.
_____. 1972. The structure of polylectal grammars. In: George-
town University Monograph Series on Languages and Linguistics,
Monograph 25, Report of the 23rd Annual Round Table. Washing-
ton, D.C., Georgetown University Press.
Black, Max. 1949. Language and philosophy. Ithaca, Cornell
University Press.
Bucca, Salvador and Alexander Lesser. 1969. Kitsai phonology
and morphophonemics. IJAL. 35.7-19.
Cedergren, Henrietta and David Sankoff. Variable rules: Perfor-
mance as a statistical reflection of competence. To appear in
Language.
DeCamp, David. 1971. Toward a generative analysis of a post-
creole speech continuum. In: Pidginization and creolization of
languages. Ed. by Dell Hymes. Cambridge, Cambridge Uni-
versity Press. 349-70.
Hockett, Charles F. 1958. A course in modern linguistics. New
York, Macmillan.
Jakobson, R., G. Fant, and M. Halle. 1952. Preliminaries to
speech analysis. Cambridge, MIT Press.
Katz, Jerrold J. and Jerry A. Fodor. 1963. The structure of a
semantic theory. Language. 39.170-210.
Labov, William. 1966. The linguistic variable as a structural
unit. Washington Linguistics Review. 3.4-22. Available
through the ERIC System, ED 010 871.
_____. 1969. Contraction, deletion, and inherent variability of
the English copula. Language. 45.715-62.
_____. 1971. Methodology. In: A survey of linguistic science.
Ed. by William Dingwall. College Park, Md., Linguistics Program, University of Maryland. 412-97.
_____. 1972a. For an end to the uncontrolled use of linguistic
intuitions. Paper presented to the Linguistic Society of America,
Atlanta, December.
_____. 1972b. Negative attraction and negative concord in English
grammar. Language. 48.773-818.

Martinet, A. 1939. Un ou deux phonèmes? Acta Linguistica. 1.94-103.

Quirk, Randolph. 1965. Descriptive statement and serial relationship. Language. 41.205-17.

Stankiewicz, Edward. 1957. On discreteness and continuity in structural dialectology. Word. 13.44-59.

Wallace, Anthony F. and John Atkins. 1960. The meaning of kinship terms. American Anthropologist. 62.58-80.

Weinreich, Uriel. 1954. Is a structural dialectology possible? Word. 10.388-400.

_____. 1962. Lexicographic definition in descriptive semantics. Problems in Lexicography. 28(4)April.

_____, William Labov, and Marvin Herzog. 1968. Empirical foundations for a theory of language change. In: Directions for historical linguistics. Ed. by W. Lehmann and Y. Malkiel. Austin, University of Texas Press. 97-195.